CHANCELLORSVILLE
1863

CHANCELLORSVILLE
1863

The Souls of the Brave

ERNEST B. FURGURSON

Alfred A. Knopf
New York

1992

THIS IS A BORZOI BOOK
PUBLISHED BY ALFRED A. KNOPF, INC.

Copyright © 1992 by Ernest B. Furgurson
Maps copyright © 1992 by William J. Clipson
All rights reserved under International and Pan-American
Copyright Conventions. Published in the United States by
Alfred A. Knopf, Inc., New York, and simultaneously in
Canada by Random House of Canada Limited, Toronto.
Distributed by Random House, Inc., New York.

Library of Congress Cataloging-in-Publication Data
Furgurson, Ernest B.
Chancellorsville 1863 / Ernest B. Furgurson.—1st ed.
p.   cm.
Includes bibliographical references and index.
ISBN 0-394-58301-9
1. Chancellorsville (Va.), Battle of, 1863. I. Title.
IN PROCESS   91-47059   CIP

Manufactured in the United States of America
FIRST EDITION

To

Robert Daniel Ferguson

1ST SGT., CO. I, 53RD VIRGINIA INFANTRY
WOUNDED AT FIVE FORKS, APRIL 1, 1865

Jesse Levi Furgurson

2ND LT., CO. C, 32ND NORTH CAROLINA INFANTRY
WOUNDED AT PETERSBURG, APRIL 2, 1865

Michael Decatur Lawrence Harris

1ST SGT., CO. C, 32ND NORTH CAROLINA INFANTRY
WOUNDED AT FORT STEDMAN, MARCH 25, 1865

Thomas Upchurch

PRIVATE, CO. G, 7TH NORTH CAROLINA INFANTRY
CAPTURED AT GETTYSBURG, JULY 3, 1863
DIED AT FORT DELAWARE, OCTOBER 1863

—and to their children,
and their children's children,
who are my parents

What history, I say, can ever give—for who can know—
the mad, determin'd tussle of the armies, in all their
separate large and little squads—as this—each steep'd
from crown to toe in desperate, mortal purports? Who
know the conflict, hand-to-hand—the many conflicts in
the dark, those shadowy-tangled, flashing moonbeam'd
woods—the writhing groups and squads—the cries, the
din, the cracking guns and pistols—the distant cannon—
the cheers and calls and threats and awful music of the
oaths—the indescribable mix—the officers' orders, per-
suasions, encouragements—the devils fully rous'd in
human hearts—the strong shout, *Charge, men, charge*—
the flash of the naked sword, and rolling flame and
smoke? And still the broken, clear and clouded heaven—
and still again the moonlight pouring silvery soft its
radiant patches over all. Who paint the scene . . . ?

WALT WHITMAN, *Specimen Days in America*

Contents

List of Maps

Maps by William J. Clipson, based on Hotchkiss and Allan's
The Battle-fields of Virginia: Chancellorsville (1867);
Bigelow's *The Campaign of Chancellorsville* (1910); and
National Park Service's Troop Movement Series (1961)

Preface

SINCE THE DAY Fighting Joe Hooker retreated across the Rappahannock River, generals and historians have studied the Chancellorsville campaign as both tactical masterpiece and human drama. In no other conflict of the Civil War did one general so completely dominate another on the battle-field as Robert E. Lee did when he met and repulsed Hooker and his overwhelmingly superior Union army. No character in that war was more celebrated than the brilliantly eccentric Stonewall Jackson, no casualty more mourned than when he was struck down at the climax of his remarkable career.

My own fascination with this particularly bloody campaign began when I was a schoolboy in southside Virginia and was granted access to a family heirloom titled *The Confederate Soldier in the Civil War*. This is a ten-pound commemorative volume of official reports and sentimental poems, pictures of smoky battles and bearded heroes, published in 1895. My grandfather bought it then to remember his departed father, who was wounded fighting with Pickett. In it, his daughters had pressed flowers; to this day there is a faded rose, a lily, and a frond of dry fern inside its back cover. At first I was excited by the book's tableaux of hand-to-hand fighting and belching cannon. Later I was captured by the prose, clear expository writing by generals whose very names had almost biblical significance in the Virginia of my boyhood. There, after the regiment-by-regiment casualty figures for Chancellorsville, is Dr. Hunter McGuire's account of Jackson's final days.

I read that account many times before setting foot on the ground at Chancellorsville. On my first visit, I was a young marine at Quantico. We studied tactics by tramping the ridges and thickets where the masters had fought. The complexity of the campaign, the audacity of the winners, the suffering of the soldiers on both sides became real when I followed

Jackson's flank march, crouched in Hooker's trenches, sighted along Barksdale's lanes of fire below Marye's Heights. That long ago, I said to myself that someday I would write about Chancellorsville.

As I read and revisited over the next decades, I discovered other reasons that made Chancellorsville special to me. Hooker had opened the campaign by swinging across Kelly's and Germanna fords; my great-grandmother Mary Georgia Kelly was born at Kellysville, on the Culpeper County side of Kelly's Ford, in 1847. Another of my ancestors, John Kemper, was among the Palatine settlers planted at Germanna by colonial governor Spotswood in 1714. My great-great-grandfather Thomas Upchurch was in the 7th North Carolina, the regiment alongside the 18th when it opened fire on Jackson's scouting party that moonlit night in May of 1863.

Participants and later students of the Chancellorsville campaign agree that it is the most complicated affair of the war. One historian wrote that "There has been doubtless more misapprehension and in consequence downright misleading of the public mind respecting this battle than of any in the long catalogue of the four years of the late war." J. Watts de Peyster, an artillery major in the battle, said that "Of all the battles of the Civil War, this writer has found Chancellorsville the most difficult to comprehend in all its terms and phases and even yet some of its movements continue to be an enigma to me." Brig. Gen. A. A. Humphreys, who commanded a division in Hooker's Fifth Corps, said, "I probably know less of this battle than of any other I ever took part in." Indeed, it was not one but a series of distinct battles, lasting a week. Since those observers wrote, other historians have imposed more retrospective order on it—particularly John Bigelow, Jr., in his diligently detailed *The Campaign of Chancellorsville*, published in 1910. But the best-known book about Chancellorsville is one in which the battle is never named: Stephen Crane's great novel *The Red Badge of Courage*.

My goal at the start was to uncover enough first-person material—letters, diaries, and memoirs—to add an authentic human dimension to the tactical studies of the past. I found far more than enough; the challenge was not collection, but selection. There are specifics here that have not been in earlier Chancellorsville books—the fact that the Confederate supply service was sabotaged by a railroad superintendent doubling as Union agent, for instance, or that Jackson's personal map of the battlefield was so inaccurate that it impelled him on his fateful last ride. And there are trench-level, private's-eye views that differ with accounts long accepted by others.

Two larger facts about Chancellorsville are insufficiently acknowledged by those who study the war. The campaign is too often remembered just for Lee's fancy footwork, an approach that does not give enough credit to the ordinary soldiers of both sides who struggled as courageously there as in any battle anywhere. Because September 17, 1862, was the bloodiest single day of the war, casual observers sometimes call Antietam the bloodiest battle. In fact, Chancellorsville altogether was worse than Antietam—and May 3, 1863, was among the worst single days.

Gettysburg is traditionally called the high-water mark of the Confederacy, the turning point of the war. Geographically, it was indeed the high-water mark, for Confederate troops never fought so far north again, and Lee never took his main army across the Potomac again. That was the last great offensive effort by his Army of Northern Virginia. But in tactics and strategy, and in impact on morale North and South, the high point of the Confederacy came at Chancellorsville. As we see here, what happened at Gettysburg was crucially affected by what happened two months earlier along the Rappahannock.

I am deeply grateful to Robert K. Krick, chief historian at Fredericksburg and Spotsylvania National Military Park, for his generous cooperation and his careful reading of the manuscript. I also want to thank Donald Pfanz, Janice Frye, and others of the Fredericksburg-Spotsylvania battlefield staff, as well as Dr. Richard J. Sommers and his colleagues at the U.S. Army Military History Institute at Carlisle, Pennsylvania. I am greatly indebted to my friend, the historian Nathan Miller, who was always ready with advice and encouragement. My appreciation also goes to my editor at Alfred A. Knopf, Ashbel Green, and his associates Jenny McPhee, Anthea Lingeman, and Melvin Rosenthal; to my literary agent, David Black; and to my most conscientious counsel, Cassie Furgurson, without whom nothing is possible.

CHANCELLORSVILLE
1863

Prologue

THE PLACE OF BLOOD
AND WRATH

AT AN OBSCURE crossroads in the Spotsylvania Wilderness, halfway between Washington and Richmond, an officer on a stumpy, reddish horse reined up beside a column of gray-clad infantry that stretched out of sight in both directions. With his forage cap tilted over his eyes, he was not much more imposing than his horse. His coffee-brown beard was fine and silky, but, like the stars on his collar and the new uniform he had put on before yesterday's dawn, it was grimed by the smoke of cannon and campfire, the dust from thousands of marching feet. Yet in the passing regiments and the cluster of officers at roadside, every eye was upon him.

Pointing, he told two cavalry officers to set up blocking positions on roads running north and northeast. His expression softened a moment as the second horseman started away; earlier on the march, they had reminisced about the time they shared at Virginia Military Institute. Raising his hand, he almost smiled as he waved and said, "Colonel, the Institute will be heard from today!"

Before riding on, he brought out a pencil stub, spread a sheet of paper over the pommel of his saddle, and scrawled a message to Robert E. Lee:

> Near 3 P.M.
> May 2d, 1863
>
> General,
>   The enemy has made a stand at Chancellor's which is about 2 miles from Chancellorsville. I hope as soon as practicable to attack.
>   I trust that an ever kind Providence will bless us with great success.
>
> Respectfully,
> T.J. Jackson
> Lt. Genl.

He started to hand the message to a courier, then pulled it back. He glanced at the lean, cocky soldiers trudging by four abreast, their muskets casually angled over their shoulders, canteens and bayonets rattling as they marched on toward the Orange Turnpike. Watching him, they murmured to one another, certain he was about to ask of them yet another impossibility, ready without question to do it. He unfolded the paper and added a postscript:

> The leading division is up and the next two appear to be well-closed.

T.J.J.

Then he nudged his horse and brushed past his foot soldiers. More than a mile ahead, he turned the column east, toward the open flank of Maj. Gen. Joseph Hooker's Union army.

Stonewall Jackson had marched his leading regiments more than 12 miles through the forest before they cut back and started deploying along a low, wooded ridge. On the way, he and his officers had constantly prodded them: "Close up! Press on! Keep moving!" After two years of war, these soldiers had so impressed their enemies that one Federal artillery officer likened them to men of iron. In the Valley of Virginia, on their way to the Peninsula, to Manassas and Sharpsburg, Jackson's infantrymen had won the reputation of foot cavalry. For them, this day's march was far from a record; it is famous in history not for its distance or its speed, but for its boldness, and what happened when it was over.

Jackson was poised in a position all generals dream of but few attain. On what seemed almost a dare from Lee, he was moving more than 26,000 troops close across the front of an overwhelmingly superior Federal army, to attack by surprise where the enemy was weakest. Snaked out through the second-growth Wilderness, his column was itself vulnerable to attack at any moment. All along the way, Union lookouts had spotted his marching troops, but failed to convince their commanders that the Rebels could be doing anything but retreating in the face of insuperable odds.

Jackson understood both the danger and the opportunity. As the head of his column started spreading through the thickets into lines of attack, most of his troops were still somewhere back along the roads through the forest. At any moment, the Yankee generals could come to their senses and realize what was happening.

Time was against him. Darkness would fall fast in the thick woods. The temptation was to throw his available troops at the enemy before the rest came up. But having risked much, he now risked more. He could roll up Hooker's flank, but that was not enough. He wanted to destroy the Union army. This day's work could win the war.

Jackson checked his pocket watch. Despite the hour, he ordered three ranks of troops to keep going into the thickets. He spread them a mile north and a mile south, so their charge would overlap every point of Union resistance. The soldiers ducked and slashed their way through the pine, scrub oak, and thorny vines. Once the attack began, close control would be impossible. Jackson issued strict instructions: When the bugles sound, the entire line will sweep forward together. Under no circumstances will there be any pause in the advance.

Five o'clock passed as the sweat-soaked infantry sifted deeper into the woods. Jackson looked at his watch again. His impatience showed in his crackling orders, his clenched jaw, his eyes like hard blue flame.

Brig. Gen. Robert E. Rodes, about to take a division into battle for the first time, looked after his brigades to see that they were aligned. Then he rode back and halted near Jackson, waiting. The warm air along the ridge began to cool as afternoon waned. Maj. Eugene Blackford of the 5th Alabama rode up with a bugler and reported that the skirmishers were out. Yet again, Jackson reached under his coat and took out his watch.

It was 5:15 P.M., Saturday, May 2, 1863—an hour and thirty-three minutes before sunset, the last moment of quiet before chaos, before the most dramatic lightning stroke of the American Civil War. The sun was low in the clear sky, and the shadow of the woods fell long across the farmhouse clearing.

Jackson looked up. Now he spoke calmly, as if he were suggesting a twilight stroll among the blossoming dogwood:

"Are you ready, General Rodes?"

"Yes, sir."

"You can go forward, then."

Chapter One

WINTER ALONG THE RAPPAHANNOCK

PROFESSOR THADDEUS S. C. LOWE leaned forward to brace his telescope against the basket of the U.S. balloon *Eagle* as it strained at its mooring cables, 1,300 feet above the river.

Up there, the cold air was quiet. Occasionally a shout drifted up through the thin haze of campfire smoke, a dog barked, or a locomotive whistled on the track running down from the Potomac landings toward Falmouth. But no sound suggested that along the Rappahannock more than 200,000 soldiers in two powerful armies confronted each other, recovering from one great battle, dreading and preparing for another.

On the western horizon, far beyond Chancellorsville and the Wilderness, stretched the hazy silhouette of the Blue Ridge, where the Rappahannock trickles from beneath a mossy rock on the flank of High Knob. To the east, past Fredericksburg, the river broadened miles wide as it flowed to Chesapeake Bay. In early 1863, nearly two years after the war began, the Rappahannock had become the strategic border between North and South. At Fredericksburg, the head of navigation, where George Washington had spent his boyhood, the new railroad and the old north-south wagon roads crossed the river. It was the crucial midpoint on the straightest route between the capital of the Union and that of the Confederacy. Almost 50 miles north, beyond Professor Lowe's sight, Abraham Lincoln was trying yet again to find a general who could lead the Union's Army of the Potomac on to Richmond. Just over 50 miles south, Jefferson Davis was confident that the Confederacy would never need a better general than Robert E. Lee, but desperate to find food and munitions for his Army of Northern Virginia.

From a quarter mile above the Rappahannock, it was plain that the Federal camps in the hills to the north far outnumbered the Confederates on the south; the stacks of supplies unloaded from Union vessels at Aquia

Creek grew higher day by day. The Confederates were spread thin, digging trenches and artillery emplacements overlooking the river, waiting shivering in the winter damp. The experienced scout could tell much more, but even after a year and a half of wartime practice, Professor Lowe's intelligence reports often failed to satisfy the snappish military men below.

One clear day aloft, he wrote a message and dispatched it by "paper express"—wrapping it around a musket ball, attaching that to a ring, and dropping it down a mooring line to a waiting messenger: "Enemy apparently still in camp about 3 mi. W of Fbg, also large camp about 8 mi. S by W. Largest is about 15 mi. S of Fbg. Smaller one E by S." Maj. Gen. Daniel Butterfield, the new Union chief of staff, sarcastically thanked the professor for his "interesting" report. But, he asked, "What do you consider a large camp—and what a small one—how many men?" "Large" and "small" meant nothing; generals wanted their spy in the sky to know the difference between company and regiment, brigade and division.

Professor Lowe and the army were still learning. The French had used balloons for battlefield observation more than sixty years before, but military bureaucrats in America balked at innovation in weapons, tactics, and technology. To them, manned flight was still a dollar-a-ride fairground novelty. Lowe, a tall, stage-handsome onetime shoemaker's apprentice from New Hampshire, had flown 900 miles from Cincinnati deep into the Carolinas, arriving the day Fort Sumter surrendered and nearly being lynched on suspicion of spying for the Union. Spying was not what he was doing, but it was what he was thinking. Two months later, he finally got past Federal bureaucrats to demonstrate his balloons' potential to Lincoln himself.

To the president, Lowe sent the first telegram from an airship on June 18, 1861. He devised a portable machine that used scrap iron and sulfuric acid to create hydrogen to inflate his tightly sewn, gaudily painted silk balloons in the field. He operated a balloon from a barge on the Potomac, which thus became the nation's first aircraft carrier. On the Peninsula below Richmond in 1862, one Union general asserted that the professor's reconnaissance had saved the army at the battle of Fair Oaks. Brig. Gen. Fitz John Porter, who went up for a first-hand look, sailed over Confederate lines and provided the Rebels some target practice before luckily drifting back to safety. A visiting German lieutenant, Count Ferdinand von Zeppelin, took a ride, found it fascinating, and decided that lighter-than-air craft had a promising future. The Confederates tried to match Professor Lowe's fleet, but could patch together only one balloon from silk dresses donated by the ladies of Dixie, and it soon dropped into Yankee hands.

Along the Rappahannock in the winter of 1862–63, Lowe learned to gauge the size of Confederate camps by counting their tents and fires, comparing them to known quantities on the Federal side of the river. Staff officers had gone aloft with him during the battle of Fredericksburg, where the Confederates had smashed wave after wave of Union infantry in December. After that, Lowe watched the hungry Southern army as it dug in and waited for the next, inevitable Union attempt to cross the Rappahannock toward Richmond. Sometimes, on windless days, he could steady his scope on the rim of his basket and fix a closer eye than Rebel officers could keep on their unsuspecting soldiers.[1]

IN THE GRAY late afternoon, a private from Mississippi slipped toward the bank of the quiet river. Behind him, a shell-pocked field cut by roads and ravines rose gently toward a stone wall, at the foot of a ridge overlooking the ruined town of Fredericksburg. Scattered across that mile of field, wooden slabs marked the shallow graves of Union soldiers. Already the winter had washed away some of the loose clay, and here a hand clutched upward, there a skull grinned out of the earth. The soldier looked away from these as he passed by.

Beside the river, he whistled quick and loud. Looking up- and downstream, he slid a crude toy boat into the water. Before he let it go, he loaded it with a parcel, three pounds of Virginia tobacco. He set the paper sail mounted on the stick that made a mast, gave the craft a shove, and waited. The gray was deepening when he saw the little boat again, angling past him to touch ground. He caught it, pulled off the sail, and held it up in the faint light. He could barely make out the nameplate of the *New York Tribune*. He lifted the packet the boat had brought back, pressed it to his face, inhaled, and sighed. It was real coffee. "Thanks, Yank," he yelled; then with the boat, the newspaper, and the precious parcel, he scuttled toward the collection of huts his regiment called home.[2]

That winter, after pounding, blasting, murdering each other by the

1. Winter in Virginia, 1863. *Lee's invasion of the North has been turned back at Antietam and Burnside's move south halted at Fredericksburg. Waiting for spring, the armies face each other along the Rappahannock, halfway between Washington and Richmond. Confederate cavalry raids Fairfax Court House, Burke Station, and other points behind Federal lines.*

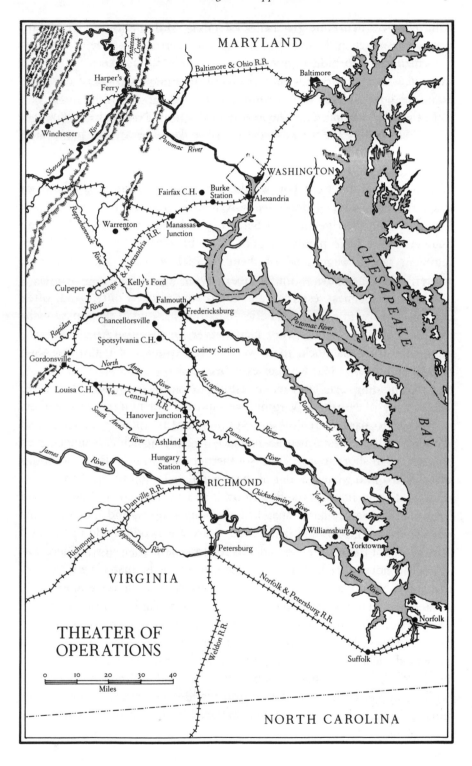

MARYLAND

Baltimore & Ohio R.R.

Baltimore

Harper's
Ferry

Winchester

Potomac River

WASHINGTON

Fairfax C.H.

Burke
Station

Alexandria

Warrenton

Manassas
Junction

Shenandoah River

Rappahannock River

Orange & Alexandria R.R.

Culpeper

Orange

Kelly's Ford

Falmouth

Fredericksburg

River

Rapidan

Chancellorsville

Spotsylvania C.H.

Guiney Station

Potomac River

CHESAPEAKE

BAY

Gordonsville

North Anna River

Louisa C.H.

Va. Central R.R.

South Anna River

Hanover Junction

Ashland

Hungary
Station

Mattapony

Pamunkey River

Rappahannock River

River

James River

RICHMOND

Chickahominy River

York River

Williamsburg

Yorktown

Danville R.R.

Richmond & Appomattox River

Petersburg

VIRGINIA

Norfolk & Petersburg R.R.

James River

THEATER OF
OPERATIONS

0   10   20   30   40
Miles

Weldon R.R.

Norfolk

Suffolk

NORTH CAROLINA

hundreds over that same ground, soldiers of North and South carried on a busy commerce in those toy boats back and forth across the river. Such fraternizing was forbidden, but no one could stop it. Yankees and Rebels shouted across the sort of wisecracks that brothers use to taunt each other. Some of them, indeed, were brothers.

In the 8th Alabama, Sgt. David Buell, an upstate New Yorker who had gone South before the war, asked Lt. Col. Hilary Herbert for permission to cross at Banks' Ford to see his brother Seth. Herbert said he had no such authority. "I know that, Colonel," said David, "but I just wanted you to say that if I went you wouldn't find out." Herbert, confident of Buell's loyalty, said, "I don't see how I could find it out"—whereupon David crossed the river to visit Seth, who offered him some U.S. Army blankets. "We have plenty of good U.S. blankets," David lied. "Our regiment sent a wagonload of them to Richmond to save until next winter." Back he came to the Southern side.[3]

The way enemies yesterday and tomorrow reached out, joked, often commiserated with each other between battles was one of the most touching parts of a war whose very fact forever touches the American soul. Along the Rappahannock, there were more examples of it in those long winter months of 1862–63 than ever before.

After holding firm at Fredericksburg in mid-December, Robert E. Lee's Army of Northern Virginia was spirited but hungry. His soldiers were used to hard marching and fighting, but for plain surviving, that winter was the hardest time they had faced. Food, medicine, blankets, even shoes were in short supply. The Southerners dug in near Fredericksburg often poked into what was left of the town after Union troops had shelled it, fought from its doors and windows, and vandalized it. Yankees had broken into wine cellars, ransacked women's closets, and danced in the streets wearing gowns and frilly underwear. Westwood Todd of the 12th Virginia went there after the Federals retired across the river. "There was scarcely a house that had not been pierced by shells, many were riddled, and some, but not a great many, were burned down," he remembered. He looked into a house that had been used as a Yankee hospital, found "amputated legs and arms lying around in a most unceremonious manner," and backed out quickly. He went into once-luxurious homes "which presented sickening spectacles; pianos and furniture smashed up, old family portraits with their eyes punched out, and slit, and walls defaced with ribald verses and maledictions on the 'd——d rebels,' letters of the most delicate and sacred character scattered in the yards and streets."[4]

• • •

ACROSS THE RIVER, the logistical state of Maj. Gen. Ambrose Burnside's thoroughly defeated army was better than its morale, but both were sagging. That place, that winter, has been called the Valley Forge of the Union army, and in terms of the soldiers' spirit it was true. Though a growing flood of supplies was sent down the Potomac, the troops got only a fraction of the food because of insurmountable paperwork and dishonest commissary officers. The hardtack and salt pork that trickled to the troops could not hold off a winter that got worse as it went on.

The Union army was in no mood to fight again as New Year's Day broke cold and clear. Soldiers dug deeper, swept ever farther in search of firewood, wrote many thousands of letters still treasured by their families. Except when their number came up for picket duty, they huddled against the cold and thought of home. Sometimes men off duty were like sullen cattle, herded together, passive, awaiting someone to prod them to move again. Now and then they flared into wild games, or violence against a bunkmate or the squad next door, and then settled back into time-killing card games, letter-writing, reading the religious tracts that poured into their camps, waiting. Professional officers as well as privates who had never seen a military map second-guessed their generals, criticizing their last battle, predicting the next. Drawing with sticks in the mud, some plotted the coming campaign as a specific operation, but in the ranks most saw it as another roll of the dice.

One soldier who had a plan was Ambrose Everett Burnside, West Point '47, major general commanding the Union's Army of the Potomac. Burnside was a chunky, genial patriot, with "a noble presence . . . a dignity and sincerity"—and a muttonchop style of whiskers that survives to this day. Despite ups and downs on the battlefield, he was still liked in Washington.[5] Earlier, after Union setbacks in the first months of the war, he had twice been offered command of the Army of the Potomac, and twice refused. At Antietam, he had led the Union's left wing attacking across what is still called Burnside's Bridge. Some blamed his delay there for allowing Lee to escape destruction. Yet, afterward, Lincoln asked him again to take over the Army in the East. Burnside still was reluctant, but his fellow generals urged him to accept because they feared that the alternative was the ambitious, self-promoting Joseph Hooker. At their insistence, Burnside became commander of the Army of the Potomac on November 5, 1862.

Despite his reluctance, he was eager to fight from the day he took over from Maj. Gen. George B. McClellan. Burnside planned to beat Lee south to the Rappahannock, cross at Fredericksburg, and drive on to Richmond. Lincoln was less than enthusiastic: increasingly he realized that the Confederacy's army, rather than its capital, should be his own army's primary target. He sent General-in-Chief Henry Halleck to try to persuade his new field commander to strike quickly at Lee's divided forces, and destroy them separately. But Burnside was stubborn.[6]

Two full corps of his men reached the Rappahannock opposite Fredericksburg before Lee's first major units arrived to face them. Because no pontoon bridges were available, Burnside held his troops back. Finally, when Burnside was ready to attack, Lee had the corps of both Stonewall Jackson and James Longstreet, his whole army, dug in behind the river. But Burnside had Lee outmanned, 122,000 to 78,000, and he forced a crossing to open the battle of Fredericksburg. Then, on December 13, he sent his troops against the Confederates defending the ridge behind the town. Federal bodies piled up in the field approaching the stone wall at the foot of Marye's Heights. Still Burnside would not back off. Grieved at how his men had been slaughtered, he wanted to atone by personally leading his old corps against the Rebels, to do or die. His generals dissuaded him; enough was enough. The Union army withdrew across the river after seeing 12,700 men killed and wounded. Lee's forces suffered fewer than half as many casualties.

It was one of the most lopsided battles of the war. It caused gloom in Washington. Knowing this, Burnside offered Lincoln a letter taking all the blame on himself. The president was gratified. This was wholly different from the alibis he had heard from earlier commanders. He tried to buck up the general and his army.

Thanking the troops, Lincoln wrote, "Although you were not successful, the attempt was not an error, nor the failure other than an accident. The courage with which you, in an open field, maintained the contest against an intrenched foe, and the consummate skill and success with which you crossed and re-crossed the river, in face of the enemy, show that you possess all the qualities of a great army, which will yet give victory to the cause of the country and of popular government. Condoling with the mourners for the dead, and sympathizing with the severely wounded, I congratulate you that the number of both is comparatively so small."[7]

The message did little to solace the Army, which had a more realistic view of the disaster. In the ranks, desertions mounted. Around their campfires, soldiers grumbled about Burnside. His generals went over his head to criticize him, to protest his plan for another river crossing. Lincoln ordered him not to move without advance approval. Burnside headed for Washington again to explain himself. On New Year's morning, he met Lincoln and learned that his generals had been complaining behind his back. Burnside defended his plan, but conceded that he did not have the confidence of his army and should be relieved—along with General-in-Chief Halleck and Secretary of War Edwin M. Stanton.[8] But that New Year's afternoon, Lincoln took a step that would forever change the war and American history, and for the moment it pushed aside the question of who should be commander and how he should lead.

FROM MORNING past noon, for at least three hours, Lincoln went through with the traditional January 1 White House reception, shaking hands with hundreds of politicians and their families, military officers, lobbyists, office-seekers, and ordinary citizens off the street. When at last the line dwindled, his right hand was swollen and trembling. As a few remaining high officials gathered around the president, Secretary of State William H. Seward unrolled a document before him. Lincoln started to sign the paper, then drew back and flexed his hand. He started again, halted again. Turning to Seward, he explained that "my right arm is almost paralyzed" from handshaking. "If my name ever goes into history it will be for this act, and my whole soul is in it. If my hand trembles when I sign the Proclamation, all who examine the document hereafter will say 'He hesitated.' "

Then he gripped the pen again, and slowly, firmly traced out his signature below the Emancipation Proclamation. Looking up, he smiled.

"That will do," he said.[9]

It was not, as most of us think of it now, a complete and sweeping order, nor did it come as a thunderbolt. The president had broached it to his cabinet in secret the previous July, and publicly promised in September, after Antietam, that it was coming. Essentially, it freed only those slaves in the occupied parts of the rebellious states. Peace Democrats were upset by the fact of it, and abolitionists by its limitations. But symbolically, the proclamation was a watershed. For the first time, it cast the war in moral terms. Southern politicians had gone to war over states' rights, and soldiers like Lee to defend the states they loved. Though pushed by the abolitionists, Lincoln had taken the North to war to preserve the Union. But whatever motivated individuals, no matter what the war had been about until then, beginning that afternoon it was about human freedom.

In the occupied South, newly freed slaves erupted in celebration. In Richmond, the *Examiner* called Lincoln's move "the most startling political crime, the most stupid political blunder, yet known in American history . . . servile insurrection is the real, sole purpose of the Proclamation."[10] Yet, among the soldiers, those who might die to decide the issue, reaction fit no predictable pattern.

Capt. Isaac Plumb of the 61st New York heard rumbles from home and told his diary, "Our Northern Traitors tell us we are fighting for the Negro. Those traitors would sooner see the country disrupted and lost than have the institution of slavery die." Later, as Congress debated the use of black regiments, Plumb wrote that "For one I would be willing to have my life saved by a black man, yes, a Nigger if you will, and I would fight by his side in such a cause as this. . . ."[11] Capt. David Beem of the 14th Indiana tried to soothe his wife: "In regard to freeing the negroes . . . the rebels ought to have their slaves confiscated, because they use the slaves to keep up the rebellion. A great many think if the negroes were freed that they would come over amongst us in the North, but this is the greatest mistake in the world. . . ."[12]

Such dutiful support for the president was not the rule among enlisted men. It was hardly surprising that a Southerner like seventeen-year-old Willie Dame of the Richmond Howitzers would ask his mother, "Did you ever hear of such a thing as the raising of the Grand Coloured Division in the Yankee army? If they bring them black scoundrels here there will be more buzzard meat in this part of the country than ever was before. And they say they are going to put them in front, just like the cowardly skunks."[13] But many Yankee soldiers were almost as annoyed.

Samuel Fisher of the 4th New Jersey wrote to his sister that "The men in our brigade have coom to the conclusion that they are fighting to free the Negroes and that is not what we came out here fore. I believe that the gratest part of the army here would hiss old Abe out of camp if he was to coom down here."[14] Charles R. Johnson of the 16th Massachusetts said of the slaves, "they are lazy and dont know what freedom means. The President Proclamation has in a measure divided the north and the army. The army hate to think that they are fighting for the negro. . . . There are officers, very few I am glad to say, who say they wont fight for the negro or under the proclamation. . . . I am glad to say that all this feeling is at present superficial and does little harm, our army being as effective as ever. . . ."[15]

Whatever spirit the Union army had that early winter came from soldiers capable of shrugging their shoulders despite the weather, impervious to snow and the greater issues. "I suppose you are all in high glee because Abe has set 3 million Niggers free (on paper)," Capt. Jacob Haas of the 96th Pennsylvania wrote to his brother. "Well, I am too if anything comes out of it. I care not if the Niggers eat the Whites or the Whites kill the Niggers, just so that the War be ended. But alas-a-lack-a-day, the Proclamation will not go even as far as our bullets go. I cannot believe that this war will ever be ended by fighting unless my plan be adopted: 'bring out all the men of the North and ram them in, and then the longest pole knocks the persimmon.' " [16]

To this shrugging, winter-droopy army Burnside returned, his resignation yet again rejected. Desertions still ran high. In the 63rd Pennsylvania, one runaway was caught and drummed out in front of his comrades as a deterrent example. He was marched out with his head shaven; his trousers were dropped and a hot branding iron was applied. The army buttons were cut off his uniform. A squad with fixed bayonets followed him as the band played the "rogues march." [17]

Yet despite their awful defeat at Fredericksburg, and their longing for McClellan, who was so careful with their lives and his own reputation, the Union troops did not unanimously resent Burnside. As they grumbled, many commiserated with their general, who one said "wears an old slouch hat as long as my arm. . . . He is quite bald-headed and not very good-looking." [18]

Beneath that hat and the gray weather, Burnside scouted up and down the Rappahannock. Everywhere he looked across he saw Lee's troops digging deeper, throwing up earthworks, covering the riverside plain beneath the heights with interlocking lanes of fire from muskets and artillery. Lee was able to cover more than 25 miles of river line with his thinly stretched divisions, and guard at least 50 miles. Burnside, grieved by his own folly in direct assault in December, determined on deception. He ordered preparations as though for crossing at scattered points, miles apart. New roads were cut, pontoons brought up, guns dug in, companies marched back and forth, cavalry sent to demonstrate under enemy eyes. [19]

Because the hills along the narrower Rappahannock upstream were the best site for his covering artillery, Burnside decided to move across United States Ford, ten miles above Fredericksburg. This sweeping maneuver would put him on the flank of Lee's army. The *New York Times*'s man on the scene reported that "The plan was an excellent one. Every military man disapproved the mode of attack adopted last time. Every military man approved the mode of attack adopted this time." As Burnside's lumbering army began to move westward, all the while carrying on an elaborate feint downstream, Lee started to strengthen his left arm to fend off the coming thrust. Burnside, with a head start, altered his plan to aim at Banks' Ford, a closer, quicker crossing. At dawn of January 21, engineers would push· five bridges across; after that, two grand divisions (temporary Union command elements of two corps each) would be over the river in four hours. Meanwhile, another grand division would distract the Rebels by repeating the December crossing at Fredericksburg.

Burnside's order said the "great and auspicious moment has arrived to strike a great and mortal blow to the rebellion, and to gain that decisive victory which is due to the country." But before Union soldiers could start hauling their guns and pontoons into place, cold rain swirled down. The *Times* man, William Swinton, looked out. "The heavens showed all the signs of a terrible storm," he wrote. It became "a wild Walpurgis night." [20]

By morning, the roads "were becoming shocking." Some 150 pieces of artillery were scheduled to be in place, and pontoons for five bridges. At the appointed hour, there were not enough for even a single bridge. Double and triple teams of horses and mules were hitched to each pontoon wagon. Long ropes were attached, and men leaned into them, sometimes 150 trying to move one boat. "They would founder through the mire for a few feet—the gang of Lilliputians with their huge-ribbed Gulliver—and then give up breathless." Night came again, and the pontoons still had not reached the river.[21] Burnside rode up and down the columns. Here, he did the work of a captain by siting an artillery piece overlooking the river. There, he all but got down and put his shoulder to a rope. As the afternoon waned he rode through the camp of Brig. Gen. Albion P. Howe's division. Burnside and his horse were "completely covered with mud, the rim of his hat turned down to shed the rain, his face careworn with this unexpected disarrangement of his plans," recalled the surgeon of the 77th New York. "We could but think that the soldier on foot, arm oppressed with the weight of knapsack, haversack and gun, bore an easy load compared with that of the commander of the army, who now saw departing his hopes of redeeming the prestige he had lost at Fredericksburg."[22]

Burnside refused to give up; he ordered food forward for two more days. Next morning he authorized a whiskey ration for everyone. But the rain kept on. Swinton rode out and reported: "One might fancy some new geologic cataclysm had overtaken the world; and that he saw around him the elemental wrecks left by another Deluge. An indescribable chaos of

pontoons, wagons and artillery encumbered the road down to the river.
. . . Horses and mules dropped down dead, exhausted with the effort to
move their loads through the hideous medium. One hundred and fifty
dead animals, many of them buried in the liquid muck, were counted in
the course of a morning's ride."[23] Burnside's problem was no longer how
to cross and fight, but how to retrieve his army from the elements.

From across the river, the taunts of Rebels sang out. Every Yankee
there remembered the sting of the broad signs put up by Lee's watching
men—"Burnside stuck in the mud" was the most frequent, and "This way
to Richmond," and "Yanks, if you can't place your pontoons, we will
send help." The Rebels had plowed the earth along their side of the river
so that if any of Burnside's men did get across, they would sink into more
mire.

But no Union soldiers would cross in the operation that history knows
as the "Mud March." Their morale sank with their wagons and animals.
That first night of rain, a captain of the 3rd New York Artillery sought
out the sergeant of the guard. He found the sergeant drunk and reprimanded him. The sergeant ran for his pistol, and "like a madman" took
out after the captain, who hid behind a tree, then stepped out and cut the
man down with his sword.[24] James Coburn, of the 141st Pennsylvania,
wrote in his diary, "Continued cold and rainy—mud growing deep, deep,
deeper—have had enough of winter campaigning. My diarhea is growing
worse. . . . This storm and exposure will kill thousands of our brave
boys."[25]

As Burnside's men dragged back toward their camps, mud-coated
regiments were indistinguishable one from another. The army had become
a disorganized crowd. And when the troops returned, they regretted the
unthinking enthusiasm with which they had set out. Many, assuming they
were on their way to Richmond, had burned their huts to the ground, so
not a plank was to be found. J. L. Smith of the 118th Pennsylvania wrote
home about passing other outfits and asking, " 'Say, did you see Burnsides
stuck in the mud back there?' They said 'h——l with Burnsides!' . . .
Burnsides has bad luck. The men have no confidence in him; they all
remember the terrible bloody Fredericksburg. If the troops don't have
confidence, why the General may as well resign."[26]

That very day, the general did.

ALREADY HUMILIATED by the crash of his hopes for reviving his
reputation, Burnside was infuriated by his generals' apparent efforts to

make things worse. Even as Burnside fumed, Hooker entertained a visiting newspaperman with bold comments about the incompetence of his commanding general, about how the president and government were imbeciles and perhaps a military dictator should take over and run the war. In anger, Burnside drew up an order dismissing Hooker and other insubordinate officers. He showed it to Henry Raymond, the *New York Times* publisher visiting his camp. What would Burnside do, Raymond asked, if Hooker defied his order? I'll swing him before sundown, the commander declared. Raymond hurried to Washington to warn Lincoln, and informed the president of Hooker's outspokenness behind Burnside's back.

True, Lincoln said, "Hooker does talk badly, but the trouble is, he is stronger with the country today than any other man. Even if the country were told of Hooker's talk they would not believe it." The president made clear that if he were forced to choose, despite everything he would have to take the popular Hooker over Burnside.[27] That is just what happened.

Burnside was about to publish the order when his aides wisely urged him to show it to the president first. He went to Washington and laid before the president General Orders No. 8—never issued, but remembered because it brought on a momentous shakeup in the Union army:

> General Joseph Hooker, major-general of volunteers and briga-
> dier-general of the U.S. Army, having been guilty of unjust and
> unnecessary criticisms of . . . his superior officers, and of the authori-
> ties, and having, by the general tone of his conversation, endeavored
> to create distrust in the minds of officers who have associated with
> him, and having, by omissions and otherwise, made reports and
> statements which were calculated to create incorrect impressions, and
> for habitually speaking in disparaging terms of other officers, is
> hereby dismissed the service of the United States as a man unfit to
> hold an important commission during a crisis like the present, when
> so much patience, charity, confidence, consideration, and patriotism
> are due from every soldier in the field. This order is subject to the
> approval of the President of the United States. . . .[28]

With this order, which also called for dismissal of half a dozen other generals, Burnside handed Lincoln his own written resignation. Accept one or the other, he told the president: he could not stay without those changes. The next day, January 25, Lincoln told Burnside he was going to relieve him and appoint Hooker in his place.

At the same time, the president heard rumors that some in his cabinet and army were scheming to replace him with a dictator. Ward Hill Lamon, his old law partner, now marshal of the District of Columbia, brought this up. Lincoln laughed. "I do not fear this from the people any more than I fear assassination from an individual," he said. "To show you my appreciation of what my French friends would call a *coup d'état,* let me read you a letter I have written to General Hooker." He opened a drawer and produced a letter that still rings in history:[29]

General:
    I have placed you at the head of the Army of the Potomac. Of course, I have done this upon what appear to me to be sufficient reasons. And yet I think it best for you to know that there are some things in regard to which, I am not quite satisfied with you. I believe you to be a brave and skilful soldier, which, of course, I like. I also believe you do not mix politics with your profession, in which you are right. You have confidence in yourself, which is a valuable, if not an indispensable quality. You are ambitious, which, within reasonable bounds, does good rather than harm. But I think that during Gen. Burnside's command of the Army you have taken counsel of your ambition, and thwarted him as much as you could, in which you did a great wrong to the country, and to a most meritorious and honorable brother officer. I have heard, in such a way as to believe it, of your recently saying that both the Army and the Government needed a Dictator. Of course it was not *for* this, but in spite of it, that I have given you the command. Only those generals who gain successes can set up dictators. What I now ask of you is military success, and I will risk the dictatorship. The government will support you to the utmost of its ability, which is neither more nor less than it has done and will do for all commanders. I much fear that the spirit which you have aided to infuse into the Army, of criticising their Commander, and withholding confidence from him, will now turn upon you. I shall assist you, as far as I can, to put it down. Neither you, nor Napoleon, if he were alive again, could get any good out of an army while such a spirit prevails in it.
    And now, beware of rashness. Beware of rashness, but with energy, and sleepless vigilance, go forward, and give us victories.

Chapter Two

MAN ON A WHITE HORSE

JOE HOOKER was six feet tall, erect and foursquare. He had a long, strong nose and pale blue-gray eyes in a clean-shaven face, pink from what many thought was overdrinking. Above his high forehead, his unruly sandy hair was brushed up and back. He sat his warhorse, a noble thoroughbred stallion, as if he were posing for a statue. He was the "beau ideal of a soldier in all physical qualities." [1]

The only weakness in his appearance was his chin. In a time when full beards, goatees, and other such adornments were in high military style, it was surprising that a man so conscious of his handsomeness did not grow a beard to camouflage this receding chin. In retrospect, looking back at his life, one may find that feature more noticeable than it must have been to his admirers in the winter of 1863. He was a blond war god, in looks and in the mind of a public hungry for a bold and lustrous captain to replace the unlucky Burnside.

But there was more to Hooker than his soldierly looks and his heroic steed. As Lincoln noted, there was ambition—it was sometimes reckless. Despite what Lincoln said, there also was politics. And there was demonstrated bravery in battle; his nickname was one of his greatest assets with the public and his troops. Although it was attributed to a typographical error, and he professed to be embarrassed by it, as he took command he had every right to be called "Fighting Joe Hooker." The more we know about him, the harder it is to believe that he truly resented it.

Grandson of a Minuteman and Continental army captain, he was born in Hadley, Massachusetts, in 1814. John Dunbar, who grew up with Hooker and whose mother taught him, said that as a boy Hooker was "somewhat mercurial." Dunbar's uncle, "notwithstanding the protest of one of his own daughters, never seemed to be willing to regard the boy as trustworthy in his dealings, some of which were well nigh being scandalous."[2] In what way "scandalous," whether in pecuniary matters or in some manner related to the protesting daughter, Dunbar did not say. Despite these traits, young Joe's mother wanted him to be a minister, but he pointed himself toward the law. Without the means for college, he turned to soldiering only because a family friend interceded to get him an appointment to West Point in 1833.[3]

Four years later, Hooker graduated twenty-ninth of fifty cadets. Among his classmates were men who would figure in the climax of his military life, including William H. French and John Sedgwick on the Union side, and Jubal A. Early and Robert H. Chilton of the Confederate army. Others critically concerned in his later career were lower classmen: future Union generals Henry W. Halleck, William T. Sherman, and George H. Thomas. As he knew them, they knew and remembered him—his carousing, his readiness to take on his Southern classmates in debate, and his habit of criticizing officers aloud, which almost got him thrown out of the academy.[4]

Lieutenant Hooker was sent to fight Seminoles and Cherokees, then in 1841 was appointed adjutant at West Point. During a later inspection trip to Newport, Rhode Island, as adjutant of the 1st Artillery, he met another soldier who would remember "What a handsome fellow he was. . . . a complexion a woman would envy, polished in manner, the perfection of grace in every movement. . . . the courtesy of manner we attribute to the old-time gentleman . . . somewhat effeminate in freshness of complexion and color perhaps, but . . . robust. He was simply elegant, and certainly one of the handsomest men the Army ever produced."[5] Such elegance served Hooker well at Newport, but soon he was transferred to Pensacola and then to duty with Zachary Taylor's army in Mexico.

FOR HOOKER and dozens of others in the fraternity of West Pointers, the Mexican War was the proving ground. In it, they first tried out the theories they had learned at the academy and would apply at places like Manassas and Chancellorsville. As Hooker took command on the Rappahannock in 1863, his mind drifted back to how he and the two most celebrated Confederate generals across the river had undergone their baptism of fire on the way to Mexico City sixteen years earlier. Hooker, newly breveted to captain, was then bracketed in seniority between forty-year-old Capt. Robert E. Lee and the freshly minted lieutenant Thomas J. Jackson. Before they fought together in the climactic battle of Chapultepec, all three had won promotions for gallantry in the field.

After action at Monterey as a brigade chief of staff, Hooker was praised for exemplary "coolness and self-possession in battle." Transferred to be adjutant of Gideon Pillow's division, he served as professional mentor to the politically appointed general. Lee, seeing action for the first time after seventeen years as an officer, won a reputation for bold reconnaissance, first as an engineer with Gen. Zachary Taylor in northern Mexico, then with Gen. Winfield Scott on the invasion route from Vera Cruz to Mexico City. Repeatedly, he found flanking routes around Mexican strongpoints and led Scott's divisions into position for attack. Scott later testified that Lee's exploits approaching the enemy capital were "the greatest feat of physical and moral courage" in the campaign. On one of those moves, Lee and the twenty-three-year-old Jackson crossed paths for the first time. It is notable that in their first work together, Lee was urging and Jackson was helping to execute a turning movement that succeeded because the enemy could not imagine an attack across such forbidding terrain. Neither of them left any record of their meeting, of whether it was as formal as a handshake or as casual as a passing salute along the trail; neither could foresee how one would become right arm to the other in campaigns to come.

Then, on the outskirts of the Mexican capital, Scott decided that the fortified heights of Chapultepec were the key to capturing the city. Lee stayed up all night positioning troops for the assault. When Pillow was wounded and the attack held up to wait for scaling ladders, Hooker asked permission to take a regiment and strike from the flank. Finding that approach too steep, he returned just in time to see his comrades break through to join marines and army regulars atop the heights. Meanwhile, Jackson took his cannon along a narrow causeway at the foot of the heights and wielded sponge and handspike in a roaring duel with massed Mexican guns above. He drove off a Mexican cavalry charge and silenced the enemy cannon. In mid-fight, he shouted to his cowering men, "There is no danger—see, I am not hit!" Later, he said that was the only lie he ever told.

There, at storied Chapultepec, the principals of a later, greater drama all fought within a few hundred yards of one another. In those months, Hooker, Lee, Jackson, and other professional soldiers could assess fellow officers whose paths they would cross again and again. When captain and future general John B. Magruder recommended Jackson for promotion, his report passed through the hands of captain and future general Hooker. James Longstreet was wounded and George Pickett picked up his colors to lead troops up the slope of Chapultepec. Hooker, Jackson, Magruder,

Irvin McDowell, and A. P. Hill were all in the same organization. McClellan, Pierre G. T. Beauregard, Joseph E. Johnston, John Pope, D. H. Hill, Benjamin Huger, Fitz-John Porter, Marcus Reno, and Richard S. Ewell were nearby. U. S. Grant took a cannon up a church steeple to chase the fleeing enemy into the capital. What they did and learned in Mexico helped assure that all would play major roles, on one side or the other, in the great civil war ahead.

After the capture of Mexico City, Hooker and other bachelors such as Tom Jackson enjoyed the society of local ladies who adapted graciously to military occupation. At the same time, the young officers created the Aztec Club, in which they studied the campaigns they had just fought, walking over the terrain, reconsidering their tactics.

Some higher officers had begun refighting their battles even while the war went on: Generals Pillow and William J. Worth, to boost their own ambitions and the political security of President James Knox Polk, wrote official reports and newspaper accounts challenging the actions of General Scott. When they persisted, Scott placed formal charges against them. Polk, siding with the insubordinate generals, relieved Scott of his post.[6] The result was a court of inquiry in the spring of 1848, Winfield Scott versus Gideon Pillow. In it, Hooker supported Pillow against the commanding general. From a professional viewpoint, as he would realize much later, it was a serious mistake—Scott had both a long career and a long memory.

Back in the States, with three battlefield promotions, Hooker requested and soon got duty on the West Coast. Peacetime army life and its modest pay scale soon paled beside the rowdy gold-boom profiteering around him. He became a regular at the Blue Wing Tavern in Sonoma, whose clientele included famous outlaws and politicians. In 1851, saddled with gambling debts, he took leave from the service. He is reputed to have borrowed from and not repaid fellow officers Henry W. Halleck and William T. Sherman; like his testimony in the Scott-Pillow dispute, that mistake would follow him. Still a bachelor, Hooker "became famous for his 'glad eye' for ladies of easy virtue," which inspired the story that those ladies took their nickname from him. "Likewise he communed with John Barleycorn and was said to be a three-bottle man."[7]

Resigning his commission when his leave ended, Hooker was appointed a colonel of California state militia. As war approached in 1861, he organized a regiment of Union volunteers. But when he found out that California regiments would not be sent east, he turned his hopes toward Washington.[8]

Hooker's first move was the obvious one—writing to offer his services to the commander of the United States Army. Unfortunately for him, the General-in-Chief was Winfield Scott. Hooker got no answer. Frustrated, he decided to go to Washington, but he had no travel money. One day he drifted dejectedly into one of his favorite saloons, Billy Chapman's in San Francisco. There the patriotic proprietor heard his woes, handed him a thousand dollars, and promised to stock his stateroom with liquor and cigars for the journey. In two days, Hooker was on his way to war. But he had no intention of merely enlisting, nor should he have. He wanted a command to fit his experience and his ego.

He used all his political contacts. Oregon's senator Edward D. Baker wrote to Lincoln that in Mexico, "No regular officer of his rank won more renown, and no man of any rank showed more gallantry. . . ." Seeing men who had served as his juniors appointed to high rank all around him, Hooker asserted that if he got a regiment he would promptly become army commander and end the war by capturing Richmond. Lincoln, impressed, passed his credentials to the War Department—where an appointment would need the approval of General Scott. Once again, nothing happened.

In July 1861, full of impatience, Hooker joined the picnickers who went to see the show west of the capital, where the Union army expected to slap down upstart Confederates near Manassas. The battle was a shocking debacle for the troops in blue, who reeled among the onlookers back to Washington. Soon afterward, one of Hooker's old Mexico comrades took him to see Lincoln, introducing him as Captain Hooker. The president was about to break off the conversation when Hooker spoke up. He was not a captain, but had been a regular army lieutenant colonel, he said. He had tried to rejoin the army, but Scott or some other obstacle prevented it. Before he left, he had to tell the president that "I was at the battle of Bull Run the other day, and it is neither vanity nor boasting in me to declare that I am a damned sight better general than you, sir, had on that field." Lincoln looked him in the eye, took his hand, and told him to sit. After they talked, the president said, "Colonel—not Lieutenant Colonel . . . I have use for you and a regiment for you to command."[9]

Thus at last Joe Hooker rejoined the army. But he thought he deserved more than a regiment. His political friends kept lobbying, and he was nominated to brigadier. On August 3, Hooker became the thirty-second ranking general in the U.S. Army.

He was back in his element, his real home. In two months, he was given a division and sent to southern Maryland to help clear the lower Potomac, a night-time freeway of Rebel spies and supplies. Hooker was anxious about enemy units across the river, potshotting at passing Union vessels. His curiosity converted him into a fan of aerial reconnaissance. Professor Lowe brought a balloon downriver moored to the U.S.S. *George Washington Parke Custis,* a former Washington–Mount Vernon steamer named for Robert E. Lee's father-in-law. When the professor's spying produced a first-class map, Hooker was so enthusiastic that he went for a balloon ride himself. Later, he would make use of Lowe in situations much more urgent.

That winter of 1861–62, Hooker's troops got into whiskey whenever it was within reach, and their general strengthened his reputation as a toper. His soldiers liked that, and revised the words of a popular marching song to make them, "Joe Hooker is our leader, he takes his whiskey strong. . . ." [10]

As 1862 began, Lincoln pressed McClellan, now in command of the Union army, to drive south. In early April, Hooker's division embarked with the cumbersome Army of the Potomac down the Chesapeake and landed near the field where Cornwallis had surrendered to Washington at Yorktown. McClellan laid siege to the town, giving the Confederates time to dig their next line of defenses before Williamsburg. When they surprised McClellan by pulling back in the night, he ordered Hooker to lead the infantry pursuit. Hooker drove the Rebels until Maj. Gen. James Longstreet turned to face him. Longstreet's brigades, led by men whose names would become increasingly familiar to Hooker—R. H. Anderson, Cadmus M. Wilcox, A. P. Hill, and George Pickett among them— pounded the Yankees back in a steady cold rain.

Hooker, for the moment doing all the Union fighting, sent for help. [11] Ahead of his main units, he rode his white horse, directing guns into place. The horse, hit earlier by a bullet, reared when the first cannon fired, throwing Hooker and falling on him. Hooker crawled out of the mud, remounted, and ordered more troops forward. Riding up and down, shouting at his men to stand, he hung on until finally reinforcements slogged up. Hooker complained that he had carried on an unequal fight all day while 30,000 troops were available to support him.

Nevertheless, in the first notable clash in the East since Bull Run, Hooker's division had held, and that was a welcome, very different story from the rout of the summer before. Legend says that an Associated Press reporter wrote about the battle of Williamsburg, sending his copy beneath an identifying line: "Fighting—Joe Hooker." In a New York paper's composing room, the dash was accidentally dropped, and "Fighting Joe" Hooker got his nickname. [12] Later, he protested that it did him "incalculable injury," making him seem "a hot headed, furious young fellow." But if he had hired a publicist to advertise him by that name, it could not have been more successful at promoting him in the public eye.

Lest Washington miss the point about who had fought and who had not, Hooker wrote to his political friends that McClellan "is not only not a soldier, he does not know what soldiership is." The commanding general, who had provoked Hooker by not giving him due credit in his battle report, was "an infant among soldiers." Those reading Hooker's letters had to recall his earlier boast that, given a chance, he would soon lead the Union army.

At Fair Oaks (Seven Pines) Hooker came up through dispirited Union regiments and confronted a swamp said to be impassable. "Get out of the way," Hooker said. "I have two regiments here that can go anywhere." After Hooker advanced, the anxious McClellan put his army on the defensive, and Hooker told him not to worry: "I can hold my position against a hundred thousand men." [13]

Such bold statements quickly spread through his division, boosting its pride, then through the army and back to Washington. Hooker's dramatic talent, displayed before Lincoln, had gotten him a prestigious command when he was being ignored in the capital. He flashed it at every opportunity, becoming the most quotable general in the army. And he was backing up his bold talk with bold action; otherwise the nickname of "Fighting Joe" would have been a joke. His division took a disproportionate number of the Union army's casualties in the Peninsula campaign—and when the fighting died down, Hooker was working his back channels to Washington again, writing his senatorial friends about the shortcomings of others, complaining that they were being promoted while he did the fighting.[14] Soon he got his promotion to major general. His next combat was on the ground of Manassas, where he had been a frustrated spectator the year before.

At the second battle of Bull Run, Hooker fought under the boastful John Pope. He looked forward to pitting his troops against those of Stonewall Jackson, who had earned his own famous nickname on the same field in the earlier battle. Hooker rode along the line on his warhorse, "the excitement of battle in his eyes, [with] that gallant and chivalric appearance which he always presented under fire." [15] At the height of the battle, one of his brigades launched a furious bayonet charge against Jackson's men in their railroad-cut defenses. Although Hooker's men cracked Jackson's line before being driven back, he later called the clash "useless slaughter."

Out of this second Union setback at Bull Run, Hooker shone as one of the increasingly few ranking generals who did not have the smell of defeat about them. In Washington, yet another reorganization was discussed. Lincoln asked Gideon Welles, secretary of the navy, who should take command of the army. "Hooker," Welles said immediately. "I like him too," said Lincoln, but "I fear he gets excited." Montgomery Blair, the postmaster general, put it more bluntly: "He is too great a friend of John Barleycorn." [16] The president was not so desperate yet that he could ignore that reputation. But in early September 1862, Hooker was given command of a corps as the Union army marched northwest to counter Lee's thrust across the Potomac.

Against Rebel delaying actions at South Mountain, Hooker advanced his divisions in a skillful flanking maneuver before the invaders pulled back. Then along Antietam Creek, Hooker was sent to open the battle by hitting Lee's left, held by Jackson. In early morning on September 17, their soldiers surged back and forth through the East and West Woods and the Cornfield, around the Dunker Church, in probably the most frenzied, sustained close combat yet seen by any Americans. Hooker was in the middle of it, "everywhere in the front, never away from the fire, and all the troops believed in their commander, and fought with a will." The two corps beat each other to bloody exhaustion. Hooker lost about a third of his troops.[17] A bullet hit his horse. He hardly noticed it. But then, as he rode over corpse-strewn ground toward the Dunker Church, his apparent immunity to gunfire ran out.

A sharpshooter's bullet pierced his foot. True to form, as he was carried off he shouted: "There is a regiment to the right. Order it forward! . . . Tell them to carry the woods and hold them—and it is our fight!" From the hospital, he wrote to his brother-in-law, "I only regret that I was not permitted to take part in the operations until they were concluded, for I had counted on either capturing their army or driving them into the Potomac. . . ."

Later, to congressional investigators, Hooker maintained that his troops at Antietam "had whipped Jackson, and compelled the enemy to fly. . . ." McClellan endorsed his self-advertising: "Had you not been wounded when you were," he wrote, "I believe the result of the battle would have been the destruction of the entire rebel army. . . ." Newspapers joined in the praise. In California, Hooker's old admirers commissioned a magnificent sword for him. To replace his wounded mount, the great white stallion that would become part of Hooker's heroic image was shipped from New Orleans.[18] Soon he went to recuperate at the Washington Insane Asylum, now St. Elizabeth's, used during the war as a hospital for ranking officers. The campaign he conducted from there was ambitious, but not insane.

Among many distinguished others, the president came calling. So did Secretary of the Treasury Salmon P. Chase, who wanted to succeed Lincoln. As Hooker described his battles, he denounced McClellan over and over. McClellan was not only the man who held the job Hooker wanted; he was the principal hero of the Democrats, while Chase was in search of political backing from the radical Republicans. Chase and Hooker fed each other's ambitions.

As they talked, Lincoln was wrestling with the choice of yet another commander to replace McClellan, who the president said suffered from "the slows." In the press, in Washington gossip, Hooker became the clear favorite. Yet there were reasons, aside from his slow recovery and his reputation for the bottle, why the president might hesitate to jump him over senior corps commanders. To pick such a blatant critic of McClellan would not sit well in the ranks, where soldiers still cheered for "Little Mac." Secretary of War Stanton and Maj. Gen. Henry W. Halleck, who had come east to succeed Winfield Scott as general-in-chief, both opposed Hooker (there was that unpaid loan from Halleck in California years before). And in the end, Hooker's unsubtle hospital campaign may have been overdone. Besides, Lincoln liked Ambrose Burnside—and so he chose him to command the Army of the Potomac, and by doing so assured future trouble from Hooker.

As if the army's table of organization could win battles, Burnside redrew it again. He created three "grand divisions" of two corps each. Hooker took the Center Grand Division. Before the battle of Fredericksburg, when Burnside held up at the Rappahannock to wait for bridges, Hooker sent a request to Burnside—and significantly to the secretary of war, too—that he be allowed to push his command over without waiting. This refused, he sent another letter complaining of Burnside's leadership. Visiting newspapermen found him angrily outspoken against his commander and the Washington bureaucracy. When Burnside detailed his plan for attacking head-on at Lee, Hooker openly called it "preposterous." [19] He urged crossing above Fredericksburg instead. He was right in what he said, if not in how he said it.

As the fight began, the command group watched from the Falmouth hills. One grand division crossed below, one above, and then Hooker saw one of his own corps go over without him. He complained mightily that his talents were being ignored, his command frittered away. Finally, Hooker was ordered to take his remaining corps into the fight. With the corps commander, his friend Daniel Butterfield, he went over to scout the situation. Officers already there advised against further attack. Hooker saw the foolishness of throwing his men into this meat grinder, and rode back to try to talk Burnside out of it. When Burnside insisted that he push on, Hooker unleashed "a torrent of vituperation" that drove some subordinate officers out of the room. One said he "made the air blue with adjectives." [20]

In a fury, Hooker recrossed the river to see a quarter of his lead division cut down. At that point, he refused to go on. As he sarcastically explained later, "Finding that I had lost as many men as my orders required me to lose, I suspended the attack." [21] Burnside called off the effort. Then came the postmortem.

Hooker went up to testify before Congress's Joint Committee on the Conduct of the War, and unloaded on Burnside yet again. Back and forth between the army and Washington, Hooker was busy talking to reporters, feeding his political friends more animosity against Burnside. The capital was full of rumor. Barely a week after the fiasco at Fredericksburg, one of the best-informed correspondents wrote that "Everywhere people are asking 'What next?' and here the rumors of another advance are snatched at with hopeful eagerness. . . . The most plausible theory of future operations is that Burnside will detach a great part of his army from its present position and cross the river at a fording point far above Falmouth, leaving enough of his force at the point now occupied to beguile the enemy . . . a brilliant success might yet attend our banners." [22] That was just what Burnside had in mind, but as his soldiers said, he was unlucky. The result, eventually, was the Mud March, and Lincoln's admonitory promotion of Joe Hooker to command the Army of the Potomac.

HOOKER DID NOT TREAT Lincoln's letter, citing his flaws and asking for victories, as something embarrassing and secret between him and the president. Rather, he offered it to others as proof of their intimacy. To a group of his officers Hooker read it aloud and said, "He talks to me like a father. I shall not answer this letter until I have won him a great victory." [23]

But Hooker took command of "an unhappy army, defeated, despondent, ravaged by desertion, unpaid, and stuck in the mud. . . ." His force on the Rappahannock theoretically numbered 256,545 soldiers. But more than 85,000 officers and enlisted men were absent from duty, and desertions mounted by 200 or more a day. The army's morning report for January 30 showed only 147,184 present and equipped for duty. Of these, nearly 30,000 were short-timers, mostly nine-month troops who had signed up the previous summer, due out by mid-May.[24]

A soldier in the 140th Pennsylvania wrote wistfully that the war should be over by July 4, and "If it isn't over by then I would not give much for this army, for it is badly discouraged and out of heart. . . . Now I hear that Burnside has been removed and Hooker has his place. He will make a failure or two and then I hope McClellan's turn will come again. . . . If they don't give us McClellan or someone the army has confidence in, this army may turn into an armed mob and throw down their arms and go home. . . . I have seen a whole regiment so drunk that they were hard put to find 15 sober men for picket duty. . . . I have seen lieutenants, captains and colonels so drunk they fell off their horses in the mud. Still the papers say this army isn't demoralized. As my messmate says, 'They don't count drunks.' "[25]

One New Englander who had known Hooker for years thought the "nervous verve and dash in his manner" inspired troops.[26] To another, the same qualities made him "a veritable Bombastes Furioso."[27] Many who had fought beside him feared he was so blustery that managing the biggest army in the country's history would be a task beyond his patience. They, and others who knew him only by reputation as "Fighting Joe," were surprised. "Administrative Joe" took over, and improvements began the first day. Some of the changes were organizational: Hooker scrapped the Grand Division concept, which had put a layer of command between corps and army headquarters, and made all his seven corps commanders responsible directly to him. They would report through Maj. Gen. Daniel Butterfield, lately one of Hooker's corps commanders, whom he installed as chief of staff.

Butterfield was not a professional soldier; he had studied law, then become a manager of his father's American Express Company before entering the New York militia. One biographer says he inherited "a genius for organization, an iron will, and a natural ability for promoting large enterprises."[28] His most lasting contribution to U.S. military tradition came during the Peninsula campaign, when he prescribed a few simple bars of music to be played by his brigade's bugler—the elegiac notes known to generations since as "Taps." A headquarters officer said Butterfield "was recognized as the brains of Gen'l Hooker, did all the difficult work for him, made out the lines of march, was virtually the executive officer of the whole army, and issued the orders to the various corps."[29] It was not the first or last time a staff chief was perceived as the brains of an army, and the commanding general the front man. Hooker's army had two great problems: management and morale. Its commander was fortunate in finding in Butterfield a man with "a natural ability for promoting large enterprises." Hooker would provide the inspiration.

While most communication up from his officers would pass through Butterfield, Hooker himself would bypass the War Department and communicate directly to the White House. On accepting the command, he had set one condition—that he deal first-hand with the president, not through his nominal superior, General in Chief Halleck. "Old Brains" Halleck was perhaps the most unpopular man in Washington, educated in both arms and law, an efficient administrator but with a shifty, irritable personality. Hooker maintained that Halleck was prejudiced in favor of the western army in which he had served, and, besides, held that old personal grudge against him. Although the official record shows no agreement by Lincoln to this bypassing arrangement, Hooker said later that he had accepted "with the stipulation that [Lincoln] would stand by me, and he swore that he would." [30]

But Halleck followed normal channels downward, and he promptly cited to Hooker the same guidelines that had been issued to Burnside just after the turn of the year: The main aim of the Army of the Potomac was to defeat Lee's army, not to capture the Rebel capital. With bloody Fredericksburg fresh in mind, Halleck said the next move should be via the fords above that town, that cavalry should be used against the enemy's communications, and in the meantime there should be constant demonstrations along the river to keep Lee from causing trouble. [31]

To Hooker, between bottomless mud and deepening snow, those were matters for the future, for a spring that seemed far away. First he had to resurrect an army.

Recognizing that between battles, homesickness and worry over family welfare can inspire desertion even by soldiers who march willingly into combat, he installed a rotating furlough system that encouraged soldierly performance as the price of visiting home. If men like Charles Littlefield and his comrades in the 21st Connecticut did well in inspections, they would be able to go check up on their worst fears. Writing to his wife, Littlefield said, "I sent my picture to you last week and did not hear whether you had got it or not. . . ." She must have worried him by mentioning a stay-at-home, however, because he said, "Tell Phil Madison to kiss my ass and to find out if he can get anything that I have got, and look out for him." The soldier wandered into strategic rumor, reporting that "Some say we are going to Washington and some say we are going to New Orleans and some say they are going to take Fredericksberg.

. . . I can't tell much about it." But he couldn't keep his mind off more intimate concerns: "When you get my picture I want you to let me know whether it makes you horny or not. . . . Strong said he saw one [woman] yesterday down to the depot and she wanted to get her pass signed to go to Washington and she said that the damn lieutenant would not sign it and I tell you she was not a baby. . . . It is a rather tough place here for women and I think that they will bring a good price. There is two regiments that have got women with them and they do washing for the officers in the regiment, but they look funny in a tent, I tell you that."[32]

Among the women who washed clothes for the army was the comely nurse Anne Etheridge, with the 3rd Michigan. When other regiments moved to the front, their camp followers stayed back, but Etheridge served through the thick of battle and had won sergeant's stripes for tending wounded on the Peninsula.[33] In fact, women were not that rare in the Union camps that winter, and they did more than nursing and laundry. H. N. Hunt of the 64th New York passed on the story that "there was a corporal taken sick on the picket line close by us the other night and the corporal was taken to a house close by and before morning there was a little corporal in the bed with her. It appears that she enlisted with her lover last fall and dressed in mens clothes and by some means deceived the doctor when examined and has been with the Army all winter and tented with her sweetheart."[34]

Some of the women who came as laundresses or masqueraded as soldiers made more money moonlighting as prostitutes, and there were also outright professionals who flaunted their trade. Capt. Charles Francis Adams, of the 1st Massachusetts Cavalry, wrote that "During the winter when Hooker was in command, I can say from personal knowledge and experience that the Headquarters of the Army was a place no self-respecting man liked to go and no woman could go. It was a combination of barroom and brothel."[35] It is possible, of course, that the blue-blooded, prematurely dyspeptic Adams made too much of what he saw, that his report was colored by Hooker's reputation.

When a soldier's turn came to go home legally, he understandably was more willing to return to the ranks than if he had slipped away. Charles Veil of the 39th Pennsylvania took a furlough back to Johnstown and walked in the dark toward his family's place outside town. "As I was coming down the hill into Scalp Level," he later recalled, "I happened to think of an old black dog we had, 'Fillmore' by name, and I knew he was cross at nights. . . . As I quietly stole up to the side gate and was about to raise the latch there stood old Fillmore. . . . For a moment I did not know how to proceed, but the next instant I snapped my finger. . . . Old Fillmore recognized me and was out over the gate with a bound, jumping up and yow-yowing, so that he woke up the whole family. . . ." For a few short days, there was chicken, turkey, mince pies, "everything that was good." Neighbors came to ask about their boys in the army. Charlie fought and refought the battles he had seen. "Finally the time came when I must start back," he wrote, "and I dreaded the goodbyes, so I had my brother smuggle my satchel out and without saying anything to anyone, stole away."[36] That Veil so fondly remembered that visit home certified his thankful loyalty to the commander who made it possible.

Hooker also recognized that an army trains as well as travels on its stomach, and so ordered that fresh bread be provided four times a week, fresh vegetables twice. He broke the system by which commissary officers were getting rich selling hard-to-get supplies to eager civilians, including some Virginians who did not let war interfere with opportunity. Hooker decreed that whenever specified rations were not delivered to regiments, the commissary officer must submit proof from the depot commander that those supplies were unavailable. He strengthened the army's inspector-general staff to see that his orders were carried out. To quash any doubt about his seriousness, he ended delays in carrying out court-martial sentences; deserters were arrested, and an exemplary few shot by firing squad. He ordered a halt to homefolks' shipment of civilian clothing packages to the troops, often accompanied by letters urging them to desert. He pushed Dr. Jonathan H. Letterman's upgrading of the medical department and his closer attention to sickness and sanitary conditions. And operationally, his major changes were to create an intelligence arm where there was none, and draw the army's scattered cavalry units together into one powerful corps.

Chief of Staff Butterfield testified that when Hooker took command, "We were as ignorant of the enemy in our immediate front as if they had been in China."[37] Soon after the war began, Lincoln's bodyguard, ex-Chicago detective Allan Pinkerton, had set up the Federal secret service and operated in the field with McClellan. But when McClellan left, Pinkerton did, too, and for intelligence the Army of the Potomac depended mostly on casual travelers through the lines, "contraband" ex-slaves, and the observations of cavalrymen who till then were far from aggressive. Nobody was charged with correlating the odds and ends that came in. On the Rebel side, Lee fought on friendly ground most of the time, so local farmers and their families functioned as his spies, and what they told

Union questioners was often misleading. Washington and Baltimore were riddled with Southern sympathizers, including bold agents who slipped back and forth across the Potomac in the dark. Jeb Stuart's cavalry scouts were always moving. The Confederates also learned a lot from the Northern newspapers swapped across the Rappahannock, which were then sent on to Richmond. For Union purposes, the Rebel army might as well have been in China, while Lee was much better informed about Union moves and intentions.

To remedy this, Butterfield commissioned Brig. Gen. Marsena R. Patrick, the army's provost marshal-general, to create a system to collect and make sense of information about the enemy. Patrick called in Col. George H. Sharpe, who commanded the 120th New York, and designated him deputy provost marshal-general. Sharpe, a sophisticated lawyer who had taken on diplomatic assignments before the war, organized a Bureau of Military Information. In short order, he had a network of agents behind Confederate lines, moving information quickly to army headquarters. Together with Professor Lowe's balloons, this made Hooker the best-informed Union general who had ever taken the field.[38] As a counterespionage measure, Patrick cracked down on deserters and stragglers within the lines.

Before Hooker took over, Union cavalry regiments had been dispersed among corps and divisions, their strength and efficiency dissipated. They were used for escort and courier service, and occasional scouting expeditions. That was in clear contrast with Lee's use of Jeb Stuart's farseeing cavalry command. Apparently the Union approach was a holdover from Winfield Scott's fear that cavalry could not operate in mass against the longer-range, rifled cannon coming into use. The cavalry had less prestige in the Northern army, while it was the glamour arm for the South, which had a tradition of country life and horsemanship. The Union cavalry's reputation for marginal operations inspired Joe Hooker's stinging query, "Whoever saw a dead cavalryman?" Hooker knew at least how to organize his horsemen. He put them into three divisions, making one cavalry corps under command of Brig. Gen. George Stoneman, a West Point classmate of Stonewall Jackson and George Pickett. Stoneman had commanded a bigger infantry corps under Hooker at Fredericksburg. With this change, Hooker had created—at least on the table of organization—his own Jeb Stuart.

Thus things picked up in the Army of the Potomac. A Maine captain recalled that before Hooker, "the higher officers had such piques and quarrels among themselves as never before or since undermined the morale of that or any other army of the United States. Soldiers, as well as officers . . . had become disheartened and discouraged. . . . A bright flame of enthusiasm was fast dwindling into a flickering torch." And then, he wrote, Joe Hooker took command, and "never was the magic influence of a single man more clearly shown."[39] One of the simple moves Hooker ordered was Dan Butterfield's idea—to give each corps distinctive insignia, both to boost spirits and to identify stragglers in the field. These were the assigned symbols: First Corps, sphere; Second, shamrock; Third, diamond; Fifth, Maltese cross; Sixth, Greek cross; Eleventh, crescent; and Twelfth, star. Within each corps, the 1st Division's badge was red, the 2nd Division's white, the 3rd's blue, the 4th's green. Suddenly caps in Hooker's army blossomed with new insignia, worn as proudly as badges of honor.

Of such little things morale is made. But there is only one way for it to last, and that is success in battle. When the Union soldiers looked at one another polishing bayonets, parading, singing, throwing snowballs, they had reason to feel better. And then they looked across the river. Over there, as one of their artillery officers saw it, was the Army of Northern Virginia, "proud, elated and confident of success. Numerically the weaker, it was strong in the absolute loyalty of its leaders to their chief. Its officers and men, long inured to privations, had been welded on the anvil of battle till they were hard as iron. . . ."[40]

Chapter Three

AUDACITY ABOVE ALL

IF THE UNION gunnery officer who thought them hard as iron could have walked among Lee's soldiers that winter, he would have seen that they were most human. They could laugh at their enemies, but they could feel hunger and cold. As shoeless soldiers of the 22nd Georgia stood picket duty in the rain, sleet, and snow, they wrapped green cowhides around their feet. Around their campfires they raked away the snow, covered the ground with wet blankets, and slept. W. B. Jennings of the 22nd wrote, "awoke before day nearly frozen; taking my blanket by the edge it would stand up like a plank, it was frozen so hard and stiff."[1]

Such living debilitated the toughest infantrymen, North or South. Henry Clay Roney of the 22nd came down with a fever that turned out to be smallpox, and was sent in a snowstorm to a hospital in the woods toward Chancellorsville. The hospital had once been a church. "There were no windows or doors," he recalled, "but the openings were chinked up with pine boughs. There were a few patients lying on cots, placed against the sides of the wall. The floor of the building, in the middle thereof, had been removed for a space to build up a fire, from the ground to the floor . . . but little warmth could come from such a source." Hungry when he felt a little better, Roney slipped out and stole biscuits from the nearby kitchen, then sneaked in the snow to a forest farmhouse and ate his fill of apples. This escapade brought on pneumonia, and he was carried out to a crude brush lean-to where a heavy-drinking young doctor concluded that he would soon die. He didn't, but all around him others did.[2]

In both armies, they died of smallpox, pneumonia, diarrhea, typhoid—there was little notion of camp sanitation. They were pestered by body lice, which both sides called graybacks, a term that soon became a Yankee nickname for the Rebels. Their stomachs growled for food. Jim Wilson of the 16th Mississippi datelined a letter home, "Camp Starvation, near

United States Ford," and said gamely, "I am used to hardships. I can do with eating once a day just as we used to do with eating three. . . ."[3] Like travel, hunger broadened men's horizons. One day the 1st South Carolina was on picket around an old barn infested by rats, and some of the soldiers chased and killed a few to "see how they would eat, broiled." It was a joke at first, more crude humor, but when the men tried their new entrée, some found that it "tasted like young squirrel."[4]

A handful of the 22nd Georgia, sent to guard a farmhouse, was rankled by the farmer's willingness to feed a passing cavalry detachment while refusing food to his infantry protectors. Jennings and his messmate Jim Jones set their eyes on the farmer's flock of turkeys. Afraid to shoot and attract attention, Jennings climbed up and chased the turkeys through the trees, trying to whack one down with his iron ramrod. After the flock escaped, Jones next morning drove it a mile away so the sound of his musket would not be heard when he shot one down.[5] The fortunate few who owned their own turkeys were possessive of them; one was Brig. Gen. William Mahone, who kept a flock fattening in a pen outside his tent. When he stepped out on Christmas morning to select one for roasting, they were all gone. "Who stole Mahone's turkeys?" was a question his Virginia brigade laughed over for the rest of the war.[6]

That winter, Mahone's sternness created a "painful and mortifying scene" that his troops remembered long after. He formed his brigade to witness the punishment of two men convicted of stealing property they had been sent to guard. The prisoners were stripped bareback and their hands tied to crossbars above their heads. Two soldiers were detailed to give them thirty-nine lashes apiece, with a lieutenant counting. But Mahone, watching from horseback, saw that the whip-wielders were merely tapping the prisoners. He ordered the lieutenant and the soldiers with the whips arrested, and picked another officer to carry out the punishment correctly. "If I may judge by the way the prisoners winced, and the appearance of their backs, the new detail did their work effectually," wrote Westwood Todd of the 12th Virginia. He wondered whether Mahone had been remembering his stolen turkeys.[7]

The tiny, dapper Mahone was hardly the most popular general in the Army of Northern Virginia, but even the best-loved insisted on discipline, painful as it could be. In February, six members of Stonewall Jackson's old brigade were convicted of desertion; three were to be executed by firing squad. Brig. Gen. Elisha Franklin Paxton pleaded that only one, chosen by lot, be shot as an example. Jackson disagreed. "Over-lenient courts" are a problem for the army, he said, and when one does its duty, its sentence should be carried out. Lee stood behind Jackson's refusal, but on the day of execution President Davis intervened to save the men.[8]

Still, even as officers insisted on discipline, they felt deeply for their suffering troops. Legend says that Jackson, riding with one of his generals past soldiers shivering about a campfire, heard his companion mutter, "Poor devils, poor devils." Stonewall corrected him: "Call them suffering angels," he said.[9] A South Carolina captain wrote sadly that thousands were on duty in the snow and mud "without shoes, often no blanket, hardly any overcoats, and many without coats, nothing often but a ragged homespun shirt."[10] A Louisiana officer wrote to his congressman that 400 of his 1,500 men had nothing on their feet. One regiment was unable to drill for lack of shoes.[11]

Even the Yankees across the river could sympathize with what they saw. A man in the 140th Pennsylvania wrote as winter waned that "The Rebs are getting hard up for grub and clothes. You can see them when they change pickets. The man on post peels off his coat and gives it to his relief and runs to his quarters. One of them told me they only had five or six coats to a company and those on duty use them. He also said lots of the men in his camp were barefooted and there was no use going around the stump about it."[12]

The wonder is that the Army of Northern Virginia retained its morale while its better-supplied enemy wallowed so deep in despond—that despite all, the Southerners fought with such spirit in those brief, bloody spurts between months of digging, shivering, and waiting. When the war began, the typical Southerner was more strongly motivated. He was fighting, as he saw it, to defend his home, whether he lived by the Virginia battlefields or the faraway Gulf of Mexico. The Northerners were invaders, and for them the concept of holding the Union together was a shade theoretical as a driving force. Yet, that winter, Lincoln's Emancipation Proclamation had made the war's root cause its public reason. A minor fraction of Southern soldiers owned slaves, but they were now cast as defenders of slavery. When Northern soldiers were sworn in, a minor fraction of them had ever seen slaves, but they were now—reluctantly, most of them—sent to set slaves free. Only later would they learn to play the role of liberator with pride.

For Confederate soldiers, the very fact of being underdogs in numbers, in weapons, and in provisions somehow contributed to morale. They looked derisively on the enemy as a dependable source of supply, and let the Union soldiers know it. As the Yankees advanced toward Jackson's men at Fredericksburg, the Southerners yelled across their stone wall,

"Take off them boots, Yank! Come out of them clothes; we're gwine to have them! Come on, blue-bellies, we want them blankets! Bring them rations along!" [13] And sure enough, after driving the Union divisions back, the Rebels deftly stripped boots and coats off enemy corpses. Even when captured, they had a cockiness that Union soldiers remembered years later. As men who still had never suffered a major defeat, the troops of the Army of Northern Virginia had an immense temporary advantage over their countrymen across the river. And as soldiers who marched with Robert E. Lee, they carried toward spring a confidence that the Union army in the East would not wear until the final stages of the war.

NAPOLEON WROTE that "In war men are nothing; it is the man who is everything. The general is the head, the whole of an army." Writing specifically of Lee's army, that accomplished military historian Col. G. F. R. Henderson added that "Even a professional army of long standing and old tradition is what its commander makes it; its character sooner or later becomes the reflex of his own; from him the officers take their tone; his energy or his inactivity, his firmness or vacillation, are rapidly communicated even to the lower ranks. . . . The history of famous armies is the history of great generals, for no army has ever achieved great things unless it has been well commanded. . . . Mutual confidence is the basis of success in wars, and unless the troops have implicit trust in the resolution and resources of their chief, hesitation and half-heartedness are sure to mark their actions. . . ." [14]

For more than a century, Americans have accepted Lee as the very monument of a soldier, all but perfect in war and peace, "the marble man." An anonymous poem to him begins: "There he stood, the grand old hero, great Virginia's god-like son / Second unto none in glory—equal of her Washington." It tells how he offered to lead Texas troops in an attack but they refused to go forward until he moved out of harm's way. When he insisted, a Texan grabbed the reins of his warhorse, assuring the soldiers that Lee would not ride on to share their danger—at which they charged gloriously ahead. Seeing this, Lee's "god-like calm was shaken, which no battle shock could move / By this true, spontaneous token of his soldiers' child-like love." [15]

The details of that incident at the Wilderness may have been exaggerated, but in repeating the description "god-like," the poem dealt with a larger truth—with the way Lee came to be regarded by his troops, his Southern compatriots, and eventually most of the country. But in the winter of 1863, that image was still building. In his psyche, in his battle record, even in his aristocratic Virginia background, there were flaws, a complexity that makes him more interesting than the figure of polished marble that has endured in the popular imagination.

Lee became a soldier with a name to live up to, and to live down. The family had been distinguished in Virginia well over a century when the dashing Henry Lee, Robert's father, won the nickname "Light-Horse Harry" as a Revolutionary cavalryman. He was a favorite of George Washington's, who gave him a command called Lee's Legion. Leading it, Light-Horse Harry fought brilliantly. An admirer said he came into the world "booted and spurred, his spurs made of the purest hand-hammered silver, twirling his saber over his head and shouting, 'Charge the bastards! Ride them down, boys!' "[16] Harry ended the war a celebrated hero, entered politics, became governor of Virginia. His future seemed ever brighter; he went to Congress, and there wrote the resolution that labeled Washington "first in war, first in peace and first in the hearts of his countrymen." He married his cousin and thus became master of the ancestral Lee homeplace of Stratford on the Potomac, and on this first wife's death took another—Anne Carter, of an equally glorified Virginia family, the Carters of Shirley plantation on the James. The couple's fifth child was christened Robert Edward.

Light-Horse Harry was daring, charming, an honored soldier and politician. But his financial ambitions outpaced his business sense. He lost repeatedly in land speculation. When Robert was two years old, Harry was sent to debtors' prison. Mrs. Lee left Stratford and had to feed and clothe the family in Alexandria.

Harry died in 1818, leaving Robert fatherless at the age of eleven. As if his father's decline were not enough of a burden, Robert's older half-brother Henry, the new master of Stratford, brought further disgrace to the family. While Henry's wife was grieving the loss of a baby, he dallied with his young sister-in-law. She became pregnant. He was also accused of misusing her money. Virginians thus dubbed young Henry "Black-Horse Harry"; he sold Stratford and left the state. The family's hopes focused on Robert. By his father's and half-brother's troubles the boy was taught meticulous restraint in matters of money and morals. But Light-Horse Harry's reputation as a soldier was still bright, and overflowing testimonials to it helped Robert get an appointment to West Point in 1825.

He was a model cadet, graduating second in 1829 without a single demerit. After seventeen years as an engineer, he got orders to join the army heading for Mexico. The high point of those years was not professional but domestic: Lee married Mary Anne Randolph Custis, great-granddaughter of Martha Washington. The couple lived at Arlington, overlooking the national capital. She eventually inherited the mansion from her father, George Washington Parke Custis, who was Martha Washington's grandson, and who had been adopted by George Washington and spent his boyhood at Mount Vernon. Arlington was a museum of Washington memorabilia. This association strengthened Robert Lee's feeling for George Washington, his father's old admirer, as not a remote and legendary figure but an everyday presence in his own life.

In Mexico, Lee was conscious of the tradition that traveled with him. In camp, he dined with George Washington's silver, brought along as part of his kit. But he made his reputation in the field. At Zachary Taylor's headquarters one day, he overheard a young captain gallop up sweating to report the approach of 20,000 Mexicans with 250 cannon. "Captain," Taylor asked calmly, "did you say you *saw* that force?" "Yes, General," said the officer. "Captain," said Taylor, "if you say you saw it, of course I must believe you; but I would not have believed it if I had seen it myself." In his mind, Lee was making notes every moment; that lesson of easy skepticism toward alarmists would help preserve another army one day.[17]

Assigned as engineer for Winfield Scott, Lee became a protégé of that grand old general, who had been a hero in the War of 1812 and would serve until 1861. Between battles, Lee listened hard as Scott, "the most scientific soldier at that time in America," taught lessons with his tales of earlier wars. Years later, before Lee and Scott were thrown on opposite sides in the Civil War, Scott would call him "the very best soldier that I ever saw in the field." Lee, breveted to colonel, headed home from Mexico with a glowing reputation and a personal knowledge of some of the men who would become generals in his future, most importantly Joseph Hooker and fellow engineer George McClellan.[18]

As superintendent of West Point in the early 1850s, Lee got first-hand impressions of many cadets who would shine in combat within a decade—men such as J. E. B. Stuart, John Pegram, Dorsey Pender, Philip Sheridan, and O. O. Howard. Then, in 1855, another of Lee's friends from Mexico, Secretary of War Jefferson Davis, assigned him to the 2nd U.S. Cavalry, on the Texas frontier. Lee thus said goodbye to the Engineer Corps to become a line officer for the first time in his thirty years in uniform—in the cavalry, the branch with which he had the least experience.

As the debate over slavery boiled higher in the East, Lee was 1,500 miles away. His earliest surviving thoughts on slavery and civil war were written to his wife: "Certain people of the North," he wrote, want to "interfere with and change the domestic institutions of the South," an object they could attain only through war. "In this enlightened age, there are few I believe, but what will acknowledge that slavery as an institution is a moral & political evil in any Country." Yet, he went on, "it is a greater evil to the white man than to the black race. . . . The blacks are immeasurably better off here than in Africa. . . . How long their subjugation may be necessary is known & ordered by a wise Merciful Providence. Their emancipation will sooner result from the mild & melting influence of Christianity than the storms & tempests of fiery Controversy. . . . While we see the Course of the final abolition of human Slavery is onward, & we give it the aid of our prayers & all justifiable means in our power, we must leave the progress as well as the result in his hands who sees the end; who Chooses to work by slow influences; & with whom two thousand years are but as a Single day." [19]

A year later, Lee returned to the seat of the debate when he took leave to straighten out matters concerning his father-in-law's estate. His stay at home dragged on for many months. Then, one morning in October 1859, Lt. Jeb Stuart rode up the hill to Arlington with an urgent message. Some unidentified radical had raided the arsenal town of Harper's Ferry, Virginia, and was inciting slaves to an uprising. President James Buchanan sent Lee to put down the insurrection. With Stuart, Lee sped west on a Baltimore & Ohio locomotive. His troops surrounded the engine house, where a man called Smith had barricaded himself and his raiders with a handful of local hostages. Next morning, Lee sent Stuart to the engine house door with an ultimatum. When a bearded man opened the door a crack, Stuart recognized him as the fiery abolitionist John Brown. Brown refused Lee's surrender demand, and a marine detachment stormed the engine house. Brown was captured, tried, and sentenced to hang. After cleaning up the military details, Lee stepped aside from the uproar created by Brown's raid and forthcoming execution.

Soon afterward, he went back to Texas. By then even the frontier was aflame with argument. Lee had little patience with the Deep South cotton states. He did not identify with the South as such, or sympathize with any potential Confederacy. During the painful months that followed, he declared repeatedly that his first duty was to Virginia. In January 1861, he wrote home that "I can anticipate no greater calamity for the country than a dissolution of the Union. . . . I am willing to sacrifice everything but honor for its preservation. . . . Secession is nothing but revolution.

. . . Still, a Union that can only be maintained by swords and bayonets, and in which strife and civil war are to take the place of brotherly love and kindness, has no charm for me. . . . If the Union is dissolved, and the Government disrupted, I shall return to my native State and share the miseries of my people, and save in defence will draw my sword on none." Deeply conscious of what his father and his idol Washington had done to make the nation, he wrote again that "I wish to live under no other government. . . . I wish for no other flag than 'the Star spangled banner' and no other air than 'Hail Columbia.' " [20]

Such was Lee's state of mind when, on April 1, 1861, he received orders to return to Washington. Reporting to General Scott, he made clear the feelings he had spelled out in his letters. Virginia had called a state convention, whose members were committed two-to-one against secession. But volunteers were drilling, fire-eaters were speechifying. Lee was given command of the 1st U.S. Cavalry. He was still hoping, and so was Scott, himself a Virginian who also opposed secession. But as general-in-chief, Scott was preparing to defend the Union. He did not expect Lee to take arms against Virginia; he likely hoped that by having him in place to lead a powerful army, he might head off what was coming.

But nothing could. After Fort Sumter, Lincoln called for 75,000 volunteers to put down the rebellion. In the president's name, Postmaster General Montgomery Blair offered Lee command of the Union army. Lee refused, saying that "though opposed to secession and deprecating war, I could take no part in an invasion of the Southern States." Scott told him, "You have made the greatest mistake of your life, but I feared it would be so."

Virginia's pressured politicians voted secession on April 18. Two days later, Lee resigned his commission. He wrote to Scott of "the struggle it has cost me to separate myself from a service to which I have devoted all the best years of my life and all the ability I possessed." He told the old general, "Your name and your fame will always be dear to me." And then he rode back to Arlington, not to cross the Potomac again until he led the thoroughly blooded Army of Northern Virginia into Maryland seventeen months later.[21]

The very day of Lee's resignation, the Alexandria *Gazette* nominated him to lead Virginia's troops in the coming conflict. "His reputation, his acknowledged ability, his chivalric character, his probity, honor, and—may we add, to his eternal praise—his Christian life and conduct—make his very name a 'tower of strength,' " the paper said. "It is a name surrounded by revolutionary and patriotic associations and reminiscences." The day after, Lee went to services at Christ Church, where Washington had been a vestryman. Those ties had to be much on his mind there, and afterward when the governor summoned him to Richmond. He left Arlington for the last time, looking out a train window at Fairfax, Manassas, and Culpeper, at Bull Run, the Rappahannock and Rapidan, villages and streams whose names would soon burn into the nation's history.

If Lee had not consciously cast himself as the Washington of the Confederacy, newspapers and politicians had. A recurring note in that praise was reference to "his Christian life and conduct." When a child up North wrote asking for his photograph, he sent his likeness back with a note that said: "It is painful to think how many friends will be separated and estranged by our unhappy disunion. May God reunite our severed bonds of friendship, and turn our hearts to peace! I can say in sincerity that I bear animosity against no one. . . . [But] I must side either with or against my section of country. I cannot raise my hand against my birthplace, my home, my children. . . . I foresee that the country will have to pass through a terrible ordeal, a necessary expiation, perhaps, of our national sins. May God direct all for our good, and shield and preserve you and yours." His personal letters had often included an invocation, especially after he was confirmed in the Episcopal church in 1853. Now, increasingly, that tone crept into his official communications, as if he were molding any remaining doubt over his painful decision into comforting certainty that he had chosen a holy cause.[22]

THE FIRST URGENCY of that cause was to organize a defense of Virginia, mobilizing her volunteers and fortifying her rivers. As commander of state forces, Lee began this task, then Jefferson Davis brought him into Confederate service as his military adviser. In his first Civil War campaign, a minor affair at Cheat Mountain, Lee failed to retake parts of western Virginia that had been captured by McClellan. This diminished his reputation with some, but not with Davis. Later, Lee prepared coastal defenses from Virginia south until early 1862, when McClellan's Union army was slogging up the Virginia peninsula. Brought back to Richmond, Lee was a general without an army, serving as buffer between Davis and the Confederate field commander, Joseph E. Johnston. Then Johnston was wounded, and on June 1, 1862, Davis appointed Lee commander of the Army of Northern Virginia.

Lee moved into his historic role at the age of fifty-five. He had never commanded troops in a major battle. When he took over, 100,000 Federal soldiers were on Richmond's doorstep. First he built a line of trenches to hold the Union divisions while he maneuvered against them. Then, for the first of many times, he turned in crisis to Stonewall Jackson. Jackson already had baffled a Federal army in the Shenandoah Valley. Lee brought him marching fast to join the offensive in the Seven Days' Battles. The day of Jackson's arrival, his uncharacteristic sluggishness cost A. P. Hill casualties in what was to have been a coordinated attack. Then, in a series of moves, Lee took the initiative away from McClellan.

But in that first campaign as commander, Lee also made a costly mistake of the kind he would not repeat until a year later in Pennsylvania. Overmatched by Lee's boldness, McClellan looked for a way out. To cover his withdrawal he massed his Union force at Malvern Hill beside the James. In the tangled terrain Lee could not coordinate his inexperienced troop leaders, but pressed a piecemeal attack. Union artillery beat down the assault, and before that July 1 was out, Lee's army had suffered more than 5,000 casualties. It was a costly mistake, but what counted in Richmond was that in one month Lee's campaign had driven the Federals from the outskirts of the capital. Morale zoomed as the South cheered its new hero.

Even before he outgeneraled McClellan below Richmond, Lee had impressed others with the aggressive energy behind his calm courtesy. Hearing the order to dig in to protect the capital, an eager young major was unhappy. He was E. Porter Alexander, who became one of Lee's best artillery officers. He did not like the passive look of those trenches. He asked a friend whether Lee had the audacity to do what was asked of him—whip a much bigger force. The friend, Col. Joseph Ives, had served with Lee and overheard his conversations with Davis. "Alexander," he said, "if there is one man in either army . . . head and shoulders above every other in audacity, it is General Lee. His *name* might be Audacity. He will take more desperate chances and take them quicker than any other general in this country, North or South, and you will live to see it, too." [23]

Lee took chances every time he collided with the enemy, because his army was consistently outnumbered. On the way to Second Manassas and Antietam, he divided his forces and relied upon his subordinate generals, especially Jackson, to arrive at the right place at the right time. Then at Fredericksburg, his experienced sense of terrain told him to let the attacking Federal divisions shatter themselves against his lines. With a sweeping view from the knob since known as Lee's Hill, he watched young Maj. John Pelham of Alabama take two pieces of horse artillery out on the flank and hold up the oncoming Yankees with sheer impudent bravery. Then, as a Southern counterattack drove Federal troops back, he turned to Longstreet and said, "It is well that war is so terrible; else we should grow too fond of it." To his biographer, that "revealed the whole man in a single brief sentence."[24]

Though his job was to map strategy and move tens of thousands of men rather than adventure out front to fight an army with a brace of cannon, Lee set an example of chivalry for his more colorful juniors like Pelham and Stuart. Wills Lee of the Richmond Howitzers recalled the day on the Rapidan when a Federal regiment marched in beautiful order across a slope beyond the river. An officer ordered his gun to fire at the Yankees. "I don't think I ever saw as many men fall from one shot," Wills Lee said. "It burst almost in the center of the force, and made such a hole as one can imagine would show in a great blanket, if some big object were blown through it. The regiment scarcely halted, closed up promptly and marched on; they were gallant men. Just then General Lee rode rapidly up, and in an indignant tone, demanded the name of the officer who ordered the shot. . . . He ordered us to cease and withdraw the gun, saying, 'This is murder, not war. Those men are only relieving their pickets.' "

After that, the gunner wrote, the weather warmed and "we had quite a pleasant time with 'our friends, the enemy.' " Although officially Lee opposed their fraternizing, his attitude seemed to approve it. They swam to meet each other at midstream to swap delicacies, and would even "cross to each other's banks and have a social smoke" until orders came to stop all that and fire on any enemy in sight: "It seems too much spying had been going on."[25]

CONFEDERATE SPYING and Confederate hunger figured in a decision Lee made reluctantly in mid-February 1863: to send a quarter of his infantry away from the Rappahannock line, to southeast Virginia. His informants had reported that a Union corps was moving down the Potomac. Its objective was unknown—perhaps to cut the Confederacy's rail line into the Carolinas, perhaps to threaten Richmond again from seaward. Lee sent George E. Pickett's, then John B. Hood's, division south. That was half of Longstreet's corps. Hearing that more Federals were moving that way, he assigned Longstreet to take command of the detached force. Its further duty was to collect food and fodder for his weakened army.

Lee hoped that in an emergency those two hardened divisions could return in time to fight along the Rappahannock. But he was unimpressed by his opponent. Soon after Hooker's takeover, Lee wrote home that "General Hooker is obliged to do something. I do not know what it will be. He is playing the Chinese game, trying what frightening will do. He runs out his guns, starts wagons and troops up and down the river, and creates an excitement generally. Our men look on in wonder, give a cheer, and all again subsides in *statu quo ante bellum.*"[26] Like his troops, Lee was more amused than frightened. He decided Hooker would do nothing serious until winter broke. He settled into a cluster of ordinary service tents, rather than impose on any of the civilian homes that would have been honored to have him. By then Lee lived plainly, his one luxury being a pet hen that traveled with him and regularly laid an egg under his cot.

During that harsh winter, he did all he could to keep his men in good spirits. He liked to tease his young officers, when occasionally they went calling together at nearby households where Virginia belles delighted at the attention of dashing soldiers. He made it seem that the soldier in the ranks was the most important man in any army. One of the stories that helped win his troops' devotion was of the private he found waiting outside his tent one day.

"Come in, Captain," said Lee. "Take a seat."

The soldier said, "I'm no captain, General. I'm nothing but a private."

Lee insisted: "Come in, sir, and take a seat. You ought to be a captain," and listened patiently to the man's troubles.[27]

His soldiers told themselves that no army could be defeated with "Marse" Robert Lee at its head. In less than a year he had led them at Richmond, Second Manassas, Antietam, and Fredericksburg—three outstanding victories and a bloody draw. With each battle, their assumption grew that they would always win, were meant to win, because they marched with Lee. The feeling was mutual, his admiration based on his troops' performance against all odds. But morale alone could not defeat the Union, and on those dark winter days Lee had more tedious things to do than jolly his troops.

The previous spring, his army's meat ration had been cut from twelve to eight ounces; an increase of two ounces in the flour allotment was scant compensation. In late January 1863, that was cut further to four ounces of salt meat and a fifth of a pound of sugar. Troops counted heavily on bacon, peas, molasses, and other staples mailed from home, most of which surprisingly got through in edible condition.

Supplies were repeatedly held up by the purported shortage of freight cars and constant delays in bridge repairs on the Richmond, Fredericksburg & Potomac Railroad. Increasingly frustrated by this, Lee asked

President Davis to fire Samuel Ruth, the railroad's superintendent. But Davis vouched for Ruth, a Pennsylvanian by birth. Much later it turned out that Lee's anger was eminently justified—Ruth was a Federal secret agent, a valued informant for Hooker's Bureau of Military Information. He was arrested in the last weeks of the war and held at Richmond's Castle Thunder prison before being released when the key witness against him backed off. But Ruth himself, petitioning the Federal government after Appomattox, told how he had passed on information about Confederate supplies and the destruction of track and rolling stock. He described how he had encouraged skilled railroad men to desert and slip away to the north. George Sharpe, head of the Union spy service, certified that Ruth and his colleagues "throughout the war . . . were constantly endeavoring by every safe channel to send military information to the U.S. government." [28]

One of the most stubborn, demoralizing enemies Lee had to contend with throughout the war seemed almost in collusion with Ruth. He was the Confederate commissary general, Col. Lucius B. Northrop. Northrop held trivial grudges against Lee and blamed conditions on the generals; "he took refuge in interminable letters of explanation when he was asked why the army was starving. He seemed satisfied if he could demonstrate that he was on record as predicting what had come to pass." [29] Although Lee was bothered as much by this stubborn bureaucrat as by any ongoing burden he carried, he controlled his anger. This illustrates another of his shortcomings: Lee's belief in civilian control of the military, handed down from his idol Washington, made him the quintessential diplomat in politely turning aside attempts at strategic meddling by the ex-soldier President Davis. But his army suffered when he failed to blast crippling functionaries like Ruth and Northrop out of the way.

After three major battles in less than four months, Lee asked Richmond for more troops, but did not get them. Repeatedly, he wrote, he had been unable to follow up successful combat because his exhausted regiments were too thin. He had to referee a long-running feud between two of his best generals, Jackson and A. P. Hill. He had to keep up with the two divisions sent below Richmond, and occasionally send cavalry to help Brig. Gen. W. E. Jones fence with Federal Brig. Gen. R. H. Milroy in the Shenandoah Valley. Because the Rappahannock-Rapidan area had been scoured clean, he had to forage his artillery horses along the North Anna River, well south of his winter lines.

Something had to be done about that artillery. Lee's guns were outnumbered 404 to 264, a margin that became 413 to 220 after Longstreet's two divisions went south.[30] About 60 percent of the Southern guns were older, smooth-bore pieces, effective mainly at close range, but more than two-thirds of the Federal artillery were rifled models, with a range up to triple that of smooth-bores. To make up for the difference, Lee's guns had to fight as effectively as his outnumbered infantry. Yet they had never fired with the impact that even their lesser numbers could have if organized properly. They were strewn out among the divisions and brigades, a battery here and another there, usually employed at the whim of the nearest infantry commander. Only rarely could a lone brave section like Pelham's at Fredericksburg make a difference in a battle.

To give his artillery more punch, Lee made a change that compared with Hooker's reorganization of the Union cavalry. He consolidated the Confederate guns into battalions, usually of 16 pieces (four batteries) each. Six battalions were assigned to each of his two corps, plus two battalions in army reserve. Each corps would have an artillery chief, directed by the army chief of artillery, reporting straight to Lee. This way the guns could be massed quickly and with much more chance to turn a battle than if they were booming away by ones and twos with no central direction. The change would pay off soon.

Along the Rappahannock line, Lee's infantry—Jackson's corps of four divisions plus the two left behind by Longstreet—kept digging. From the fords above Fredericksburg downstream to Port Royal, riflemen cut into the winter earth long trenches that tied in with stone walls and fences. Jackson's divisions watched the river line roughly from Hamilton's Crossing down, and Longstreet's from there up.

When not on work details, soldiers found other ways to fight the cold and tedium. They bowled, using bricks for tenpins and 12-pound shot for balls. They organized minstrel shows, starring slaves brought along as officers' orderlies. One Virginian counted twenty-seven snowfalls that winter, and like their brotherly enemies across the river, the Rebels mounted formal snowball battles as if they were in mortal combat—regiment against regiment, maneuvering and attacking. Tempers flared, and there were casualties, broken noses and arms.

Once, troops of E. A. Perry's Florida brigade, excited at the novelty of a snowstorm, joined Carnot Posey's Mississippians to challenge Mahone's Virginians. They appeared with officers mounted and color-bearers waving scraps of red blanket for battle flags. The Virginians seemed to be overrun by numbers, but had held back their 6th Regiment, hiding in reserve with haversacks packed with snowballs. The surprise counter-attack hit the Deep South attackers on their flank, and as they retreated, one of their colonels seized his regiment's colors and called on his men to stand. Virginians grabbed his reins and pelted him till he surrendered. Then Mahone's officers rescued him and took him to their tent. "He came out about an hour or two later 'as high as ninety,' hurrahing for 'Old Virginia.' "[31]

Pushing back the foreboding, the certainty of what awaited beyond the winter, regimental bands on both sides of the river played patriotic airs and sentimental tunes that reminded troops of happier times. The Yankee bands were superior, particularly those of the German regiments. With the winter wind down from the northwest, the Rebels could listen to them, and even shouted requests across the river. One of the lasting scenes of the war has been described by so many soldiers that it might seem to have happened nightly. James Buckham romanticized it as "The Common Chord." His poem began with the Northern band near sunset playing "Hail Columbia," and tent flaps parting as men came outside to listen. When they cheered, there came back from the other shore a Rebel band's answer, "Bonnie Blue Flag," met by "The Star-Spangled Banner," and then from the Southern side, "Boys in Gray." Buckham went on:[32]

> *Deeply the gloom had gathered 'round, and all the stars had come,*
> *When the Union band began to play the notes of "Home Sweet Home."*
> *Slowly and softly breathed the chords, and utter silence fell*
> *Over the valley and the hills, on Blue and Gray as well. . . .*
> *Then what a cheer from both the hosts with faces to the stars;*
> *And tears were shed and prayers were said upon the field of Mars.*
> *The Southern band caught up the strain, and we who could sing, sang.*
> *Oh! what a glorious hymn of home across the river rang. . . .*

Chapter Four

THE COUNTRY SAYS "MOVE"

MUD-COATED, DOG-TIRED, and laughing, Jeb Stuart rode into camp New Year's morning with another tale of high jinks behind Yankee lines. Rampaging north, he had led 1,800 cavalrymen with four cannon and surprised the telegraph office at Burke Station, 14 miles from the White House. From there, he sent a message to the Union quartermaster general, complaining about the poor quality of the mules he was capturing of late.

That five-day outing was known as the Dumfries raid. The names of this and other cavalry exploits—Fairfax Court House, Chantilly, Aldie, Olive Branch Church, Dranesville, Raccoon Ford, Hartwood Church— do not ring in history like those of mass collisions between infantry and infantry. That winter, they were sideshows, exploratory sparring before the main action to come. But the horsemen had immensely more fun than did soldiers with muskets crouching on picket with cold feet, waiting for the snow and rain to stop. Aside from gathering tactical intelligence, cavalry operations had an inordinate impact on morale, in the trenches and in both Washington and Richmond.

The dash, the flamboyance, that goes with the word "cavalry" had never attached itself to Union troopers. It belonged to the South, to the plumed knight, Jeb Stuart, and his eager lieutenants like Fitzhugh Lee and John Pelham. When Joe Hooker made his stinging remark about never having seen any dead cavalrymen, he was talking to and about Yankees. No one in the Army of the Potomac had earned the reputation for speed and daring that all cavalrymen covet; Philip Sheridan was still out west. Stuart and his brigadier Fitz Lee both liked to taunt their ineffective counterparts in blue.

Impudence, as in complaining about the quality of captured mules, was Stuart's trademark, part of the devil-may-care flair that has made him the most fabled cavalryman in American history. Between battles, his aide Sam

Sweeney played banjo and his mulatto footman Bob rattled bones and danced to entertain his camp by firelight. Such "claptrap" did not enchant some of his infantry colleagues: the sober Maj. Gen. Lafayette McLaws of Georgia, for example, called Stuart's showmanship "the act of a buffoon to attract attention."[1] Attract attention it certainly did. But McLaws's observation was egregiously wrong, because Stuart was no buffoon; he was superb at his job. While at it, he made fun of war, and that spirit rubbed off on his men.

As March snows swept over the awakening armies, Stuart's brigadiers on hand were the commanding general's son, W. H. F. "Rooney" Lee, and his nephew, Fitzhugh Lee. (The other cavalry brigadiers, Wade Hampton and William E. "Grumble" Jones, were detached south of the James River and in the Shenandoah Valley.) Rooney Lee was the serious soldier, Fitz the "laughing cavalier," in the Stuart mold. John Pelham drove Stuart's horse artillery with unmatched élan. And a towering, swaggering Prussian staff officer, Heros von Borcke, was always there at promise of a good time or a good fight.

Although Von Borcke magnified his military role in his memoirs, he left delightful accounts of the social side of cavalry life. One was about setting off with Stuart on a spontaneous ride to a plantation wedding forty-five miles away; another concerned the time when, after a snowy night ride to Culpeper, he and Pelham met ladies who made their stay so pleasant that in mid-March Pelham wangled an order to go back that way to inspect artillery batteries.

By that time, esprit was rising in the reorganized Federal cavalry. Union officers were ready to answer the taunts the Rebels had tossed at them for so long. Fitz Lee, for example, had crossed the Rappahannock in late February to jab past Federal pickets and check rumors that Hooker was shifting his main force to thrust at Richmond from the south and east again. The Rebel horsemen charged through fresh snow and panicked the New York and Pennsylvania cavalry protecting Hooker's right at Hartwood Church. As the skimpy Southern force retired with about 150 prisoners, rumors magnified the probe into a major attack, and Union brigades rushed in all directions to counter it. But Lee got away, leaving behind Union officers embarrassed once more by their outclassed cavalry. To rub it in, he had dropped off a message for his West Point classmate Federal Brig. Gen. William W. Averell. "I wish you would put up your sword, leave my state and go home," it said. "You ride a good horse, I ride a better. Yours can beat mine running. If you won't go home, return my visit and bring me a sack of coffee."[2]

Averell was eager to crack back when he got orders to take his cavalry division across the river, to destroy Fitz Lee's force based at Culpeper. He told his men to sharpen their sabers and use them—their turn had come. With about 3,000 horsemen, he moved out on March 16, and at dawn the next day confronted Rebel sharpshooters across the swift, swollen Rappahannock at Kelly's Ford. After an opening clash, Averell crossed to scout the gently lifting farmland for a place to fight. Lee waited briefly near Brandy Station with his brigade of some 1,100, then moved forward. Toward noon, the two forces made contact. It was a day to remember: Kelly's Ford would be the first all-cavalry fight in the East involving more than a battalion of troopers on each side.[3]

Jeb Stuart was at Culpeper for a court-martial. John Pelham, "as grand a flirt as ever lived," ostensibly was inspecting batteries but more likely visiting ladies at Orange. He hurried to join Stuart when he heard of battle brewing.

Pelham, not yet twenty-five, looked younger. At Williamsburg, the Seven Days, and Second Manassas, his elders had marveled at the way he placed guns and got them into action before others knew they were there. At Antietam, he had held Jackson's left, a ridge that looked across the Union right flank. From it he pounded each successive wave of attack. Stonewall may have remembered his own earliest moment of glory, at Chapultepec, when he saw Pelham run his guns out under the enemy's nose. After Antietam, Jackson purportedly said, "With a Pelham on each flank I believe I could whip the world."[4] And then Pelham had done it again at Fredericksburg, delaying the Federal attack. During the winter he had gone along on Stuart's raids, running his cannon through creeks and rivers where no one thought artillery could pass. But on that St. Patrick's Day below Culpeper, Pelham's official role was merely to oversee somebody else's fight. He could not resist any more than Stuart could, so they rode on borrowed horses to see how they could help as Fitz Lee felt out Averell's powerful regiments.

The Yankees faced north, spread across the road half a mile from Kelly's Ford. Their left was in a grove of woods, their right reached into a field and farmyard, ending behind a tall stone fence. Lee sent a regiment at Averell's troopers, who were dismounted, crouching and waiting. When some of Lee's men briefly wavered, Stuart himself rode forward to rally them. Pelham, helping position Lee's guns, saw the Virginians in full gallop, yelling as they closed on the stone fence. He drew his sword and spurred after them, catching up as they flowed along the fence, looking for an opening.

"Forward!" Pelham shouted, reining up as the troopers bunched and pushed through a barnyard gate. He stood in his stirrups, waved his saber, and yelled again.

At that moment a shell burst bright above him, his horse reared, and Pelham fell as the Virginians rode on. A comrade struggled to lift the body across his saddle. Stuart, told Pelham was killed, bowed to his horse's neck and wept. But on the grass beyond the action, friends found that Pelham's heart was still beating. He had a small entry wound at the base of his skull, but was otherwise unmarked. His comrades sent him in an ambulance to Culpeper. Surgeons found that the fragment, the size of a fingertip, had penetrated about two inches. He died soon after.[5]

Women and soldiers cried at the news. Poets and generals wrote in his praise. Stuart's camp was dejected, although Fitz Lee's outnumbered brigade had finally sent the Federals back across the river. Stuart reported that "the enemy, broken and demoralized, retired under cover of darkness to his place of refuge (the main army), having abandoned in defeat an expedition undertaken with boasting and vainglorious demonstration."[6] But across the river, morale was flying because the Union troopers had dared take the offensive against Fitz Lee, and had withdrawn only after pushing the gray cavalry back nearly two miles. Averell had set the tone by leaving behind a note answering Lee: "Dear Fitz: Here's your coffee. How is your horse?"[7]

The battle of Kelly's Ford is best remembered for the death of the heroic Pelham. The *New York Times* called it "The first real cavalry battle of the war . . . a decisive victory on the part of the national forces." The Richmond *Whig* claimed for Fitz Lee "a complete victory, because we clearly succeeded in frustrating the evident design of our enemy, which was to make a long cavalry raid à la Stuart. . . ." But the battle was important not because either side won or lost heavily. Kelly's Ford mattered because there the Union cavalry demonstrated to itself, and to the whole army and the country, that at last it could go head-to-head with Jeb Stuart's storied riders. That gave the Union horsemen a confidence they had never before experienced, and an ambitious role in the campaign ahead.

DOWN THE RIVER, soldiers on both sides heard the mutter of guns 20 miles away at Kelly's Ford and stopped to wonder whether something big was happening. On the Northern side, it was no ordinary Tuesday in camp. There were enough Irish soldiers and Irishmen-for-a-day to tickle

Saint Patrick, wherever he was. They set out on one of the most uproarious and nearly disastrous celebrations in the history of the Union army.

The Irish themselves already were celebrated in the Army of the Potomac. They not only loved to laugh and sing, they loved to fight, on and off the battlefield. Before the war began, they were largely pro-Southern, and they were the main protesters in the furious antidraft riots that were to rock New York in the summer of 1863. But once they were in, they did not hold back. The Irish Brigade (63rd, 69th, and 88th New York, 28th Massachusetts, and 116th Pennsylvania) had won glory when it was almost wiped out in its desperate attacks on the stone wall below Marye's Heights at Fredericksburg. Its brigadier, Thomas Francis Meagher, was a rollicking patriot banished from the old country. There were dozens of other regiments predominantly Irish, and dozens of other companies heavily manned by men with Irish roots. They, and all around them who liked an excuse to forget camp routine, cut loose on March 17, 1863.[8]

There were sack races, pig chases, Irish jigs, reels, and hornpipes, more fun because the quartermasters had brought in barrels of whiskey and rum. The Irish Brigade erected a greasy thirty-foot pole with a thirty-day furlough and a twenty-dollar gold piece on top, and the man who could reach the prize could have it. One got within ten feet, then slid wailing back to earth. But the great event was the steeplechase. Generals from Hooker down sat in the judges' stand. General Meagher wore white hat, blue swallowtail coat, buckskin knee breeches, and high boots, and carried a heavy ornamental whip. The riders were in full jockey dress, with silks and boots.[9] At first they rode horses in more or less standard form over hurdles, ditched fences, and "artificial rivers." Later races were aboard army mules, and when the riders climbed up they were already as sloshed as when they flew head over heels into the moat. One surgeon was reported killed when his mount threw him, but the gala gathered momentum until afternoon, when suddenly far drums sounded the long roll, the call to arms.

"You ought to have seen them run for their camps and fall in line of battle," wrote a Connecticut soldier. The cause of the alarm, he said, "was the crossing of some of the rebels over the river on our right flank—but I believe it didn't amount to much."[10] What it amounted to was the battle at Kelly's Ford, its rumble blown downriver by the wind. When the alert was canceled, the party resumed until deep in the night. And then next day the army groaned and went on, trying to recover from a day it would always remember and a winter it would rather forget.

. . .

JOE HOOKER was pleased with what he had done. By the end of March, his soldiers were coming out of their deep doldrums. Watching them parade past, Hooker said to the officers around him, "If the enemy does not run, God help them." At another review, he maintained that "I have the finest army the sun ever shone on. I can march this army to New Orleans. My plans are perfect, and when I start to carry them out, may God have mercy on General Lee, for I will have none." He didn't intend merely to drive Lee, he would "bag him." [11]

Even officers who managed to restrain any personal admiration for Hooker were impressed. As John Robinson's division prepared to pass the reviewing stand, Abner Small and his comrades in the 16th Maine watched other regiments ripple by, admiring "the pageant of blue and steel and scarlet." Small remembered "the trimly clad men with their burnished guns, the proudly mounted and gayly uniformed officers, the brilliant standards fluttering in the breeze and the measured tramp of veterans marching to the crash of bands. . . ." Hooker obviously was satisfied, and "conscious power" was plain on "his handsome but rather too rosy face." All this lifted the army and its commander. "Despondency and doubt had given way to pride and confidence." [12]

One of Hooker's more controversial improvements after the ignominy of the Mud March was ordering pack mules to take over from wagons on tactical marches. For one review, Averell's 1st Brigade saddled up, loading a day's forage and three days' rations on its horses and assorted camp and kitchen gear on its mules. The result was "splendid laughs for the boys," wrote Albinus Fell of the 6th Ohio Cavalry. "The pans would rattle and the mules would kick and pull away then you would see them get every jump a kick and every kick a jump; packs scattered for a mile and mules ran wild like mad. . . ."

Things back in Ohio were less amusing to Trooper Fell. He had heard that an erstwhile friend was now "a regular secesh, that he is mad at every U.S. soldier in the service . . . if he will only come down here and join the Rebels I will settle any account that he has against me. Such men are a curse to our cause. . . ." [13]

There were a lot of them. Loyal Unionists called them Copperheads. The dissatisfaction of the past winter, of Fredericksburg and the Mud March, had mounted higher against the Emancipation Proclamation and yet higher with passage of the Enrollment Act to enforce conscription in the North. There was talk in the Ohio and Mississippi valleys of another secession, to create a new Northwest separated from abolitionist New England. In Illinois and Indiana, the lower houses of the legislature passed resolutions calling for an armistice and retraction of the Emancipation Proclamation. They offered bills to take control of state troops away from their Republican governors. Soldiers along the Rappahannock received letters describing Copperhead agitation. Regiments held meetings to pass resolutions opposing Copperhead activities back home. The weekly paper from Beaver, Pennsylvania, put one soldier in a rage. "We think it is a curious thing that there are not enough union men left at home to tear that darned *Star* office down and tar and feather the editor," he wrote. "If this company was there it would be done in short order." If the local peace Democrats "were only here to see the feeling the soldiers have for them and their policy of compromise, they would hide themselves. The soldiers are determined to conquer or paint this country with blood and they are the ones who have the hardships and danger to face. The peace Democrats are not here and nothing but a draft will bring them here. . . . I believe old Abe is the wisest man living for making that draft and not exempting the Quakers, for if he had the Democrats would have all got wide brimmed hats and gone to peddling garden seeds."[14]

In most armies, almost any incentive to gripe is welcomed by the troops, especially in long weeks of waiting and uncertainty. That spring, eagerness to "paint this country with blood" was not widespread on either side. A boy from Connecticut wrote home that "I don't wish to cross that river agin for it is a hard place to tackel you can bet & I hope when we move that we shall move back toards Washington. We have only two months and a half longer to surv where ever we go and then we shall move towards New haven. That will sute mea you Can bet. . . ."[15]

A New Yorker from Onondaga wrote that "Our camp is in sight of the city of Fredericksburg and are within 62 miles of Richmon our army can march this distance in a little less than three days. But the question is are they going to do it? No it will take 8 months and then it has got to be at the sacrifice of many a poor fellows life. If you could see the Rebs fortifications on the opisit bank of the Rappohanock you would say at once that it will be imposible for any army to break through them." He had seen the Southern boys playing ball and pitching quoits, close enough to hear them talk and call each other by name. "They seem to be quite friendly," he wrote. "They say that if they could have their way they would hang Lincoln and old Jef Davis and that would end the war. . . ."[16]

In both armies, every rumor that the other side was discouraged was repeated with hope. A lieutenant of the 21st North Carolina reported that he had talked across the river to a Union picket. "He seemed to be tired of the war and said his Regt will go home this week but doubt whether he knows much about it or not. . . . I have seen no one that understood the meaning tho I expect Gen Lee does."[17]

GENERAL LEE understood what was ahead, and feared that his men might not be in sufficiently good physical condition to handle it. There were signs that, considering the weakness of the Confederate supply system, he had decided to turn logistics over to a higher power. He ordered the army to join the rest of the Confederacy in observing Friday, March 27, as a day of fasting and prayer. Routine duties would be suspended, religious services encouraged. "No portion of our people have greater cause to be thankful to Almighty God than yourselves," his order said.[18]

That Friday, a Georgia infantryman wrote to his wife that "It was the only bright day we have had since my return" from leave. "It seems significant that the sky should be so unclouded on the day set apart for fasting . . . the only one in several weeks."[19] At the same time, Lee was writing to James A. Seddon, the secretary of war, about how his men fared on ordinary days. Their current daily ration, he said, was 18 ounces of flour and four ounces of bacon "of indifferent quality," occasionally supplemented by rice, sugar, or molasses. Few complained, but he was afraid they would not be able to stand up under the coming campaign. Scurvy was showing up; to replace vegetables each regiment was ordered daily to collect sassafras buds, wild onions, garlic, lamb's-quarter, and poke sprouts, "but for so large an army the supply obtained is very small."[20] In the 17th Mississippi, Cul Cummings was the first man sent on this foraging duty. "When he got back he smelled like a Dutch restaurant," a friend recalled. "Just fancy the commander in chief of a great army sending out his troops by details to gather wild onions. . . . Anybody who does not think we did not have much to eat can form his own conclusion from this. . . ."[21]

Lee's plea to Richmond was remarkably courteous, considering its content. The other Southern armies reportedly fared better, he said: "I think this army deserves as much . . . and, if it can be supplied, respectfully ask that it be similarly provided." Lee's old nemesis, the commissary L. B. Northrop, predictably replied with a shrug rather than supplies.[22]

In Richmond early that winter, steak and oysters had seemed plentiful in the restaurants and hotels patronized by politicians, profiteers, and rear-area officers. But prices went up and up, and clerks and laborers could not eat decently. As winter stretched on and supplies tightened, Secretary Seddon sent the Southern capital into a fit of nerves by ordering all the flour in Richmond seized to feed the army. Fear rose among those who were not plugged in to wartime prosperity.[23]

On April 2, fear turned to anger. A crowd of chanting women gathered before the Capitol in Richmond, demanding bread to feed their families. Jeff Davis himself came out and tried to quiet them. They shouted him down: "Bread! The Union! No more starvation!" The mob broke into the commissary depot, looting it. The government called on Richmond papers "to avoid all reference directly or indirectly to the affair," lest it "embarrass our cause and encourage our enemies."[24] The appeal didn't work; embarrassment inevitably followed.

The Richmond riot forced into print alarming facts the South already knew. Food was short and famine was near. Later that week, Davis told the Confederate Congress that "There is but one danger which the government of your choice regards with apprehension." The previous year's droughts and poor crops had hurt, especially in the upper Confederacy where the army had fought. Bread and fodder were short. "Grovelling speculators" and winter-ravaged roads had cut off supplies of meat. Thus, he pleaded, "Let your fields be devoted exclusively to the production of corn, oats, beans, peas, potatoes and other food for man and beast. . . . Is it not a bitter and humiliating reflection that those who remain at home, secure from hardship and protected from danger, should be in the enjoyment of abundance, and that their slaves also should have a full supply of food, while their sons, brothers, husbands and fathers are stinted?"[25]

Around Fredericksburg, soldiers searched the greening fields for wild vitamins and herbs to cut the taste of what one Virginia boy called "old rusty bacon and musty flour & not half enough of that."[26] North of the Rappahannock, soldiers in blue ate better despite the huge backup of provisions at their supply base at Aquia. The Union army was inundated with clothing, weapons, and ammunition as the overwhelming Northern industrial machine gathered speed. But between drills, reviews, and friendly cross-river conversations, the Northern soldiers read of unhappiness and confusion back home. Their relatives were not united in hunger, they were divided among plenty.

Lincoln understood that the longer his army sat still, the wider those political divisions would grow. On the first Saturday in April, he started down the Potomac to give Hooker a nudge.

Chapter Five

WHEN WE GET TO RICHMOND

THE PRESIDENTIAL PARTY had hardly started south from the Washington Navy Yard on the dispatch boat *Carrie Martin* when a wet, swirling snowstorm blew down from Maryland. Visibility was nil, so the boat took shelter for the night in a Potomac cove. The group seemed casual: Mr. and Mrs. Lincoln and their frolicksome son Tad, celebrating his tenth birthday on this great adventure; Attorney General Edward Bates; an old Illinois friend, Dr. Anson G. Henry; and Sacramento *Union* correspondent Noah Brooks, who had become a Lincoln intimate and left some of the best first-hand accounts of the wartime president. That night the men sat up late talking strategy and politics, Lincoln worrying about what might be happening at Charleston, where the Union navy was about to launch an attack on Fort Sumter.

Easter morning, April 5, with snow still falling, their vessel slipped downstream to the mouth of Aquia Creek. There it pulled between boats and barges that crowded the riverbank, and Lincoln boarded a bunting-bedecked freight car on the 15-mile rail line to Falmouth Station and Hooker's army.[1]

Chief of Staff Dan Butterfield met them, and they were driven over muddy roads to Hooker's tented command post. Next day, there was a grand review of George Stoneman's consolidated cavalry corps. The president and Hooker headed a brilliant troupe of generals, colonels, and assorted staff officers, escorted by the gaudy Philadelphia Lancers. After a 21-gun salute that alerted both armies to the president's presence, Lincoln and his assembly watched squadrons of horsemen roll past, "winding like a huge serpent over hills and dales, stretching far away out of sight."[2]

Later, because Tad wanted to see some Rebels, the visitors went quietly down to join the pickets opposite Fredericksburg. The president and his

son looked out over the town and the "painfully famous" fields where so
many Union troops had died in December, and saw the Confederate Stars
and Bars flying over one of the surviving mansions. A troop of Gray
infantry marched in and out of sight, a train of wagons passed, Southern
soldiers clustered around a headquarters tent, and a swarm of slaves played
a noisy game. At the base of a chimney, all that was left of a house by the
river, two Rebel pickets warmed their hands at the fireplace. One wore a
captured blue overcoat. They spotted the presidential party, waved, and
yelled something the president could not understand. A Southern officer
appeared, looked across through his spyglass, then made an elaborate bow.
Later, when the wind tapered, the pickets yelled again, and the Union
sentries heard them: Rebels had fought off the naval attack at Charleston.[3]

Between reviews, Lincoln strolled through the camps and visited sick
and wounded soldiers in field hospitals. When the Lincolns passed a
collection of hovels, dozens of black refugees swarmed out. "Hurrah for
Massa Linkum!" they shouted. Mrs. Lincoln wondered how many of
"those pickaninnies" were named Abraham Lincoln.

"Let's see," said the president. "This is April, 1863. I should say that
of all those babies under two years of age, perhaps two-thirds have been
named for me."

Again, as they bounced in a hard-bottomed ambulance to visit the First
Corps eight miles away, their driver muttered salty criticisms of his six
cantankerous mules.

Lincoln leaned forward, tapped him, and said, "Excuse me, my friend,
are you an Episcopalian?"

"No, Mr. President," said the teamster, "I'm a Methodist."

The president cracked gently, "Well, I thought you must be Episcopalian, because you swear just like Governor Seward, who is a church-
warden."

The driver drove on, mute.[4]

No field was big enough to hold the entire Army of the Potomac, but
on April 8, after work parties dug stumps, leveled, drained, and filled for
days, there was a broad parade ground on which four of the seven infantry
corps, more than 60,000 men, converged to pass in review. When a gun
salute announced the president, the troops surged into motion, "their arms
shining in the distance, and their bayonets bristling like a forest on the
horizon."[5] The president enthused over the polished cannon and the
fancy-dress Zouaves. He touched his hat to salute passing officers but
removed it to respect the enlisted ranks.[6] On an undersized horse beside
the magnificent Hooker, he "would have presented a comical picture had

it not been for those sad, anxious eyes, so full of melancholy foreboding, that peered forth from his shaggy eyebrows."[7]

Those reviews were as much to impress the troops themselves as for the generals and politicians. Confidence builds in soldiers who feel part of a huge, smooth machine, who can look left and right and see their friends, their regiment, thousands of men marching shoulder to shoulder, and then look up and see their general erect on his charger, ready to lead. In the Eleventh Corps, an Ohio soldier recalled that "Each regiment, its flag rippling gracefully as it bent to the wind, advanced in a double line, a quarter of a mile long. Bands played. Men cheered. The wide cove was black with soldiers. The hard damp earth throbbed with the pounding of their feet." The president's "expression was kindly, yet firm and serious, even sad. General Hooker beamed with satisfaction and pride. . . . His eyes sparkled with confidence. He held his chin up a little too high to suit me. . . . Such a great army! Thunder and lightning! The Johnnies could never whip this army!"[8]

Hooker exuded confidence not only in his public bearing but in private conversation with Lincoln and his entourage. Reviewing his own success, Hooker was like "a gay cavalier, alert and confident, overflowing with animal spirits, and as cheery as a boy"—a general who "seemed to regard the whole business of command as if it were a large sort of picnic." Over and over, as he talked with the president, he told of what he would do "When we get to Richmond," and "After we have taken Richmond." Lincoln said to Noah Brooks, "That is the most depressing thing about Hooker. It seems to me that he is overconfident."[9] But Maj. Gen. Darius Couch, who ranked second to Hooker, walked in on a conversation between the commanding general and the president in which Hooker was not so ebullient. They had been talking about the action to come. As Lincoln excused himself, he said to both generals, "I want to impress upon you two gentlemen—in your next fight, put in all of your men."[10]

Another night, when Hooker and newspaperman Brooks were alone, the general produced the letter Lincoln had written to him on his appointment in January. Lincoln had read it privately to Brooks then; now Hooker read it to him again. The general reached the lines about his having thwarted Burnside, committing "a great wrong to the country." He looked up and insisted that he had never worked against Burnside in any way. As he finished reading, Hooker said emotionally, "That is just such a letter as a father might write to his son. It is a beautiful letter, and although I think he was harder on me than I deserved, I will say that I love the man who wrote it." Then he added, "After I have got to Richmond, I shall give that letter to you to have it published." [11]

When Lincoln returned to Washington, he wrote a memo for Hooker about the campaign ahead. Again he insisted that "our primary object is the enemy's army in front of us, and is not with or about Richmond. . . ." As long as Lee's army was intact, Hooker should not attack him directly, but "continually harass and menace him, so that he shall have no leisure nor safety in sending away detachments. If he weakens himself, then pitch into him." [12]

That same day, April 11, Hooker sent Butterfield to Washington, hand-carrying to Lincoln a confidential letter—his plan to do much more than "harass and menace" Lee.

Hooker had mapped a strong cavalry raid looping far beyond Lee's rear, cutting the Rebels off from Richmond, tied in with a concealed move across the upper Rappahannock by most of his infantry. (See Map 2.) That infantry would sweep down on Lee's western flank and rear while other divisions came straight at him just below Fredericksburg, across the fields where they had been turned back in December. Hooker expected that once Lee realized he was caught between such powerful forces, he would have no choice but to retreat toward Richmond—and that way, he would be blocked by the long-riding Federal cavalry:

> I have concluded that I will have more chance of inflicting a heavier blow upon the enemy by turning his position to my right, and if practicable, to sever his communications with Richmond with my dragoon force and such light batteries as it may be advisable to send with him. I am apprehensive that he will retire from before me the moment I should succeed in crossing the river, and over the shortest line to Richmond, and thus escape being seriously crippled. I hope that when the cavalry have established themselves on the line between him and Richmond, they will be able to hold him and check his retreat until I can fall on his rear, or, if not, that I will compel him to fall back by the way of Culpeper and Gordonsville, over a longer line than my own, with his supplies cut off. The cavalry will probably cross the river above the Rappahannock Bridge, thence to Culpeper and Gordonsville and across the Aquia [Richmond, Fredericksburg & Potomac] Railroad, somewhere in the vicinity of Hanover Court-House. They will probably have a fight in the vicinity of Culpeper, but not one that should cause them much delay or embarrassment. I have given directions for the cavalry to be in readiness to commence the movement on Monday morning next. While the cavalry are moving

I shall threaten the passage of the river at various points, and after they
have passed well to the enemy's rear, shall endeavor to effect the
crossing. I hope, Mr. President, that this plan will receive your
approval. . . .[13]

It did, promptly. Hooker's "Monday morning next" was April 13.
Brig. Gen. George Stoneman started up the Rappahannock with the Army
of the Potomac's entire cavalry corps, minus one brigade. Each trooper
carried three days' rations and 60 rounds of ammunition—40 for his
carbine, 20 for his pistol. The accompanying pack train would carry
another five days' rations, plus forage.

Stoneman had finely detailed orders, aimed at "turning the enemy's
position on his left, and of throwing your command between him and
Richmond, and isolating him from his supplies, checking his retreat, and
inflicting on him every possible injury which will tend to his discomfiture
and defeat. . . ." Hooker told him where to cross streams, what railroads
and canals to destroy, and repeated that his objective was "the cutting of
the enemy's connections with Richmond by the Fredericksburg route,
checking his retreat over those lines"—reinforcing the Union assumption
that Lee's reaction this time, against all precedent, would be to retreat
before fighting.

"Let your watchword be fight, and let all your orders be fight, fight,
fight," Hooker told Stoneman. "It devolves upon you, general, to take the
initiative in the forward movement of this grand army, and on you and
your noble command must depend in a great measure the extent and
brilliancy of our success. Bear in mind that celerity, audacity and resolution are everything in war, and especially is it the case with the command
you have and the enterprise upon which you are about to embark." [14]

Thus challenged, Stoneman took his heavily provisioned horsemen and
their cannon upriver. They made 24 miles the first day, no thanks to that
cantankerous innovation, the pack mule, which was supposed to take over
from cumbersome wagon trains. In the 16th Pennsylvania Cavalry, a rider
detailed to help keep the mules moving said later that the whole effort was
"a living curiosity." The green mules, this Yankee wrote, "did very much
as they please. . . . When a mule wanted to rid himself of his load, he
would resort to many devices. He would rub against the trees, fences or
against another mule, and when all these failed, he would lie down and
roll. This last resort generally did the business. Oats, corn, hard bread,
pots, kettles, pans, etc. would be strewn along the road. Frequently these
animals would take to kicking. A mule can kick the highest of any animal

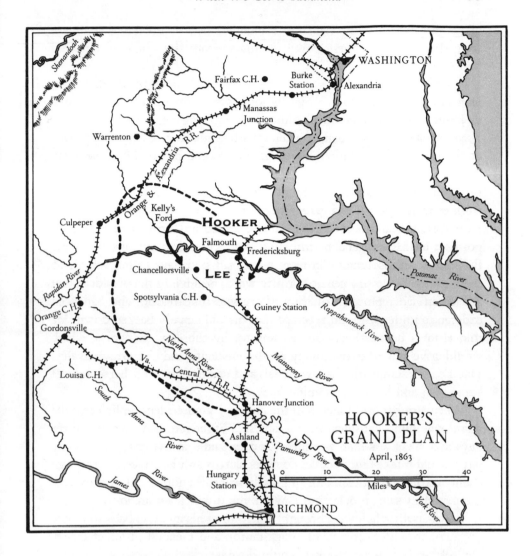

HOOKER'S
GRAND PLAN

April, 1863

2. Left Jab, Right Hook. *Hooker's plan is to send his cavalry (broken line) to cross the upper fords of the Rappahannock, then loop far south, cutting the railroads north of Richmond. His main infantry force will then cross at Kelly's Ford and swing down behind Lee while a secondary attack distracts the Confederates below Fredericksburg. After Stoneman's first excursion bogs down, Hooker restarts his infantry and cavalry at the same time. He expects supply boats to greet his advancing divisions at the Pamunkey River.*

of his size by all odds. I do not remember how many times we were compelled to repack these pesky varmints' loads, but patience deserted pretty early in the march." [15]

Soon after that, luck deserted, too, along with determination. Stoneman's cavalry, only somewhat less ignominiously than Burnside's infantry in January, got caught in the rain.

Stoneman sent Col. Benjamin Davis's brigade to cross the Rappahannock far upstream at Sulphur Spring, then sweep down and chase away Southern pickets so the rest of his expedition could move across Beverly Ford untroubled. But before Stoneman could finish shifting his supplies from wagons to mules and get his main force over, a rainstorm struck. The river rose, fast and deep. Creeks and roads were flooded, and Stoneman got cold feet. Back at Falmouth, Hooker was assuring Lincoln that while the rain was unfortunate, Stoneman had had two days to get across, so there should be no problem. Soon afterward, he advised the president that Stoneman had reported that his artillery was mud-bound, and had been ordered to go on without it. But Stoneman had already backed down. He told Hooker he was lucky he had not got his whole force across, which would have put it at the mercy of the elements and the Gray cavalry. Davis's brigade surprised a few Rebels and had to fight off others, and lost some men and horses swimming back.

When Hooker told Lincoln of the holdup, the president replied that the news gave him "considerable uneasiness." Stoneman had been out three days and made less than 25 miles, Lincoln said—at that rate, how many days would it take him to cover 60 miles, across another river and through enemy territory to Richmond? "I greatly fear it is another failure already," the president said in dejection. "Write me often; I am anxious." [16]

It *was* another failure; it brought Lincoln, in his anxiety, back to Aquia on April 19 with Secretary of War Stanton and General-in-Chief Henry Halleck, to hear what Hooker would do next.

Hooker elaborated a revised plan, which he would execute as soon as weather permitted. At Lincoln's urging, this time he intended to "strike for the whole rebel army" rather than merely scaring Lee into retreat.

Although the cavalry's venture upriver had alerted the Southern side, Lee was still guessing where Hooker would move. He discussed with Stuart whether Stoneman had been headed to the Valley or toward Richmond. He told Jeff Davis that he suspected the Federal cavalry was meant to draw the Rebel army upstream so Hooker could seize Fredericksburg. He also told the president that provisions were so low that if Hooker did not move by May 1, the Confederates would have to move first. Stoneman reported to Hooker that Southern sympathizers to the west were expecting the Union army to move that way, to take the rail junction at Gordonsville. To compound this useful confusion, Hooker sent a division downstream to Port Conway, 21 miles below Fredericksburg, where it put on a show of preparing to cross, while cavalry and infantry units posted upstream showed themselves to mislead the enemy.

Hooker still planned to send the cavalry off on its mission around the Rebel rear, but the infantry would start moving at the same time. He would push O. O. Howard's Eleventh Corps, Henry W. Slocum's Twelfth, and George G. Meade's Fifth, in that order, far up to the right, crossing at Kelly's Ford. They would hasten across the Rappahannock, then across the Rapidan, and march down from the west toward the crossroads of Chancellorsville. As they cut behind Rebel outposts at the fords closer to Lee's main army, they would secure those crossings for other Union forces.

Couch of the Second Corps was ordered to send two divisions to Banks' and United States fords, while holding another within view of the enemy near Fredericksburg. Hooker assumed that Couch's movement, though ordered to be made quietly, would be seen by Lee's troops. That would convince Lee that the Union effort was following the route of Burnside's Mud March, toward the closer fords. Meanwhile the main flanking force would move unseen, well back from the river, to cross farther up at Kelly's Ford. When that force swept down behind Lee, Couch would drive over United States Ford, just below the juncture of the Rapidan and Rappahannock.

At the same time, Hooker's left wing—John Reynolds's First Corps and John Sedgwick's Sixth—would cross near the December battlefield just below Fredericksburg. Daniel Sickles's Third Corps would stand ready to move either way. This action downstream would hold Lee's attention and prevent his confronting the flanking force until Hooker's trap was set.

Except for sending most of the Union cavalry away from the focus of battle, the whole complex of moves and feints was brilliantly planned. If it worked, Hooker would get across the Rappahannock and Rapidan before Lee could shift to block him. Then he would hit Lee with overwhelming force before Longstreet could be brought up from below Richmond to join the battle.

Consciously or not, Hooker's plan with its sweeping maneuvers demonstrated the influence of the Napoleonic wars on American military thinking of the time. Though there was no broad, coherent strategic doctrine in either the Northern or Southern army, what ranking officers on both sides shared was a West Point education. In the late 1820s, Professor Dennis Hart Mahan had studied in France under officers who had served with Napoleon, and his teaching dominated theoretical classes at the academy for decades afterward. Mahan for a while headed a Napoleon Club, in which officers stationed at West Point discussed the master's battles. He maintained that, after Napoleon, there was nothing new to be learned about the art of war.[17] Then in 1836, Baron Antoine Henri Jomini, a Swiss who had campaigned both with and against Napoleon, published his classic *Précis de l'art de la guerre*. It was rich with maps and diagrams, and had become the standard analysis of Napoleon in western Europe by the time Mahan's student, Henry Halleck, toured the continental battlefields as a promising young lieutenant. On his return, Halleck wrote *Elements of Military Art and Science*, based on Jomini, which influenced American officers during and after the Mexican War. In the 1850s, George McClellan also studied in Europe and wrote treatises endorsing Jomini's version of Napoleonic warfare. And Lee, who had graduated from West Point before Mahan introduced strategy to the curriculum, independently studied Napoleon when he was superintendent at the academy.

Although Jomini acknowledged the virtues of offensive action, what impressed his disciples was his scientific approach, emphasizing logical, geometrical precision more than the human elements of battle. As Lynn Montross has written, Jomini outlined a system of war, while Karl von Clausewitz, the Prussian interpreter of Napoleon, produced a philosophy. Though Clausewitz was not translated into English until after the Civil War, Lee and Jackson carried out his version on the battlefield. Jomini's work abounded in maxims; Clausewitz disdained them. He wrote: "There is no human affair which stands so constantly and so generally in close connection with chance as war. . . . Pity the warrior who is contented to crawl about in the beggardom of rules! . . . What genius does must be the best of rules, and theory cannot do better than show how and why it is so."

Today, Jomini is seldom quoted, while Clausewitz is taught at every academy of arms. In April of 1863, Hooker's meticulous diagram for success was about to be tested against chance and genius.[18]

AS HE TRIED to focus on the opportunity of his lifetime, Hooker was repeatedly distracted by events in Washington, especially in the public prints. On April 17, the pro-Lincoln *Chronicle* did the Rebels a favor by printing a report from medical director Letterman to Hooker on the status of the Army of the Potomac. It disclosed that 10,777 troops were sick, a rate of 67.64 per 1,000. From these figures, a quick calculation showed that on the verge of battle, Hooker had 159,329 troops minus the sick, or 148,552 potentially available for duty. He raged to Secretary of War Stanton that "The chief of my secret service department would have willingly paid $1,000 for such information in regard to the enemy." Hooker demanded an investigation, which found that Maj. Joseph R. Smith, an army surgeon, had innocently handed the document to reporters. Smith's apology did little to calm Hooker. Soon afterward, as the offensive opened, Hooker demanded to know the names of *New York Times* and Philadelphia *Inquirer* correspondents who wrote of "a submarine cable said to be in use by the enemy between Falmouth and Fredericksburg." He tried to end the "frequent transmission of false intelligence and the betrayal of the movements of the army" by ordering that, henceforth, correspondents must sign their names to all dispatches from his army, or be ejected from the zone of war.[19]

Plotting what lay ahead, Hooker still burned over what had gone by. Somehow the never-issued General Orders No. 8 presented to Lincoln by Ambrose Burnside, demanding Hooker's dismissal, was published. In response, Hooker sent a furious letter to Stanton. He described Burnside's order as "stupid." He said Burnside's "moral degradation is unfathomable," and condemned him for "cowardice . . . follies . . . blundering sacrifice . . . madness" in earlier battles. Hooker regretted that he could not "call him to account for his atrocities, swallow his words or face the music, before going into another fight. I like to feel easy at such times, with a name and character unclouded, and cannot bear to go into battle with the slanders of this wretch uncontradicted and the author of them unchastised. He must swallow his words as soon as I am in a condition to address him, or I will hunt him to the ends of the earth."[20] As Hooker well knew, Burnside at the time was across the Appalachians in Cincinnati, commanding the Army of the Ohio.

Despite the distractions, Hooker's rehabilitated army was creaking into motion. Rations and ammunition were issued. Professor Lowe's portable generators exhaled hydrogen and his balloons tugged at their moorings. But not all Union soldiers were impressed by the professor's advanced technology. The rains kept coming, and a Pennsylvania soldier suggested, "If old Hooker wants to move here he had better get some shoemakers pegs and take his balloon and go up and stop the holes in the clouds so it wont rain," and added, "I believe his balloons are a humbug."[21]

Another soldier, whose opinion mattered, bore official rather than merely personal skepticism of the chief aeronaut's irregular operations. He stepped in and made demands that soon would end Lowe's career with the Union army. This skeptic was Capt. Cyrus B. Comstock, Hooker's engineer officer, who insisted that Lowe, though still a civilian, go strictly by the military book. Comstock would oversee and be ready to second-guess all Lowe's operations. All balloon corps correspondence and requisitions henceforth would run through him. The professor's daily pay would be cut from ten dollars to six dollars.

After putting up with Comstock's harassment for days, in mid-April Lowe finally said he could not stay on at reduced pay, but since he was committed to Hooker, he would serve gratis through the imminent campaign.[22] And so his balloons were up, watching the Rappahannock fords, as cavalry and infantry began the bold sweeping movement that would take the Union army to Chancellorsville.

Chapter Six

THAT CRAZY OLD PRESBYTERIAN FOOL

THE FIVE-INCH SNOWFALL that had delayed Lincoln's Easter arrival on the Rappahannock freshened the trenches and huts, the rutted roads and stripped fields, where nearly a quarter million soldiers and camp followers were awakening. In the Reverend Beverly Tucker Lacy's tent at the headquarters of Stonewall Jackson's corps, the canvas overhead drooped with the weight of the snow as Jackson and his staff gathered for services. They listened as Lacy spoke from Jackson's favorite text, Romans 8:[1]

"And we know that all things work together for good to them that love God, and to them who are the called according to his purpose."

Beyond those familiar words, that chapter of Romans says more that strikes home for the soldier. It ends: "For thy sake we are killed all the day long; we are accounted as sheep for the slaughter. Nay, in all these things we are more than conquerors through him that loved us. For I am persuaded that neither death, nor life, nor angels, nor principalities, nor powers, nor things present, nor things to come, nor height, nor depth, nor any other creature, shall be able to separate us from the love of God. . . ."

From United States Ford downstream to Port Royal, Baptists, Methodists, Episcopalians, and Presbyterians of the Southern army were in the midst of a religious revival that defied the weather. Catholics, too: In the camp of the 14th Louisiana, Father Joseph Sheeran looked out into the snow early that April 5, glum at the prospects for his eight o'clock mass. But when the hour came, he stepped outside and found soldiers, most of them hell-raising Mississippi River boatmen who still bucked army discipline, surrounding his tent. It was "one of the most consoling sights of my life," he wrote. As he led the service, the rough soldiers knelt to pray in the storm, flakes wetting their bare heads.[2]

The great revival had begun months earlier, before winter deepened.

Across the river, the Union army was having the same experience, though less intensively. Religious enthusiasm was a reaction against what happens to young men torn away from family ties when they have surplus time to admire and copy the cursing, gambling, and dissolution flaunted by older, worldly soldiers. Dozens of preachers from back home joined the regiments as chaplains. Colporteurs sent by religious associations passed out thousands of Bibles and tracts like "A Mother's Parting Words to Her Soldier Boy." Services were held throughout the week. Occasionally a Rebel regiment asked that a morning's drill be canceled in favor of a prayer meeting, and the request was granted. As the weather eased and brought the spring campaign near, the revival spread faster than the diseases that had dragged the army down during the winter. Troops used precious logs and pine branches, brought from miles away by volunteer teamsters, to build regimental and brigade chapels.

One Virginia minister reported in 1863 that "Modern history presents no example of armies so nearly converted into churches as the armies of Southern defence. On the crest of this flood of war, which threatens to engulf our freedom, rides a pure Christianity; the Gospel of the grace of God shines through the smoke of battle with the light that leads to heaven. . . ."[3] A Georgia soldier sent home some Christian Association literature and said it proved that "Christians in the army are doing more than those at Home, who have scarcely nothing to do. I have heard more preaching here in two weeks than I heard at home in four months."[4] And behind it all was that fierce Presbyterian deacon, Stonewall Jackson himself, pressing the revival forward as he pressed his troops into battle.

With Longstreet still away south of the James, four of the six Confederate divisions along the Rappahannock were Jackson's. He concerned himself as much for their spiritual health as for their feeding and training. He urged each denomination to send distinguished ministers to the army. He was ecumenical: "As a general rule, I do not think that a chaplain who would preach denominational sermons should be in the army. His congregation is the regiment."[5] At Jackson's request, the Reverend Mr. Lacy became unofficial chaplain to his corps. Jackson had moved his headquarters upriver from Moss Neck to Hamilton's Crossing, about four miles below Fredericksburg. Around this new command post, rude seats and a temporary pulpit were set up in the open.[6]

But Jackson's religious imprint was not made by official orders and organizing efforts. It was by his personal piety, some said fanaticism, on and off the battlefield. No fight was commenced, no trivial duty undertaken, without asking a blessing first. He tried not to march or do battle on Sundays; when he had to do either, he tried to set aside the following Monday for worship. After a victory he specified an hour for his soldiers to gather and offer thanks. He even carried on a losing campaign against moving the mail on Sunday. A friend told an army chaplain:

"The truth is, sir, that 'old Jack' is crazy. . . . I frequently meet him out in the woods walking back and forth muttering to himself incoherent sentences and gesticulating wildly, and at such times he seems utterly oblivious of my presence and of everything else."

Jackson admitted to the chaplain later, "I am in the habit of going off into the woods, where I can be alone and speak audibly to myself the prayers I would pour out to my God. I was at first annoyed that I was compelled to keep my eyes open to avoid running against the trees and stumps; but upon investigating the matter I do not find that the Scriptures require us to close our eyes in prayer, and the exercise has proven to me very delightful and profitable."[7]

His most remarked, least understood gesture was to hold a hand aloft, palm forward, especially as he watched his men move toward the enemy. One of his biographers says it was merely to ease the pain in his left hand, wounded as he made just such a gesture at First Manassas. Another believes it was meant to balance his blood circulation. Another says it was to stretch the arm, which Jackson believed was shrinking. Many insist he was reaching up in prayer. Conceivably the habit came from his fascination with Joshua, the great battler of the Old Testament. Jackson sometimes cited Joshua's struggle against the Amalekites, reported in Exodus 17, verses 9–13:[8]

"And Moses said unto Joshua, 'Choose us out men, and go out, fight with Amalek: tomorrow I will stand on the top of the hill with the rod of God in mine hand.' . . . And it came to pass, when Moses held up his hand, that Israel prevailed; and when he let down his hand, Amalek prevailed. . . . But Moses' hands were heavy . . . and Aaron and Hur stayed up his hands . . . and his hands were steady until the going down of the sun. . . . And Joshua discomfited Amalek and his people with the edge of the sword."

Jackson left no doubt that he identified with the biblical forces of righteousness. In his calm wrath, his certainty and determination, he was an Old Testament character—one historian said, "a reincarnated Joshua, he lives by the New Testament and fights by the Old."[9] But off duty there was a gentleness, too, a concern for his men expressed in his willingness to eat, dress, and worship as they did. Every Sunday when troops gathered at that outdoor chapel, he was there, an unobtrusive member of the congregation. When no minister was present, he did not hesitate to lead prayers or sermonize. His talented mapmaker, Jedediah Hotchkiss, remembered that on the Sunday before Easter, in the evening in Lacy's tent, Jackson had "prayed fervently for peace and for blessings on our enemies, in everything but the war." [10]

In response to this spiritual upwelling, the Presbyterian Rev. William J. Hoge came to preach to Virginians of the proud Stonewall Brigade. Once he approached the brigade chapel to find hymns soaring from a packed house before the service was scheduled. Jackson arrived quietly with Frank Paxton, who had taken over his old brigade. The two generals looked in, then quietly backed away when they saw that if they sat, two soldiers would have to stand.

Later, Hoge was invited to preach to William Barksdale's Mississippi brigade, holding Fredericksburg. There in the ruined city, soldiers filled a battered church's auditorium, stairs, and balconies. "We had a Presbyterian sermon, introduced by Baptist services, under the direction of a Methodist chaplain, in an Episcopal church," Hoge reported with pleasure. Afterward, "a little before sunset," he wrote, "I ascended the spire of the Episcopal church, which still gapes with many an honorable wound received as the tempest of shells swept over it. There I had a fine view of the Federal camp, the dress parade, the hills whitened as far as the eye could reach by their tents, the heights malignant with cannon menacing yet more wrath to this quiet old town. . . ." [11]

ON MONDAY, APRIL 20, there was more rain. As the mail train from Richmond puffed into Guiney Station, the usual crowd of off-duty Confederate soldiers milled about hoping for letters and food from home. But this time, Jackson was among them, and the troops stood back to watch him hug his wife and the five-month-old daughter he had never seen. Protecting Anna and little Julia from the rain, he helped them into a carriage that took them to a quiet interlude unique in Jackson's spartan wartime experience. [12]

The muddy road north from Guiney to the Yerby plantation near Hamilton's Crossing ran nearly ten miles. On the last stretch, the carriage bounced through the camps of Jackson's corps, between the divisions of Jubal Early and Robert Rodes. His other two divisions, under A. P. Hill and R. E. Colston, were closer to the river, downstream toward Moss Neck. Farther up, behind and beyond Fredericksburg, R. H. Anderson's and Lafayette McLaws's divisions of Longstreet's corps overlooked the river and the town. As Jackson's carriage rumbled along, the rain held up, and thousands of soldiers eased into the sunshine to resume their infinite ways of killing time.

Morale among Lee's troops was lifting despite the boredom. Anticipation was part of it; they knew something would happen soon. Spring was much of it; not only fresh greens, but fresh fish were suddenly bounteous as the shad and herring began their run up the river and creeks. So generous were the troops in their relative plenty that few grumbled when Lee asked that a day's rations be given up by his whole army to help the poor civilian survivors of Fredericksburg. "On that day there was not a bite of meat, a dust of meal or flour in Lee's army," recalled a Mississippi soldier. On another occasion, Jackson had urged his corps to take up a collection for the people of the ruined town, and they gave some thirty thousand dollars.[13] Their religious mood must have helped the troops feel good about playing benefactor after so many months in need. "Someone asked what kind of religion the boys got at the revival," said a man in the 17th Mississippi. "I don't know what kind of religion [they] had, but they had a hell of a fight in them."[14]

R. A. Pierson, a young Louisiana officer, visited Fredericksburg and walked over the ground where he had fought in December. In late winter, he had been impressed by seeing that "The graves of those who perished in the action are scattered around in all the little groves. Many of the Yankees were left on the field and our troops were so worn down with fatigue from the three days fight, that they took but little pains in burying them; they are still exposed to view in many places, some with their hands and arms sticking out, while others heads are projecting and present the most hideous features; their teeth glistening as though grinning at the passers by." In April he came back to town and looked nervously on the brighter side, seeming surprised to find that "There is still a number of the citizens living there many ladies may be seen promenading the streets and I learned that there was a ball nearly every night in some part of the city given by the soldiers. This will sound very harsh on your ears," he wrote to his sister, but "the Yankee batteries command the city and could set it on fire at any moment. This reminds me of the story told of 'Nero's fiddling while Rome was burning.' "[15]

It is distinctly possible that what Pierson heard from Barksdale's Mississippi boys, whose posting in the shambles of the town made them the army's urban sophisticates that spring, exaggerated the social whirl. But spirits were indeed up. In the clearings, baseball was becoming the national pastime, played with makeshift balls and bats on both sides of the river. Pierson said that baseball in the 9th Louisiana was "quite a show, sometimes as many as one hundred are engaged at once." [16]

Soldiers stopped to cheer Jackson as he brought Anna and the infant Julia to the Yerby house, near which he had tented since mid-March. Eager as he was to hold his wife and child, he spent only a short time installing them before returning to headquarters to catch up on paperwork. He had sat much of the winter editing official reports of his battles as far back as the Valley campaign of the previous spring. He was so secretive that he would not disclose in those reports any details that might help the enemy the next time. His officers believed he was too stingy with commendations; in the absence of medals, such mentions were their chief means of recognition. Jackson concluded his long report on Winchester, for example, by saying simply, "The conduct of officers and men was worthy of the great cause for which they were contending." [17] In this official chariness, as in so many things beginning with birth, he stood in contrast with the man to whom his name is forever linked, Robert E. Lee.

LEE WAS a consummate Tuckahoe. Jackson was a Cohee.

Tuckahoe is what early western Virginians called those from Tidewater, where the tobacco economy was founded on slave labor and the Anglican aristocracy had been dominant since the founding of Jamestown. Jackson was the cultural opposite, a Cohee, which is what upcountry settlers called themselves. Many were Scotch-Irish pioneers like Jackson's great-grandfather, an immigrant who stopped only briefly in Maryland before pushing on into the mountains. Jackson's grandfathers fought in the Revolution and against the Indians. He was born in Clarksburg in 1824. His father died when Tom was three, his mother died when he was seven, and he grew up with an uncle. He went to a rude school, where he was conscientious but not quick, except in math. When he was sixteen, he got a job as county constable. Two years later the sincerity of his application outweighed his academic shortcomings, and he was appointed to the U.S. Military Academy.

At West Point, he started near the bottom but worked hard to move steadily upward in class standing. Later, he said he did not remember even speaking to a woman during his whole time as a cadet. In 1846, he graduated seventeenth in a class that included McClellan and others he would come to know better later. He had shown his diligence and stubbornness. His boldness would make its mark next. He was assigned to the

1st Artillery and ordered to New Orleans, where reinforcements were gathering for the war in Mexico.[18]

Jackson, though one of the most junior officers in the field, was not outdone by anyone on the way to Mexico City. Then, on the flank at Chapultepec, he took his guns and put on a display of bravery that stirred everyone who saw or heard about it. For him, as for Lee, the sweetest praise came from the commanding general, Winfield Scott himself. At a reception in Mexico City, the general heard Jackson's name as he approached, and ostentatiously stuck his hands behind his back. "I don't know that I shall shake hands with Mr. Jackson," Scott said. Jackson blushed, uncertain what to say. Then Scott, so everyone could hear, said, "If you can forgive yourself for the way in which you slaughtered those poor Mexicans with your guns, I am not sure I can." Smiling, he extended his hand. Another officer said that was as high a compliment as a general could pay, and that Jackson did not know he had done anything special until he was told so. But Jackson was not unconscious; much later, when someone asked if he had been afraid at Chapultepec, he said his only fear was "lest I should not meet danger enough to make my conduct conspicuous."[19]

Like Lee and Hooker, Jackson came home with battle-won credentials for a bright army career. Though not working at the staff level where they had been involved in strategy and tactics, he had learned to perform under fire with troops, especially nonprofessional volunteers like those who manned most Civil War regiments. And he had learned to know himself. As his heart pounded in the chaos of battle, he felt more in control, more steady than ever.

In Mexico after the fighting, Jackson developed two other interests he had never indulged before. One was women. He studied Spanish, took dancing lessons, squired the elegant señoritas of the capital, and apparently got serious about one of them. The rest of his life, he used little Spanish endearments to his loved ones. The other new interest was church. Influenced by his regimental commander, Col. Frank Taylor, and perhaps by those young women, he started studying religion. He considered Roman Catholicism, asked for and had interviews with the archbishop of Mexico. But he remained undecided. He was still exploring his own mind when his regiment was posted to Fort Hamilton, Long Island.[20]

There, feeling sickly after Mexico, he became a chronic hypochondriac. He adopted and urged on others a regimen of plain meat, stale bread, salt, and water, varied only with an occasional vegetable or fruit. Searching New York's bookstores, he also began absorbing history, including Napoleon's campaigns. But religion was still his major subject. After further talks with Taylor, he was baptized in the Episcopal church. Yet he was still groping, studying alternatives. Then he was transferred to Florida, to help put down the persistent Seminoles.

There he had a clash of wills with his commander at Fort Meade, William H. French, who accused him and other officers of insubordination. After Jackson and French brought charges against each other, the post commander was overruled in Washington. The confrontation illustrated Jackson's stubborn pride in matters of military protocol, and foreshadowed a more serious feud with one of his most valued officers that lasted to the edge of death. But even winning left Jackson with a sour feeling about the military career that Mexico had made seem so promising. He liked campaigning, but was frustrated in barracks life. When a timely offer came to leave the army and teach cadets at Virginia Military Institute in Lexington, he clutched it. In 1851 he began a decade during which he studied the theory of war more closely than did most of his comrades who stayed in the army.

At VMI he taught physics and artillery tactics, but without eloquence. At first, cadets joked at his stiffness and rectitude, but in time he won their respect. He sampled services at all the churches of the little Shenandoah Valley town, and after long discussion joined the Presbyterian congregation. He became a deacon, and organized and taught Lexington's first Sunday school for blacks (at tense moments in the war to come, he would still remember to send back his contributions to it). In 1853, the shy and courtly soldier married Elinor Junkin, the daughter of a preacher, the president of next-door Washington College; a year later, she died with their stillborn child. Three years after that, he married Mary Anna Morrison, daughter of a North Carolina minister and college president. He became a father, but in less than three months that baby daughter died of jaundice.

Jackson lectured on the techniques of war, and they were on his mind in the summer of 1856, when he made his only trip to Europe. He visited England, France, Belgium, and Switzerland, and delighted to talk on his return about their cathedrals. But it is likely he concentrated hardest at the battlefield of Waterloo, analyzing each side's moves and countermoves. Back home, he still believed Napoleon the greatest of commanders, but second-guessed the French master's opening thrust against Wellington.[21]

In 1859, Jackson's and the world's attention was seized by John Brown's raid at Harper's Ferry. Fear of slave insurrection spread through the South. Virginia mobilized its militia, and the governor called up the

VMI cadets to stand by at Brown's hanging in Charlestown. Jackson commanded the cadet artillery there, and was moved by what he saw.

To his wife, he wrote an eloquent description of how Brown died—how he "behaved with unflinching firmness," how he stood on the gibbet for ten minutes while final arrangements were made, how the rope was cut and Brown fell, and "There was very little motion of his person for several moments, and soon the wind blew his lifeless body to and fro." Jackson, a solid Democrat who preferred some kind of compromise on slavery, totally disagreed with Brown's politics. But it is easy to see in his account some inward admiration for John Brown, for an uncompromising man dying with head up for what he thought was right. Indeed, as Jackson watched, he offered a prayer for Brown's salvation.[22]

From Harper's Ferry, it was downhill to war. When Lincoln was elected, Jackson wrote to his nephew explaining how he felt as war threatened: "I am in favor of making a thorough trial for peace, and if we fail in this, and the state is invaded, to defend it with a terrific resistance. . . ."

IN MID-APRIL of 1861, on the day Fort Sumter surrendered, a street debate in Lexington flared into a fight, and VMI's cadets poured into town brandishing their muskets. Their officers herded them back, and lectured them about upholding law and order. Then "Old Jack" was called on to speak. There was a new fire in his eye when he told the cadets, "The time for war has not yet come, but it will come, and that soon; and when it does come, my advice is to draw the sword and throw away the scabbard!" Within a week, Virginia seceded and the VMI cadets were called to Richmond. Jackson knelt in prayer with Anna, kissed her, and marched his boys to war.[23]

Ten days later, Major Jackson was appointed colonel of the Virginia line and sent to organize the defense of Harper's Ferry. He shaped the militia and volunteers who had clustered there into well-drilled units. He also acquired a companion that would see him through his war: When his men captured a B&O train, he liked the looks of a smallish red-brown horse and took it as a gift for Anna, making sure to pay the quartermaster for it. But then, pleased by its easy gait, and finding himself unable to send it to Lexington right away, he decided to keep it as his own warhorse, and it became the "Little Sorrel" known to his admirers. In the 4th Virginia, an officer just getting acquainted with Colonel Jackson said he was "considered rigid to the borders of tyranny by the men here and some of them have been greatly surprised to get an insight into his character as a

Christian man. He enjoys I hear the entire confidence of his command."[24]

When Virginia's forces went under Confederate command, Brig. Gen. Joseph E. Johnston took charge at Harper's Ferry. He assigned Jackson the 1st Brigade of Virginia troops. Johnston chose to abandon Harper's Ferry when Union forces threatened, and westward in the valley Jackson fought his first infantry skirmish, a skillful delaying action at Falling Waters. Promptly afterward, he was promoted to brigadier general. Writing to Anna, he said, "Look how our kind Heavenly Father has prospered us!"[25]

He prospered further a month later, when he led Johnston's swing across the Blue Ridge to reinforce Gen. P. G. T. Beauregard at the first battle of Manassas. From Piedmont (now Delaplane), Jackson's troops moved by train—history's first use of rail to achieve strategic mobility.[26] Against a Union flanking movement, Jackson formed a second line of defense along Henry House Hill.

Brig. Gen. Barnard E. Bee, who had been out front with him at Chapultepec, galloped up sweating and shouted, "General, they are beating us back!"—to which Jackson said, "Then, sir, we will give them the bayonet." Bee rode to his broken regiments and pointed his sword toward Jackson.

"Look!" he shouted. "There is Jackson standing like a stone wall! Rally behind the Virginians!"

As the Yankees came on, Beauregard and Johnston raced to bolster the defenders, and Jackson rode back and forth across his brigade front, repeating "Steady, men! Steady!" When the fighting was fiercest, he threw up his hand while talking to artilleryman John D. Imboden and jerked it down bleeding, nicked by a bullet. A moment later, as the outnumbered Confederates struggled with fresh Union regiments, an officer said in alarm, "General, the day is going against us!"—to which Jackson said quietly, "If you think so, sir, you had better not say anything about it."[27]

Jackson had become Stonewall, a name he always insisted belonged to his brigade, not himself. Bearing it, he was made major general that fall, and given command in the Shenandoah Valley. There he put on a campaign that Douglas Southall Freeman called "the most remarkable display of strategic science, based on accurate reasoning, correct anticipation of the enemy's plans, rapid marches and judicious disposition of an inferior force, in all American military history."[28]

Not every clash was a victory, but in his daring Jackson repeatedly outmarched and outfought Generals James Shields, Nathaniel P. Banks, Robert H. Milroy, and John C. Frémont. Thrusting his "foot cavalry" back down the valley toward the Potomac, he alarmed Washington and prevented the reinforcement of McClellan at Richmond. About that time, his admirer Lee took command. With the enemy largely cleared from the valley, Lee ordered Jackson to march quickly to join him outside Richmond.

His aim was an attack by Jackson, coordinating with A. P. Hill, against Union forces along Beaver Dam Creek. But Jackson, groggy from lack of sleep and moving through thick, unfamiliar country after a forced march of more than 130 miles, delayed his approach, and Hill made a costly assault without his support. Through five more days, Jackson moved his troops sluggishly, frustrating Lee's effort to coordinate attacks at Gaines's Mill, Savage's Station, and White Oak Swamp. It was the worst week of Jackson's career. He failed in just those particulars where he had won his reputation—fast movement, precise execution of orders, reliability in independent command. Lee's use of vague sketches of the terrain rather than accurate maps could be blamed, too. So could Hill's impetuosity, and the slowness of some other officers. In the Seven Days' Battles ending with repulse at Malvern Hill, Lee's army suffered some 20,000 casualties.

If Jackson's disappointing performance lowered Lee's confidence in him, the commanding general hid any sign of this. Detaching Jackson's force, he sent it to confront the Federal army led by the bombastic John Pope, newly arrived from the west. At Cedar Mountain near Culpeper, Union troops attacked Jackson after his plan was confused because he kept its details secret too long from his own generals. Jackson himself had to wave his sword for the first time in the war, rallying his men to stand. Although A. P. Hill roared in with a counterattack that prevented disaster, Jackson remained furious with him for misunderstanding his orders on the approach march. Infantry and wagon trains had been mixed, division columns crossed each other, and Hill made only two miles the day before the fight. The feud between Jackson and the fiery Hill would soon flare again. But before that happened, Jackson's entire command would make a forced march still marveled at by soldiers.[29]

Lee, learning that McClellan was moving his army north to join Pope, decided to strike Pope before McClellan got there. Bringing Longstreet up from Richmond, he sent Jackson on a sweeping left hook to get between Pope's army and Washington. Jackson's men marched 26 miles one day and 28 the next to reach and destroy the vast Union supply base at Manassas Junction. Then they fell back and awaited Pope along a ridge at Groveton. As part of Pope's superior force marched past, Jackson opened fire and brought on the second battle of Manassas. Fighting from a protective railroad cut, his men beat back repeated Federal assaults. Then

Longstreet, though attacking late, swung like a gate against Pope's left. Jackson had more than made up for his lapses on the Peninsula. Lee, emboldened, turned north to Maryland.

Along the way, A. P. Hill's division started behind schedule one morning, and straggled. In an angry confrontation, Jackson relieved Hill of command and placed him under arrest. The army pushed on across the Potomac, to Frederick (where, contrary to John Greenleaf Whittier's poetic imagination, Jackson neither saw nor heard of a gray-haired lady named Barbara Frietchie). From there, Lee ordered Jackson to recross the river and take Harper's Ferry. Moving out early the next morning, Jackson ostentatiously asked citizens of Frederick for directions to Chambersburg—the other way, in Pennsylvania. Then he marched west to Martinsburg, Virginia, where he was set upon by admirers who clipped the very buttons off his coat. As the force turned toward Harper's Ferry, Hill asked that he be restored to command of his division in the coming battle, and Jackson consented. That decision may have saved Lee's army.[30]

Jackson knew the territory. After marching a hot, circuitous 60 miles from Frederick, he captured Harper's Ferry. Jackson's troops cheered their commander, and even many of the captured Union soldiers uncovered and saluted when they saw the dusty, ordinary-looking Rebel legend ride by. With minimal bloodshed, Jackson had taken more than 12,000 Northern soldiers, 13,000 rifles, and 73 artillery pieces. Then, leaving Hill's division behind to deal with the captives, he marched to rejoin Lee. By that time, Union general McClellan was pushing through the South Mountain gaps toward the outnumbered Southern army along Antietam Creek.

There Jackson's exhausted troops held the left against repeated attacks by Hooker, then other Union corps. His center was cracked at one point before the Yankees were driven back over a "landscape turned red." The battle shifted south, to Bloody Lane and then Burnside's Bridge. When Federals finally forced their way across the bridge, McClellan had his chance to cut Lee off from the Potomac. But in the absolute nick of time, A. P. Hill rode up wearing the red-checked shirt he always donned for battle. After driving his Light Division on a blistering 17-mile march from Harper's Ferry, he threw its lead brigades straight in on the right. They stopped Burnside's momentum and he fell back. The battle was over, and Lee's army lived to fight another day.

Hill was always better in combat than between battles. After distinguishing himself at Antietam, he refused to forget the way Jackson had treated him. That fall, Jackson was made lieutenant general and given command of Lee's Second Corps. Hill filed charges against him and

Jackson filed charges in answer. Lee tried to smooth over their feud, but Hill would not back off. In November he wrote in confidence to Jeb Stuart: "I suppose I am to vegetate here all the winter under that crazy old Presbyterian fool—I am like the porcupine all bristles, and all sticking out too, so I know we shall have a smash up before long. . . . The Almighty will get tired of helping Jackson after a while, and then he'll get the d—ndest thrashing—and the shoe pinches, for I shall get my share and probably all the blame, for the people will never blame Stonewall for any disaster."[31]

Hill characterized himself perfectly—"like the porcupine all bristles"— but he was wrong about any thrashing in Jackson's future. As he wrote, Lee started gathering his divisions to confront Burnside along the Rappahannock.

The day before the battle of Fredericksburg, amid bursts of fire between pickets and occasional salvos from cannon, Jackson inspected his positions facing the river and rode back whistling confidently.[32] On December 13, with Hill's division in front, Jackson's corps defied stubborn Union attacks against the Confederate right while Longstreet scythed them down on the left. Hill's line was pierced, but the hole was sealed after desperate seesaw fighting. Intending this time to follow up success, Jackson planned an all-out night attack to drive the Union troops into the river. Only after his first units had edged forward did he call off the effort because the field would be so completely dominated by Federal artillery across the river. Back at headquarters, Dr. Hunter McGuire asked Jackson how the Southern army could ever deal with an enemy of such overwhelming numbers. "Kill them, sir!" said Jackson. "Kill every man!"[33]

WHEN A FALSE alarm about a Yankee crossing down the Rappahannock pulled Jackson's corps that way soon after the battle of Fredericksburg, he bivouacked in the open but awoke later with a painful earache. Nudging one of the officers who had tried to persuade him to shelter at a nearby plantation, Jackson said he had changed his mind. In the dark, they groped their way to Moss Neck, the spacious home of Richard Corbin.

Though Jackson had intended only to spend a night, the family insisted that he stay—and he did, for three months, headquartering in an office on the lawn. There on Christmas he entertained Lee, Stuart, and some of his staff at dinner, and the visiting generals joshed their austere host about having such a luxurious spread.[34]

Jackson was smitten with five-year-old Janie Corbin, and spent many intermissions from work playing with her. But work there was made harder by his continuing bitter dispute with A. P. Hill. Each of them gathered testimony from uneasy fellow officers; Jackson was further infuriated when he found out that Hill had told his division's officers not to respond to any orders unless routed directly through him. Lee, not wanting to offend Jackson, not wanting to lose Hill, kept trying to resolve the matter, but it was still unsettled as the winter wore on.

By then, what Jackson had done in the Valley, at Manassas, Antietam, and Fredericksburg had made him a public idol ranking with Lee himself. In the *Southern Literary Messenger,* Peter Alexander wrote that winter that Jackson might be undistinguished to the eye, but "let the cannon begin to thunder, the small arms to rattle, and the sabres to flash in the sunlight—and . . . the awkward, calculating pedagogue becomes a thunderbolt. . . . He is the idol of the people, and is the object of greater enthusiasm than any other military chieftain of our day . . . notwithstanding the fact that he marches his troops faster and longer, fights them harder, and takes less care of them than any other officer in the service. Indeed, some say that if he had no enemy to encounter, and nothing to do but march his troops about the country, he would yet lose one-third of them in the course of a year. This indifference to the comfort of his men is only apparent, however—not real. No man possesses a kinder heart or larger humanity; but when he has anything to do, he is so earnest, so ardent and energetic that he loses sight of everything but the work before him. . . ."[35]

His fame spread abroad, partly via the steady stream of foreign officers and journalists who toured the Southern camps. Col. Garnet Wolseley, later Lord Wolseley, was a veteran of faraway wars. After visiting, he wrote that with a leader like Jackson, "men would go anywhere, and face any amount of difficulties; and for myself, I believe that, inspired by the presence of such a man, I should be perfectly insensible to fatigue, and reckon upon success as a moral certainty. Whilst General Lee is regarded in the light of infallible Jove, a man to be reverenced, Jackson is loved and adored with all that childlike and trustful affection which the ancients are said to have lavished upon the particular deity presiding over their affairs." Comparing Lee's army to highly polished troops he had witnessed abroad, Wolseley said, "I never saw one composed of finer men, or that looked more like *work*. . . ."[36]

. . .

LITTLE JANIE CORBIN was ill with scarlet fever when Jackson left Moss Neck to move his headquarters upriver near Hamilton's Crossing. Departing, he gave her the gold braid off his forage cap to twine in her hair as a remembrance. Soon afterward, he got word that she had died. Jackson wept; for a while the girl had filled the place of the baby daughter he had never seen. When his wife and the infant Julia arrived in late April, he realized their visit could not last long. Though Julia was five months old before her father saw her, Stonewall was luckier than most of his men to see his family at all.

As the Southern army readied itself, Lee was recovering from a painful illness, apparently a throat infection that had settled into pericarditis, an inflammation around the heart. He had not been sick for years, and this attack sent him to shelter a week or more at Yerby's shortly before Jackson's wife and child arrived.

While there, Lee told President Davis that unless Hooker moved first, he intended to attack the Union army in the Valley, which should either draw Hooker away or at least prevent his sending reinforcements to the war in the West. That would mean bringing Longstreet back from southern Virginia to watch the Rappahannock line. Meanwhile Lee had to fend off Longstreet's appeals for more troops for his secondary operation around Suffolk, and inquiries from Richmond about sending one of the divisions with Longstreet west to strengthen the Confederate Army of Tennessee. Secretary of War Seddon noted that the Southern force there was outnumbered more than two to one, and "should we encounter defeat in Tennessee for want of additional strength at this time, we can well imagine what would be the effect of such defeat to our cause." Lee gently pointed out that Southern forces were outnumbered everywhere, "and it is difficult to say from which [region] troops can with safety be spared." He wanted Pickett's and Hood's divisions with Longstreet to be kept near the railroad so they could be dispatched to the Rappahannock if Hooker attacked. On April 16, Lee said, "There is some movement in agitation now" in Hooker's army.[37]

Jackson, who was not a born diplomat, had the good fortune to concern himself with tactics more than strategy, to deal with soldiers rather than politicians. In mid-April, obviously motivated by his feud with Hill, he issued an order spelling out how his troops would march. If a division was not ready at the precise time ordered, the next would move in its place. Troops would make two miles in 50 minutes, stop, stack arms, and rest for 10 minutes of each hour. Company officers would march at the rear of their troops to keep them moving; "a day's march should be with them a day of labor; as much vigilance is required on the march as in camp."[38] Soon afterward, Jackson ordered unnecessary wagons and baggage to the rear. Now he was ready, and confident. Talking with one of his officers, he explained why: "My trust is in God"—and then, impatiently, "I wish they would come!"[39]

But before the Yankees came, Anna and baby Julia came to visit, and there at Yerby's, where Lee had recuperated, the Jackson family spent almost nine precious days together. The wives of other generals often joined their husbands between battles, but since the first winter of the war in the Valley, Jackson had resisted this pleasure, partly because Anna was pregnant, then because he feared Julia might catch the smallpox so common in the camps.

Now in spring the dour, reserved soldier let his heart go. He called Julia his "angel." Before the mirror in their bedroom he bounced her, talking as if she could understand. On April 23, the day she was five months old, he arranged for Chaplain Lacy to baptize her there in the Yerbys' parlor. Jackson's whole staff attended. Later Lee came to call, admired Julia and charmed Anna. On Sunday, April 26, Lee and Jubal Early joined the Jacksons beneath a tent as Lacy spoke to hundreds of soldiers on the parable of Lazarus and the rich man. Jackson spent that afternoon in reverential bliss, speaking to Anna of this life and the next.

As the days grew longer, dogwood and lilac were blooming. Jackson, at ease with his loved ones, looked up to see Professor Lowe and his aides watching from bright-colored balloons above the Rappahannock. He and Anna knew their time together would be short. Reports from scouts across the river told of cavalry on the move, of marching rations issued to Union infantry. Lee urged Longstreet to hurry his restocking operations and be ready to march north.

At dawn on April 29, someone came stomping up the stairs and banged at the Jacksons' bedroom door. It was a courier from Early. Jackson got up, pulled on his boots, and stepped outside. Returning, he said to Anna, "It looks as if Hooker were crossing."[40]

Chapter Seven

INTO THE WILDERNESS

HOOKER WAS indeed crossing—with more men, at more points, in a wider, bolder, more smoothly executed maneuver than Lee or Jackson had imagined. The Army of the Potomac, spit-shined and thoroughly drilled, marched farther faster than it had ever marched before. Along the way, despite rain and fatigue, somebody in the 75th Ohio had the spirit to start a chorus of "Battle Hymn of the Republic"—"Mine eyes have seen the glory of the coming of—"

Suddenly, a shout rolled forward through the column—"Hooker! Hooker is coming!" The infantry swayed onto the roadside to let the commanding general pass, riding hard, his party's horses spattering mud onto the foot soldiers. Ignoring it, the troops raised their caps and shouted hurrahs as Hooker rode on, with his escort of decorative lancers. "His bright blue eyes sparkled with pride and confidence," one of the Ohioans recalled. "He waved his black hat high overhead. His thick blond hair jolted in rhythm to the galloping of his horse."[1]

Pride and confidence: Pride in its own strength tingled through Hooker's army as horsemen headed upriver, divisions broke camp to march in different directions, signalmen wigwagged messages from hilltop to hilltop, and Professor Lowe's balloons drifted above the Rappahannock. Confidence in themselves and in Hooker rose as troops believed that this time they were getting the jump on Lee, though less than a handful knew exactly what their commander had in mind.

Even as Hooker's divisions set out, his generals had been told only what their opening moves would be, not how they fit into the overall strategy. By a series of planned feints and accidental false starts, Hooker already had confused both his enemy and his own troops, which served his purpose of secrecy. In the runup to battle, Hooker and his staff had performed at a higher professional level than any Union generals so far in the war. By hard marching, his infantry carried out his first objective as well as any commander had a right to expect.

THROUGHOUT THE CAMPAIGN, indeed throughout the war, Union generals consistently overestimated Lee's troop strength, and Lee often underestimated theirs.

Personnel figures for both sides were notoriously approximate, varying from day to day; the number of men in any given action was far lower than the total on the books. The best accounting shows that as Hooker's men marched to battle, they outnumbered Lee's by slightly more than two to one: 133,868 Federals to 60,892 Confederates. Hooker had seven infantry corps, averaging three divisions each. Those divisions averaged three brigades, or about 5,600 men, including organic artillery. Lee had on hand only a corps and a half—six infantry divisions against Hooker's 21. But the Confederate divisions were bigger, averaging more than four brigades, about 9,000 men per division. With fewer generals reporting directly to him, Lee had a simpler command structure, easier to manage in the confusion of battle. By the spring of 1863, Union regiments in the field averaged 433 men, against the Confederates' 409. Thus at a nominal ten companies per regiment, the typical mid–Civil War company numbered about 42 men, barely the strength of a modern rifle platoon. (See Appendix 1, Order of Battle.)

Hooker's available cavalry also outweighed Lee's, by some 11,540 to 4,450. So did his artillery—413 guns against 220.[2]

The classic rule is that to succeed, an attacking force should outnumber the defenders by three to one. But that applies to the point of attack, where advancing troops must expect heavy casualties against a ready enemy. In a campaign of maneuver, in which each army shifts back and forth from tactical offense to defense, no such simple rule applies throughout. Along the Rappahannock, Hooker had the overall advantage of numbers in troops, guns, and supplies. His horses were in much better condition, and his cannon were superior. To those assets, Hooker's master plan added the strategic initiative.

Lee had the advantage of defending prepared ground, but Hooker meant to maneuver him out of it. Lee also had interior lines, the ability to shift strength quickly and directly to any part of his loosely linked position facing the river. At the outset that was enhanced by the route of the Rappahannock and Rapidan, with Lee inside and Hooker outside their curve. But on a smaller scale, at the very height of the fighting, Hooker

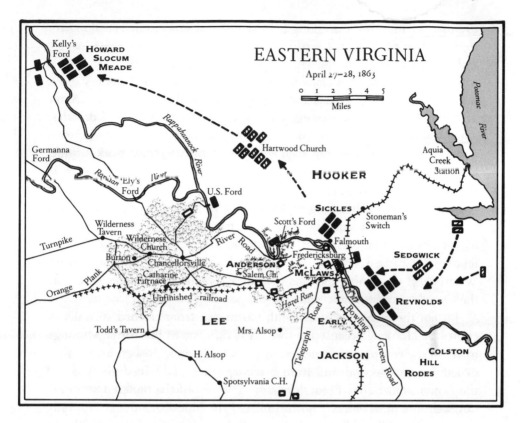

EASTERN VIRGINIA
April 27–28, 1863

0 1 2 3 4 5
Miles

3. Hooker's Opening Moves. *The Union commander succeeds in his bold plan to move most of his infantry onto Lee's western flank via Kelly's Ford, while holding the Confederates in place with diversionary crossings below Fredericksburg.*

would be thankful that the ground gave this asset to him. Hooker's overall plan, with its bold arrows swinging far beyond the armies' existing lines, exaggerated the attacker's normal need to march farther to gain surprise and leverage. Thus, when they set out early that Monday morning, April 27, the three Union corps ordered upriver had to push themselves hard before they got their chance to fight.

Before daybreak, the 75th Ohio scrambled to get ready to march with O. O. Howard's Eleventh Corps, heading northwest behind the rolling hills that screened the maneuvering divisions from the enemy. Into their packs troops crammed eight days' rations—crackers or hard bread; bacon and raw pickled pork wrapped in paper; coffee, flour, brown sugar, and salt, each tied in a little cloth sack like the ones soldiers had carried their toy marbles in as boys not long before. Live cattle were driven along for fresh beef on the march. Cartridge belts and cartridge boxes were loaded, and another 20 or more rounds stuffed into each man's pockets. Pup tents were rolled outside gum blankets and strapped across the shoulders above the haversack. "Frying pans and coffee pots clinked and rattled. . . . Some of the boys looked like moving vans on legs, they took the gol-darndest loads. Including the rifle, each man carried from sixty to eighty pounds. Some tucked away a prized daguerrotype, a breast-pin, a pocket knife. . . ." Cannon lumbered past, and harness creaked as mules strained to pull the regiment's overloaded wagons along the soft road.[3]

Helping one another sling packs, shouldering their weapons, the Ohio men filed onto the road. Ahead of them, troops with German names, led by officers like von Steinwehr, Buschbeck, von Schluembach, Schimmel-fennig, Rolshausen, and Koenig, already had settled into a steady stride. Where they were going they did not know, only that when they got there they would have to fight again.

To put the men of this Eleventh Corps out front seemed an unlikely choice by Hooker, because they were the outcasts of his army. Although many of the troops were veterans of John C. Frémont's western Virginia expedition and Second Bull Run, as a corps they had joined the Army of the Potomac just after Fredericksburg. The rest of the battered army did not welcome newcomers who had missed the bloodbath there. Not only that, but the Eleventh Corps was a "foreign" outfit. Franz Sigel, the general who had commanded it until recently, was German-born, and so were many of his troops—perhaps a bare majority spoke German, but they gave the corps its flavor and reputation. They had a proud boast, "I fights mit Sigel," that others had turned into a taunt, mainly because the accent was so easily mocked. Sigel himself, like dozens of other distin-guished Union officers, was a career soldier who had fought in Germany's revolution before being exiled. He had led a corps since mid-1862, but his pride was hurt when Hooker's reorganization made his the smallest corps, and so he resigned the command.

His replacement was Maj. Gen. Oliver Otis Howard. A thirty-two-year-old West Pointer, Maine Yankee, and devout Congregationalist, Howard had lost his right arm in fighting below Richmond the year before, yet had come back for every battle since. Except for the profession-alism he shared with those European-trained officers, he was a misfit with the Germans of the Eleventh Corps. They resented him because he had replaced their darling Sigel. His straitlaced ways were laughable to men brought up to Continental-style free thinking and free drinking. So Howard and his troops had something to show the army and each other on this, their first march to combat together.

By 9:00 A.M., the corps had been on the move for three hours. In the 55th Ohio, Luther Mesnard's pack straps cut deep into his shoulders, and overburdened troops had started throwing away coats and blankets, things they thought they would not need. "Even the strongest and toughest begin to fear they will give out, can not stand it. A halt, and every man drops down and leans back on his knapsack. After a short rest start on, then comes the worst of all, it seems as though we could not, but soon we get warmed up to the work and the aches and pains subside, and we are yet alive, and some fellow begins to joke, and we get through the day in pretty good shape. . . ."

Mesnard learned the trade of the infantry the only way: "I do not think there is any labor, any physical trial as severe as hard marching to the man who carries the musket," he wrote. "No place or situation in life where men get so tired, and still plod on after being completely tired out, hour after hour, perhaps, like an ox in the furrow, not knowing when the misery will end, but doggedly stagger on, seemingly more dead than alive, yet keep going on because the rest do. It's the orders."[4]

A Connecticut private was glad the roads that morning were "too wet for dust and too dry for mud." But soon the weather turned hot and here and there men stumbled out of column, collapsing by the road amid the mounting piles of coats, blankets, skillets, and tents tossed away by straining soldiers. The Yankee from New Canaan watched as "Sambos and Phillises [recent slaves] collected in squads, grinning and bowing, they would gather up an armful of clothing and march off in great delight."[5]

At three-thirty that afternoon, an anxious Lincoln telegraphed Hooker: "How does it look now?"

Ninety minutes later, Hooker replied: "I am not sufficiently advanced to give an opinion. We are busy. Will tell you as soon as I can, and have it satisfactory."[6]

About that time, a chill rain moved in. The Eleventh Corps slogged on with Henry Slocum's Twelfth Corps close behind, followed by George Meade's Fifth. The whole flanking force spent the night of April 27 near Hartwood Church. Next day, as it neared Mount Holly Church, two miles short of Kelly's Ford, officers at the head of the column passed the word for strict silence. The march was so well concealed up till then that Jeb Stuart, unequaled as a scout and judge of enemy numbers and intentions, could tell Lee only that "a large body of infantry and artillery was passing up the river"—that, and apparently no more.[7]

Slocum, senior to Howard and Meade, had overall command of the flanking column. A West Point roommate of Union cavalryman Phil Sheridan, he had been wounded at First Manassas and risen to command brigades and divisions through the Peninsula, Second Manassas, Antietam, and Fredericksburg. Only on the twenty-eighth, as he approached Kelly's Ford, did Slocum get detailed instructions for his move beyond the Rappahannock. Hooker told him to push on across the Rapidan and back past Chancellorsville if the Confederates were not confronting him in force. If they were, Hooker said, "you will then select a strong position, and compel him to attack you on your ground." Hooker desired that "not a moment be lost until our troops are established at or near Chancellorsville. From that moment all will be ours."[8]

Ahead of Howard's Eleventh Corps, the 154th New York put out skirmishers to protect the engineers hurrying forward to throw a pontoon bridge just below Kelly's Ford. Manning rowboats that had been hidden in Marsh Run, a Rappahannock tributary, the advance guard crossed and cleared the opposite bank. The pontoons were square-ended boats about 30 feet long, clumsy but so buoyant that one soldier compared them to "an open umbrella inverted, and resting on the water."[9] Across them, timbers and planks were laid from shore to shore. Hooker had ordered the pontoons for Kelly's Ford brought by rail from Washington to Bealeton, a dozen miles north, so slow and noisy transit by road from near Falmouth would not attract Rebel attention. Once the pontoons were launched and linked, the engineers spread pine boughs over the planking, so the footsteps of troops at route march, even the rumble of artillery wheels, could hardly be heard. At ten that night, April 28, the Eleventh Corps started crossing.[10]

By midnight, Charles Devens's division was over, spread out in a loose perimeter facing west and south as the rest of the Eleventh Corps and Twelfth Corps followed. Before dawn, troops built fires and balanced coffeepots and cups on the coals, fried bacon, and poured hot grease over their hardtack to make it chewable.

As the Eleventh Corps loaded up to move on, it fell in behind Slocum's Twelfth for the march to the Rapidan. William Southerton of the 75th Ohio was detailed as a "moving picket," pushing through the woods alongside the column as it headed south to Germanna Ford. He had to struggle through "a desolate wilderness of pine and cedar and scrubby blackjacks, all matted and entangled with vines and underbrush. . . . I tore and clawed at the vines, trampled and crashed through scratching briars and high prickly weeds." Gnats pestered him as he "kept a sharp eye for Johnnies," but he "couldn't have seen one beyond ten or fifteen feet."

Out front rode the 6th New York Cavalry, one of only four horse regiments held back when Stoneman undertook his expedition around Lee. But Stoneman's main force, intended to swing farther upriver, was again discouraged by high water, so what was assumed to be the army's fastest-moving arm trotted back down to Kelly's Ford. There, some of the horsemen forded the river and others crossed on the pontoon bridge between divisions of infantry, snarling things and earning very little good will from the foot soldiers.

One of the riders in the 16th Pennsylvania Cavalry was angry that some of his comrades had plundered Kelly's house at the ford. True, John Follmer conceded, "He is said to be a rank rebel, who fired on our men as they were crossing." But "Plundering does not seem to be right. The house was entered and ladies insulted. The men also broke into a sick lady's chamber, and insulted the husband in her presence. These men claim to come from an enlightened country, but are a disgrace to the army. . . . The man who did the deed should be punished and made an example." Follmer's indignation was long out of style among Yankee riders a year later, in the Shenandoah Valley and Georgia.[11]

As the powerful Blue infantry column pushed along the 11-mile way from Kelly's to Germanna Ford, Rebel cavalry dashed at its edges, picking off a few prisoners and losing a few. In the early fog on the twenty-ninth, a Belgian officer wearing a Union uniform as observer with the Eleventh Corps rode unawares into Jeb Stuart's pickets. Captured, he was reluctant to talk, but when Stuart's aide von Borcke questioned him in French, he said, "Gentlemen, I can only give you one piece of advice—that is, to try and make your escape as quickly as possible; if not, your capture by the large army in front of you is a certainty."[12]

From this conversation, Stuart telegraphed Lee that the Eleventh Corps was across the Rappahannock. But he still did not know where it was heading. (Throughout the war, prisoners from both sides were remarkably free in disclosing whatever military secrets they knew from their limited perspective. There was nothing like the twentieth-century regulation that tried to limit conversation with captors to name, rank, and serial number. Speaking the same language made casual talk between prisoners and captors the natural thing. There was an understandable hope that cooperating would mean a better chance of parole, or at least gentler handling. Close to battle, front-line soldiers who might themselves be captured in

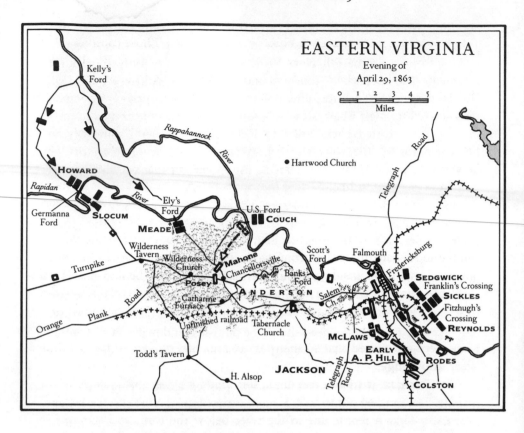

4. Across Two Rivers. *Before Lee can decide how to react, the two wings of Hooker's army are across the Rappahannock below Fredericksburg and the Rapidan far above town. Federal columns moving toward Chancellorsville clear U.S. Ford for more direct crossings by Couch's and other corps arriving later.*

the next day or hour were consistently kinder to their captives than guards at the overcrowded, undersupplied prison camps to the rear. And besides, the rules of this particular war, with its paroles, exchanges, cross-river commerce, and cease-fires for burial parties, made it seem a game to many soldiers when actual shooting was not going on. All this is why Hooker went to such lengths to restrict any advance knowledge of his plans to senior officers who absolutely had to know where and when he was going. But occasionally, the casual dribble of intelligence from prisoners could lead its recipients astray. That would happen later in the coming battle.)

In the afternoon Stuart's horsemen jabbed repeatedly at the flank of the Union force. They took prisoners from the Eleventh and Twelfth as well as the Fifth Corps, which trailed the first two across Kelly's Ford and then angled southeast toward Ely's Ford on the Rapidan. Those captives gave Stuart the first clear intelligence on what Hooker was up to. By the time he questioned his prisoners and realized the scale of the Union move, Blue infantry had taken Germanna Ford, and the courier Stuart sent to warn the Southern detachment there was captured on the way.

Hooker's move so surprised Lee that there was nobody guarding the vital Germanna crossing except a bridge-building party of about 125 soldiers. Fifty of these were posted on the north bank when the Union advance guard from Brig. Gen. Thomas H. Ruger's brigade made contact. Ruger spread a regiment far off each side of the road and pushed them through the thickets to envelop the Rebel outpost, capturing most of the fifty. As the Rapidan bent around the ford, this put the rest of the Rebels on the south bank under fire from two sides. They resisted briefly but with spirit, firing from inside the old Germanna mill and behind stacks of bridging timber on the bank. Then a few got away through the woods, but about 100 prisoners were taken by the converging Federal regiments. As these Confederates marched back past the advancing Union column, they were astonished that so many thousands had moved so far without their knowledge.

The Rapidan ran swift and high, and this time there was no pontoon bridge. Determined not to halt, Slocum ordered cavalrymen on the biggest horses to form a rescue line in the river below the ford, and started his infantry across. Thousands of soldiers imitated John Marshall of the 123rd New York, who crammed his pack, cartridge boxes, boots, and pants into one tight bundle, fixed his bayonet to his rifle, stuck his bundle on its point, and started wading. The current pulled at him, and many around him slipped on slick rocks.[13] The water reached the troops' armpits; most of those washed off their feet were fished out by the cavalrymen, and by guards in a few boats below. Husky riflemen carried some boy musicians over on their shoulders. As this risky business went on, an officer suggested using the timbers left by the departed Rebels to throw up a temporary bridge, and the engineers went to work. Eventually more fording was halted while the bridge was completed. Some troops were detailed to unsling ammunition from pack mules and tote it over the bridge while the little animals struggled to swim across. Even stripped of its load, one mule, "with suicidal intent, accomplished drowning in three feet of water." With everyone doing his part, the Eleventh and Twelfth Corps pushed on across the Rapidan.[14]

Farther down that river, after Federal horsemen chased away a few

Rebel cavalry pickets, the infantry went through the same kind of dangerous comedy when the Fifth crossed at Ely's Ford. A Pennsylvania chaplain who risked this "universal kind of baptism" said he had "never
witnessed a scene in which the sublime and ludicrous were so completely
blended as in this undress parade. . . ." [15] "We got there just as the sun
was going down," a Michigan soldier recalled. "The water was waist deep
and very cold. We had to take off our catrige boxes and haversack and
hold them up out of the water and then plung in of all the yelping and
yelling mingled in with some horid oathes. Any one would think that the
devels school was out for noon. We was nearly two hours getting across
and there we was in the dark wet, tired, hungry & cold and our company
had to go out on picket all night. A cold chilly wind blew from the
northwest all night. We was right glad to see the sun rise the next
morning." [16] Dr. Cyrus Bacon, a Michigan surgeon, came to the river and
stood looking across at the slope where the army's campfires "made the
night resplendent." [17] After sloshing across, most of the Fifth Corps
marched a few hundred yards up the muddy slope and flopped for the
night.

The closest Confederate infantry to these major crossings was William
Mahone's and Carnot Posey's brigades guarding United States Ford,
named for an old gold mine just below the juncture of the Rapidan and
Rappahannock. In late afternoon two sentries galloped into Mahone's
command post and told him the Yankees were coming in force down the
road from Ely's Ford. Soon Mahone got word of the Federal column
marching east from Germanna. He and Posey immediately realized these
heavy columns were flanking them out of defending U.S. Ford. Across the
river, two divisions of the Union Second Corps approached the ford to
be ready for a pontoon-bridge crossing the next day. Within an hour
Mahone and Posey decided to quit the position they had held for months,
leaving about 600 men behind to try to delay the enemy at the ford. After
pulling back, they set up new lines just west of Chancellorsville—Mahone
across the Ely's Ford road, Posey across the Orange Turnpike, squarely
facing the oncoming Yankees. Hooker did not realize it yet, but his plan
to uncover U.S. Ford by pushing down behind it had worked perfectly.

That night, as Yankee chaplain J. W. McFarland lay down after crossing Ely's Ford, he smelled coffee cooking over huge bonfires and listened
to soldiers make predictions about the battle they expected the next day.
There was swearing, joking, and laughter. When it died down, he heard
only "the lonely voice of the whippoorwill. The moon and stars look
down as peacefully and sweetly as if there were no strife on earth." [18] Later,

a drizzling rain began, but it could not damp the spirit of the tired, soaked infantry. Satisfaction overrode exhaustion from three days' hard marching, almost wiped out tension over what was to come. Under the chill rain, the right wing of Hooker's army slept, proud of a job extremely well done.

"Since we crossed the Rappahannock in such style, fording the Rapidan shoulder deep by moonlight, Hooker's stock is rising," a New York soldier wrote to his mother. "He furnishes the brains, the Army the legs, and I think legs have won. Hooker is a brick of the genuine kind."[19]

THAT WEDNESDAY, April 29, one to three miles below Fredericksburg, the other wing of Hooker's army made its opening move in the face of Lee's carefully laid defenses. Maj. Gen. John Sedgwick of the Sixth Corps had command of this left wing. His orders were to cross and go through the motions of attack against the Rebels around Fredericksburg, to keep them busy and prevent their moving. If they pulled back, he was to go after them. If they headed upstream to confront Hooker's flank approach, he was to take their positions, block the Telegraph Road from Richmond, and send reinforcements to Hooker.[20]

Filing down ravines that hid them from Rebel pickets, Sedgwick's men started toward the river late Tuesday. Until dark, he kept his infantry and pontoons in the cover of woods a thousand yards back from the river. Brig. Gen. Henry W. Benham of the Engineers was in charge of laying the bridges; he also thought he was in charge of the initial crossing. Brigadier generals William T. H. Brooks and James S. Wadsworth, commanding the lead infantry divisions, did not think so. This provoked a hot argument over getting the boats to the river and troops into the boats after midnight. To hold down noise in the dark, most of the boats were dragged by hand along the ground. Farther back, the rumbling wagons had awakened dozing troops, who thought they heard artillery.

The regiments waiting near the river lay on their arms, eyes wide open. A New York soldier remembered it as "a peculiar night, moonless, clouds in heavy masses drifting across the sky, through numerous rifts in which the stars twinkled a moment and were gone, occasional drops of rain fell, large and noisy. Away off to the right the boom of cannon was heard, and the track of the shells could be traced by their burning fuses as they sped on their way. . . . Back and forth the mind wanders, memories and anticipations mingle; what life has been and whether it shall continue to be over the morrow. . . ."[21]

Benham had been ordered to complete the bridges by 3:30 A.M., but at

Franklin's Crossing, where Brooks's division was ready to cross and cover the bridging operation, the boats were not at river's edge until 1:30. Brig. Gen. David A. Russell maintained that crossing was impossible in the dark, and refused to let his brigade embark before dawn. When Benham ordered him arrested, Russell ignored it. Finally at 4:20, more than 1,200 men of the 95th and 119th Pennsylvania—45 troops plus officers to each boat—loaded up and disappeared into the river fog. The boatmen raced to be first to hit the Rebel shore.

Minutes later, out of the thickness ahead rang the command, "Fire!" and a bright horizontal flash lit the fog. "Bang whiz bang—we were saluted by a volley of musketry," said a Pennsylvania captain waiting to go over with the next brigade. But "the greater portion of the balls flew too high over the men in the boats and too low to do us much damage." The troops in boats were too tightly packed to return the Rebel fire, and besides could see nothing until the boats scraped ashore. Soon those waiting behind heard a string of cheers, and boatmen returned out of the fog to pick up more troops. Once ashore on the Confederate side, the Pennsylvanians formed quickly despite the defenders' fire, and got up the riverbank and into the Rebel rifle pits within minutes. With the riverbank secure, bridge-building began at 5:50 and was done at 7:00. Another span was run alongside a half hour later, a third by 9:45.[22]

A mile downstream at Fitzhugh's Crossing, troops of Maj. Gen. John F. Reynolds's First Corps did not get into boats until about 9:00 A.M. Benham was in a ruckus there, too. An artillery officer asserted later that the engineer was talking boisterously, "had been up all night and taken so much whiskey to keep himself awake that he was tight as a brick; had fallen off his horse once and scratched his face badly."[23] Hooker demanded that Benham explain his performance, and as soon as these first bridges were done Benham replied that very day with a long narrative that apparently forestalled any charges against him. Still more bridges were needed at other crossings—up and down the river, there would be fifteen in all—and before the campaign was over Benham had redeemed himself with most of his fellow generals by the way he laid, picked up, and moved them from point to point. Without them, there might have been disaster.

Back of Fitzhugh's Crossing, Brig. Gen. James S. Wadsworth's infantry lay all night expecting orders to fall in at any moment. They looked back on the months of despair that had turned to confidence before they marched down toward the river. "Perhaps before another sun would rise half of our now joyous companions would be stretched cold and lifeless on the bloody field," a Wisconsin soldier thought. Somebody said aloud that he hoped tomorrow's battle would be the Waterloo of the war. "So do I," said a friend, then one after another echoed him. If this were to be Waterloo, they were convinced that this time Hooker would play Wellington to Lee's Napoleon.[24]

Wadsworth picked as his division spearhead the famous Iron Brigade, northwesterners who had won their reputation at Second Bull Run. He sent them close to the river before midnight. But at daylight the thoroughly awakened Confederates opened fire and chased away the boatmen, who left their boats half in, half out of the water. Brig. Gen. Solomon Meredith sent two regiments to shoot back from behind stone fences and trees along the bank, but after two hours they withdrew until orders came to load the boats to take the Rebel positions from the flank. By then Meredith's men had to double-quick across a wide span of open ground before reaching the river, and the watching Confederates opened on them again. With the rest of the Iron Brigade laying down a heavy covering fire, the 6th Wisconsin and 24th Michigan leaped into the boats and pushed across "right merrily, the bullets hailing around all the time." They took only light casualties and started up the steep bank toward the Rebel defenses. Crossing close after them came their generals and the rest of the Iron Brigade—Meredith standing in one boat, swinging his hat and hurrahing; Wadsworth gripping the reins of his horse, which swam behind.

Opening fire on the first Union regiments leaping into knee-deep mud along the riverbank, the 13th Georgia held out until the 6th Louisiana, coming on picket duty, moved forward to help. But once the Iron Brigade's regiments were across, the defenders had to stand at least halfway out of their rifle pits to aim down at them, and so exposed themselves to heavy fire from the other side of the river. Many Rebels who tried to run were cut down; those who crouched deeper in their holes were captured.[25] "The secesh wir scamping across the field at a tearing pace," one of the Wisconsin attackers wrote. "It was the greatest fun we have ever had, but at first it was considered the most desperate thing we had ever undertaken."[26] The Georgians and Louisianans were overrun. "I never saw men run faster," wrote the First Corps artillery chief. "It was amusing to see our men too rush on. Two of them pushed up the bank alone and took the men out of the smaller pits; they would only take their muskets away from them, tell them to run to the rear, and then, throwing down the captured muskets, rush on to the next pit. . . . Such is the excitement of success, and so much does a man's bravery depend on the fact that his enemy are running away from him."[27]

Once the pickets along the river were driven off, the Union line pushed on close to the Old Richmond Stage Road, also called the Bowling Green Road, which ran in a cut about two feet deep. At first the leading Yankees were exuberant about what they had done, but as they halted and lay panting they saw dark lines of Southern infantry moving along the low hills before them. In the 2nd Wisconsin, Elon Brown looked around, considered the scant number of comrades close by and the river behind. He thought of the disaster that had struck another Federal force when it crossed the Potomac above Washington back in 1861. Involuntarily, he said aloud, "Another Ball's Bluff!" Somebody nearby agreed: "You're right, Brown. I fear so, too." Brown told him to "Hush!"—suddenly afraid his own words might create a panic. Nobody else had heard. When the regiment pulled back along the riverside bluff, the fog lifted and Brown was relieved to see two bridges completed and Federal artillery zeroing in to protect the bridgehead.[28] Eighty Union guns were sited overlooking the two crossing points, with 42 more ready for use against any Rebel move on the attackers' flanks.

At Franklin's Crossing, Russell's men in the earlier bridgehead pushed about 300 yards from the river. Flushing pickets of the 54th North Carolina out of two lines of rifle pits, they reached left to tie in with Meredith at Fitzhugh's Crossing. By early afternoon of April 29, both wings of Hooker's great offensive had made their opening moves without serious casualties, and with only slight delay.[29]

Hours before that, Lee had started moving troops in response, and asking Richmond for reinforcements. But he still was not sure what Hooker was up to.

Chapter Eight

HURRAH FOR OLD JOE!

IN THE MORNING darkness of April 29, the crackle of gunfire that met the Union boats appearing out of the fog half waked Lee in his tent three miles south of Franklin's Crossing. But he fell asleep again, assuming that if the fuss was anything more than nervous troops shooting at shadows, someone would tell him soon enough.

Jubal Early, whose regiments picketed the riverbank, did not wait for orders before sending the rest of his division into line along the Richmond, Fredericksburg & Potomac Railroad, a mile back from the river. He anchored his right on Massaponax Creek and his left on Deep Run, ready to refight December's battle. Before his troops started to move, he dispatched Maj. Samuel Hale to arouse Jackson at Yerby's plantation house.

Jackson heard the news, went back upstairs, and told his wife she might not be safe there, and to get ready to go to Richmond. If he could, he would come back to say a proper goodbye. If not, he would send his staff officer, her brother, Joseph G. Morrison, to take her to the train at Guiney Station. He embraced her and the baby, then rode to battle.[1]

By that time, Jackson's aide, Lt. James Power Smith, was on his way to Lee. When Smith arrived, Lee sat up on the edge of his cot. He was calm, gently joking even then. "Well, I thought I heard firing," he said. "I was beginning to think it was time some of you young fellows were coming to tell me what it was all about. Tell your good general that I am sure he knows what to do. I will meet him at the front very soon."[2]

A courier rode off to Fredericksburg and at five-thirty the Episcopal church bell started ringing the alarm. Barksdale's brigade had had a prayer service inside and pep rally outside the church the night before, with Mississippi ex-governor Albert Gallatin Brown and other politicians speaking before Barksdale himself gave "a very interesting 'family talk.' "

One of his soldiers wrote, "He is very much attached to the boys, as the boys are to him."[3] After falling asleep with this inspirational rhetoric in their minds, Barksdale's men were startled awake by the bell and scurried to their Fredericksburg defenses. Most of the residents who had hung on in the battered town grabbed a few valuables and left their homes, some fleeing west toward Chancellorsville.

Drummers stood in company streets and beat the long roll. It carried from camp to camp through the river fog and back into the low hills that run up from the Rappahannock. Still half sleeping, Bartlett Malone of the 6th North Carolina "herd a horse come threw the camp in a full lope." In a few minutes, someone said, "Boys you had better get up we will have a fight hear to reckly." Malone told his diary, "Befour I got my close on they comenced beating the long roal and it was not but a minnet or too untill I herd the Adgertent hollow fall in with armes. . . ."[4] The chill of anticipation touched the sophisticated as well: In Joseph Kershaw's brigade, a South Carolinian recalled "the ominous sound of the long roll to the soldier wrapped in his blanket and enjoying the sweets of sleep. It is like a fire bell at night. . . . A battle is imminent. The soldiers thus roused, as if from their long sleep since Fredericksburg, feel in a touchous mood. The frightful scenes of Fredericksburg and Marye's Hill rise up before them as a spectre." Troops rushed about, asking one another what was about to happen, guessing where the Yankees were coming. They fell in along damp camp roads, listening to the first sparring of far cannon.[5]

As the Union troops started their second crossing, the 13th Georgia played its picket role by fighting hard to hold up the Yankees before falling back, losing dozens as prisoners. Henry Walker wrote home that "we fought there about two to three hours untill our cartridges gave out and we never lost but one man while we was in the rifle pits but when we went to leave they swept our boys down like they was chaff. The North Carolinians above us [at Franklin's Crossing] let the yankees surprise them they fired one volley and runaway as fast as there heals would carry them."[6]

Lee looked out from a bluff that commanded the developing Union bridgehead. His riverside guards fell back past the Old Richmond Road, where Early had posted three regiments of new pickets. Along the railroad a mile from the river, Early's main units started digging in. Troops in blue were spreading along the plain, approaching the very ground where Lee and his generals had hoped, but hardly expected, the enemy might attack again. He telegraphed Richmond that "it looks like a general advance, but where [Hooker's] main effort will be made, I cannot say." Troops not needed below Richmond should be sent his way, he said. As the fog thinned and Sedgwick's men began their second crossing at Fitzhugh's, at about 10:00 A.M. Lee wired Richmond again. The enemy "is certainly crossing in large force here," he said. He had heard nothing of other moves "except below Kelley's Ford, where General Howard has crossed with his division, said to be 14,000, six pieces of artillery, and some cavalry."

This was day-old intelligence from Stuart; although three of Hooker's corps upriver were across the Rappahannock on their way to the Rapidan, Lee still had word of only Howard's troops, less than a third of the flanking force—and he assumed they were headed west toward Gordonsville rather than turning back toward him. Nevertheless, he repeated that "All available troops had better be sent as rapidly as possible. . . ." Shortly afterward he sent another message asking that a force be sent to Gordonsville, adding, "Longstreet's division[s], if available, had better come to me. . . ."[7]

When Jackson saw the size of the Union force crossing the river, he realized a serious fight was imminent. He scrawled a tender note to his wife, urging her to leave for Richmond at once. He handed the note to Lieutenant Morrison, his wife's brother, asking him to take an ambulance and see her to the rear. Morrison, speaking as if to his brother-in-law rather than his commander, said he would rather stay for the battle— couldn't Chaplain Lacy go instead? Jackson agreed and sent Lacy, who took Mrs. Jackson and daughter to the southbound train at Guiney Station.[8]

Then Stonewall rode forward, abrupt and businesslike. Moving quickly to shorten and strengthen his line, he brought Brig. Gen. Robert E. Rodes's division in on Early's right, with Brig. Gen. Stephen Dodson Ramseur's brigade angling toward the river along Massaponax Creek. Jackson's other two divisions, under Maj. Gen. A. P. Hill and Brig. Gen. Raleigh E. Colston, were farther away, down near Moss Neck. They had to march hours through drizzling rain, soldiers slipping and falling and cursing, to come up behind Early. Hill's division deployed in a second defense line, and Colston was held in reserve. As Jackson rode past inspecting their positions, his troops cheered and waved their hats and muskets. They were as ready as he was.

Lee waited for the situation to develop, eager for some word from Stuart that would help him decide whether the force in front of him was the main Union effort or a diversion. As the day cleared, Early saw the slopes across the Rappahannock "semi-covered" with troops, from opposite Fredericksburg almost to a point opposite Massaponax Creek, a good four miles. "The question was whether they were ostentatiously displayed as a feint, or whether they were massed for crossing," he wrote. While the Union regiments already across were throwing up breastworks and artillery emplacements, it was impossible to tell their numbers because they were shielded by the steep dropoff to the river. Occasionally artillery boomed, but except for pickets putting out feelers, neither army's infantry moved beyond the positions taken early that morning.[9]

When Lee rode toward Fredericksburg to check the positions of Maj. Gen. Lafayette McLaws's division on Early's left, McLaws thought the commander seemed "very confident of his ability to beat back the enemy should our troops behave as well as they have usually done." "General McLaws," Lee said, "let them know that it is a stern reality now, it must be victory or death, for defeat would be ruinous."[10]

Only toward dusk did a cavalryman bring word to Lee that the Union force upriver was moving across the Rapidan toward his flank. Lee was more and more concerned that the enemy had cut between him and Stuart, the eyes and ears of his army. Still without clear warning of how big Hooker's flanking force was and where it was headed, he called his artillery up from Chesterfield Station and Bowling Green. Later he ordered Maj. Gen. Richard H. Anderson to take Wright's brigade west, to join Mahone's and Posey's brigades in a blocking position around the crossroads of Chancellorsville. That evening he got his first detailed message from Stuart—that Howard's Union corps was not continuing west, but was part of the force coming down across the Rapidan.

With that, Lee finally made up his mind what Hooker was trying to do. He wired President Davis that "Their intention, I presume, is to turn our left, and probably to get into our rear. Our scattered condition [i.e., Longstreet's absence] favors their operations." Once again, Lee politely pleaded, "I hope if any reinforcements can be sent, they may be forwarded immediately." During the night, Davis answered that minor units were on the move. However, Longstreet near Suffolk, Maj. Gen. Samuel French at Petersburg, and Maj. Gen. D. H. Hill in North Carolina "have been telegraphed to on the subject of reinforcements, but have not yet been heard from."

Substantively, they never would be heard from: Lee would have to fight this battle with what he had on hand. That was less than half the enemy's strength—and now Hooker, with his opening moves, had skillfully taken away the river-line advantage that Lee had held so long.

. . .

SUE CHANCELLOR was fourteen that spring. She was one of ten Chancellors, all but two of them women, who lived in the brick house eleven miles west of Fredericksburg. There, five roads came together and two armies were about to meet.

This Chancellorsville was not a village but one imposing farmhouse, a two-and-a-half-story brick building with an inset, columned front porch. A few outbuildings and an irregular clearing of about 100 acres spread around it. For years it had been an inn for travelers, and refugees from Fredericksburg had fled December's fighting to take shelter there and at other country houses scattered in the thick Virginia forest. Rumors swept through with each move and feint of the armies up and down the Rappahannock. Then as the rumors came true, Confederate soldiers marched past and began digging trenches west of the house. Late on April 29, Dick Anderson met his brigadier Carnot Posey there, and Jeb Stuart rode in to counsel with them about the Union force descending on Chancellorsville. Anderson decided to pull back again, away from Chancellorsville and the surrounding forest, so he would have clear fields of fire at the advancing Federals.

Of the twenty Chancellor family slaves, all but one little girl had fled to freedom with the Yankees across the river. Thus Sue and her sisters cooked and proudly set a meal for the generals and their aides. But no sooner had the officers settled down than a courier rode in warning that the enemy was moving across United States Ford. "Immediately all was confusion," Sue remembered. The generals got up to leave, "but General Stuart, always so charming, took time to say to my sister, 'Thank you, Miss Fannie, for the good supper, and as it is always my custom to fee the waitress, take this from me as a little remembrance.' And he gave her a little gold dollar," which would be kept for generations as a family treasure. Expecting the Yankees any moment, the women and girls layered on as much clothing as they could wear, fastened the family silver inside their hoopskirts, and hid other valuables about the farm.[11]

But, fast as the Yankees were marching, they would not get to Chancellorsville that night. Nor were they crossing, yet, at U.S. Ford. Hooker's main force had to move first through the dense woods locally called the Wilderness. It was second-growth forest, grown thicker and thicker for almost 150 years since colonial governor Alexander Spotswood planted a stockade of Palatine ironworkers at Germanna, on what was then the unsettled frontier. In ever-widening arcs, their furnace consumed wood for charcoal, and as soon as trees grew up they were cut again. Other furnaces were opened, each demanding fuel, until about 70 square miles from the Rapidan east past Chancellorsville were cut-over woodlands. Thickets of new growth, blackjack oak and scrub pine, sprouted among tree stumps. Between cuttings, the sunlight reached the forest floor and encouraged brambles and catbriers. Regiments hurrying through this Wilderness could hardly push flank guards alongside; infantry, artillery, supply trains, cattle on the hoof, division after division had to move in tight column along the roads that ran to Chancellorsville from the fords of the Rappahannock and Rapidan.

Soon after dawn on the cool drizzly morning of April 30, Maj. Pennock Huey led three squadrons of his 8th Pennsylvania Cavalry from Ely's toward U.S. Ford to make contact with the Second Corps infantry approaching from the Union side. Where the road forked, his advance guard appeared out of the woods to surprise most of a company from the 12th Virginia Infantry asleep inside a country schoolhouse. The detachment had been left behind by Mahone to watch U.S. Ford. Unable to see around the building, the Confederates did not realize that the Yankee riders surrounding them numbered only eight. Three Rebel officers and 22 men came out one by one, each surrendering his weapon as he stepped through the schoolhouse door, and all were furious at themselves when they saw their captors. Sgt. John F. Sale, a sentry posted in the woods, was overrun by the Union cavalry before he could sound an alarm, but got away into the thickets with five comrades. Looking back at the horsemen searching for them, they thought at one point that capture was certain, so they emptied their pockets of letters and documents, tore them up and ran on. Through the woods the Yankees caught an occasional sight of the sprinting sentries and sent hurried carbine shots zinging past them, but were reluctant to push their horses into the undergrowth. At last the panting Rebels hit a path that one of them recognized, and followed it back to their regiment.[12]

After Union cavalry surprised that outpost, the Confederate rear guard fought a series of sharp engagements to protect Dick Anderson's command as it withdrew past Chancellorsville. With two skirmish lines alternately firing and dropping back, the 12th Virginia repulsed the 8th Pennsylvania's charging horsemen around the McGee farmhouse, on the Turnpike a mile east of Chancellorsville. (To add confusion in the coming battle, there was another McGee a half mile east of this, and another a half mile east of that one.) This stand enabled Mahone and Posey, plus

Wright's newly arrived brigade, to carry out Anderson's decision to pull back four miles from Chancellorsville toward Fredericksburg. Anderson would dig in at another crossroads, beyond the thickets, where his men would have a clear shot at Union columns as they felt their way out of the Wilderness.

There his three brigades spread out near Zoan (miscalled Zoar or Zion by some mapmakers) and Tabernacle churches, facing west along the Old Turnpike and the Orange Plank Road. The Turnpike ran from Orange Court House to Wilderness Tavern, where it joined the road eastward from Culpeper Court House and Germanna. A gravel-surfaced dirt road, the Turnpike was corduroyed with earth-covered poles in the many creek bottoms it crossed. The Plank Road also ran east from Orange, roughly paralleling the Turnpike but looping south of it, then merging with it, then looping south again east of Chancellorsville. It was covered with two-inch-thick planks; in rotten spots, the feet of men and horses broke through into the mud beneath. Nevertheless the Plank Road and the Turnpike were the best routes from the west toward Fredericksburg and Lee's main army. At Anderson's location they were linked by the Mine Road, the direct way from U.S. Ford. Digging in and looking toward Chancellorsville, Anderson's brigades thus covered the likeliest avenues of enemy approach. Late that morning, 28 artillery pieces sent by Lee rolled up to join the new blocking position.[13]

Maj. Gen. George G. Meade, with Griffin's division of his Fifth Corps, was the first senior Yankee into Chancellorsville. When he rode up to the big house about eleven that morning, he saw four of the Chancellor women on the upper veranda, giving the approaching troops an angry welcome. General Lee was just ahead, the women warned, and he would offer the Yankees the "hospitality of the country." Ignoring their fury, Meade's officers told the family that the house would be Hooker's headquarters, so all ten Chancellors would be confined to one room at the back. The women made pallets on the floor, and depended on Union soldiers to bring them food. Whenever they tried to leave the room, they were ordered back. But Hooker was not there yet, and the Chancellors had no inkling yet of how many thousands of Yankees would surround their clearing before nightfall.[14]

As Hooker's right wing drove toward Chancellorsville, the sheer weight of its three full corps pushed aside the Rebel cavalry detachments trying to feel out its strength and purpose. Neither did the Federal troops' quick forays at roadside henhouses slow the advancing columns; the old Virginians still trying to make crops on those scattered farms were taken along lest they sneak away to tell the Confederates what they had seen.[15] Jeb Stuart's riders had nicked the Union columns, briefly panicking a stretch of one with a tattoo of cannon fire. They captured prisoners with a dispatch that showed the Union force was carrying five days' rations and driving cattle for fresh beef along the way. "These items placed it beyond doubt that the enemy was making a real movement to turn Fredericksburg," Stuart recalled.[16] But by then Hooker had done it; the question was how he would follow through his opening success.

Hooker's orders two days earlier to Slocum, who commanded the flanking force, called for him to push on past Chancellorsville toward Banks' Ford. That ford was at a bend where the Rappahannock dipped southward behind Fredericksburg. It was no more than seven marching miles above the town by roads north of the Rappahannock, and even closer by the River Road along the southern side. It was guarded only by one of Anderson's brigades, under Brig. Gen. Cadmus M. Wilcox. Pushing Wilcox away would enable Hooker to move more troops quickly, close on Lee's flank, and put the two wings of his army within easy support of each other. Slocum's orders told him to keep going that way as long as the Confederates did not confront him in force—and if they did, then "you will select a strong position, and compel him to attack you on your ground." But on the morning of April 30, Hooker's chief of staff, Dan Butterfield, sent new directions. Rather than pushing on, the flanking force should establish a defense line around Chancellorsville, and "be in readiness to take the initiative in the morning."[17] Having seized the initiative with a grand movement onto Lee's flank, Hooker would hold up to consolidate, trusting that the initiative would still be his to resume the next day.

Meanwhile, U.S. Ford would be the main Union crossing point, making the line of operations between Sedgwick's wing and Chancellorsville 12 miles longer than it would have been via Banks' Ford. Brig. Gen. Gouverneur K. Warren, Hooker's chief topographical engineer, rode early April 30 past Second Corps troops who had moved up from near Banks' Ford and waited to cross at U.S. Ford. Finding the approach too rough for pontoon wagons, he borrowed a 500-man working party from the

5. Halt at Chancellorsville. *As the bulk of four Union corps arrives at the crossroads 11 miles west of Fredericksburg, Hooker orders them to hold up rather than pressing on eastward. Anderson's Confederates dig in at a blocking position linking Zoan and Tabernacle churches.*

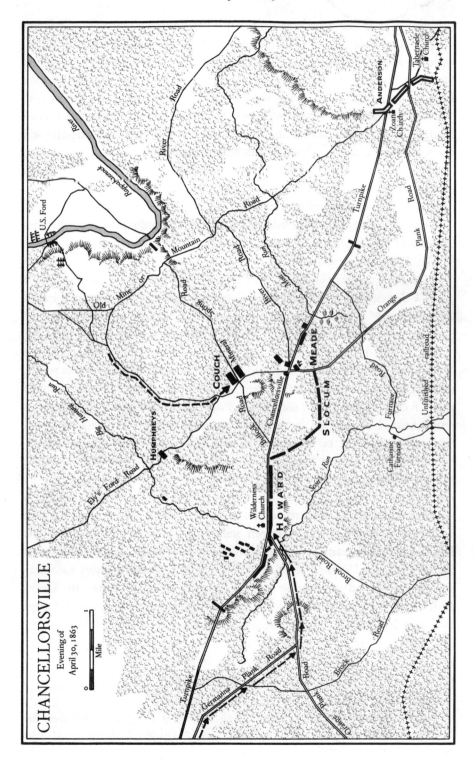

CHANCELLORSVILLE

Evening of
April 30, 1863

Mile

infantry to clear the way. Not till the fog lifted and he saw Union cavalry on the other side did he realize that the Southern pickets guarding U.S. Ford were gone. At midafternoon a bridge was ready, and the engineers' band led the crossing, jauntily playing "Dixie." To Union troops, after looking across the river at the enemy for so many months, it seemed the Rappahannock rather than the Potomac had become the border of Dixieland. Promptly, two divisions of Darius Couch's Second Corps crossed the ford and headed toward Chancellorsville. Thus by late afternoon, Hooker had three and two-thirds corps—more than 50,000 men—at and around the crossroads, astride Lee's possible retreat route toward Gordonsville. More were on the way.

General Meade, already installed at the Chancellorsville house, was elated and eager to press on when Slocum came up with the vanguard of his Twelfth Corps at about 2:00 P.M.

"This is splendid, Slocum!" Meade said in greeting. "Hurrah for old Joe! We're on Lee's flank, and he doesn't know it. You take the Plank Road toward Fredericksburg, and I'll take the Pike, or vice versa, as you prefer, and we will get out of this Wilderness."

Meade had not yet heard of the order to hold up for the night, but Slocum had. "My orders are to assume command on arriving at this point, and to take up a line of battle here, and not to move forward without further orders," he told Meade. That obviously deflated his colleague's enthusiasm, but most of the troops around them were ready to celebrate. So, indeed, was the commanding general of the Army of the Potomac.

Hooker had ordered Maj. Gen. John Sedgwick, in command of his left wing and the bridgehead below Fredericksburg, to make an early-afternoon demonstration against the Rebel lines to find out whether Lee's troops were still in strength there. But then, in late morning, Hooker withdrew that order. He was not yet ready with his right wing, the flanking force, presumably the hammer that would crush Lee against Sedgwick's anvil downstream. He ordered two of the bridges to Sedgwick's bridgehead to be taken up during the night and shifted to Banks' Ford by morning. Meanwhile, he directed Dan Sickles's Third Corps to leave its position overlooking the crossings below Fredericksburg and march under cover to Chancellorsville by way of U.S. Ford. When the Third Corps camped just before midnight, it was halfway to the ford. Well before that, Hooker himself had assumed command at Chancellorsville.

He left Falmouth about four o'clock and rode hard to reach his new headquarters in early evening. By then Meade had pulled back the troops he had sent poking beyond Chancellorsville until they ran into Anderson's pickets on the Turnpike. At Slocum's order they formed a short defensive line across that road, facing east just inside the Chancellorsville clearing. Slocum told Howard to spread his Eleventh Corps along the road to the west. Between Meade and Howard, Slocum's own Twelfth Corps threw an arc south and west, toward an open plateau called Hazel Grove. Couch's two divisions of the Second Corps were on the northeast, between the crossroads and the Rappahannock. Into this loosely forming perimeter Hooker galloped before sunset.

Brig. Gen. Alpheus Williams recalled the "gay and cheerful scene" at the Chancellorsville house, with hundreds of officers gathered, laughing and slapping backs. "We had begun to think we had done something heroic," Williams wrote later. "All was *couleur de rose!* How many joyous hearts and bright cheerful faces beat and smiled happily for the last time on that delightful moonlight night at Chancellorsville!"[18] Most of Hooker's flanking force had forgotten by then that President Lincoln had designated that day, April 30, to be one of "fasting and humiliation." Hooker effectively superseded the president's proclamation with General Orders No. 47:

> It is with heartfelt satisfaction the commanding general announces to the army that the operations of the last three days have determined that our enemy must either ingloriously fly, or come out from behind his defenses and give us battle on our own ground, where certain destruction awaits him. The operations of the Fifth, Eleventh and Twelfth Corps have been a succession of splendid achievements.[19]

So ebullient was Hooker's mood that he told one of his favorite newspapermen, "The rebel army . . . is now the legitimate property of the Army of the Potomac. They may as well pack up their haversacks and make for Richmond. I shall be after them. . . ."[20] The correspondent, William Swinton, had been around a while, and may have been skeptical. So were some veteran soldiers, who had heard generals' rhetoric before. Others who had pursued the Rebels through Chancellorsville in the morning were grumbling about being pulled back. But the mass of the army—and the editorialists who exhorted the civilian masses—seconded George Meade's "Hurrah for old Joe!"

Regiment by regiment, thousands of troops cheered and tossed their hats as Hooker's order was read. One New York soldier said the only thing that worried him was that the Confederates, seeing they were licked, would retreat and the war might be over before he got in his two cents' worth.[21] Bands played, and General Couch recalled that "the general hilarity pervading the camps was particularly noticeable; the soldiers while chopping wood and lighting fires, were singing merry songs and indulging in peppery camp jokes."[22]

Hooker could not know that that evening was the peak of his mercurial career.

EVERYWHERE THEY HEARD Hooker's congratulatory order, Union troops cheered, even if some of them were a little puzzled. In Dan Sickles's corps, on its way to join the flanking force, one soldier said, "We allowed, of course, that considerable of it was for 'Buncom,' but hoped that it was half true at least."[23]

Below Fredericksburg, troops across the river wondered what had happened when they heard the hurrahs of those left behind on the Union side. While soldiers in Sedgwick's left wing were willing to join any celebration, they felt ignored in this one. On their seemingly forgotten front, they were not too elated to remember Lincoln's day of reverence. That afternoon, after repeated rumor that they were about to cross and strengthen the Union bridgehead, soldiers of Col. Adrian R. Root's brigade in the First Corps stacked arms and formed a hollow square near the river. Four regimental chaplains led a prayer, and followed with morale-boosting predictions about what lay ahead. The whole brigade joined in hymns and heard a reading from Deuteronomy. Charles Parker, who was there, could not remember the chapter, but was impressed by "the grand and inspiring sight, in the hearing of the rattle of musketry and cannonading, and between two contending armies waiting to hurl the iron messengers of death at each other."[24]

Abner Small of the 16th Maine was there, too, but less reverent. He wrote of how the chaplains urged the men "to shrink not from the terrible ordeal through which we were called to pass, to be brave and heroic, and God being our shield we would have nothing to fear—when came a slight puff of smoke, followed by another, and yet another . . . just across the river, and then a rushing sound like trains of cars and terrific explosions all around us." The shellfire and confusion "were almost drowned out by the shouts and laughter of the men as the brave chaplains, hatless and bookless, with coat-tails streaming in the wind, went madly to the rear over stone walls, through hedges and ditches," followed by laughing shouts of 'Stand firm! Be brave and heroic and put your trust in the Lord!' "[25]

But Sedgwick and his lieutenants were miffed that Hooker's praise of the flanking force did not even mention their own successful bridging of the Rappahannock in the face of Lee's thorough defenses. Advised of this, Hooker had Butterfield assure Sedgwick that "all would come right"— that he, Hooker, would "be on the heights west of Fredericksburg tomorrow noon or shortly after, and if opposed strongly, tomorrow night."[26]

After ordering Sedgwick to demonstrate against Southern lines below Fredericksburg, Hooker canceled the order when he heard from Maj. Gen. John F. Reynolds, commanding the First Corps facing the downstream crossing at Fitzhugh's. Reynolds told Sedgwick that the Southern force facing him was undiminished, and "a demonstration will bring on a general engagement." Thus Hooker held that left wing motionless on the thirtieth, while Reynolds dispatched an all-day stream of nervous messages warning of Confederate moves and concentrations.

Large bodies of troops were coming up across Massaponax Creek, he said—"I think it must be troops from Richmond." Hooker said he hoped they were from Richmond, "as the greater will be our success." One of Professor Lowe's aeronauts reported, "The woods directly opposite our bridge on the left full of rebel troops." Reynolds said, "This is either bravado, in order to get up troops from Richmond, or they are really in force. They have never shown their troops in this way before"—mirroring what Early had said as he watched the Union divisions mill about the day before. Reynolds wondered: "It may be that the artillery is simply horses arranged to look like teams. . . ." Again: "They are passing troops up to our right. . . . The railroad seems to be busy. . . ." This got Butterfield's attention—"Could it be transportation trains?" If the railroad was involved, that might reinforce the Union generals' hope that Lee, bowing to Hooker's master stroke, was sensibly retreating. But from all this message traffic, Sedgwick concluded that "The enemy seems to be in heavy force in front of both Reynolds and Brooks, and to be forming for an attack. We are ready for them."[27]

Neither steady "Uncle John" Sedgwick nor the usually confident John Reynolds was a fluttery type; both had shone in increasingly responsible jobs under fire. But uncertainty was the norm on April 30, on both ends of the developing battle. For a while that included R. E. Lee, who telegraphed President Davis that Hooker's "object [is] evidently to turn our left," and "If I had Longstreet's division, would feel safe." Richmond ordered Longstreet, that day, to move "without delay" to join Lee, but Longstreet was still skirmishing with the Federal force around Suffolk.

Lee had told Lafayette McLaws, whose division covered the ground between Early and Fredericksburg, that "We may be obliged to change our position in consequence of the enemy's having come in between us and General Stuart." McLaws should leave only a light detail of sharpshooters in the town and along the river, "so as to have as strong a force as possible to strengthen our left." On the thirtieth Lee urged Dick Anderson, at his blocking position west of town facing Chancellorsville, to "Set all your spades to work as vigorously as possible." Ordering Anderson to "hold your position firmly," he promised to send more troops if possible. But at the same time, he said Anderson should "be prepared to pack your trains and move off at any moment when ordered." [28]

That morning, Jackson was up before dawn, breaking camp to move his corps headquarters forward. When bustling staff officers approached Jackson's tent, his black orderly, Jim Lewis, stepped in front of them. "Hush," he said. "The general is praying." The little glade fell quiet. Then, after fifteen minutes, Jackson came out, the bustling resumed, and he rode to the front. [29] As so often, prayer seemed to steel him. Even while his family had been with him, during those gentlest days, he had talked with his staff about making the coming campaign "exceedingly active." "Only thus can a weaker country cope with a stronger," he said. "It must make up in activity what it lacks in strength. A defensive campaign can only be made successful by taking the aggressive at the proper time. Napoleon never waited for his adversary to become fully prepared, but struck him the first blow, by virtue of his superior activity." [30]

Now, as he and Lee surveyed the enemy bridgehead together, Jackson wanted to attack immediately, before Sedgwick's busily digging troops built up their strength any further on the Confederate side of the river. Lee, ever polite, almost deferential to his boldest lieutenant, said it would be hard to get at the Union force, and much harder to get away if his troops drove all the way to the river. That plain was covered by masses of enemy cannon sighted in from the other side. "But," he said, "if you think you can effect anything, I will give orders for the attack."

Unlike some of Lee's other generals, Jackson always caught his meaning through his calm courtesy. He hesitated, asked if he could study the ground further, and rode away in the rain. During his reconnaissance, Jackson watched the clouds blow off, and realized that anyone moving over those fields that night would do it in bright moonlight. Returning to Lee, he agreed that it would be "inexpedient" to attack there. [31]

By then, all Lee's uncertainty was over. He had decided on his first major countermove against Hooker's opening success: against all military dogma, he would split his army in the face of a greatly superior enemy. He issued Special Orders No. 121, which had two main points: McLaws would leave one brigade (Barksdale) to hold the line behind Fredericksburg, and take the rest of his division west to reinforce Anderson on the Plank Road toward Chancellorsville. Jackson would leave one division (Early) to hold the lines facing the Union bridgehead. At daylight on May 1 he would take the rest of his corps west to Anderson's location, "and make arrangements to repulse the enemy."[32] At and below Fredericksburg, that would leave Early commanding only one division plus one brigade—just over 10,000 men—facing Sedgwick's two full corps plus one division—more than 45,000. To meet Hooker, Lee sent west about 40,000 troops, plus the cavalry already operating in that direction. When Hooker got his entire right wing together, he would have more than 80,000 available to confront Lee there.

AS ON MANY a battle's eve, Jeb Stuart and his staff were partying with hospitable Virginians when the Union flanking force began crossing at Kelly's Ford. Their hostess at a plantation near Culpeper was an elderly poet. She had written earlier verses lauding Lee and Jackson, so that night the gathering assumed it was Stuart's turn. After dinner, the lady read her latest work—not about Stuart, but about his gaudy Prussian lieutenant, Heros von Borcke. When she was done, von Borcke gallantly knelt and kissed her hand, but Stuart told him, "That won't do, Von," and bussed the lady's cheek. "General," she said in full tremolo, "I have always known you to be a very gallant soldier, but from this moment I believe you to be the bravest of the brave." In this mood, the dancing went on till late, and the laughing cavaliers had hardly turned in when, about 3:00 A.M., came word of the Yankee crossing. The bugle sounded "To horse!" and away they rode.[33]

They were too late to do anything about the Federal move across the Rappahannock, and the messengers Stuart sent to warn the bridge-building party at Germanna and pickets at Ely's Ford were captured en route. One of his brigadiers, W. H. F. Lee, spread his troopers across the road from Kelly's Ford to Brandy Station, as if the Union force were continuing west toward Culpeper. The 13th Virginia Cavalry, out front, skirmished with the Federal advance guard as the main crossing force turned back toward Germanna. Stuart harassed that column on the way, striking into its flank and picking off prisoners near Madden's farm. Like R. E. Lee, he realized with concern that the Union flanking force was cutting between his cavalry and the main Confederate army. About this time orders arrived from Lee to detach part of Stuart's mounted division westward to protect the Orange & Alexandria and Virginia Central railroads, threatened by Stoneman's Federal cavalry. The rest of Stuart's horsemen would hurry east to join Lee.

Stuart sent W. H. F. Lee with the 9th and 13th Virginia toward Culpeper, and rode east to Raccoon Ford with Fitz Lee's "jaded and hungry" troopers. Most of them rested after crossing the Rapidan the night of the twenty-ninth, but Stuart sent Col. Thomas H. Owen's 3rd Virginia to try to delay the Union force advancing from Germanna. Next day, part of Owen's lone regiment got in front of the Federal column near Wilderness Tavern, where the Orange Turnpike joins the road from Germanna five miles west of Chancellorsville. Owen attacked, opening up with his horse artillery and forcing some of Slocum's regiments to deploy. One New York infantryman remembered being "surprised by a strange noise that sounded like a great bird fluttering over the regiment, and then there was a crash in the woods followed by a loud explosion." "The boys took this baptism pretty well," Rice Bull wrote, "but this first shot was followed by others that hissed and shrieked over our heads and made everyone jump and duck, a nervous habit very few ever got over." [34] After about two hours' delay, the overwhelming Yankee force drove on. Owen's cavalry dropped back to Anderson's blocking position east of Chancellorsville while Stuart and Fitz Lee's other regiments moved along the Federal south flank. That night, Stuart halted the command at Todd's Tavern, five crow-flight miles south of Chancellorsville but farther by the winding wilderness roads. Stuart himself, eager to join Lee, pressed ahead with his staff toward Fredericksburg. [35]

He had ridden less than a mile when he collided with Union troopers and triggered a wild cavalry fight, in and out of dark woods and moonlight, that no two of the soldiers involved would ever describe the same.

The outfit he happened into was the 6th New York Cavalry, commanded by a fiery, red-haired Scot, Lt. Col. Duncan McVicar. Probing south out of Chancellorsville, McVicar had come to a junction in the woods northwest of the H. Alsop house, and held up while he sent scouting parties in three directions. One of them, about 30 men, was riding west toward Todd's Tavern when Stuart set out east along the same narrow road. Stuart's party heard a pistol shot ahead, and its point rider came galloping back, saying he had been fired on by Yankee cavalry pickets. Stuart scoffed, and sent von Borcke to take a look. The Prussian and one comrade rode ahead and soon saw horsemen in the shadowy moonlight. From about 50 yards, he shouted, asking what regiment they were. "You'll see soon enough, you damned rebels!" a voice answered as the Yankee detail thundered forward. Von Borcke and his friend raced away, firing their pistols back as they leaned low over their horses' necks.[36] Stuart and the rest of his party took flight toward Todd's Tavern; as one of his colonels told it, the general "escaped by the fleetness of his horse," and "was more excited than I ever saw him."[37]

The Yankee pursuit slacked off before Stuart got back to his main body. He dispatched a captain with orders for Fitz Lee to send a regiment forward immediately and follow with his whole brigade. The 5th Virginia, which had led the march, was ordered to "take the road and open it." By then the Union horsemen had broken through a gate into a field at Alsop's, turned, and formed a line facing the gate. The 5th Virginia came forward in a column of fours, all that could ride abreast along the narrow woods road. It knocked McVicar's pickets aside and crowded into the gate. The waiting Federals, firing their carbines from the saddle, riddled the Virginians as they pushed through. Stuart rode up and sent in reinforcements, but they too were stopped as they tried to squeeze through the gate.

McVicar, realizing he was outnumbered, decided he had to cut his way out. He drew his sword, stood in his stirrups, and yelled, "Sixth New York, follow me! Charge!" Before he got to the gate, he was shot through the heart. But the regiment, with sabers slashing, broke through onto the road and scattered the Rebel troopers trying to reorganize in the darkness.[38] Borcke wrote that Stuart himself, when his first attacks were shattered, waved his saber and called for another charge, but his broken regiments dribbled to the rear. Just then the bugle sounded McVicar's charge, which drove Stuart and his staff into the black woods in "a wild, exciting chase in which friend and foe, unable to recognize each other, mingled helter-skelter in one furious ride."[39]

As Yankee Capt. William L. Heermance remembered it, the 5th Virginia's bugle sounded at the same moment as McVicar's, and the regiments rode headlong into each other. Heermance came galloping through the Virginians and slashed his saber down across the face of Benjamin Medina, almost cutting off his nose. At that moment Capt. Reuben B. Boston of the Virginia regiment jabbed his pistol into Heermance's side and fired, putting a ball through his left arm and into his body. From somewhere a blow on the head knocked the Yankee officer out of his saddle, and he was captured.[40]

Col. Thomas T. Munford of the 2nd Virginia Cavalry wrote that after the other Confederates were thrown back and McVicar's regiment charged through the gate at Alsop's farm, Stuart turned to him and said, "I'm sure the gallant Second will open the way." If not, Stuart said, he would have to take another route to reach Lee. That would mean further delay, sure to affect Lee's move to meet Hooker. Munford wanted no one to hang back; he told his officers he was going to call the roll on the other side. Yelling and swinging pistols and sabers, the 2nd Virginia charged "with a zeal never excelled," slamming into the 6th New York and cutting it almost in half.[41] About midnight, the way was open for Stuart, and most of his stragglers rejoined as he moved on via Spotsylvania Court House. The outnumbered 6th New York had delayed him for hours as he hurried to reach Lee. The collision in the dark also prevented the New Yorkers from continuing to Spotsylvania Court House, where they could have raised hob in a train of Rebel wagons passing through unprotected. Leaving 51 men including their brave colonel on the field, the Union troopers returned through the blackness to Chancellorsville.

Around them in the Wilderness, whippoorwills chanted. Hooker's troops bedded down after dragging logs, stumps, and stones into line for breastworks and starting to fell long rows of trees with branches interlocking pointing outward to make abatis, the effective forerunner of defensive barbed wire. Almost 15 miles east, soldiers of each army lit bright bonfires on the river slopes below Fredericksburg to make the other side believe they were staying put. The Confederates did not know about Hooker's congratulatory order when they heard the enemy cheering. But they hollered back, under orders.

"We privates thought this meant something," a soldier in Joseph B. Kershaw's South Carolina brigade recalled. "We soon found out that it did."[42]

Chapter Nine

KEEP CLOSED ON
CHANCELLORSVILLE

NO DRUMS, no bugles sounded this time as Jackson's troops shook each other awake in the morning darkness. Quietly, they rolled their equipment into their blankets and fell in to march toward Chancellorsville. As they awaited orders to move, Lt. Thomas Herndon of the 14th Tennessee sat and wrote carefully in his daybook:

> Before battle, May 1, '63—
> In the event I am killed you will please write to Jos. C. Anderson, Durham, N.C. I owe Lieut. Collins $235 dollars. Jno. King, Dcd., owes me about 148 dollars. I have received pay by Capt. Allensworth to 31st day Jany., 1863. Ephraim Mason will please make the proper disposition of one gold ring in my pocket book, also all of the things in my possession belonging to Jno. King, Decd. E.P.M. will also present my watch to Miss Eliza. Bowe.

Many soldiers like Herndon tucked new wills into their pockets before each battle, revising the figures of debts, sometimes changing beneficiaries, perhaps because there had been no mail from a dear one named earlier. A few months before, Herndon had written in his diary:

> . . . a calm and beautiful evening. Wish that I could spend it with Miss M.E.S. if she is now the same. If she is true and has not forgotten me, how merrily I could spend the evening. But if she has forgotten me, alas; how painful would be the meeting to me. But I am sure no one with such an Angelic face could be false. Bright Star, your light will ever Shine around me. Distance, absence, and even my Struggles for liberty have not changed my feelings. You, Ella, I still hold as the Bright Ideal of My heart.

Herndon would survive Chancellorsville, and write another will a month later—not mentioning either M.E.S. or Eliza Bowe, but leaving a lock of hair to Miss Ellen T. Long. To maintain his morale, a soldier had to be flexible.[1]

Stonewall Jackson himself, adrenaline pumping, was up shortly after midnight. Something told him to impress on his men that this would not be just another day's work. Instead of the familiar uniform with the dust and mud of a dozen campaigns ground into it, he put on the new set of grays in which he had posed for a photograph for his wife during her visit.

All his divisions except Early's would pull back silently in the dark, then Rodes, Hill, and Colston would head west in that order. Along the roads behind Fredericksburg, McLaws's troops already were marching, carrying out Lee's decision to throw most of the Confederate weight against Hooker's flanking force.[2]

In Rodes's division, the 2nd North Carolina was awakened at two o'clock and in five minutes was on the road. "We had no idea where we were going," William Calder wrote. "A soldier never knows where he is going, nor what he is going to do, until the moment for action comes. They have only to trust in their commanders and blindly 'follow their leaders.' On we went through mud and over stumps, stumbling about in the dark, to the great danger of our heads and shins." Shortly after daylight, the regiment took its first break along a creek bank, and the word swept up the line, "Stonewall's coming!" "Soon the old hero came dashing by, his horse at full speed, and hat in hand, followed by a single courier. He cast his eyes from one side of the road to the other, his head working as if it were on wires."[3]

The troops spoke of "Old Jack" the same way they did of "Old Bob" Lee, though Jackson had only turned thirty-nine in January. In his seriousness, he was much older. But "the old hero" was called that out of reverence rather than longevity. Lt. William Norman thought "he seemed to be anxious as he rapidly rode by, as if to say, 'There is heavy work ahead.' " The troops yelled and waved when they saw him, their cheers rolling forward along the column. Norman recalled that as they fell in to move on, everyone knew there was a big fight at hand, for they could "see it in Stonewall's eyes."[4]

FOG HUNG OVER the river and blanketed the slopes on both sides, so neither army below Fredericksburg could tell in early morning whether the other was still there.

Chief of Staff Dan Butterfield, running the Army of the Potomac's message center at Falmouth, advised Hooker at 5:30 A.M. that a deserter had said Jackson's whole corps still faced the Union bridgehead at Franklin's Crossing. This Rebel who crept into Union lines reported camp rumors that Longstreet had come up from Suffolk to Culpeper, and that Lee was saying this would be the only time he had fought against equal numbers. Troops in Colston's division had told the deserter they would march to Culpeper the next day.[5]

From his balloon above the lower crossings, Professor Lowe could see nothing of the Confederate positions until the fog burned off a sunny May Day morning. His first message to Butterfield, at 9:15, said, "Heavy columns of the enemy's infantry and artillery are now moving up the river, accompanied by many army wagons. . . ." But "There is also a heavy reserve on the heights opposite the upper [Franklin's] crossing, and all the rifle pits are well filled." Forty-five minutes later he reported that a Confederate column was crossing a run near Banks' Ford, and that "One of the columns . . . required thirty minutes to pass a given point. . . . Long trains of wagons are still moving to the right."

All morning, this pattern of confusion had Union officers thinking first one way, then the other. Did the balloon reports and others from signal stations confirm what the Rebel deserter said, or contradict it? A little of both.

On the ground, General Reynolds passed word that Confederate batteries were moving along the ridge overlooking his lower bridgehead, apparently toward the Telegraph Road, back toward Richmond. Reynolds was becoming a worrier. He wrote to Sedgwick: "If they have not detached more than A. P. Hill's division from our front, they have been keeping up appearances, showing weakness, with a view of delaying Hooker, in tempting us to make an attack on their fortified position, and hoping to destroy us and strike for our depot over our bridges." This was the first official expression of any Union general's fear that Lee would drive the Yankees back over their lower crossings, then push his army over the Union pontoon bridges to loot and destroy the vast supply bases on the Potomac. Considering this possibility, Reynolds suggested to Sedgwick that "We ought, therefore, in my judgment, to know something of what has transpired on the right. Do you not think this is the correct view?"[6]

Hooker still was not disclosing to his left hand what his right was doing, or vice versa. Only hours after the fact would Sedgwick learn that the commanding general had ordered him to make a threatening demonstration below Fredericksburg. Hooker also had ordered Brig. Gen. John Gibbon of Couch's Second Corps to take his division across the river at Banks' Ford. In the flurry of messages back and forth, even Butterfield was unsure whether that move was intended for May 1 or the next day. Whenever it happened, some of Gibbon's men wanted no part of it.

Two years after the first shots were fired at Fort Sumter, the Union army was still plagued by the near-universal assumption at the beginning of the war that it would soon be over. Troops had enlisted not for the duration but for fixed tours of duty. As the battle of Chancellorsville approached, thousands of two-year terms were about to run out. So were nine-month hitches that commenced with the War Department's "pseudo-draft" of the previous summer. In the 34th New York, six companies of infantrymen maintained that their terms were over two years from the day they signed up, while the government insisted that their service had not officially begun until their regiment was mustered into Federal service, in mid-June. Mutiny threatened.[7]

Gibbon, a "steel-cold" West Pointer who had fought on the western frontier, had no patience with shirkers. A Pennsylvania-born North Caro-linian, he saw his duty as lying with the Union, though three of his brothers fought for the Confederacy. He had led the Black Hat Brigade to earn the nickname of Iron Brigade before he was seriously wounded as a division commander at Fredericksburg in December. Now he ordered Brig. Gen. Alfred Sully to enforce discipline in the mutinous New York regiment, but Sully said he could not. With that, Gibbon himself ordered 50 to 75 still-unyielding soldiers brought under guard before their com-rades. He ordered the best-disciplined regiment in the brigade to load muskets and stand by. Standing before the balky troops, Gibbon told them flatly that they were mutineers, no better than the Rebels across the river. From among them, a sergeant stepped out to give their side of the argument. Gibbon told him that such cases already had been heard in other units, and rejected. Reconsider and do your duty, he told the New Yorkers—if they did not, the guard regiment would open fire and kill them all.

"Every man who is ready to do his duty, step forward!" the general said. One of their officers urged them, "Step forward, men!" But Gibbon said, "Silence, sir . . . let them put themselves right." At that, the entire unit broke into cheers and stepped forward together. "Stop your cheer-ing!" Gibbon ordered, restraining his anger. "Go to your regiment and do your duty."

Gibbon relieved Sully for insisting that "it was not in his power to enforce discipline in his command."[8] After the battle, a court of inquiry found that Sully probably doubted his authority to "order extreme measures," and so reversed Gibbon's order relieving him, but Sully was sent west to the Dakotas soon afterward.[9]

Such discontent had popped up here and there throughout Hooker's divisions. But once troops crossed the Rappahannock, those outbreaks were mooted in the excitement of a great army going into battle. Early that morning of May 1, Hooker sent his engineer, Gouverneur Warren, to scout from Chancellorsville out the turnpike toward Fredericksburg. Warren passed the pickets of the 8th Pennsylvania Cavalry and came within sight of the Rebel blocking position set up by Dick Anderson near Zoan and Tabernacle churches. While he was forward, other generals strolled in and out of Hooker's headquarters at the Chancellorsville house, gossiping and wondering about their next move. Dan Sickles rode in ahead of his Third Corps, which was pouring across U.S. Ford. When Warren returned from his reconnaissance, he found that the commander had not waited for his report. With 70,000 men and 184 cannon already on Lee's flank, Hooker ordered an advance eastward.[10]

Meade's Fifth Corps would march along River Road and the Turnpike, to uncover Banks' Ford. Slocum's Twelfth Corps would push along the Plank Road toward Tabernacle Church, with Howard's Eleventh following closely. One division of Couch's Second Corps would set up at Todd's Tavern, to the south. The rest of it would hold back near Chancellorsville. Sickles's Third Corps would mass in reserve behind Chancellorsville. Except for regiments already assigned to work with individual corps, Pleasonton's cavalry would stay back at Hooker's disposal. Hooker's headquarters would displace forward to Tabernacle Church.[11] In sum, his columns would march about two miles east along the main roads until they emerged from the Wilderness. Then they would link up across clear ground and press on toward Banks' Ford and the line that Confederate Dick Anderson now held facing west. Hooker ordered these moves to be completed between noon and two o'clock, but like many of his orders, this one was delayed in delivery. Couch recalled that instead of being issued the night before, it "was not received by the corps commanders, at least by me, until hours after light."[12]

AT ABOUT EIGHT that morning, Jackson arrived and took command of the Confederate force deployed across the Turnpike and Plank Road. Anderson's troops were still digging formidable breastworks across

Hooker's path—and making history doing it, for it was the first time Lee's army had built fortifications in such a fluid situation, in the open field.[13] The line bent from south of Tabernacle Church to cross the Turnpike just east of Zoan Church and the Mine Road junction. McLaws's troops had doubled Anderson's strength, and he used them to lengthen his line as they arrived in the darkness after midnight. Brig. Gen. Paul J. Semmes's brigade, then Brig. Gen. Joseph B. Kershaw's and Brig. Gen. William T. Wofford's, were put in north of the Turnpike. The last two swung back toward the river to face any threat against Anderson's right flank.

As Jackson rode up ahead of his own three divisions, Anderson briefed him. Jackson realized that once all his brigades arrived he would have at least 40,000 to defend a strong position, anchored at one end on Mott's Run and the river, at the other below the Plank Road. That would give him seven or eight men per yard along three miles of front. But most of those troops were still on the road. At the moment, only about 10,000 were between him and Hooker's powerful force. Hooker had more corps at hand than Jackson had divisions. He might attack at any moment.

Lee had ordered Jackson to "make arrangements to repulse the enemy." Jackson quickly decided that the way to do it was to attack first.

Stop digging and pack up, he ordered. McLaws would take a column straight down the Turnpike toward Chancellorsville. Mahone's brigade would lead it, followed by McLaws's division, with Brig. Gen. Cadmus M. Wilcox's and Brig. Gen. Edward A. Perry's brigades pulled down from the Rappahannock to bring up the rear. Jackson, in overall command, would take a heavier column along the Plank Road that swung gently south, then back up to Chancellorsville. Brig. Gen. Carnot Posey's and Brig. Gen. Ambrose Ransom Wright's brigades would lead it, followed by Hill's and Rodes's divisions. Colston's division, still on the way from below Fredericksburg, would follow as reserve.

Three hours after Jackson's arrival, his force had shifted onto the tactical offensive. An hour before noon, it was in motion. Within fifteen minutes, Federal pickets opened fire on McLaws's troops along the Turnpike. Then they started peppering the skirmishers ahead of Jackson on the Plank Road. As Jackson sent patrols to feel the Federal flanks, a message from McLaws said heavy forces were confronting him, and more ranks were deploying behind them. Jackson's column, on the left away from the river, had more maneuvering room and the best chance to swing against Hooker's flank. Jackson told McLaws to hold where he was, and called Col. E. P. Alexander's artillery battalion forward to try to drive the Yankees back into the thickets of the Wilderness. A Union captain in the

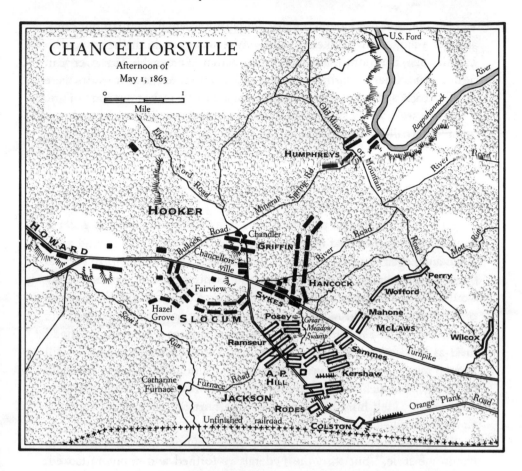

6. Collision and Recoil. *Jackson, sent west to confront Hooker, orders his Confederates out of their defenses to meet the Federals head-on. When the two sides collide on the Turnpike and Plank Road, Hooker angers his generals by pulling their divisions back around Chancellorsville.*

Twelfth Corps, moving toward Jackson on the Plank Road, saw a shell burst over the forest, checked his watch and said, "Twenty minutes past eleven; the first gun of the battle of Chancellorsville." [14]

Along the Turnpike, McLaws's column was in what Brig. Gen. Billy Mahone with the lead brigade called "quite a brisk little engagement." [15] Skirmishers of Mahone's 12th Virginia struck their familiar opponent, the 8th Pennsylvania Cavalry, which was screening Meade's right division, Maj. Gen. George Sykes's U.S. Regulars. As the Virginia infantry moved down the road with a company of horsemen "to flush the game, as it were," a musket fired and a cavalry lieutenant shouted, "Hurry up, boys, and get a shot at the Yankee cavalry!" Westwood Todd of the 12th, who had the pleasure more than once, recalled that "If there is any poetry in fighting, it is infantry fighting cavalry." The horsemen on both sides were pushed back against the foot regiments, and the 12th came out of the woods to see Yankee skirmishers "in a beautiful line." That brought on what Todd called "the most satisfactory fighting in which I had any share during the war." After doing little damage at Seven Pines, Malvern Hill, and Manassas, Company E now had "a fair, square, stand-up, open-field fight." With the rest of the 12th, it spread out as skirmishers and went in yelling.

Sykes's U.S. veterans gave way slowly as the Virginians drove them back at close quarters. Atop a low ridge, the Rebels dropped behind a rail fence and began pouring fire into the retreating Blue riflemen. A Federal soldier fell 50 yards from the fence, and as his comrades ran on he lay waving his handkerchief in surrender. Nobody "was so cowardly as to fire on a fallen foe," Todd recalled. One Yankee officer stood his ground and by his lone example kept his company from fleeing with the rest. Todd fired at him several times and missed. A Rebel cavalry lieutenant, Hill Carter, asked for Todd's weapon and took a shot at the Yankee who was behaving with such "splendid courage." He missed, too, remarking that the musket's kick hurt him worse than he hurt the enemy. Hours later, Carter was killed.

Todd was proud that "we had thrashed a whole line of Regulars in handsome style," but then the Federals re-formed and counterattacked. The Virginians expected an order to fall back, because "resisting their serried ranks with our then disorganized ranks [was] simply impossible." Company E's captain, Robert Banks, had been killed in what Mahone called "beautifully heroic" action leading the attack.[16] His soldiers blazed away until a lieutenant took the responsibility of ordering a retreat, but as they turned back, 80 exhausted men of the regiment were captured by the swarming U.S. Regulars.

Todd was dragging; he could hardly climb over the rail fence with his blanket and haversack. Stumbling farther back, the remnants of the company splashed into swampy ground that kept the Yankees from pursuing. They flailed on till they ran into troops of Paul Semmes's brigade, advancing along the left of the Turnpike. For a moment, but only a moment, they thought of joining Semmes's Georgians in the attack. Taking cover by a little creek, they filled their canteens and huddled in safety, listening to Minié balls cut the branches overhead.[17]

The fight seesawed away from them as McLaws's men retook the initiative and pressed the Union force steadily back within a mile and a half of Chancellorsville.

To their left, Posey's Mississippi brigade leading Jackson's advance had pushed two miles along the Plank Road before striking main units of the Union Twelfth Corps near the Alrich farmhouse. There Posey deployed the 12th Mississippi and drove the Yankee skirmishers until he hit solid lines of waiting troops along the road that led to Catharine Furnace, below Chancellorsville. Lt. Col. M. B. Harris, commanding the 12th, was badly wounded in this collision. The determined Mississippians broke the Furnace Road line and kept going through thick woods on the right of the Plank Road till they hit a marsh and started taking rapid artillery fire from their open flank. Posey halted then, with Wright's brigade formed to his left across the Plank Road.[18]

Just after noon, a courier brought Jackson word that Jeb Stuart's cavalry was screening his southern flank, and Fitz Lee was watching for any enemy turning movements in that direction. "I will close in on the left and help all I can when the ball opens," Stuart wrote. "May God grant us victory."

Jackson scrawled on the back of Stuart's message: "I trust that God will grant us a great victory. Keep closed on Chancellorsville."[19]

The ball had formally opened. After stiff firefights on first contact with Hooker's advancing infantry, the Southerners had turned the Yankees back along both main roads. But most of the Union troops had withdrawn in good order, from position to position. Jackson and McLaws had to assume that their own troops' aggressiveness had carried the field again. They could not know what was happening in Joe Hooker's command. Hooker's generals could not understand it, either.

GEORGE SYKES had been through nine fights with his U.S. Regular Infantry, but none had been in territory exactly like the Spotsylvania Wilderness. When his division, moving out the Turnpike, ran into McLaws's men coming the other way, he sent forward his three brigades and quickly recovered the ground he had lost in the first skirmish. He put cannon on the crest of the low ridge and pounded Mahone's brigade, whose cannon pounded back. For a while Sykes held his own against head-on Rebel attacks, but he was worried about his flanks. Before him he had a clear field of fire, but on the north and south his regiments disappeared into thick woods. The Confederate battle line reached beyond his on both sides. Two aides sent to make contact with Slocum's column on the Plank Road ran into Rebel skirmishers and barely escaped. Sykes was afraid the Confederates would sift through the forest and fall on his rear. He sent Gouverneur Warren, the engineer, back to Chancellorsville "at all possible speed" to tell Hooker of his situation.

Meanwhile Hooker, when he heard cannon fire in Sykes's direction, had turned to Maj. Gen. Darius Couch, commander of the Second Corps, standing by at Chancellorsville with two of his divisions. He told him to take Hancock's division out the Turnpike to help Sykes. Couch was a West Pointer and Mexican War veteran who had taken leave from the army to become a naturalist with a Smithsonian expedition to Mexico in the 1850s. An outspoken New Yorker, he had led a division in combat on the Peninsula and in the Second Bull Run and Antietam campaigns, and a corps at Fredericksburg. He was the man with Hooker when President Lincoln had told them less than a month earlier to "put in all your men" next time. Now he was eager to put in all his corps, to complete Hooker's brilliant opening stroke against Lee. He rode along the Turnpike for a mile and a half and found Sykes pulling his brigades back in succession, line by line. At that point, Couch heard from Hooker what Sykes already had heard in an order delivered by Warren:

> General Sykes will retire to his position of last night, and take up a line connecting his right with General Slocum, making his line as strong as he can by felling trees, etc. General Couch will then retire to his position of last night.[20]

Couch was furious. He could not believe the order. Hancock, Sykes, and Warren agreed with him that their commanding position with open country in front should not be abandoned. They sent Maj. John B. Burt back to Hooker to make their case, but in half an hour Burt returned with a direct order for withdrawal. According to Couch, Warren suggested that he disobey the order, though Warren's official report understandably says nothing about offering such advice. Sykes's troops headed to the rear, followed by Hancock's. Much later, when all but two of Hancock's regiments had passed, Couch got another order from Hooker—"Hold on until 5 o'clock." Still angrier, Couch replied that Hooker was too late, that "the enemy are already on my right and rear. I am in full retreat."[21]

Sykes's troops understood the order no better than the generals, but at first they took it better because they were glad to get away from the confrontation with McLaws. J. Ansel Booth of the 140th New York, in

Sykes's only non-Regular brigade, realized the Rebel guns were ranged precisely on his outfit. The ground trembled at an explosion behind him, and he turned to see a dozen men struck down like "a tuft of grass flattened by the wind." To escape this, the New Yorkers double-quicked forward and into a cornfield. They lay on their faces for an hour, waiting to go forward, then got orders to withdraw. The Confederates followed so fast that most of the fleeing Yankees lost everything that was not tied on— "haversacks, overcoats, blankets, guns, caps, everything."[22]

Slocum, in charge of the Union advance along the Plank Road, got the same order as Couch, and if possible he was even more furious. In his official report, he covered the day in four terse sentences: "On Friday, at 11 A.M., pursuant to orders, I moved the Twelfth Corps from Chancellorsville toward Fredericksburg, on the Plank road. We met the skirmishers of the enemy about a mile from the Chancellor house; formed in line of battle and advanced, the enemy falling back toward the heights of Fredericksburg. At about 1 P.M. orders were received to return to our original line. In this movement our loss was only 10 killed and wounded. . . ."[23] Those who were there said the dialogue was more colorful.

Slocum reported that when his advance skirmishers first ran into Jackson's oncoming column, they pushed the Southern vanguard back. He deployed Brig. Gen. John W. Geary's division on his right, Brig. Gen. Alpheus S. Williams's on his left, six brigades in two lines of battle. By the time Slocum got this formation ready to move again, Jackson had put Ramseur's brigade in the center of his Confederate advance, with Posey to his north and Wright to the south. These three brigades forced Slocum back on his main line near the Alrich farmhouse. Jackson opened with 14 cannon before additional Union guns could roll into play. Slocum did not have his reserves up and the artillery duel was not fully developed when he got Hooker's stunning order.[24]

Washington Augustus Roebling, who later would carry through his father's plan to build the Brooklyn Bridge, was an engineer officer at Hooker's headquarters that morning. He recalled that "Shortly after noon Gen. Hooker sent for me, saying 'I have determined to receive the enemy on my bayonets here at Chancellorsville. I want you to ride ahead to Gen. Slocum and tell him to stop the advance and return here with his command.'

"To hear was to obey," Roebling wrote. "I rode perhaps too fast. . . . When I gave my orders from Hooker, Slocum turned on me with fury, saying, 'Roebling, you are a damned liar! Nobody but a crazy man would give such an order when we have victory in sight!' " Others say Slocum sent a staff officer, Maj. E. W. Guindon, to ask Hooker's permission to stay. Roebling wrote that Slocum personally rode back to headquarters, warning as he left, " 'I shall go and see Gen. Hooker myself, and if I find that you have spoken falsely, you shall be shot on my return.' Off he went, the advance was stopped. . . . In the course of an hour Gen. Slocum returned, having labored in vain with Hooker to make him rescind his change of plan. Casting a scowl at me, he turned the head of his column. . . ."[25]

The Federal thrust closest to the river moved farther and met less resistance than either of those along the Turnpike and the Plank Road. Had it gone on, it might have been the most important, might perhaps have changed the course of the battle. It was George Meade's march along the River Road toward Banks' Ford. If Sykes's push down the Turnpike had continued past Mott's Run, he was to angle north and join Meade with the rest of the Fifth Corps to close on the ford. Success would have opened that critical direct crossing between the two wings of Hooker's army. It would have squeezed Lee into much tighter quarters, limiting his room to maneuver. While Sykes collided with McLaws on the Turnpike and had to do more fighting than any other Union column, Meade had met no resistance at all when he got the order to return. At that time his advance regiments had reached the Decker house, within sight of the undefended ford.[26] As he turned about, Meade grumbled, ". . . if we can't hold the top of a hill, we certainly can't hold the bottom of it."[27]

THE ORDER to pull back on Chancellorsville was the most important decision of the campaign, and of Joe Hooker's life. It was his first response to the boldness and flexibility of Lee, and his deepest look inside himself. It was his moment of truth.

With mass, position, and momentum on his side, after one of the most successful opening moves in American military history, Hooker bowed and handed the initiative to Lee. Biographers, strategists, and psychiatrists have spent more than a century wondering why. Some present said Hooker had broken his vow to quit drinking during the campaign, but Couch, who was at his side, thought not—"it would have been far better had he continued in his usual habit in that respect."[28] Hooker's own later explanation, to Maj. Gen. Abner Doubleday on the way north weeks later, was that "for once I lost confidence in Hooker, and that is all there is to it."[29] While he obviously lost confidence, that could not have been all there was to it. All the tangibles of that day should have made him supremely confident, as his subordinates asserted they were. The answer is not in the tangibles, but inside Joe Hooker.

In boyhood games and in the White House, he had advanced himself by puffing his chest and saying "Look at me." In the field, from Mexico onward, his performance had backed up his bluster. But it is easier, in a way, to ride a white horse out front in battle, where all can see, than it is to command from an army headquarters. Out front, the display of bravery is seen as bravery itself. There a man can subdue inner doubts by putting himself where hesitation would be obvious to all, and so impermissible. There the enemy is shells and ranks of soldiers, brightly visible with regimental flags; before them, impetuosity is cheered more than calculation. At headquarters, a commander is surrounded by other officers, but he is alone in command. Hooker, especially, was alone with the knowledge that now at last, the battle was his own to win or lose. There would be no one above for him to blame later. He had given himself such a buildup that his soldiers and his country expected great things from him.

He had outmaneuvered the vaunted Lee, and led the applause for himself. Any sensible opponent should have conceded his brilliance, and retreated as Hooker counted on him to do. If that had happened, Hooker would have cut him off as planned, and marched on to Richmond. But this opponent was Lee, whose reflex was not retreat. Had Hooker pushed on to Banks' Ford the day before, Lee would have had to consider retreat more seriously. But Hooker had hesitated, waiting for still more reinforcements. While he waited, Lee acted. When Hooker then moved on May 1, his troops met those of McLaws and Jackson. Hooker himself, in his mind, met Robert E. Lee.

He had time to wonder whether prisoner reports that Longstreet had come up from Suffolk were true, whether Fitz Lee's cavalry harassing his right rear preceded some surprise action, and whatever happened to the offensive demonstration he had ordered John Sedgwick to mount downriver. He remembered the Peninsula, Bull Run, Antietam, and especially Fredericksburg. He remembered how Lee's waiting army had cut down Burnside's attacking troops there. And so, all things considered, he decided to dig in and let Lee play Burnside's role this time at Chancellorsville. At 2:00 P.M., he telegraphed to Butterfield:

> From character of information have suspended attack. The enemy may attack me—I will try it. Tell Sedgwick to keep a sharp lookout, and attack if [he] can succeed." [30]

Hooker had begun with the strategic and tactical initiative. At the moment of truth, he folded. At no other time between Sumter and Appomattox did moral character so decisively affect a battle.

BUT THE BATTLE was yet to be fought. Hooker still had Lee's whole army between the two arms of his own, had Lee outnumbered two to one, had more guns and supplies, had the option of swinging some of the five corps in his flanking force around Lee's rear, still had options galore. Lee understood this perhaps better than Hooker did. Unlike Hooker, he knew that help from Longstreet was nowhere near. As Lee headed west to take command where most of his outnumbered army was now concentrated, he was thinking just as Jackson had when he rode up in early morning. The way to remove Hooker's options was to exercise his own, first.

On a last inspection of the defenses behind Fredericksburg, Lee had added artillery there, where it would be of more use than in the Wilderness. Leaving Jubal Early in charge, he told him not to let the enemy know how thinly his lines were manned, and to try to hold against any attack. If forced out of his defenses, Early was to fall back to the south and protect the supply trains in that direction. If most of the Union troops facing him were withdrawn, Early was to send as many men as he could spare toward Chancellorsville. If the enemy before him pulled out entirely, he was to march west immediately to join the rest of Lee's army.[31]

These contingencies covered, Lee took the Plank Road and caught up with Jackson as the head of his column was clashing with Slocum's Federal skirmishers. As the two generals went forward, tired Southern troops sensed that their favorite leaders passing by together meant great things about to happen, and cheered them on the way. With the Union columns pulling back along both the Plank Road and the Turnpike, Lee trotted north toward the river to do some scouting of his own, to be sure Hooker's troops were not slipping along the River Road toward Fredericksburg. What he found was rough country, low thick woods crosshatched by small streams and spotty swamps. Though retreating, the Federals had their front efficiently picketed, with cannon laid along the narrow forest roads. It was no place to attack an enemy thoroughly dug in. Besides, Lee was curious why the Union troops were withdrawing in such good form, as if by plan. Hooker might be trying to draw the Confederates that way while swinging his several corps against Lee's other flank, or westward toward Gordonsville.[32]

In that direction, Jackson's steady pressure threw Slocum's retreat into brief disorder. Skirmishers out front somehow either invented or picked up a rumor that Hooker was abandoning Chancellorsville. Lee, Jackson, and Hill looked over their maps and thought they saw a way to slice between the Federal defenders on the two main roads. Hill ordered Brig. Gen. Henry Heth to angle three brigades from the Plank Road to the Turnpike, and then drive on with McLaws toward Chancellorsville. Jackson sent word to McLaws to resume his advance on the Turnpike as well. Meanwhile Jackson would keep pushing along the Plank Road, with Ramseur's North Carolina brigade leading. Wright's brigade, which had been sharing the point on the Plank Road, would veer off to the left, probing for Hooker's flank and rear.[33]

As Ramseur's Tar Heels pounded against stiffening resistance, Wright hurried his troops along an unfinished railroad right-of-way that would figure repeatedly in the fighting ahead. In late afternoon he reached Catharine Furnace, beside a soggy creek bottom a mile and a three quarters south-southwest of Chancellorsville. It was owned by Col. Charles C. Wellford, whose home in Fredericksburg had been destroyed in December, so the family was sheltering at a house near the furnace. Over and over, Virginia civilians had fled the war only to see their refuge become more dangerous than the home they had left.

At the furnace, Wright found Jeb Stuart with the 1st Virginia Cavalry, already scouting the enemy flank. Stuart told him the woods north of the furnace toward Chancellorsville were thick with Yankees. Wright sent the 22nd and 48th Georgia Infantry into the "almost impenetrable forest," where they ran into blazing musketry from outposted Union regiments of Alpheus Williams's division. The Georgians crashed on, chasing the Federals across a farmhouse clearing into a pine grove. Fearing a trap, Wright held up and asked Stuart for help from his horse artillery.[34]

By the time Rebel cavalrymen dragged four guns through the woods, Federal artillery was there to respond. Capt. Marcellus N. Moorman, bringing his Lynchburg battery forward, could not find space to unlimber in the dense scrub oak. Then the Federal guns started, "apparently all over the woods." Once in place, the Rebel cannoneers drove the Yankee infantry farther back to trenches beside another clearing, at Hazel Grove. But they were outgunned. Ten Federal pieces fired from the Fairview plateau near Chancellorsville, two from Hazel Grove, sweeping the woods with shell and canister. "It was warm work certain," recalled a Georgia sergeant.

Just before the cannon opened, Jackson cantered up from the Plank Road behind the Rebel guns. With Stuart, he rode to a spot of high ground to look at what lay west, farther around the Union flank. But the first Rebel salvo provoked such a blast from the Yankees that Maj. R. F. Beckham, commanding Stuart's guns, said, "I don't think that men have been often under a hotter fire."

Stuart, realizing just that, said, "General Jackson, we must move from here." As they turned, Stuart's adjutant, Maj. R. Channing Price, was hit by a tiny shell fragment. He said he was not hurt badly—then reined out of the line of fire, dropped from his saddle, and soon died. After this cannon duel, Wright decided it was getting too dark to send the 48th Georgia up an overgrown ravine on the Yankee flank as he had planned. As his men pulled back to bivouac, their stomachs were knotting; they had been issued no rations for two days.[35]

Jackson returned to check on progress along the Plank Road. There Hill told him Union resistance was hardening. Jackson sent this word to Lee, then rode with Hill toward the sound of guns on the Turnpike. Brig. Gen. Samuel McGowan's South Carolinians were leading the three brigades shifted by Hill from Plank Road to the Turnpike. When they reached the Turnpike they were a half mile ahead of McLaws's force. Striking enemy skirmishers immediately, they realized Hooker was by no means abandoning his position around Chancellorsville.

Henry Heth, commanding the three brigades, had just come from the West to join the Army of Northern Virginia, and did not intend to hang back in his first battle under Lee. He told his staff he had his orders from Hill, and would press on through Chancellorsville regardless. One of McGowan's staff officers, Capt. A. C. Haskell, suggested that he be allowed to ride back and ask McLaws to come up in close support. But when McLaws heard Heth's request, he turned to his chief of staff and said curtly, "Order my division to halt here and bivouac for the night." McLaws obviously was peeved that Heth had been sent to cut in front of his column.

Heth nevertheless ordered McGowan to deploy and push ahead. The South Carolinians faced an open field before the thick woods resumed toward Chancellorsville. Haskell, fearing what waited in those woods, asked Heth to let him take two regiments forward. If the woods were clear, he could keep going. If not, the rest of Heth's command would come up for the serious fighting. Heth consented, and Haskell put the 14th South Carolina on the right of the road, Orr's Rifles on the left. "We swept ahead as if on dress parade," he recalled, "really not having an idea we would meet anybody until we got well into the forest." But they were barely halfway across the field when cannon and muskets opened up. In an instant, Haskell's mare skipped nimbly off the road and behind the 14th. The infantrymen laughed and cheered—and at that moment got the command to charge.

They rose up yelling, and pushed the enemy skirmishers back. As the Rebels re-formed, Haskell found a little rise from which he could make out three lines of firmly entrenched Yankee infantry, waiting. He was torn between warning Heth of these defenses and sticking with his temporary command. About that time, Jackson arrived with Hill and a string of staff, once again personally reconnoitering beyond his main forces. The anxious Haskell hastened to meet him.

"Ride up here, General, and you will see it all," said the captain. Jackson studied the Federal lines with his field glass as shells burst around him. After musing a minute, he said, "Hold this position until nine o'clock tonight, when you will be relieved. . . ."

Then, leaning toward Haskell, he said quietly, "Countersign for the night is: challenge—Liberty; reply—Independence." Young Haskell wrote it in his notebook and kept it for years afterward.[36]

DAYLIGHT was dwindling.

Hooker's army was digging in and slashing brush to make a dense abatis, fortifying the Chancellorsville surroundings. Hooker had ordered his generals at 4:20 P.M. to reoccupy the previous night's lines, "and have them put in condition of defense without a moment's delay." His order said he trusted that "a suspension in the attack today will embolden the enemy to attack." Over and over, he repeated this hope. To Butterfield, he telegraphed:

> After having ordered an attack at 2 o'clock, and most of the troops in position, I suspended the attack on the receipt of news from the other side of the river. Hope the enemy will be emboldened to attack me. I did feel certain of success. If his communications are cut, he must attack me. I have a strong position.
>
> P.S.—All the enemy's cavalry are on my flanks, which leads me to suppose that our dragoons will meet with no obstacle in cutting their communications.[37]

Anyone reading that message, even then, must have noted a certain past-tense wistfulness in it—he "did feel" sure of success. Hooker's hope of being attacked was as well founded as any hope ever expressed in warfare. But his suppositions about the cavalry were based more on hope than fact. The Union dragoons were yet nowhere near cutting Lee's main links with Richmond, and whether they were or not seemed no factor in Lee's thinking.

The "news from the other side of the river" that Hooker said caused him to pull back must have been the intelligence from Confederate prisoners. What sounded like the firmest of these reports was first forwarded by Butterfield at 2:05, about the time Hooker made his decision, though likely not received till later. It said two deserters from Hays's Louisiana brigade, below Fredericksburg, reported that John B. Hood's division had arrived the previous day from Richmond. One deserter said he actually had questioned Hood's troops as they marched past. Butterfield credited this information because the prisoner was, like himself, a New Yorker, "an intelligent man." This prisoner also said there were not one but three divisions facing Sedgwick downriver.[38] All this meant that reinforcements were arriving from Longstreet below Richmond; if Hood was on scene, Pickett must not be far behind. It also might dissuade Union attack on Jubal Early's thinly manned lines below Fredericksburg.

There is no proof, but in retrospect a strong belief among historians, that such "deserters" were sent across by Lee to cause just this kind of concern. They had much more impact on Hooker than his own professional spy's realistic report from behind Lee's lines later in the day. At 7:20, Butterfield telegraphed to Hooker that "Sharpe's Richmond man returned." This was one of the agents operated by Col. George Sharpe, head of Hooker's recently created information bureau. He reported on Confederate defenses around Richmond, which suggested the Union cavalry would find little opposition if it ever got there. He also gave an accurate picture of what Lee had in hand to fight Hooker. Fifty-nine thousand rations were issued to Lee's army, not counting his cavalry, the spy reported. Longstreet's force was still at Suffolk, and D. H. Hill still in Carolina, though there was talk of moves to reinforce Lee.[39]

In Hooker's frame of mind, each conflicting report magnified the confusion of handling seven corps, complicated by a river and a pugnacious enemy. To make things worse, his vaunted logistical backup was malfunctioning. Though his telegraph crews had strung dozens of miles of wire, some messages between wings of his army would have moved faster by broken-down mule.

At 11:30 A.M., Hooker had telegraphed Butterfield to "Direct Major-General Sedgwick to threaten an attack in full force at 1 o'clock and to continue in that attitude until further orders. Let the demonstration be as severe as can be, but not an attack." This, of course, was intended to cooperate with Hooker's push east from Chancellorsville.[40] Sedgwick had not received this order when another came from Hooker at one o'clock, telling him to "throw your whole force on the Bowling Green road and no other." Forwarding it, Butterfield semi-apologized: "My telegraphic communication to the general is roundabout, and takes three hours' time." Sometimes it took longer. At 4:00 P.M. Butterfield reported that he had informed Sedgwick of Hooker's pulling back—but Sedgwick still had not gotten the 11:30 order for a one o'clock demonstration. Butterfield himself did not receive it for forwarding until 4:55. He reported that as of 6:45, Sedgwick was advancing. Two hours after that, Hooker told Butterfield: "The telegram for Sedgwick's demonstration reached him too late. Order it in immediately." At 10:30 P.M., a tired and exasperated Butterfield sent a long dispatch to Hooker about the flurry of messages he had received. "The character of these dispatches received leaves no doubt in my mind that my dispatches to you have either been mutilated or tampered with," Butterfield said. Thus he sent a special messenger to hand-carry copies of all the day's dispatches to the commanding general.[41]

On into darkness, Hooker's flanking division kept digging and slashing, putting a second night of labor into most of the fortifications they had started on Thursday. They created an irregular line more than five miles long, facing almost entirely east and south. It began just over a mile northeast of the Chancellorsville crossroads, ran south, and then hugged the Turnpike back to the Chancellorsville clearing. From there it made a gentle mile-wide arc south and west, returning to the Turnpike near where Bullock Road joins, and then stretched along the Turnpike for a good two miles westward. There were reserves behind Chancellorsville and outposts at the fords and road junctions still farther back. But except for a small hook at its westernmost point on the Turnpike, none of the main line looked either west or north.[42]

On the east, the valley of Mott's Run separated Hooker's troops from Lee's. The Confederate line was anchored on its right where the run crosses Mine Road. It angled southwest across the Turnpike and Plank Road, pressing closest to the Yankees along the west of Great Meadow Swamp. Between those main roads, Lee had brigades stacked one behind another. Only an outpost was left at Catharine Furnace, where Wright's sortie had been rejected in late afternoon.

Hooker had ordered his divisions to keep building fortifications all night. Some soldiers without shovels dug with bayonets, tin plates, and cups.[43] Glad to break contact when Rebel guns were booming, they realized now that pulling back and digging so furiously meant they were on the defensive. All the happy furor about having Lee just where Hooker wanted him seemed overtaken by events.

Philadelphians in Meade's Corn Exchange Regiment felt "as discomfited as if they had been checked by a serious repulse. All enthusiasm vanished, all the bright hopes of success disappeared." [44] T. A. Meysenberg, an adjutant with the Eleventh Corps, mused unhappily over the Napoleonic maxim that says, "The strength of an army, like the power in mechanics, is estimated by multiplying the mass by the rapidity: a rapid march augments the morale of an army and increases its means of victory. Press on!" "Instead of pressing on," Meysenberg wrote, "the corps spent late Friday losing from hour to hour that morale which promptness of action produces." [45]

JUST BEFORE DARK, Lee and Jackson met at the Plank Road–Furnace Road junction. As they dismounted to talk, bullets hummed past from a treetop Yankee sharpshooter aiming at artillerymen nearby. The generals stepped off the road into the edge of the pines. Lee sat on a log and motioned Jackson down beside him.

Both men understood the urgency of grabbing the initiative Hooker had handed them, and assumed that soon Sedgwick's Union troops downriver would discover what a sparse force Lee had left behind to hold them. Lee wanted to know what Jackson had found on the left. Jackson described the heavy fire met by Stuart's artillery and Wright's infantry near the furnace. But he was suspicious. Hooker, after taking favorable terrain, had fallen back too quickly. This whole flanking move might be a huge feint, or else Hooker saw already that he had lost the advantage of surprise, and was calling off his offensive. Jackson predicted that "By tomorrow morning, there will not be any of them this side of the river."

Lee disagreed. Hooker's maneuver was too big to be a mere feint, and too ambitious for him to give it up so soon. Suppose Hooker is still here in the morning, said Lee—then we must attack him, but where?

In automatically looking for the spot to strike, Lee was carrying out on the tactical level the approach he had prevailed on Jefferson Davis to adopt as overall strategy. It was impossible for the outmanned Confederacy to defend its long coast and river lines by merely waiting for the enemy to attack. The South must adopt the offensive-defensive, keeping its main forces concentrated, threatening the enemy's capital, drawing his armies away from vital points, forcing him into "an overwhelming thunderclap of combat" in the field.[46] On the battleground itself, Lee repeatedly took great risks to seize the initiative, because only thus could he defeat an active and superior Union army. And yet, with all this said, it remains a merely logical explanation of what he and Jackson were about to do. The truer reason is that, as Porter Alexander had said the year before, Lee's "very *name* might be Audacity."

Lee and Jackson sent their engineers, Maj. T. M. R. Talcott and Capt. J. K. Boswell, to scout the ground for a possible drive directly on Chancellorsville. Lee kept the discussion of options going. If he could not go straight at Hooker, he would have to go around. He had seen what lay to the right, toward the river, and had no intention of sending men into that morass. About that time Jeb Stuart galloped along the Furnace Road bringing precisely what Lee wanted to hear.

Fitz Lee, his horsemen unhindered by Federal cavalry, had probed far around the left. Feeling for Hooker's west flank, out the Turnpike, he realized it was hanging "in the air"—unanchored on any hill, river, swamp, or other natural obstacle. It just seemed to peter out along the road. Lee quickly saw the opportunity to swing that way and strike where least expected—the opportunity and the risk, because Hooker's flank was a long march away, and to attack it without being discovered en route was most uncertain.[47]

How to get there? Lee's decisiveness was momentarily delayed again by his casual attitude about maps. He had been hampered by vague maps when he brought Jackson down from the Valley to surprise McClellan outside Richmond the year before. He was an engineer by training, a specialist in terrain. His army had been camped along the Rappahannock, with units operating in and out of the Wilderness, for nearly half a year. He had long considered a Union move from that direction likely. He had skilled mapmakers available, notably Jedediah Hotchkiss of Jackson's staff. On Thursday, Jackson had ordered maps of the region between the Rappahannock and Rapidan, but for most of the winter and spring Hotchkiss had labored over drawings to accompany overdue reports of the 1862 campaigns. Now Lee had only a rough sketch map of the terrain where he proposed to fight. To find out what forest roads lay around Hooker's flank, he had to send Stuart to reconnoiter in the darkness with a local guide.

As staff officers ran errands in and out of the pine grove that had become the Confederate command post, they heard snatches of the conversation that would determine the next day's battle. Rebel soldiers, behind the trenches they had dug so hastily, lay with their muskets and murmured about the day past. Occasionally cannon flashed and boomed, and conversation halted. The two engineers sent to scout the ground for a direct attack toward Chancellorsville returned to say that such an assault would be foolish. The Federals were strengthening their line every hour; the approaches were through chaotic undergrowth, except for the roads, which were covered by Union cannon.

After listening to this report, Lee peered at his rough map, tilting it to catch the candlelight. He looked at Jackson. "How can we get at those people?"

Leaning over the map, Jackson made clear that regardless of his earlier doubts about whether Hooker would be there in the morning, he was ready to do whatever Lee decided. Lee swung his finger left, then tapped the point where the cavalry had said Hooker's flank was wide open. He did not have to say what he was thinking. Jackson understood at once that he meant another broad sweep like the one at Second Manassas—except this time it would be more dangerous, because having divided his army once, Lee would now divide it again, directly in the face of a much stronger opponent. This time he would outflank the enemy flanker.

Lee did not have to say who would do it. Jackson did not have to ask. He nodded.

If Jackson remained unsure whether Hooker was there in the morning, Lee suggested, he could drop in a few artillery rounds to see if they stirred anything. The flank move would have to be fast and quiet. Tactical details and exact line of march would be up to Jackson. "General Stuart will cover your movement with his cavalry," he said.

Jackson stood, smiled, and saluted, saying, "My troops will move at four o'clock." That was less than four hours away. And then Jackson, who had been awake and driving his troops since before dawn that Friday, made a grave mistake. Without issuing warning orders to his division commanders, he went a few steps into the darkness of the pines and spread his saddle blanket to sleep. He unbuckled his sword and propped it against a tree. As the general lay down, his young aide Alexander "Sandie" Pendleton offered him his overcoat as a blanket against the spring night. Jackson refused it. Pendleton then in effect split the coat, unbuttoning its long cape and offering that. Jackson thanked him, pulled the cape about his shoulders, and quickly fell asleep.

Lee was still up when Jackson's chaplain, Tucker Lacy, came into the circle of firelight. Stuart had found out that Lacy's brother lived nearby and that the minister knew the back roads of the Wilderness, so he sent him to Lee. Lacy assured the commanding general that there were such roads, that what he wanted to do could be done. Lee, gratified, spread his own saddle blanket and propped his head on his saddle. He had drifted asleep when Jackson's aide James Power Smith returned from scouting the Federal right. When Smith waked him, Lee thanked the officer and put his arm about his shoulder, saying it was too bad he had not spotted some Union guns that had annoyed his troops. "Young men of my generation," he joked, "would have done better." When Smith pulled away, unsure whether to feel chastened, Lee laughed aloud, his voice mingling in the pines with the whippoorwills' calls.

Barely an hour later, Jackson awoke, his bones chilled, damp from dew that tipped the pine needles above. He got up, draped Pendleton's cape over its sleeping owner, and went to warm himself by the low fire. In a moment Lacy walked up and Jackson insisted that he sit beside him on a cracker box left behind by the Yankees. For some reason Jackson talked a while about general problems of the Confederate army before wandering back to the matter at hand. He asked Lacy about roads toward Hooker's rear. When the minister assured him they existed, Jackson asked him to trace what he meant on his pocket map.

As Jackson watched, he shook his head. "That's too near," he said. "It goes within the line of the enemy's pickets. I want to get around well to his rear without being observed. Don't you know another road?"

The Wilderness could be friendly, enabling a shorter march covered by the woods. Too long a march could waste time and exhaust the troops before they went into the assault. Lacy suggested that Charles Wellford at Catharine Furnace would know the back roads, and his son should be able to guide them through. Urgently, Jackson told Lacy to go with Hotchkiss to the furnace, send back young Wellford as guide, and be sure Hotchkiss picked a road that could take artillery.

He was alone again, hands stretched out to the fire, when Lee's aide, Col. Armistead L. Long, awoke and saw him. Long went to a company camp nearby and brought back a cup of coffee, and Jackson sipped it as they talked. Suddenly, for no apparent reason, Jackson's sword clattered to the ground from where it was propped against the tree. The colonel picked it up and handed it to Jackson, who buckled it on. Afterward, Long recalled that incident as an omen.

At the first ray of light, Lee was up. He and Jackson talked about the roads Lacy had described, and what Lacy and Hotchkiss would find out. Soon the preacher and the engineer were back. Hotchkiss sat on another cracker box between the generals and showed them a rough wagon trail he had sketched in on his map. It paralleled the route already shown, but

ran farther back in the forest. Then it joined a better road that struck the
Turnpike beyond where Hooker's line was believed to end. After the
generals had listened to Hotchkiss, Lee asked Jackson, "What do you
propose to do?"

Jackson, fixed on the map, said, "Go around here." He ran his finger
along the route Hotchkiss had found.

"What do you propose to make this movement with?" asked Lee.

He was one of history's most unshakable generals, but the answer
startled him:

"With my whole corps," said Jackson.

Since the moment Lee suggested it, the move had grown in Jackson's
mind. He had no intention of merely rattling Hooker, of trying to distract
the Federals before they concentrated their superior strength against
another part of Lee's divided army. He meant to destroy the Union army,
to drive Hooker back across the river. For Lee to approve this version
would mean not only redividing his army, but separating it into three
pieces, each outnumbered by the Union force confronting it. For once,
Lee's own boldness had been trumped.

"What will you leave me?" he asked Jackson.

"The divisions of Anderson and McLaws."

If Jackson took three divisions—his whole corps, minus Early below
Fredericksburg—Lee would have just two divisions to face Hooker where
Hooker was strongest. Jackson would take some 28,000 men around the
flank, leaving Lee with about 14,000. Hooker with some 65,000 would be
squarely between them—and Sedgwick with another 40,000 might drive
up from Fredericksburg behind Lee at any hour. Lee considered all this,
then met Jackson's eyes.

"Well," he said, "go on."

Jackson's troops had not been alerted for an early march. After he and
Lee talked over particulars of their plan, Jackson set out to get his
divisions moving. McGowan's South Carolinians spied him coming and
got ready to cheer as usual, but up close they saw his intense look and held
back, wondering what it meant. Time flew as word passed down the Plank
Road for troops to bolt their sparse rations, roll their packs, struggle out
of the woods, and fall in to march. While they were assembling, Lee told
Anderson and McLaws what had been decided. Their divisions would
have to dig in and build parapets to fortify the line thinned by Jackson's
departure. Later they would launch noisy attacks against Hooker's lines to
distract him from what Jackson was doing.

It was nearing seven o'clock, not at four as Jackson had promised, when the lead regiments of his force came trooping past Lee's command post, down the road toward Catharine Furnace. Lee watched as Jackson appeared, riding just behind the head of Rodes's division. Jackson stopped, and the two generals talked briefly. Nobody nearby could hear what they said. Then Jackson thrust his arm forward, pointing. Lee nodded, and Jackson rode on.[48]

They never saw each other again.

Chapter Ten

You Can Go Forward, Then

THE RANGY TROOPS filing past Lee's command post looked nothing like the innocent boys, brave and wide-eyed in their fancy uniforms, who had posed for ambrotypes before heading off to war two years before.

Somewhere back in the Valley, on the Peninsula, on the way to Sharpsburg, they had thrown away knapsacks, overcoats, pistols, daggers, extra underwear, and other nonessentials. Now each man rolled his blanket in his groundcloth and looped it in a horseshoe over a shoulder, tied at the opposite hip. Personal odds and ends, writing paper, precious apples or squares of cornbread, were in his haversack slung over the other shoulder. His wooden canteen, or a tin one taken from the Yankees, hung beside it. A cup might dangle from his belt or by a thong from the blanket roll; here and there a frying pan rattled with its handle stuck into the muzzle of a musket. Most of the time his weapon was carried casually over a shoulder: the .58-caliber Springfield rifle musket and the British-made .577 Enfield, the most common weapons of the war, were just under five feet long—over six feet with bayonet fixed—too unwieldy to be carried comfortably at sling arms. They weighed between nine and ten pounds complete. Cartridges, a dozen to the pound, were more often crammed into pockets than in ammunition boxes where they were hard to pinch out in the hurry of battle. For many infantrymen, the broad-brimmed slouch hat had succeeded the stiff-billed forage cap. Polished boots were a remote memory; the troops who wore shapeless brogans thought themselves lucky as they set out around the flank of the Union army.[1]

Brig. Gen. Alfred H. Colquitt's Georgia brigade, marching four abreast, led the column swiftly toward Catharine Furnace. But far back in the woods along the Plank Road, some regiments had to wait for hours before stepping out in turn. Others fought brisk skirmishes first, supporting a daybreak cannonade ordered by Lee to be sure the Yankees were still where he had left them the night before. Moving in open country, a division's wagon trains usually took the middle of the road while the foot soldiers marched alongside. Here, the track through the woods was so narrow there was barely room for a horseman to pass by, running messages up and down the column. Each division's light train—artillery, ammunition, and ambulances—directly followed its infantry, ahead of the next division.

The route Jackson had traced with his finger as he talked with Lee ran westward past the intersection where the generals had spent the night. Then it curved southwest toward the furnace in the valley of Scott's Run. From the furnace it veered left, south, for almost two miles before swerving right to the Brock Road. If Jackson had been willing to risk the most direct route to reach the Union line beyond Chancellorsville, he would have marched north from there on the Brock Road. Instead he headed his column south again—the second time his turns seemed to take him away from the enemy, toward Orange Court House and Gordonsville, just the way Hooker had hoped the Confederates would retreat. Heading in that direction for three-fourths of a mile, Jackson would then turn north along an obscure farm track, jog briefly left along the unfinished railroad, and take another path northward through the woods before rejoining the Brock Road. This was the better-hidden route found after he objected that the Reverend Mr. Lacy's first suggestion did not clear the enemy's picket line. After following the Brock Road north for another mile, Jackson intended to cut right along the Orange Plank Road and strike the Union flank near Dowdall's Tavern on the Turnpike. His heavy wagon train of provisions would follow via Todd's Tavern, taking the Catharpin Road, more than a mile south of his march route.[2]

Even under ideal battlefield conditions, for a general to divide his army and march most of it this way across the front of a superior enemy is considered either foolhardy or desperate, forbidden in every textbook of war. Conditions in the Wilderness were anything but ideal. Once troops settle into route step, their column lengthens despite constant urging to close up. To avoid stepping on the heels of those in front, ranks seldom follow closer than five feet. Spaced thus, 26,000 infantrymen moving through that forest four abreast—3 divisions, 15 brigades, 70 regiments—would cover six miles of road, even without the inevitable stretchout between troops and units. Add to them Jackson's 16 batteries of artillery, plus ambulances and ammunition wagons: altogether they made a thin, winding, vulnerable procession whose tail would just be under way when his advance guard approached the enemy on the far flank. Should it be attacked, he could not deploy his infantry or use his cannon effectively in the thickets.

If Lee, outnumbered and initially outmaneuvered, had been someone else, he might have tried anything else rather than a venture so dangerous. After all, there was a prudent alternative, honorable under the circumstances: retreat to a more defensible position. Instead of that, he chose to risk disaster—because he was Lee, and because the man beside him was Jackson. Whether it was also because his opponent was Joe Hooker is less clear. Lee had known Hooker in Mexico, where the younger officer earned his reputation before he earned his nickname. But Hooker had not been in a command position there—instead, he was the eager executor of others' decisions. Yet Hooker's record since as an aggressive division and corps commander, in head-on fights against Lee's army, should have told any sensible opponent that it was foolish to chance destruction in detail by his powerful force. For Lee, however, Hooker's performance in the previous two days, twice pulling back on Chancellorsville when his generals wanted to drive on, must have outweighed the rest of that war record. If Lee had not firmly concluded that Hooker would stay behind his fortified lines, he was willing to gamble on it. The clinching reason was Stonewall Jackson.

American history offers no other pair of generals with such perfect rapport, such sublime confidence in each other. Jackson had said, "Lee is the only man I know whom I would follow blindfolded."[3] Lee, from the beginning, had insisted that he was fighting to protect the Virginia of his fathers; Jackson could say he was fighting now to recover his own Virginia, the mountainland that on April 20 was cut off as a new Federal state. But both by then were fighting as much for their soldiers, for each other, for the Chancellorsville crossroads, as for strategic and political goals beyond the immediate battlefield. There was a synergism in their mutual confidence. It inspired them to dare things together that they would not have tried with anyone else. Jackson had quickly jerked the Confederates facing Chancellorsville out of their rifle pits, off the defensive, and sent them probing for a weak spot in Hooker's lines before Lee even arrived. But Lee upped the ante when he proposed going all the way around to hit the Union army from its far flank. Jackson, as if challenged, upped it again when he told Lee he not only would go, he would take all three of his divisions along to do it right. Lee, fully realizing that that would leave him to hold Hooker's overwhelming force with about one-fifth its number, met that challenge when he said calmly, "Well, go on." This was the climax of two great military careers, each made greater by the other.

But neither Lee nor Jackson would have dared as they did without their shared confidence in the common soldier of the Army of Northern Virginia. Repeatedly, their troops had outmarched and outfought an enemy superior in numbers, guns, and provisions. The generals' devotion was plain to the regiments; the soldiers' infinite trust in their commanders was both inspiration and burden to Lee and Jackson. And so as they talked and watched their soldiers march by, as their soldiers saw Lee nod and Jackson ride forward, a genuine love moved back and forth among them. It is a feeling understood best by soldiers who have been there.

ACROSS THE WAY, Hooker was admired if not yet loved. He was the man who had recharged the Army of the Potomac, regularized its furloughs, improved its rations, reorganized its cavalry, made the whole army glitter and strut, and then moved it boldly onto the flank of the enemy. Despite the army's letdown after pulling back on Chancellorsville the day before, Hooker was showered by cheers as he rode his lines that early morning, hoping Lee would oblige him by attacking.

By any objective measure, he had much more reason for confidence than Lee. With five corps already on hand, at 1:55 that morning he had ordered John Reynolds to pull the First Corps back across the river below Fredericksburg and bring it up to join his flanking force. That would increase his odds to about 83,000 against Lee's 40,000 around Chancellorsville. When the First Corps arrived, Hooker would stretch it over the Union rear, between the Rapidan and the Turnpike, to cover what seemed the least likely direction of enemy attack. That would make his line an unbroken arc from the Rappahannock on his left to the Rapidan near Ely's Ford.[4]

Hooker set out at sunrise, trotting amid his staff to inspect the rifle pits and breastworks reaching west along the Turnpike. Slocum's Twelfth Corps still held a crescent that dipped south to enclose the open eminence called Fairview. To Slocum's right was David Birney's division of Sickles's Third Corps, spread along the edge of a farther clear plateau called Hazel Grove. On its right, O. O. Howard's Eleventh Corps stretched past Wilderness Church and Dowdall's Tavern, using the latter as corps headquarters. Howard's line, looking south, ran another mile past the Turnpike–Plank Road junction. There, where it petered out, two artillery pieces pointed west along the road and two infantry regiments were swung back to face in that direction—Howard's gesture toward what seemed the most remote eventuality.[5]

Howard heard the cheering as Hooker rode his way. "It was a hearty sound," he recalled, "with too much bass in it for that of the enemy's charge." With his staff, he was waiting at Dowdall's and joined "the ever-increasing cavalcade." As they rode together looking over the lines, Hooker was pleased by the breastworks built by Carl Schurz's and Charles Devens's divisions. "How strong, how strong!" he said.

But his engineer, Cyrus Comstock, occasionally pointed out gaps. Howard said, "The woods are thick and entangled; will anybody come through there?" "Oh, they may," said Comstock. According to Howard, "his suggestion was heeded." [6]

Regiment after regiment, luxuriating over breakfast, sore from marching and digging, stood to shout as Hooker and his entourage trotted by. When he got back to Chancellorsville about nine o'clock, messengers from Birney were waiting. Lookouts in the treetops at Hazel Grove had been watching a Confederate column moving west across the army's front for at least an hour.

They could see the glint of sun on bayonets as the Gray column crossed high ground just before Scott's Run, a mile and a half away. After dropping into the valley toward the furnace, the column reappeared to the south. That meant Lee was doing what Hooker originally intended him to do—retreating. Or did it? Hooker pondered aloud as he stared at a map spread on his bed. There, apparently for the first time, it dawned on him that Lee might not retreat, and might not follow Hooker's reconsidered plan by attacking where the Federals were strongest. It finally occurred to him that to retreat without a fight was unlike Lee. Yet there were Lee's soldiers, steadily trooping south. If not retreat, what was it? Was Lee trying to flank him? [7] At 9:30, remembering how the Eleventh Corps line trailed off at its far point, Hooker dispatched this to Howard and Slocum:

I am directed by the major general commanding to say the disposition you have made of your corps has been with a view to a *front* attack by the enemy. If he should throw himself upon your flank, he wishes you to examine the ground, and determine upon the position you will take in that event, in order that you may be prepared for him in whatever direction he advances.

He suggests that you have heavy reserves well in hand to meet this contingency.

J. H. Van Alen,
Brig. General and A.D.C.

We have good reason to suppose that the enemy is moving to our right. Please advance your pickets for purposes of observation as far as may be safe in order to obtain timely information of their approach.[8]

Despite the confusion of personal pronouns, the message was clear. What was disputed in the hours and years ahead was whether it ever reached Howard. Even if he did not get it, he and his brother generals heard a rising volume of other reports to the same effect as Jackson's men kept moving across their front.

Now that Lee had committed himself, Hooker had another opening to prove his earlier boast that the Confederate army was "the legitimate property of the Army of the Potomac." He could have retaken the initiative by abandoning his Chancellorsville defenses and lighting into his exposed, outnumbered opponent. Instead, he sat tight and turned his attention back toward Fredericksburg. He reversed what seemed to be his original concept, of using his own force as the hammer to pound Lee back against the anvil of Sedgwick's bridgehead. At the same time he issued Howard and Slocum the warning about a possible flank attack from the west, he sent Sedgwick strangely conditional orders to take the offensive in Lee's rear. This was his message to Butterfield:

> The general commanding desires you to instruct General Sedgwick, if an opportunity presents itself with a reasonable expectation of success, to attack the enemy in his front. We have reliable information that all the divisions known to us as having belonged to the army at Fredericksburg, except Early's, are in this vicinity. It is impossible for the general to determine here whether it is expedient for him to attack or not. It must be left to his discretion.[9]

While things were happening on Hooker's front and right, he entertained himself all that day and into the next with the idea that Sedgwick had become the key to his success. Once again, the leisurely pace of his communications eliminated any prospect that the idea would convert into quick, decisive action. But even if Sedgwick had received that message immediately, he could have been forgiven for missing any sense of urgency in it.

MAJ. GEN. DAN SICKLES rode the lines with Hooker that morning, then returned to his Third Corps command post. "Colorful" was a pale adjective for Daniel Edgar Sickles: His past was garish, never without controversy in politics or the army. He had been a diplomat in London and a congressman from New York. In Washington in 1859, he was cuckolded by Philip Barton Key, son of the author of "The Star-Spangled Banner," and shot him dead across the avenue from the White House. Defended by a lawyer named Edwin M. Stanton, soon to be Lincoln's secretary of war, Sickles used the defense of temporary insanity, was acquitted, and remained in office. On the outbreak of war, he volunteered his services to the Union and organized New York's Excelsior Brigade. Fighting on the Peninsula, at Antietam and Fredericksburg, he rose from colonel to major general and commanded Hooker's old division. After early differences, he became Hooker's favorite corps commander, the only non–West Pointer among them.[10]

Two of Sickles's three divisions were camped in reserve behind Chancellorsville—the other, Birney's, held the ground between Slocum and Howard. When Hooker returned to headquarters, he was still concerned about what was happening to the east, where Lee's artillery dropped in sporadic salvos during the morning. Hooker had Sickles send two regiments beyond the lines, one along the Turnpike and one down the Plank Road, to see what was stirring in that direction. The 26th Pennsylvania, returning from the Plank Road, brought back a few stray Confederates who said their division was moving west. Soon afterward, more reports came from Birney about the column still marching across the Union front. Sickles went out to Hazel Grove to take a look and saw the Confederates plainly, only about 1,600 yards beyond Birney's artillery. Capt. A. Judson Clark's gunners got in some "excellent practice" that chased Jackson's infantry off the exposed stretch of road into deeper woods and hurried the Rebel artillery and wagons into the valley toward Catharine Furnace.

As Sickles watched, he realized this was no mere feint, to set up a direct assault from the east. The column had been watched for three hours and was still passing. It could be heading toward the Orange & Alexandria or the Virginia Central railroad. He ventured a new analysis: The Confederates were either retreating, or going to attack the Union flank—*or both*. The two were not mutually exclusive; if a flank attack failed, Lee could continue south and west. Sickles passed on what he saw to Hooker, and to Howard and Slocum on his flanks. He wanted them to cooperate if, as he urged, Hooker let him attack the enemy column.[11]

Sickles pleaded, and eventually Hooker said go ahead. Getting his orders at noon, Sickles sent Birney's division south from Hazel Grove to "follow the enemy, pierce the column, and gain possession of the road over which it was passing." [12]

On each flank, Birney would be shielded by a battalion of Berdan's Sharpshooters, one of the occasional "elite" outfits that deserve the adjective. The two Sharpshooter regiments were commanded by Col. Hiram Berdan, a New York engineer who for fifteen years before the war had been the country's best rifle marksman. In the first September of the war, Berdan was pushing for adoption of the Sharps rifle. This was a breechloader opposed by crusty old Brig. Gen. James Ripley, head of the Union arsenal, who objected to most technical advances and dreaded having to supply ammunition for a plethora of different weapons. (At least 18 different muskets, rifles, and carbines, of at least 10 different calibers, were issued to various Federal units between 1861 and 1865.) After Lincoln watched a spectacular test-firing at Washington, he drove away chuckling. "Colonel, come down tomorrow and I'll give you the order for the breechloaders." Now, armed with the Sharps and special target rifles, some with telescopes, Berdan's Sharpshooters headed into the woods wearing their distinctive green jackets and black-plumed caps. [13]

Philip Regis Denis de Keredern de Trobriand—duelist, novelist, memoirist, poet, son of a French baron, husband of an American heiress, colonel of the 38th New York—encountered Slocum behind Birney's line just before noon. "Let me recommend that you fortify yourself as well as possible," Slocum told him. "The enemy is massing a considerable force on our right. In two or three hours he will fall on Howard, and you will have him upon you in strong force." As de Trobriand was about to follow that advice, he got the order to move out with Birney. With the 20th Indiana in front, Birney's division headed into "a network of branches and briars" south of Hazel Grove. The troops had to throw bridges over Scott's Run and some of its tributaries as they pushed into the thickets. [14]

As Jackson passed Catharine Furnace, he ordered Rodes to detach a regiment from Colquitt's leading brigade to guard a woods track coming down from the north toward the furnace. Colquitt picked the 23rd Georgia. Almost from the start of the march, Jackson had realized the Yankees were watching. When their guns let fly from Hazel Grove on his men in the open stretch before the furnace, he ordered his infantry to double-time past the danger. For the wagons, he sought out a safer detour farther south, which rejoined a mile or so onward. Jackson's corps artillery, with its ammunition train and other wagons, was still passing the

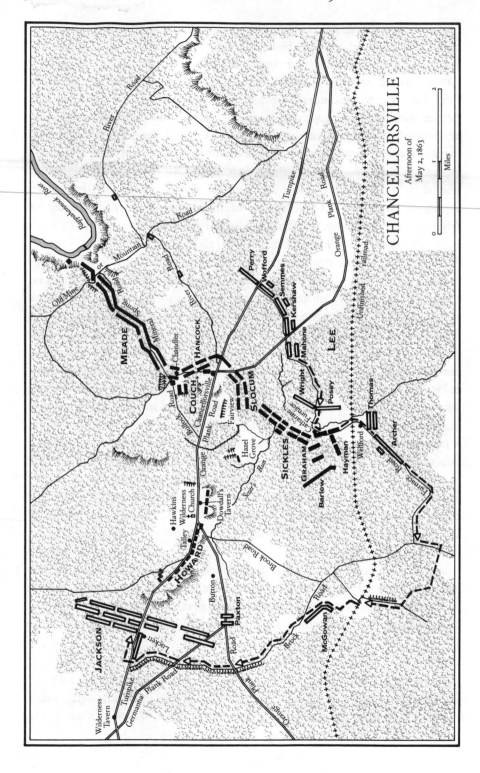

CHANCELLORSVILLE

Afternoon of
May 2, 1863

furnace when Berdan's Sharpshooters came crashing through the under-growth. Afterward, one of the workers at the furnace caught the excitement of those minutes better than any official report.

He was a country boy named Sprig Dempsey, who helped Ab Chewning, the "boss blacksmith." Sprig said Ab was not in the army because he had such bad rheumatism he had to be carried in a chair and sometimes hoisted in a sling to check on jobs under way. They were working on the furnace roof when Jackson's men marched by. Then "here came a Georgia regiment . . . moving fast. The woods were full of Yankees, they said, and they couldn't stand them off much longer." But the ironworkers "had no doubt for a minute those Georgians could whip a woods full of Yankees anytime," so they kept working while the Georgia troops got set for a fight in and around the foundry.

"All of a sudden up on the bluff there broke out such a racket of shooting and yelling that Sprig and Ab got uneasy and then—Whooee! Georgians began to pour over the bluff like a waterfall and the sky behind them clouded up and rained Yankees." Sprig took off for Scott's Run as the Georgians, firing from behind trees, fell back toward the railroad cut near Wellford's house. Sprig was about to splash into the creek when he remembered poor Ab back on the roof. He stopped and wondered what to do "when a man shot by him like a bat out of a barn and made a leap that carried him clear across Scott's Run, which was more than Sprig could do or had thought of doing. It was Ab."

Sprig was so astonished that he just stood there, and as he gazed at where Ab had vanished through the forest, "a parcel of Yankees that thought they were chasing Ab came running and captured Sprig. . . . To his dying day, Sprig Dempsey said he had never seen anything like how those Yankees had cured Ab Chewning of that rheumatism, which even bee-stinging had failed to cure." [15]

Col. Emory F. Best and the men of the 23rd Georgia didn't think it was that funny. When his pickets in the woods were driven in, Best realized he was flanked on his right. Hearing the firefight, Lee sent a brigade from Anderson's division to counterattack the Federals. These were Posey's men, who poured heavy fire into the left of the Union thrust and later were

7. Jackson's Flank March. *When Lee's cavalry finds Hooker's western flank hanging "in the air," he sends Jackson looping through the Wilderness to strike there. Sickles heads a Union thrust to cut off Jackson's vulnerable column at Catharine Furnace. This leaves a gap in the Union line between Howard and Slocum.*

joined there by Wright's brigade. Together they hammered at Sickles's flank as he pushed south.

Striking such stout resistance, Birney ordered all three of his brigades forward. Sickles brought Maj. Gen. Amiel W. Whipple's division down in support, and borrowed Brig. Gen. Francis C. Barlow's brigade from Howard's corps. Brig. Gen. Alpheus S. Williams's division was hurried out of its position along the right of Hazel Grove to face Posey and Wright, thus leaving a wide undefended gap in the Union line between Sickles's salient and the Eleventh Corps.[16]

After pushing the outnumbered Georgians back, Birney's force was halted by well-aimed fire from Confederate Napoleon 12-pounders emplaced near Wellford's house, half a mile beyond the furnace. Col. J. Thompson Brown's battalion of Virginia artillery had turned and unlimbered as the 23rd Georgia was falling back. Two companies of the 14th Tennessee, left on picket back along the Plank Road, had just passed, hurrying to catch A. P. Hill's division. As they were taking a break, several officers rode up in alarm and urged them to turn around and help the Georgians. Arriving at the hill south of the furnace, they ran into the retreating 23rd and together they rallied against the Yankees until the rest of the artillery train jolted on. Colonel Best, withdrawing to the railroad cut, was confident that they had saved everything but one broken-down artillery caisson whose horses were wounded.[17]

When the Georgians were being driven through the woods, Lt. Col. W. R. Carter of the 3rd Virginia Cavalry had galloped ahead to catch the tail of Jackson's infantry column and ask for help. Without time to consult higher command, Brig. Gen. James J. Archer turned back his own and Brig. Gen. E. L. Thomas's brigades from Hill's division. Archer arrived and "found that the enemy had already been repulsed."[18] He ordered Colonel Best to hold at the railroad cut. But after hunkering down while an artillery duel was fought overhead, Archer's skirmishers withdrew and exposed the Georgians' left. Although Best was ordered to pull back at the same time, he did not get the message before Yankees poured into the cut, nearly surrounding his command. He got away with his regimental colors, and with help he had successfully carried out his rearguard mission. But 26 officers and 250 men, about three-fourths of his command, were captured. (Berdan said his Sharpshooters took 365, including 19 officers, and added, "Our loss was trifling.")[19] A few months later, a Confederate court-martial cashiered Best for his performance at the Furnace.

Archer and Thomas marched southwest again to follow the rest of Hill's division. Though Jackson's column had paid a minor price to protect its rear and march on, Sickles reported that his own movement was "successfully completed" because Birney's troops eventually reached the road and poured cannon fire on "the retreating column of the enemy."[20]

HAD SICKLES seen Jackson and his men up close, all his impression of retreat would have vanished. There was haste but no panic in the Confederate column as it pushed on past splotches of pink azalea in the deep woods. Spring warblers were flitting through the branches overhead. In the occasional open spots, brambles arced from the roadside and Virginia cedars put out new green shoots. In those places troops fearful of being seen sometimes skulked beside the greenery, half bent, at trail arms. When they spotted one of Professor Lowe's balloons to the north, they were sure of being watched.[21]

Despite the urgency of the march, Jackson's forward brigades apparently began the day expecting to obey the road discipline he had laid down for more routine travel: two miles in 50 minutes, then 10 minutes' rest. That did not last long. A. P. Hill's trailing division, which had not passed Lee's command post until about eleven o'clock, covered perhaps ten miles before taking a two-hour rest. (The routine obviously varied, depending on how far back a given unit started; artilleryman E. P. Alexander reported that "During the day there were three halts for rest of perhaps 20 minutes each.")[22] The roads were just right for infantry—damp enough to hold down dust but muddy only in low spots, so the wagon trains did not make ruts that turned the ankles of marching men. The sun was bright above the forest, and in early afternoon the temperature reached about 80 degrees. For even Jackson's lean troops, hurrying forward under arms, this was hot. Many were hungry. Sweating, they grew thirsty, for there were few farms and wells along their way. Hundreds were like William Calder in the 2nd North Carolina, who wrote that "I suffered exceedingly. I was several times on the point of giving out, but persevered, and succeeded in keeping up."[23]

Jackson's troops remembered his steely look as he rode by, constantly urging them to "Press on, press forward." His intensity squelched any reflex to cheer as he passed, and he did not have to say so for them to know they were on the march of their lives. Stopping occasionally to watch regiments pass, he spoke to their colonels and captains: "Keep the column closed. . . . Permit no straggling. . . . Press on, press on."[24]

Yet despite the pace and the heat, the troops kept up what was by then a tradition of amusing themselves at the expense of young mounted officers passing by. If a fuzzy-cheeked lieutenant was cultivating a mustache, they were sure to gibe at him, "Look, there he goes with a mouthful of mice! Don't tell me he ain't, look at their tails sticking out!" If he had an impressive hat or outsized boots, they would say, "Come out, I know you're in there, come on out!" In early afternoon, Jackson's aide Lt. James Power Smith pushed his horse along the column to catch up with the general. The foot soldiers were as sassy as if they had just finished a full meal in a shady bivouac. "Here's one of Jack's little boys," they cracked. "Let him by, boys! . . . Have a good breakfast this morning, sonny? . . . Better hurry up, or you'll catch it for getting behind. . . . Tell Old Jack we're all a-coming. . . . Don't let him begin the fuss till we git thar!"[25]

In this spirit, the springy, confident infantrymen were not confused when their winding march route occasionally seemed to take them away from the enemy. The sun told them they were heading west, south, west, south, west, then north, but their own inner bearings told them what Jackson was up to. Many of the Yankees watching suspected the same thing. One of the Georgians captured at the furnace told them: "You may think you have done a big thing just now, but just wait till Jackson gets round on your right."[26] But Hooker seemed to think his warning to Howard about what might come from that direction was all he needed to do for the moment.

THOUGH SICKLES kept thrashing around near the furnace, overall Hooker preferred to keep his powerful force in place around Chancellorsville until he was ready to take off after Lee's supposed retreat. Other suppositions were at work: Stoneman's cavalry was supposed to be in Lee's rear, between him and Richmond. And Sedgwick, miles away downstream, was supposed to pick up the Union offensive.

From the hills overlooking the Federal bridgehead below Fredericksburg, generals of each army got the impression early that Saturday that just maybe the enemy was pulling out. At 6:15 A.M., Professor Lowe took a balloon aloft, but the wind was so strong he was unable to steady his glass to see whether any Confederates were moving upriver. Most opposite Falmouth seemed still to be in place. At 7:45, he reported Lee's cannonade 12 miles away in front of Chancellorsville. At 8:30, he added: "I cannot say that the enemy have decreased, but they do not show themselves quite so much this morning, and I can see no reserves on the opposite heights."

In the morning darkness, a messenger had gotten lost with Hooker's
1:55 A.M. order for Reynolds to withdraw his First Corps, move up, and
recross to Chancellorsville. It was not forwarded by Chief of Staff Butterfield until 5:00, and Reynolds finally got it at 7:00.[27] Reynolds was slow
in pulling back across the river because Early's artillery kept pummeling
his bridgehead, but at 11:05 that morning he reported that all his troops
were on the Union side, and on the march toward U.S. Ford. They made
no effort at concealment as they pulled away, but a division of Sedgwick's
corps came down the slope to make a show of force to impress the
Rebels.[28]

Jubal Early was watching all this from the hill where Lee had overseen
the battle of Fredericksburg. With William Barksdale, whose brigade still
held the town, and artillery brigadier William N. Pendleton, Early was
trying to decide what the Federal move meant. Before they drew any
conclusion, Lee's chief of staff, Col. Robert H. Chilton, rode up at about
eleven o'clock and gave Early a verbal order to move his force immediately toward Chancellorsville. He was to leave behind only one brigade,
with eight or ten guns; the rest of his artillery should be sent south to
safety.

Early was astounded. He told Chilton he could not possibly pull out
without being seen, and as soon as he did the enemy would take the town
and the heights. Chilton said he assumed Lee knew all this, and that
Early's division was needed more upriver than here. Noting the movement
of Union troops beyond the river, he said they were doubtless going to
reinforce Hooker. Early recalled that Chilton repeated the order "with
great distinctness," denying that there could be any mistake. Early believed his division was holding many more enemy troops below Fredericksburg than it could fight or divert if it moved to Chancellorsville. But
there was no "if" in Lee's order as delivered by Chilton. Puzzled but
obedient, Early ordered a brigade and a regiment to stay behind, and
began to withdraw the rest of his troops as inconspicuously as possible.[29]

Because of the wind, Lowe's balloons were grounded in early afternoon, but later he could see that something was happening. Before 5:00
P.M., he reported that "the enemy have entirely withdrawn their advanced
line, with exception of a small picket force . . . they have also disappeared
from opposite our extreme left, below the town crossing."[30] By then Early
was well on his way. But in late afternoon, as his division approached the
Plank Road intersection, a note came from Lee making clear that Chilton
was indeed mistaken; rather than delivering a peremptory order to head

for Chancellorsville, he had been sent to repeat essentially what Lee had told Early before. Lee did not expect Early to join him unless he could do so safely.

If ever Early had an excuse for swearing, this was it. The decision of which way to go now was left to his judgment—and that judgment, with his division already so far along the road, was to keep going west. He assumed the enemy already had discovered his withdrawal, and it would be too late to retake his old positions by turning back. But a mile later, another courier caught up, with word that a strong Union force had advanced against Harry Hays's Louisianans, the brigade left behind. Barksdale, with the trailing brigade, had been told that the artillery would be captured if help was not sent immediately. On his own initiative, he had turned his brigade back. Early, with his command thus subdivided, halted his column and put it in reverse. When he countermarched to the heights below Fredericksburg, he found the situation not as desperate as he feared. It was well after dark when his troops moved back into most of the emplacements they had left in such a hurry.[31]

HONEST CONFUSION botched communications between the separate wings of each army. Union artillery and supply wagons blundering over telegraph lines, knocking down poles, slowed message traffic among Hooker, Butterfield, and the troops still below Fredericksburg. But efforts to communicate urgent tactical intelligence from Federal soldiers to their generals ran into trouble of a higher order: a stubborn refusal to listen to anything that contradicted more convenient assumptions. While Sickles was slashing at the tail of Jackson's column near the furnace, the head of that column pressed on, angling back north toward the Turnpike. There it was crossing the front of Howard's Eleventh Corps, and all along that front, Union pickets and lookout stations spotted it, heard it, and sent back word.

Howard's leftmost division, commanded by Brig. Gen. Adolph von Steinwehr, had but two brigades. Only one of those—Col. Adolphus Buschbeck's—was on line. The other was Barlow's, assigned as corps reserve but now sent to reinforce Sickles's venture toward the furnace. Maj. Gen. Carl Schurz, commanding the next Eleventh Corps division, on von Steinwehr's right, could see the hard-marching Confederates himself. He rode to Howard's headquarters at Dowdall's Tavern and urged that the corps' line be pivoted north from that point, to face a possible attack from the west. But Howard was of Hooker's mind, that the Rebels were

retreating and Sickles was doing them heavy damage. After at first object-
ing to sending away Barlow's brigade, his only general reserve, Howard
had dispatched it to support Sickles's foray. He and von Steinwehr rode
toward the furnace with Barlow, to see what he believed was the main
show and perhaps "capture a few regiments."

Schurz decided on his own to drop three regiments behind his south-
facing line, turning them 90 degrees west. He also told Brig. Gen. Alexander von Schimmelfennig to run patrols out to the front and right, down
the Plank Road. These sorties bumped into Rebel pickets protecting
Jackson's move, and could not penetrate to get a closer look. A Pennsylvania major returned from one of them and was sent to corps headquarters
to report the enemy massing. Officers there laughed and told him not to
worry; obviously Howard was unconcerned, because he was still on his
excursion with Barlow.[32]

Beyond Schurz, at the Eleventh Corps' westernmost extension, the line
was manned by Brig. Gen. Charles Devens's division. Devens had taken
command only twelve days earlier, in place of the popular Col. Nathaniel
McLean, who had been bumped down to lead the division's 2nd Brigade.
A Harvard-trained lawyer, Devens was an ardent Massachusetts abolitionist. He had been wounded twice, at Ball's Bluff and Fair Oaks, as he moved
up from major to division command. He was confident that he knew more
than the pickets out front of the Ohio regiments to his right, and the
officers who relayed their notices.

Starting before noon, pickets of the 55th Ohio had been sending
half-hourly reports of Confederate troops moving across their sector. The
outposts, facing south, heard a few shots to their left, then their front, then
their right. They sent back word of artillery moving in that direction. As
their reports became more specific and urgent, Col. John C. Lee of the
55th took some of those pickets to McLean, and McLean rushed them up
to division. He was frankly worried, and pushed for some quick response
to the Southern movement.

Three times the 55th brought this news to Devens, who was lying
down resting at the Talley house, and Devens disdained it. The third time,
he told Lee, "You are frightened, sir," and added something about western colonels being more scared than hurt. Then Col. William P. Richardson of the 25th Ohio brought in four scouts who reported Confederates
massing on the right of the Eleventh Corps. Again, Devens brushed them
off, telling McLean to send Richardson back to his regiment. When Col.
Robert Reily of the 75th Ohio sent Lt. Col. C. W. Friend to Devens with
yet another such bulletin, the general said he did not believe it because

corps headquarters had reported no such thing. Friend promptly went on to Howard's headquarters—where he was laughed at, and warned not to start a panic.[33]

Farthest to the Union right, beyond McLean, was Col. Leopold von Gilsa's brigade, one more of the outfits that gave the Eleventh Corps its unwanted reputation as the "foreign contingent" in Hooker's army. Two of the corps' three divisions (Schurz and von Steinwehr), four of its six brigades (von Gilsa, Schimmelfennig, Buschbeck, and Krzyzanowski), twelve of its twenty-six regiments, and six of its eight artillery units were commanded by men with Central European names. According to Howard's post-Chancellorsville tabulation, 8,345 officers and men, more than two-thirds of the Eleventh Corps troops available for duty, were in eleven exclusively German and four "mixed nationality" regiments.[34]

Most of these were first-generation Americans, not yet acculturated or adept in English; they had been born in the old country and come here in the surge of immigration following the German revolutions in the late 1840s. Many of the officers had European military schooling and combat experience before they came to America. Schurz, who would later be celebrated as a reform senator, cabinet secretary, and editor, was one of the least professionally trained soldiers among them. He had served as a lieutenant and staff officer in the revolution, so had to flee Germany when the movement collapsed. In this country, he settled in Wisconsin, supported Lincoln in the 1860 election, and was rewarded with a diplomatic post in Spain. Returning in 1862, he got a brigadier's commission and did his best.[35]

Von Gilsa, heading that lonely rightmost brigade, was a former Prussian officer who had been a major in the Schleswig-Holstein war. As a civilian in New York, he had supported himself in distinctly unmartial pursuits: lecturing, singing, playing piano in music halls along the Bowery. In uniform, he enforced his strictness with a superb talent for profanity in his native Deutsch. As a contemporary put it, "When in difficult straits he was wont to be overcome by a lingual diarrhoea of sonorous expletives in the Bismarckian vernacular."[36]

At the very end of his line, von Gilsa bent back two regiments to face west—the 54th New York across the road angling down from Ely's Ford, and the 153rd Pennsylvania between it and the Turnpike. Facing south along the Turnpike were the 41st and 45th New York. Although von Gilsa's pickets were active, feeling toward Jackson's column, Capt. (acting Maj.) Owen Rice of the 153rd recalled that along the brigade line, there were only "a few trees, felled forward . . . a not very formidable nor systematic abatis . . . nothing in the manner of breastworks or redoubts on the right and at the angle." At that angle, two cannon were sited looking west out the Turnpike.

Rice led a detail of pickets to silence Rebels sniping from the woods, and had to struggle through "a very Hades of thickets." When he ran into aggressive Rebel artillery and infantry, he sent back a message to von Gilsa: "A large body of the enemy is massing in my front. For God's sake make dispositions to receive him!" Von Gilsa reported this to corps headquarters, but was told no force could push its way through the tangled woods.[37]

Perhaps the most conclusive evidence came from the impetuous Capt. Hubert Dilger of the 1st Ohio Light Artillery, who was called "Leather Breeches" for the outfit he wore in battle. He had learned to handle guns in his native Germany, and some considered him the best cannoneer in the Union army. On this afternoon he decided to inquire personally into the rumors of enemy movement on the right. Riding out with an orderly, he kept going until he ran smack into Jackson's force and barely escaped capture by Rebel horsemen. Racing back into the lines, he reported his finding at corps headquarters and was sent to alert Hooker at Chancellorsville. There, he said, a long-legged cavalry major laughed at his story and refused to let him see the general.[38]

IF THAT LONG-LEGGED cavalryman had been in the saddle, screening Hooker's army out beyond the infantry pickets, he would have been less amused and the Union army would have been better prepared. Hooker had sent most of his cavalry away from the battle; what was left was misused, and ignored when it did show some initiative. Late in the afternoon, a squadron scouted out the Turnpike and came back, its captain reporting to Devens that he had gone only a short way before meeting enemy infantry. Devens was getting jumpy by that time, and said, "I wish I could get someone who could make a reconnaissance for me"—as if the rider before him had not done just that. The cavalryman said, "General, I can go further, but I cannot promise to return." Devens told him to go to bivouac in the rear.[39]

To scout, screen, and guard his whole army, Hooker had kept back just Alfred Pleasonton's 2nd Brigade of four cavalry regiments. The remaining twenty-three regiments were in two contingents flailing around with little profit far to the west and south of the battlefield.

George Stoneman's main force rode south to cut the railroads between

Lee's army and Richmond, destroying supplies and communications on the way. William Averell's division, some 3,400 sabers, was to mask Hooker's flanking movement and the main cavalry strike. First it would head west and keep W. H. F. "Rooney" Lee's Confederate horsemen busy around Culpeper. Then it would hurry south along the Orange & Alexandria Railroad to join Stoneman at the Pamunkey River just above Richmond, where Hooker had ordered supply boats to await his army's triumphant arrival. But around Culpeper, Rooney Lee's smaller force tied up Averell, rather than vice versa. Muddled messages from Stoneman further confused Averell, and Hooker was surprised to find out that he had frittered away two days at Rapidan Station, about 25 miles west of Chancellorsville, staring across the river at cavalryman Lee. Furious, at 6:30 P.M., May 1, Hooker ordered this message to Averell:

> I am directed by the Major-general commanding to inform you that he does not understand what you are doing at Rapidan station. If this finds you at that place, you will immediately return to United States Ford, and remain there until further orders, and report in person.
>
> P.S. If this reaches you at one o'clock in the morning you will start immediately.[40]

But communications were not that swift. The order took twelve hours to reach Averell, and another 16 hours passed before he arrived, at 10:30 P.M. on May 2, at Ely's Ford. His division was therefore useless in either following Jackson's move or spanning the wide gap on Hooker's western flank between the Turnpike and the Rapidan.

If Hooker had prudently used all his superior cavalry strength, or any part of it, the climax of the battle would have been different. Jeb Stuart's horsemen performed almost perfectly during Jackson's march, providing a moving screen along the column's right. Without it, at least one of those many Federal probes was likely to have got close enough to convince even Devens, Howard, or Hooker of what was happening.

Fitz Lee's brigade formed that screen for Jackson, with Col. Thomas T. Munford's 2nd Virginia Cavalry in the van. Munford was a loquacious, contentious VMI man who had been a planter before the war. He fought with Jackson in the Valley, taking command of his cavalry after the redoubtable Turner Ashby's death, and was in every engagement, large and small. Twice wounded at Second Manassas, Munford liked to ride out front. One of his favorite tales shows how Germans were taunted in both the heterogeneous Yankee ranks and the relatively homogeneous Army of Northern Virginia.

Munford obviously was jealous of Stuart's aide Heros von Borcke, and related how once on the road the enthusiastic Prussian had brought him a message from Stuart. Lingering, von Borcke spotted some blackberries along the roadside. "He gathered a hand full," recalled Munford—"many of them black and well ripe, others red and very bitter. I saw him make a 'rye' face. When I smiled he said, 'What for you laugh?' I remarked, 'They are green.' 'Vot you zay? Ze black berry is green? Ven he is rad? How can a man ever learn so dam languish as dis? Ze black berry is green? He is no green, he is red as fire. . . .' "[41]

Protecting Jackson's right flank, Munford's regiment followed trails through the woods parallel to the infantry route. For a while he rode alongside Jackson and Brig. Gen. Robert Rodes, who commanded the lead division. Brig. Gen. Raleigh Colston came up to report all going well in his division, which followed Rodes. Briefly, Jackson let his conversation wander to more relaxed times. He recalled that all four of them had VMI connections—Rodes and Colston had been teachers, and Munford cadet adjutant, when Jackson arrived there.

Rodes, a militia general's son from Lynchburg, had graduated from the Institute in 1848, and hoped for the professorship that was awarded Jackson instead. Disappointed, he left to become a civil engineer on an Alabama railroad, married an Alabama girl, and at the outbreak of war came into service as colonel of the 5th Alabama, the regiment he chose to lead his division's march that day. Since then, Rodes had been badly wounded while distinguishing himself at Seven Pines, South Mountain, and Antietam, and any long-ago rivalry was forgotten.[42]

Trotting along together, the four officers spoke of the many other VMI alumni in the long column behind, and that brought Jackson back to matters at hand.

"I hear it said that General Hooker has more men than he can handle," he mused. "I should like to have half as many more as I have today, and I should hurl him in the river! The trouble with us has always been to have a reserve to throw in at the critical moment to reap the benefit of advantage gained. We have always had to put in all our troops and never had enough at the time most needed."[43]

As Jackson rode up the Brock Road, a courier caught him, bringing a message from Lee, back beyond Chancellorsville:

> General: I have received your note of 10½ to-day. I have given directions to all the commanders to keep a watch for any engagement which may take place in rear of Chancellorsville and to make as strong

a demonstration as possible with infantry & Artillery & prevent any troops from being withdrawn in their front. I sent a dispatch to Gen. Stuart a short time since to your care saying that the enemy had reached Trevilians & was tearing up the R.Road Central there. Force stated from one to four thousand. Everything is quiet in front at present.

Very respectfully, your obedient servant,

R. E. Lee
General[44]

Jackson obviously had advised Lee of his progress after passing Catharine Furnace, and wanted to be sure Lee would distract Hooker on the Union left flank. Reassured, he pressed on. About one o'clock, Munford's cavalrymen reached the Orange Plank Road, where it angled northeast toward the Turnpike and Howard's line. This was the way Jackson expected to aim at the Federal flank. Turning up that road, Munford's regiment stopped at Hickman's farm, a mile and a quarter from the Turnpike. Munford sent a squadron farther on, which struck a picket of the 8th Pennsylvania Cavalry and drove it in. The Rebel squadron got a good look at Howard's line, and reported back to Munford and Fitz Lee, who had just ridden up. Shortly afterward Jackson appeared, leading his infantry up the Brock Road. Fitz Lee galloped to meet him.

"General," he began, motioning Jackson a few steps off the road, "if you will ride with me, halting your columns here out of sight, I will show you the enemy's right, and you will perceive the great advantage of attacking down the old Turnpike instead of the Plank Road, the enemy's lines being taken in reverse. Bring only one courier, as you will be in view from the top of the hill."

Jackson felt young Lee's concern, and halted the infantry. He followed Lee across the Plank Road and into the woods, across the Germanna Ford Road, to clear ground at the Burton farm. From there, across a little creek valley, they could see Howard's line along the Turnpike.

Lee swept his arm in that direction. Jackson was close enough to see individual soldiers. He could see their trenches, with fallen trees in front. With their arms stacked, the Federal troops were relaxed, talking, smoking, lighting campfires. None seemed worried or even conscious that 28,000 Southern troops were swinging onto their flank.

All this had to exhilarate Jackson, to come so far and risk so much and find the enemy unsuspecting, wide open to attack. "His eyes burned with a brilliant glow, lighting his sad face," Fitz Lee recalled. But as Lee talked, Jackson was looking west beyond the Union troops directly before them. Where was the end of Howard's line, where it reportedly dangled in the air?

To the east, Jackson had spotted freshly thrown earth just over half a mile away at the Melzi Chancellor farm (the same Dowdall's Tavern where Howard was headquartered—not Chancellorsville itself, which was another two miles in that direction). Seemingly that was where the Federals meant to stand. If that had been the end of Howard's line, Jackson could do what he intended, turn up the Plank Road to hit the enemy's flank and rear. Now he realized the line ran on west beyond that.

Fitz Lee was right. Clearly, unless Jackson wanted to angle into the enemy's line after marching all day to get around it, he would have to keep going another mile and a half up the Brock Road and turn back when he reached the Turnpike. That would cost more precious time, an hour or even two with such a long column to bring up and deploy, but it could not be helped.

His decision made, Jackson sent his courier back to tell Rodes to move on across the Plank Road and stop at the Turnpike. There, Jackson would join him. With another glance toward the unaware Union troops, Jackson turned back down the knoll. Lee remembered how the general's arms flapped up and down as he rode; he was afraid Jackson would pitch right over Little Sorrel's head, so far was his mind from horsemanship.

Back at the Brock Road, Jackson saw that Rodes was pushing on. Snapping orders, he told Fitz Lee to take Brig. Gen. Frank Paxton's Stonewall Brigade with a cavalry detachment and guard his right flank, blocking the Plank Road at its junction with the Germanna Ford Road. He told Munford to protect the other flank by moving his 2nd Virginia Cavalry up the Ely's Ford Road once the attack was under way. As Munford nodded, Jackson remembered their conversation about VMI and sent him off by saying, "Colonel, the Institute will be heard from today!" [45]

Beside the long infantry column, Jackson realized that R. E. Lee to the east was expecting to hear the guns of the flank attack at any time. Without bothering to dictate to an aide, he produced a pencil and spread a sheet of notepaper over the pommel of his saddle. Little Sorrel fidgeted, stretching down to reach the tender spring grass. In a rough hand, Jackson wrote to Lee:

Near 3 P.M.
May 2d, 1863
General,
  The enemy has made a stand at Chancellor's which is about miles
from Chancellorsville. I hope as soon as practicable to attack.
  I trust that an ever kind Providence will bless us with great success.

Respectfully,
T.J. Jackson
Lt. Genl.

Scanning the message, Jackson inserted a "2" between "about" and
"miles." Before handing it to a courier, he looked up at the troops moving
past and turned to watch more still coming, as far as he could see back
down the Brock Road. He scrawled:

Genl. R.E. Lee
  The leading division is up and the next two appear to be well-
closed.

T.J.J.[46]

Capt. Marcellus Moorman and his battery of Stuart's horse artillery
trotted ahead of Rodes's lead regiment, Col. J. M. Hall's 5th Alabama
Infantry, when they reached the Turnpike about 2:30. At Jackson's direction, the column turned east on the pike for less than a mile and stopped
on a long, low north-south ridge near Luckett's farmhouse. That was six
miles west-northwest of where the Alabamians had started their day. To
get there, they had tramped more than 12 miles through the woods in
roughly eight hours. It was nowhere near a record march; many a day,
Jackson's foot cavalry had covered twice as many miles. It is famous not
for its time or distance, but for its daring, and for what those troops and
their general did at the end of it.

  Jackson had studied and prayed for what lay before him. Every professional soldier, from cadet to commander, dreams of bringing his troops to
the line of departure against an unsuspecting enemy, with the battle and
perhaps the war in the balance. Few, however long their careers, get there.
Jackson knew that, and meant to make the most of the chance by thoroughly preparing his assault. But time was against him. He had started
late. He had added more than two miles and two hours when he found out
the Union line extended farther west than he expected. The head of his
column was ready to deploy, but most of his troops were still strung out

on the Turnpike, down the Brock Road and along trails in the Wilderness. Those enemy lookouts and pickets had been tracking his movement and pecking at it all day, and kept on even as he ordered his generals to deploy their regiments through the woods. At any moment some Yankee in authority could come to his senses and take his sentries seriously.

The hour grew late; the sun would set at 6:48, and darkness would fall swiftly in the thick woods. To spread battle lines through those woods was a tedious process. Close control of troops half-hidden in the thickets would be impossible. Any general in his place would be tempted to throw his forward troops into the attack immediately, before all these elements turned success into disaster. But Jackson, having risked so much, now risked more. He could roll up Howard's flank, but that was not enough. He could rout Hooker's army, "hurl him in the river." He wanted to destroy it. This day's work could decide the war.

He had reached not only Hooker's flank but his rear, the unprotected span between the Turnpike and the Rapidan. If Jackson were willing to attack on a narrow front along the Turnpike, he could get his assault under way quickly. But in that case, once he penetrated far enough, the depth of Hooker's force would allow Yankee brigades beyond the flank to sag in on the sides of Jackson's spearhead, and possibly surround his lead units. To make sure that did not happen, Jackson would sacrifice more time. He would go at Hooker on such a broad front that whenever his troops hit a strongpoint they would flow around and envelop it—so broad that their own flanks would not be exposed as they advanced.

Jackson ordered three lines of battle, extending a mile into the woods on each side of the Turnpike. Rodes would form the first line, with sharpshooting pickets some 400 yards to his front. Colston's smaller division came next, about 100 yards behind. Following it by 200 yards, commanding an abbreviated third line, was A. P. Hill.

From left to right, the brigades in Rodes's front line were Alfred Iverson's North Carolinians and Edward O'Neal's Alabamians north of the Turnpike, and George Doles's and Alfred Colquitt's Georgians to the south.

Colston's second line had Francis T. Nicholls's Louisianans on the left, then John R. Jones's Virginians and E. T. H. Warren's mixed Virginia–North Carolina brigade. Dodson Ramseur's North Carolina troops dropped back from Rodes's front line on the right, to cover that flank of the advance.

Hill's third line started to form with Henry Heth's Virginians and W. Dorsey Pender's North Carolinians both north of the Turnpike. Of Hill's

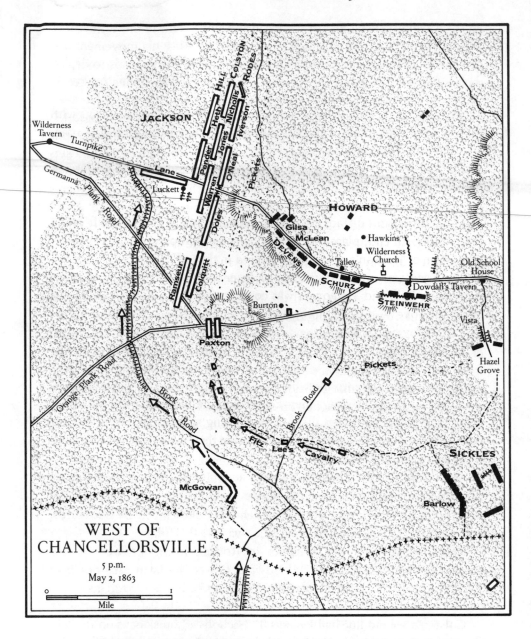

WEST OF CHANCELLORSVILLE

5 p.m.
May 2, 1863

0   1
Mile

8. Poised to Strike. *Jackson spreads his infantry through the undergrowth for a mile on each side of the Turnpike, positioned to overlap and roll up Howard's unsuspecting corps. Three of Jackson's brigades and most of his artillery are still strung out in the Wilderness.*

other brigades, James H. Lane was still arriving on the Turnpike and Samuel McGowan was farther back. Only about this time did Jackson find out that the last two, Archer and Thomas, had turned around to help fight off Sickles at the furnace, and were barely halfway along the march route.

The Turnpike was wide enough for only two cannon to move abreast. A pair from Capt. James Breathed's Stuart Horse Artillery lined up with Rodes, while two more of his plus Moorman's two followed in the road, ready to move up and take turns firing. The 20 guns of Rodes's division artillery, commanded by Lt. Col. T. H. Carter, assembled in a clearing right of the road near Hill's line. The rest of Jackson's artillery was still back along the way.[47]

Thus, the weight of Jackson's three assault waves was on the left of the road, the north end, placed to come down on the open rear of Hooker's army. Ten of Jackson's 15 brigades arrived in time to deploy in those three waves. Lane was on the Turnpike close enough to advance in column, supporting Hill, and McGowan was coming up behind Lane. Paxton was ready to move in on the right when the attack cleared the Plank Road.

But deploying those thousands of troops for a mile in each direction, off the road through that Wilderness, took infinitely longer than diagramming where they would go. Most of the infantry got a brief rest on arrival, then regiments sifted into the woods, men sometimes losing sight of those ahead. Crouching, twisting, they kept going and could hardly believe it when their officers prodded them to keep going still farther. They did not need orders to be quiet; they knew how close they were to the enemy, and some of the enemy knew, too.

About four o'clock, the two Yankee cannon at the angle of von Gilsa's line let go at Fitz Lee's screening horsemen.[48] This salvo, fired without orders, alarmed Col. George von Amsberg's 45th New York, and its infantrymen grabbed their muskets and sent a volley toward the Southern cavalry. But the noise did not alert the rest of the Eleventh Corps any more than the rest of the potshotting that had gone on all day. Von Amsberg sent two picket details into the woods.

After waiting with one of them, listening a while, Lt. A. B. Searles "began to hear a queer jumble of sounds, a confusion of orders." He even thought he remembered "their bugles sounding the call to deploy. It was only now and then that we caught the notes, but they would come with startling distinctness at times, and we could hear an order occasionally, too, quite plainly." Searles sent a sergeant in to warn von Amsberg of "an immense mass of men on our flank," but got no response. He sent other soldiers to follow up, until the last of them came back and reported that

General Howard had scoffed, "Lieutenant Searles must not be scared at a few bushwhackers."[49]

All fell quiet again. Back at Chancellorsville, Joe Hooker still thought he was riding high. As Jackson was preparing to strike the Union army from flank and rear, Hooker's mind was at play in the other direction. At 4:10, he had sent yet another in his series of messages to Sedgwick, urging the Sixth Corps to take Fredericksburg "and vigorously pursue the enemy." "We know the enemy is fleeing, trying to save his trains," he said confidently.[50]

Beyond the thickets, beside Luckett's farmhouse a few hundred yards out the Turnpike, Jackson kept looking at his pocket watch. From far back east, the sound of gunfire drifted and helped cover the unavoidable rustling of his troops deploying through the undergrowth. Captain Moorman of the horse artillery asked Jackson what that gunfire might be. "How far do you suppose it is?" Jackson asked. "Five or six miles," Moorman estimated. "I suppose it is General Lee," said Jackson, and it was. Even as his men stretched out through the woods, on Hooker's other flank Lee was hammering away, just as he had said he would. Hooker was responding as if Lee and Jackson had written his part—still sending units away from the center of his lines to help Sickles against Lee's counterattacks.

Jackson, after keeping his plan quiet during the march, made certain that each brigadier had clear instructions for the assault. Issuing new orders, shifting regiments, would be nearly impossible in that forest. Everyone must know what to do, and it must be simple:

Guide on the Turnpike. Aim first for Talley's farm, just over a mile ahead, on a gentle leftward bend in the road. The rise there seemed to command the next objective—Melzi Chancellor's house, Dowdall's Tavern, Howard's headquarters. The Yankees might make a stand there, as Jackson guessed when he viewed their line with Fitz Lee. If so, the leading infantry would take shelter while the artillery moved up to blast them out. Ramseur would keep close watch on the right, allowing Colquitt to push ahead without worrying about that flank. One of Iverson's regiments, the 23rd North Carolina, would face outward for the same purpose on the far left. When the bugles sounded, the entire line would sweep forward together. Above all, "Under no circumstances was there to be any pause in the advance."[51]

Five o'clock passed as the regiments stretched through the woods. Jackson's blue eyes were alight. He checked the time again, looked right and left. Rodes had seen to the alignment of his division as its ranks disappeared in the undergrowth. He rode back and halted his horse near

Jackson, tense, waiting. Maj. Eugene Blackford of the 5th Alabama trotted up with a bugler and reported that the skirmishers were out. One last time, Jackson reached under his coat and took out his watch.

It was 5:15 P.M., Saturday, May 2, 1863. The sun was low in the clear sky, and the shadow of the woods behind them fell long across the farmhouse clearing.*[52]

Jackson looked up. He spoke calmly, almost gently:

"Are you ready, General Rodes?"

"Yes, sir,"

"You can go forward, then."[53]

---

*Various accounts start the advance as early as four and as late as seven o'clock. Colston reported it at "6 o'clock precisely," Hill at "about 6 P.M." Few Civil War soldiers carried watches; those who did could not synchronize them before action. Minutes elapsed between Jackson's order, his troops' movement, and their reaching the Union lines. For soldiers judging the time by sun and light, much depended on whether they were in thicket or clearing.

Chapter Eleven

SUCH A STAMPEDE NEVER WAS SEEN

OUTSIDE HIS Eleventh Corps command post at Dowdall's Tavern, Oliver Otis Howard told a battery of gunners to "Unharness those horses, boys, give them a good feed of oats. We'll be off for Richmond at daylight." On Howard's western flank, in a tone almost as confident, Devens's division headquarters passed the word to eat supper. The troops needed no order. They had already stacked their muskets back of the firing pits by the Turnpike, and some of the German soldiers were slaughtering the cattle that had been driven along to provide fresh beef.

Music began to drift from clearing to clearing, regiment to regiment. In the 75th Ohio, a private with a fiddle was playing the doleful "Tell My Mother When You See Her." Somebody told him to get into the prevailing mood—"Play something cheerful . . . something we can sing!" The smell of sizzling bacon and frying potatoes lifted spirits. Field officers, having thoughtfully managed to bring extra baggage and rations, dined around a table, seated in proper chairs. The regimental supply wagon rolled up the Turnpike, and applause broke out. Hollis Brooks mixed flour and water in his tin cup, then twisted the dough into a long snake, wrapped it around his ramrod and browned it over the coals of his squad campfire.

As he bit into the hot, crisp roll, somebody shouted, "A deer!" Ordinarily, when a deer blundered into camp, hungry soldiers fell all over themselves laughing and trying to corral it, and now and then they actually tackled one and turned it into venison for supper. But this deer was bounding away in panic. There came another out of the thickets to the west. A flock of turkeys flapped out of the woods. Songbirds and scared rabbits followed. A crackle of rifle fire sounded beyond them. Somebody said he didn't know there were pickets that close.[1]

At five-thirty, General Devens had just started along the line and stopped behind the 55th Ohio to talk with a cavalry captain when a shell whooshed down the Turnpike and burst directly over their heads. Another round landed in the 153rd Pennsylvania at the far western hook of Howard's line, killing one man; the next ripped a Private Rupley's arm into shreds at the elbow. The first round to strike the 45th New York alongside killed two privates and temporarily disabled Colonel von Amsberg.[2]

As the Yankee troops scrambled for cover, they heard something many had not experienced before, but recognized immediately. A high, screeching yell, yipping, then long drawn out, rose out of the woods, seeming to come from front, left, right, and behind. One of Hooker's soldiers spelled it "*Yyyeee-ooohhh! Yyyeee-ooohhh!*" Others on other days heard it differently, because it varied from regiment to regiment, battle to battle, but one New York soldier said that here it seemed more shrill than on any other field. Jackson himself had called it "the sweetest music I ever heard." The Georgia poet Sidney Lanier, who heard it on the Peninsula, called it "a single long cry, as from the leader of a pack of hounds who has found the game . . . a dry harsh quality that conveys an uncompromising hostility . . . the irresistible outflow of some fierce soul immeasurably enraged, tinged with a jubilant tone, as if in anticipation of a speedy triumph and a satisfying revenge . . . a howl, a hoarse battle-cry, a cheer, and a congratulation, all in one."[3] All who heard it remembered it.

"Johnnies! Johnnies!"

Pots and pans clattered, troops raced for their muskets as Yankees shouted the alarm. The underbrush before them came alive, trembling and crackling as if a storm of buffalo were rolling onto the Union positions.

Jackson's infantry had waited kneeling in the thickets until at last the order came to move ahead. But the skirmishers on their left did not get the word to advance until Rodes's battle line was upon them. This confusion brought a minute's halt while the skirmishers reopened their distance ahead. Then bugles sounded up and down the line and it drove on. As the attackers came close enough to see light ahead in the clearing, they forced their way through the dark undergrowth, holding their muskets out front at high port to protect their eyes from branches that switched back in their faces. Catbriers strong as cable ripped their arms and legs, tore their hats away. The troops' long hurry-up march had been one challenge, their deployment and struggle through the thickets another, and when they burst out of the woods and the cannon fired that first salvo the foot soldiers let go their Rebel yell, sounding already triumphant at the battle's beginning.

Lieutenant Searles of the 45th New York, beyond von Gilsa's line with his picket detail, took the first shock of the assault. "We fired upon them and preserved a line of battle among the trees," he recalled, "—although there are those who say we didn't. They returned our fire. . . . When they fired the leaves came fluttering down upon us as though a thunder storm had broken loose and torn them from the branches with its spiteful hail." As his pickets dropped back toward the regiment, their own comrades fired on them, not knowing who they were, killing one man. Moments after the pickets rejoined, the 45th fell back with the rest of the line.[4]

Out on that most exposed flank, a company officer in the 153rd Pennsylvania watched the "wild enthusiasm" of the oncoming Rebels with awe. The attackers' lines, already broken up by the thickets, "compacted again and again . . . by the ceaseless 'Close up' of the officers, swept forward like a cyclone. . . . Obstacles that had harassed our advance, and hampered our retreat, yielded to the fierce momentum of an army in three-fold volume of masses, all saturated with the spirit of their almost superhuman leader. . . . they did not even reply to the resolute skirmish fire which was vigorously maintained at stand after stand, from tree to tree. . . . The confident enthusiasm and resolute ardor of that massive attack, clad in ashen gray and simple trappings, have never been surpassed. The wrath of God pervaded it. . . ."[5]

Von Gilsa sent a captain forward to tell his enveloped brigade to withdraw. When that officer was shot down he sent another, who was shot down in turn. Then von Gilsa rode forward himself, pistols drawn, screaming commands in both English and German. In the left half of the 17th Connecticut, Maj. Allen G. Brady at first told his men to hold; the regiment was divided, straddling a battery pointed south from the Turnpike. But those guns had taken off without firing. The major had no new orders, so was unsure what to do. With Rebels coming from front and flank, his men could neither change front nor fire back. Brady told them to take to the woods—and as young Justus Silliman said, "I believe there were [a] few who started before the order was given. Many of us stuck to the major, however, as he made about as good time as any of us through the woods."[6] Major Brady took command of the regiment after the colonel was wounded and the lieutenant colonel killed. He said that "not a man belonging to the battery stood at his post when the attack commenced, and neither did they undertake to fire a gun."[7]

After von Gilsa's men launched a few volleys, mainly over the heads of the oncoming Rebels, they reeled back onto McLean's brigade behind them. There, Sergeant Major Lowe of the 55th Ohio had just pointed out a deer fleeing from the woods when a ball scorched his scalp, and attackers came piling out of the timber. A Rebel color-bearer crashed through the skimpy abatis waving his flag. Luther Mesnard fired five shots, then scuttled across the road between charges of canister. Wounded and dead troops lay in the Turnpike, and he tried to squeeze into the earth as pellets raked the road and rolled one of the bodies over.[8]

Confederate Maj. R. F. Beckham, with Stuart's horse artillery, had put two guns abreast under Capt. James Breathed in the Turnpike, to move forward just behind the skirmishers. Moorman's battery followed, ready to come up. For many Union survivors, that opening burst from Breathed's Napoleons was the first they heard of the onslaught, so they thought it was a signal gun. Many also thought they had been singled out as targets for that burst. First Sgt. James Peabody of the 61st Ohio, more than half a mile back at the Turnpike–Plank Road intersection, looked westward up the line and saw a chunk of iron ricocheting along the slope. He watched it coming and could not dodge as it struck his ankle, knocking him down. He thought he had lost his heel, but couldn't see anything missing. By that time, the line was peeling back past him. "It would have not been good generalship on my part to have stopped and made a close examination," he said, "so I followed the rest."[9]

That night and in reminiscing years later, most soldiers of the Eleventh Corps were frank about what happened; there was no point in denying it. They had never witnessed anything like it before, not even in the flight from First Bull Run. Von Gilsa put the best face possible on the rout, but to do it he had to magnify the few brief steady moments.

He maintained that before the onslaught, he had seen that without any reserve he would have to pull out if attacked strongly. He told of asking Devens to send him some backup force, and getting none except the 75th Ohio behind his left wing. He said that fifteen minutes after cavalry had ridden in reporting no enemy at all out front, the patrol of the 45th New York told of Rebels massing opposite his line. Even as he passed this on to Devens, his skirmishers were driven in by "overwhelming forces of the enemy."

> The whole line was at once engaged furiously, and my brigade stood coolly and bravely, fired three times, and stood still after they had outflanked me already on my right. The enemy attacked now from the front and rear, and then, of course, my brave boys were

obliged to fall back. . . . Retreating, I expected surely to rally my brigade behind our second line, formed by [Schurz's] Division, but I did not find the second line; it was abandoned before we reached it.

I am obliged to express my thanks to the men of my brigade, with very few exceptions, for the bravery and coolness which they have shown in repulsing three attacks, and they retreated only after being attacked in front and from the rear at the same time; but I am also compelled to blame most of my line officers that they did not or could not rally their companies half a mile or a mile more back, no matter if it could be done under the protection of a second line, and I hope that in the next engagement every officer and man of my brigade will try to redeem this unsoldierlike conduct.[10]

McLean, over whose brigade those men fled, put up a stiffer fight. Though his own position began a good half mile behind the western angle of von Gilsa's line, the Confederate attack came on so broadly that almost from the first it struck both his front and rear. The two cannon pointed west from the angle with von Gilsa fired only a few times before breaking back down the road behind the rifle pits.

At that moment, McLean realized "from the rush of fugitives from the right flank" that von Gilsa's brigade had given way, and ordered the 25th Ohio to pivot rightward and deploy against the oncoming Southerners. Col. William P. Richardson turned the 25th "with as much precision as if on parade." Richardson was severely wounded as his outfit, like the 75th Ohio, kept firing till ordered back. McLean reported that all five of his regiments stood as long as possible "under the circumstances"—"They were all exposed to a tremendous fire of musketry and grape and canister from artillery." Four of his regimental commanders were wounded.

The generals lifted some of the onus from themselves and their soldiers by repeatedly speaking in awe of the attack, of its breadth and ferocity. Later, even their critics acknowledged that no force so deployed could have stood up to such an assault.

When Bill Southerton of the 75th heard someone yell "Johnnies!" he and the men around him rushed for their stacked weapons. Before they could untangle the muskets, some troops were shot down by a sheet of Rebel fire. Bill hid behind a clump of trees, gnawed the paper from his cartridges and loaded his musket. Aiming at a billow of smoke, he fired. A Confederate officer galloped across the clearing, took a shot at him and wheeled his horse about. Southerton fired every cartridge he had, but could not tell whether he hit the Rebel officer. Suddenly beside him his friend Perly fell, then the tree where Perly huddled toppled over on him, smoking. Branches came crashing down, sheared off by shellfire. Southerton called his messmate Nat Green, looked around, and saw him lying dead. Gray soldiers, their flagstaffs angled forward, sprinted cursing and yelling along the Turnpike. Solid shot and canister swept the Yankee lines.

Southerton was alone, his friends dead around him. Dodging from tree to stump, tearing through brambles, he scrambled away. When he hurdled a log he came down on the belly of a German soldier hiding in the brush. *"Mein Gott in Himmel!"* the man cried, and Southerton recognized him as a soldier of the 41st New York, von Gilsa's brigade. "Get out of here!" Bill yelled. "The Rebels will get you. . . . They'll run the bayonet right through you!" The man refused to move. Bill ran on and bumped into a black boy crying as he tugged at the bridle of an injured mule, an officer's tent strapped to its back. "Let the mule go!" Southerton shouted. "A foot is shot off! Get out! The Rebels will kill you!" Then at last he came on somebody trying to fight back.

Col. Robert Reily of the 75th was screaming orders through his cupped hands, forming a skimpy battle line abreast a shed in a Wilderness clearing. Southerton joined it, and for perhaps ten minutes Reily's men held on. The Rebel yell knifed through the din. Streaks of red fire flared in the white smoke ahead, and Gray infantry rolled up like an unstoppable wave. Mules bellowed, wounded horses screamed.

Reily was killed and his little knot of resistance was surrounded. Southerton fell to the ground, felt for cartridges. They were gone. He plunged back into the tangled woods. The ground shook as cannon boomed. Clawing at vines, Southerton ran with an arm up to shield his face. Eventually he stopped, gasping for breath in the dusk, and realized his blanket roll and haversack were gone. He had only his musket, his empty cartridge belt, and his empty canteen. He had no idea how far he had run.[11]

Early in the war, Northern soldiers had a pet word to tell how Rebels ran in retreat. After Chancellorsville, the Rebels used it to describe the Yankee rout, and the Yankees used it on themselves: Southerton, Mesnard, and thousands of Northern troops around them *skedaddled* away from Stonewall Jackson's oncoming battle lines. Journalists and historians solemnly discussed the etymology of "skedaddle." One British nobleman maintained that it was old Scottish, but the London *Spectator* insisted it came from the Greek *"skedannumi,"* to disperse or retire tumultuously. The Louisville *Journal* found variants in Homer, Hesiod, Herodotus,

Thucydides, and Xenophon, and concluded it was "a classic word, full of expression." Hooker's troops in the Wilderness knew nothing of its origin, but everything of its meaning.[12]

Among the few on Howard's flank who did not skedaddle were the cannoneers of "Leather Breeches" Dilger's 1st Ohio Light battery. If anything besides confusion slowed Jackson's attack in the early going, it was Dilger's guns, posted where the Orange Plank Road angled into the Turnpike. Gunner Darwin Cody wrote his parents how, when the Rebels attacked, "we poured the shell into them" until the attacking artillery opened with two batteries and the Union infantry alongside his guns started to run. "Our support was all Germans," Cody complained. "They run without firing a gun. Such yelling I never heard before as the Rebs made." The battery was left alone. When the Confederates came within 80 yards, Dilger ordered the guns to limber up. The battery fell back toward Wilderness Church and set up again, aiming straight down the road.[13]

STONEWALL JACKSON himself rode close behind his attacking troops. This was the chance he had lived for, asked God for. The calm with which he had ordered the advance was long gone. As his soldiers surged around him, his eyes flared and he shouted again and again, "Press on! Press on!" When a cheer rose from the assault line, he tilted his head back and said thanks as he rode on. Now and then he looked upward and raised that arm like Joshua, as if reaching up to touch another hand for strength. When he came upon a heap of fallen Gray soldiers, he stopped and raised the arm again, seeming to pray—and then slashed it ahead toward Chancellorsville. "Forward, men, forward! Press forward!"[14]

Jackson's soldiers, after marching all day and struggling through the thickets to their line of departure, attacked as wildly as any fresh troops in the whole war. When George Doles gave his Georgians the word, they started running and yelling, stopping to let go a full volley that scattered the first line of Yankees. A soldier in the 44th said, "When we once got them going, we pressed them back over and farther and farther, untill they got up a perfect stampede, leaving behind, in our hands, every thing that was cumberous . . . quite a number of fine horses, as well as all of their killed & wounded, and a grate many firearms."[15]

"Unprecedented chaos!" another of the attackers called it. There was "unparalleled confusion" among the surprised Yankees, but "excitement reigned high in our own ranks," he recalled. "One man near me was almost *non compos mentis,* emitting ear-splitting yells and firing aimlessly into the air." When his outfit struck the enemy pickets, "their arms were stacked and their astonishment was far beyond flight. So sudden was our appearance among them that they did not even rise from over their steaming suppers"—suppers that tempted the hungry Rebels to stop. The Federals "surrendered seated or half-bent, in speechless wonderment." As the attack pushed on past Devens's breastworks, one Union gunner, "perhaps daring beyond the insistence of his conscience, lingered to discharge at us (I could have sworn at me)," the Rebel recalled. "The heavy charge of iron, loosed but 30 yards away, rent the air above my head with multi-hideous sound. But on we rushed, and in their unexampled, mad attempt at flight, men, horses and cannon, obstructed by the dense second-growth jungle, were captured like entrapped rats."

Leaping a ditch, this Rebel looked down and saw it "literally congested with large and small blue-bodied sardines—very frightened Yankees who sought frantically to hide beneath our feet. I recall very clearly the facial expression of a little man directly under me. Pale-faced, out of arm-shielded and fear-dilated eyes he stared up at me. . . . How tenaciously that picture of piteous fear has clung to my memory."[16]

Companies, whole regiments of Union troops, were careening backward before Jackson's onslaught. As one brigade piled onto another, the weight of the fleeing units multiplied. Horses, wagons, caissons, frantic cattle became part of the rush, bearing down on the yet unpanicked commands behind. Some of the front-line Northern commanders fled with their troops. Each time an officer turned around and tried to organize a new line, he was quickly overwhelmed. The generals who had allowed the disaster, guilty of willful blindness rather than cowardice, realized that not only their commands, their army, but their precious reputations were being demolished. So they faced the enemy, trying to stop the flood of fleeing soldiers and save what was left of their futures. But even as the Confederate attack exploded through their lines, some still refused to admit what was happening.

Jackson's men were driving onto the flank of the 55th Ohio when Col. John C. Lee galloped to tell Devens, and ask permission to change front to face the enemy. Devens's only response, even then, was "Not yet." When Lee returned to the line and saw that von Gilsa's brigade had given way, he rode to Devens and asked again. "Without getting any orders whatever," he raced back to his regiment and turned it on his own. They could not hold long, but their effort helped save Hooker's army from worse defeat. Colonel Lee's companies fell back to join Maj. Jeremiah

Williams, who had taken command of the 25th Ohio when Colonel Richardson was wounded. Williams had managed to pivot the 25th, keeping its left on the road. Together the Ohio regiments stood with platoons of men falling until the wave of Rebels was only steps away. In those minutes five of Williams's 16 officers and more than 130 of his 333 enlisted troops were killed, wounded, or captured. After that clash, Lee said of his 55th, "As a regiment it could not rally." [17]

When Colonel Lee's men made their brief stand with the 25th, Luther Mesnard crouched against "a perfect hail storm of lead flying, a perfect mass of rebs not 20 feet away." The men on both sides of him fell, the regiment's right was overlapped and crumbled, and he ran—"how I did run." He overtook Paul Jones, who had picked up the regimental colors. Jones had the flag in one hand and with the other arm supported General Devens, who had been shot in the foot as he belatedly tried to rally his division. Soon Jones caught up again, now without the general. "Oh, damn him," he explained. "He is drunk." [18]

Although his 55th Ohio was shattered, Lee tried yet again to rally some fugitives at a low breastworks overlooking a little valley. There, Mesnard thought the Confederates seemed badly mixed up, but they rampaged on in three lines, taking turns firing over one another's heads as they came down the opposite slope. A Union battery on the right "plowed great gaps through their ranks," and Mesnard thought sure that this time the defenders would hold. But suddenly the battery was gone, and so were the infantrymen around him. Mesnard started to run again. "I think it was the most dangerous place I was ever in," he recalled. "I had always thought somehow that the Lord was not going to let me be killed in the war, and I remember thinking this was the test case. 'If the Lord was ever going to do anything for old Ira, now's the time,' to quote from a well known negro story which came into my mind at the time, as I saw the dead and wounded so thick on the ground and heard the lead and cannon shot so filling the air." Running on, he stumbled into a clearing. "To the right or left or in front as far as I could see, everything was fleeing in panic. It seemed to me that the whole army had gone to pieces in a panic. All was lost—Oh my country, can this be? There was no one near whom I knew. I look back to this as the darkest day in my war experience. . . ." [19]

A CONFIDENT O. O. HOWARD was at his headquarters at Dowdall's when Jackson struck. He and von Steinwehr had just returned from Sickles's front when he told the gunners nearby to unharness their horses and get a good rest. Then he heard cannon to the west, and a rattle of musketry. He sent his chief of staff, Col. Charles Asmussen, to see what was happening in front of Devens. Howard himself rode toward Schurz's division, hoping to turn its two brigades to face the apparent attack. As soon as he entered the clearing along the ridge at Talley's house, he realized the Confederates had driven in his front and enveloped his right, and von Gilsa's men were fleeing.

Before he could issue any order, he was surrounded by the rout—

> not the few stragglers that always fly like chaff at the first breeze, but scores . . . rushing into the opening, some with arms and some without, running or falling. . . . The noise and the smoke filled the air with excitement, and to add to it Dieckmann's guns and caissons, with battery men scattered, rolled and tumbled like runaway wagons and carts in a thronged city. The guns and masses of the right brigade struck the second line of Devens before McLean's front had given way; and more quickly than it could be told, with all the fury of the wildest hailstorm, everything, every sort of organization that lay in the path of the mad current of panic-stricken men had to give way and be broken into fragments.[20]

On his horse amid Schurz's troops, Howard tried to redeploy the regiments around him to confront the attack. But all his efforts to turn back the retreat were in vain as the avalanche of fleeing men, horses, cattle, guns, came down upon him. In his report, he said it bluntly: there was "blind panic and great confusion."

Howard jammed the staff of a U.S. flag under the stump of his amputated arm, the colors streaming across his heart. He waved his pistol in his good hand and rode at the fleeing horde, trying to stop it, turn it around. His horse reared and fell, throwing him. Orderlies helped him remount. Later, Howard said, "I felt . . . that I wanted to die. It was the only time I ever weakened that way in my life, before or since, but that night I did all in my power to remedy the mistake, and I sought death everywhere I could find an excuse to go on the field."[21]

With his staff officers, Howard tried to make a barrier against the frantic retreating troops. His aide, Capt. Francis A. Dessauer, was killed beside him. Maj. T. A. Meysenberg, his assistant adjutant general, and Lt. Col. Joseph Dickinson of Hooker's staff stood with him, swinging their sabers, cursing, threatening, firing their pistols overhead.[22] One Ohio captain, shot in the foot, limped by and looked up to see Howard "on his horse in the roadway, as cool as if on parade, but urging and insisting and entreating the flying men to go slower. . . . He was the last man off the field."[23]

Jim Peabody, of Schurz's division, ran past as Howard was trying to rally his shattered corps. His enlisted man's view of Howard was less charitable. He remembered hearing the general crying, "Halt! Halt! I'm ruined, I'm ruined! I'll shoot if you don't stop. I'm ruined, I'm ruined!" Howard clearly was "rattled," the Ohio soldier said. As Peabody watched this, suddenly at a gap in the crowd a lone Rebel soldier appeared, with no weapon. He obviously had got ahead of his outfit and confused in the woods. Some of the calmer Yankees asked what he was doing, where he came from, but the scared intruder would not answer. He edged away and started running, ignoring calls to halt. Before he had gone 50 yards, two or three Union troops raised their muskets and cut him down. As he fell, the men around Howard saw a mass of Rebels surging out of the woods on their right. Howard saw them, too, and spurred to the rear. Peabody said, "I thought he was going there to impart the same information to them he had given us; that is, 'I'm ruined.' None of us knew or cared where he went."[24]

Howard was headed to his reserve artillery. There Dickinson looked back and said, "Oh, General, see those men coming from that hill . . . there's the enemy after them. Fire, oh, fire at them; you may stop the flight!" But Howard said, "No, Colonel, I will never fire at my own men." As the fleeing troops swept past and cleared the field, the Union gunners opened on the following Rebels first with shell, then canister. Still the attackers came on, one rank halting to aim its muskets and fire, then reloading while the next line ran past, stopped, and fired. They came "in such multitudes," Howard wrote, "that our men went down before them like trees in a hurricane."[25]

By then, much of Schurz's command plus fragments of Devens's regiments, officers whose commands had disappeared, individual Yankees suddenly ashamed when they saw someone standing to fight—these scraps fell back on a line before the Wilderness Church. From the barnlike little church, rifle pits stretched north facing Hawkins's farm and swung south to end near Dowdall's Tavern. Dowdall's—Howard's headquarters, also called Melzi Chancellor's house—was the second objective Jackson had cited in his attack order; the rise at Talley's was first, and had fallen quickly. Confederate General Rodes, close behind the leading assault line, saw what seemed to him 5,000 Yankees right and left of the church, most of them facing west. For that moment they crouched and waited rather than running. Rodes called up Col. E. T. H. Warren's brigade from

Colston's division in the second assault wave. Already that second rank was on the heels of Rodes's lead division, mixing with it as the attackers charged, flowed around thickets and knots of Yankees, and drove on. Now Warren's and J. R. Jones's brigades surged forward with the leading wave.

As the Gray line came closer, Dilger's Ohio gunners loaded double canister and fired over the Union infantry in the pits ahead.[26] With each blast, the 12-pounders sprayed inch-round slugs like huge shotguns, cutting a swath through the oncoming troops. But the Confederate momentum was barely slowed. Out on the right end of Schurz's line, the 26th Wisconsin stood until it was lapped on both sides. Schurz said that without this delay, the Rebels would have converged behind his line and taken his artillery. Alongside the 26th, Capt. Frederick Braun was shot off his horse, mortally wounded, as he deployed his 58th New York. Col. Frederick Hecker of the 82nd Illinois held his regiment's colors high and ordered his men to charge with bayonets. At that instant he was shot, and within minutes Maj. Ferdinand Rolshausen, who relieved him, was struck down. Nearest the Turnpike, Col. Elias Peissner of the 119th New York was shot twice as the clash began. These brave moments were dutifully reported by Schurz, as if to prove that not all the Germans of the corps had fled.[27] But soon Jackson's troops surged around the line and the church and drove over Schurz's works.

Again the supporting riflemen abandoned Dilger, and the Rebels concentrated on his destructive cannon. They were running yelling between Dilger's guns when he ordered his men to displace again. Dilger's horse was shot from under him. Three horses with one of his pieces were shot down. Dilger tried to drag this gun along with the dead horses hanging in the harness before leaving it to the attackers.[28] Capt. Michael Wiedrich's battery of the 1st New York Light Artillery was put out of action the same way. After holding fire while retreating infantry fell back masking his guns, Wiedrich opened on the Rebels with canister, but was promptly flanked. All but one of the cannoneers manning one of his pieces were wounded. On another, four horses were killed. He had to leave both those guns behind, but dragged off another after cutting away two dead horses.[29]

When Dilger's wheelhorses were shot, wrote gunner Cody, "then we was down. We done all we could to save it. Our infantry had all left us. We had one killed and nine wounded there, and six horses killed and 10 or 14 wounded. We fell back for half a mile. . . . I say dam the DUTCH. . . . A coward will soon play out here. We had one in our battery. The Capt soon ordered charges made out against him. I hope they will shoot him. If I ever run I am willing to have them shoot me."[30]

Confederate Colonel Warren was severely wounded leading his yelling troops into the thick artillery and musket fire, but in twenty minutes the attackers had driven Schurz back, captured five cannon, and planted their battle flags on the second Federal line.

THE THICKNESS of the forest, some trick of the breeze, kept the sound of the fighting from the ears of Joe Hooker at Chancellorsville. On the pillared veranda of the house, he and his aides, Captains William Candler and Harry Russell, were sitting chatting in the balmy dusk. Occasionally they heard noise from the other direction, where Lee was jabbing at the Union lines. But for perhaps an hour after Jackson's attack began, they heard nothing from the west, and strangely nobody came to raise the alarm over what was happening there. When the faint sound of cannon fire drifted by, they assumed it was from Sickles's venture toward Catharine Furnace. They were wondering aloud how that operation was going when something caught Russell's eye west toward Dowdall's Tavern. Stepping off the porch, he lifted and focused his spyglass.

"My God!" he said. "Here they come!"[31] Hooker ran to his horse, and with Russell and Candler rode out the Plank Road toward the firing. (Of the two-mile stretch where the Orange Plank Road and the Turnpike run together between Wilderness Church and Chancellorsville, most historians have called it the Plank Road.) Washington Roebling, who was at the Chancellor house, recalled that gradually "a confused roaring sound seemed to penetrate the air, ominous and alarming, but mysterious withal." Then "a curious sight met the eye, for all the world like a stampede of cattle, a multitude of yelling, struggling men who had thrown away their muskets, panting for breath, their faces distorted by fear, filled the road as far as the eye could reach."[32]

Hooker, like Howard, was quickly surrounded by fleeing soldiers, wagons, frantic pack mules with their loads thrown and dragging in the dust. Many of the panicked troops were Howard's Germans, who screamed to the officers trying to block their way, *"Wo ist der pontoon?"*— eager to put the river again between themselves and the oncoming Rebels. Hooker and his staff turned their horses broadside to the fleeing mass, whacking at the passing men with the flat of their swords. They ordered cavalrymen to form a line across and beyond the road. Later, Hooker said that in fear that "the devils would demoralize our whole army," his staff actually killed "some of Howard's people."[33] But at that point, neither swords nor pistols could even slow the footrace.

After this first surge of excitement, the angry reaction that fit his nickname, Hooker realized that his desperate personal effort was useless, and started thinking as a general about how to prevent destruction of his army.[34]

Lee had obliged him by attacking on Hooker's chosen ground, though from the least expected direction. But was this onslaught from the west Lee's main stroke? East beyond Chancellorsville, the Confederate commander had awaited the sound of Jackson's attack. At first, he was not sure what he heard. Those guns could easily be mistaken for renewed fighting at Catharine Furnace. But as soon as the volume rose, McLaws and Anderson carried out Lee's orders to press the Union lines without overcommitting their divisions. W. T. Wofford's Georgia brigade, attacking on the left of the Turnpike, got so heavily involved that McLaws had to order it back. With Billy Mahone's brigade, pushing along the Orange Plank Road southeast of Chancellorsville, Capt. W. Carter Williams led two companies of the 6th Virginia over a Yankee abatis, took the colors of the 107th Ohio and prisoners from four different regiments. Confederate cannon banged down the Turnpike, up the Plank Road, along every byway toward Chancellorsville.

To Hooker it seemed that at any moment, along any of those routes, Lee might strike another blow. Longstreet, reported by prisoners to be arriving from below Richmond, could materialize as forcefully as he had at Second Bull Run. Hooker rode back to his headquarters. Penetration, turning movement, double envelopment—he could imagine all the possibilities in the lexicon of war, and now the choice among them was not his. He could only react. He had three corps—Meade, Couch, and Slocum—in prepared positions facing Lee on the east and south. But Lee's noisy demonstrations there might be more than show; Hooker did not dare risk withdrawing a whole corps to face Jackson's attack from the west. The biggest uncommitted Union force was Reynolds's First Corps, and its lead divisions were just starting to pitch camp after crossing the Rappahannock at U.S. Ford.

At about six-thirty, John Reynolds rode into the Chancellorsville clearing a good four miles ahead of his corps. From a quiet, rustic setting where the commanding general had been able to relax a few minutes before in the admiration of his junior aides, the clearing had turned into a frieze of chaos. Amid it a band was playing "Hail, Columbia," "The Star-Spangled Banner" and every other patriotic tune in its repertory, trying to inspire the fleeing troops to stand and fight. On the roads, organized units shifting to meet the Confederate attack had to push through the disorganized mob of fugitives. As soon as he arrived, Reynolds was turned around with orders to move his First Corps onto "the ground vacated by a portion of the XI Corps." Hooker and his staff mistakenly thought Howard's Eleventh Corps position ran farther north toward the Rapidan than it did.[35]

From Wilderness Church, what was left of Howard's command fell back another quarter mile to the "Buschbeck line," a shallow, thousand-yard north-south trench just east of Dowdall's. At a less frantic time, it might have been an effective dam against the wave of Confederates sweeping from the west. In it were jammed Buschbeck's four regiments, six other regiments of Schurz's division, plus pieces of Devens's shattered division. They stood for what seemed to some Federals an hour. Behind the rifle pits, Schurz tried to rally the confused mass of men for a charge. Yelling "Hurrah!," he started forward. After a few steps, he was alone. He tried two or three more times, then gave it up.[36] James Emmons of the 154th New York watched the Rebels swarming "like flies on a dead horse" as they turned the Union left. At that, "such a stampede never was seen," he said, but "before we run we give the rebels enough. . . . The rebs would march up to the cannons mouth in solid columns and our gunners loaded them with double charged grape and canister and let them have it. It would mow a road clear through them every time but they would close up with a yell and come on again. But they drove us at last. We run you better believe. . . ."[37] The weight of Jackson's attack spilled over and around this third and last stand by elements of the Eleventh Corps. With one of Dilger's guns in the Plank Road covering their retreat, Schurz's and von Steinwehr's men tumbled back toward Chancellorsville.[38]

The next potential line of resistance was just before Bullock Road, where Henry Slocum's original Twelfth Corps position began. There, Alpheus Williams's division had extended the barricade called "Slocum's log works" into the woods for a quarter mile north of the Plank Road. Felled trees made a thick abatis in front of it. But Williams's troops had been pulled out of their prepared position to join Sickles in his effort to cut Jackson's column at Catharine Furnace. Still unaware of what was happening west of Chancellorsville, Williams was two miles away near the furnace. He was shouldering his division in beside Birney and Whipple to resist Confederate pressure on the far side of Sickles's salient when a courier brought orders for him to forget that flank and move back into his old position at once. Before Williams got anywhere near it, Schurz and the remnants of the Eleventh Corps had retreated past the log works; some stopped there briefly, as if considering another stand, then moved on.

Jackson's advance troops surrounded four companies of the 28th New York left behind the barricade by Williams to guard the division's knapsacks, and captured half of them with hardly any fight. The Confederate troops, now leg-weary, confused, and with regiments hopelessly mixed, still knew which way to push. With Jackson close behind, they drove on.[39]

One by one, the other Federal forces sent on Sickles's adventure got hurry-up orders to return and help against Jackson. David Birney's division had just started to bivouac when Sickles sent word that the Eleventh Corps had caved in and Birney must come back immediately. Sickles dispatched recall orders to Whipple about the time Williams was turned around by his corps commander, Slocum. But Francis Barlow's brigade, originally intended to be Howard's corps reserve, belonged to a headquarters that had effectively ceased to function. Howard wished the brigade had been kept in place, but in the chaos nobody thought to retrieve it. Until a messenger from Birney caught up, Barlow pushed on southward while the friendly outfits on both his flanks hurried back to the main stage.[40]

When Sickles took most of his Third Corps toward the Furnace, two brigades of Hiram Berry's division were kept back near Chancellorsville. Now, with Hooker's east-facing troops frozen in place by Lee's aggressive jabs, Berry's was the only uncommitted, unrattled force the Union commander could put his hands on. This was Hooker's old division, and he still felt he could rely on it to save his army. As a mob of demoralized men flooded back through the Chancellorsville clearing, Hooker rode out to Berry and yelled, "General, throw your men into the breach! Receive the enemy on your bayonets! Don't fire a shot, they can't see you!"

Berry, one of the Army of the Potomac's best soldiers, flung his brigades toward the oncoming Rebels. William Hays's brigade from the Second Corps was sent to support him. Bulling their way past their fleeing comrades, the fresh reserves were cheered on by Hooker on his white stallion, shouting, "Receive 'em on your bayonets, boys! Receive 'em on your bayonets!"

SICKLES, as he slashed at the tail of Jackson's column, had called for cavalry to follow up his expected triumph. Brig. Gen. Alfred Pleasonton brought three mounted regiments plus a battery of horse artillery to Hazel Grove, awaiting Sickles's call. Sickles was about to order them into action southward when the first messenger came with word of Jackson's attack on Howard. He refused to believe it until another galloped up with a request that he send a regiment of cavalry to help on the west flank. Pleasonton turned to Maj. Pennock Huey of the 8th Pennsylvania and told him to take his regiment to Howard.

Huey's horsemen were lounging along the north edge of the Hazel Grove clearing. Under a tree, Maj. Peter Keenan, commander of the 1st Battalion, and three other officers were playing high-stakes draw poker on a cracker box. Keenan must have been winning, for when Huey told them to mount up, he laughed and complained, "Major, you've spoiled a good game." Nobody seemed excited as the regiment rode at a walk through the woods toward the Plank Road. None but Huey knew that Howard's line was giving way, and even he had no idea what really had happened.[41]

Just before the regiment reached the Plank Road, Huey, Keenan, and those leading the column saw gray uniforms ahead. Suddenly they realized that the woods on both sides were thick with Confederates, Jackson's flankers. There was no way to reverse the long, thin column of horsemen. Huey shouted, "Draw sabers and charge!"

Keenan and the others echoed him and, with sabers aloft, the 8th Pennsylvania galloped toward the Plank Road. There, the right seemed packed solid with Rebels. Huey's cavalry turned left, into the oncoming Confederates, "both men and horses in a perfect frenzy of excitement, which nothing but death could stop." They slashed and trampled through the enemy for about 100 yards. It took that long for Jackson's troops, as surprised as the horsemen, to react. As one said later, "an encounter with cavalry in that dense country seemed to be as unlikely as an attack from a gunboat."[42] Some of the Confederates thought the entire Union cavalry was upon them, and yelled, "I surrender, I surrender!" But most recovered and leveled muskets at the mass of riders along the narrow road. One crashing volley cut down Keenan, Capt. Charles Arrowsmith, Adjutant J. Haseltine Haddock, and perhaps a third of the leading battalion. When Keenan's body was recovered, it was said to bear thirteen bullet wounds.

In the second, trailing battalion of the cavalry regiment, Capt. Andrew Wells and his comrades galloped through the smoke into the Plank Road. They charged over horses and men and luckily struck the Rebel line at a pause, when most of its muskets were empty between volleys. The collision created "a jam of living and dead men, friends and enemies and horses, and the weight of the rear of our squadron broke us into utter confusion, so that at the moment every man was for himself."[43] John Collins's horse was shot as he tried to turn away. He hid in the woods, then tried to stop one of two panicking ammunition pack mules, tied together. Collins thought a mule thus coupled would be easy to catch, but

just as he ran toward them a shell blew both animals to pieces. Some
surviving cavalrymen in their flight caught up with the mass of retreating
Eleventh Corps troops. Collins did, and then joined the picket line formed
by General Howard, trying to stop the rout, but it was soon overrun.*[44]

THESE FEW HOURS were the high point of Jackson's career, still envied
and studied by soldiers worldwide more than a century later. But after the
attack's late start, there were other imperfections.

When Jackson told Rodes to go forward, George Doles's brigade led
the way, with the 4th Georgia guiding on the Turnpike. At the first clump
of resistance, Doles ordered the 4th and 44th to drive straight on and sent
the 21st and 12th Georgia around its left and right. Within minutes, they
carried that position, then the next and the next. One took longer than
another, but none halted the Georgians' momentum. Off to the north,
where the Union lines petered out to nothing, Alfred Iverson's brigade
and Edward O'Neal's leftmost regiments looped around and behind the
enemy, repeatedly enveloping Blue positions before Doles's men could
strike them head-on. But on the Confederate right, A. H. Colquitt broke
the overriding rule of Jackson's attack order: Under no circumstances was
there to be any pause in the advance.

Rodes said, "As there was possibility of pressure on my right flank,
Ramseur was directed to watch that flank carefully, thus leaving Colquitt
free to push ahead without fear from that quarter."[48] If and when Ram-

---

*The charge of the 8th Pennsylvania, the gallant but only way out of a desperate
situation, was described in flamboyant terms by General Pleasonton. In his official report,
Pleasonton maintained that he had "ordered the 8th Pennsylvania Cavalry to proceed at
a gallop, attack the rebels, and check the attack at any cost till we could get ready for
them."[45] He made himself out a hero, too, in telling how he then managed an artillery
counterblow that halted Jackson's attack. Firsthand accounts from the 8th Pennsylvania
disproved his version. As Huey wrote, Pleasonton ordered him to take his regiment to
Howard as quickly as possible, and "There were no other orders given to me or to any
officer of my regiment." Captain Wells asked later, "Can any man who was a soldier for
one moment imagine an officer deliberately planning a charge by a regiment of cavalry,
strung out by twos in a column half a mile long in a thick wood?"[46]

In 1866, Huey wrote to Pleasonton from Jackson, Mississippi, where he had reviewed
the battle with Southern veterans and become "satisfied they [the 8th Pennsylvania]
drove him [Jackson] back on his own column, when he was wounded mortally. Of these
facts I am entirely satisfied, with the amount of information I have on the subject, and
if such is the case beyond a doubt, I have often thought our command should have the
credit of it, at least in the history of the war." Pleasonton forwarded this letter to the
chief of staff, eager to have the official history show "that Jackson was mortally wounded
by our troops in his attack upon our right at that time."[47]

seur's troops were called forward as reinforcements, they had orders to run up yelling, to make the enemy think they were a much bigger force.[49] But Colquitt acted as if Jackson's order to keep going were merely optional. He reported that "intelligence was communicated to me by the skirmishers that a body of the enemy was upon my right flank. I ordered a halt, and called back the 6th Georgia, which had continued to advance. The regiment upon the right (the 19th Georgia) was quickly thrown into position to meet any demonstration upon the flank, and ordered to advance about 100 yards to the summit of a hill. The enemy's force proved to be a small body of cavalry, which galloped away as soon as the regiment advancing toward them was discovered, and a picket of infantry, which was captured by my skirmishers."[50]

Colquitt was a man of substance, a states' rights Democratic congressman before the war, later a teetotaling Methodist minister and governor of Georgia. But by his own official words, he made plain that he was guilty of not following orders. Twenty-five-year-old Brig. Gen. Stephen Dodson Ramseur, whose North Carolinians were assigned specifically to protect the right flank of the attacking force, was furious.

Colquitt's advance along the right was the least obstructed either by woods or enemy troops. But his error took his and Ramseur's men out of the attack, and delayed Paxton's entry from the Plank Road. Since A. P. Hill's third wave eventually re-formed to march in column along the Plank Road rather than trying to keep up in the woods, that meant only six of the 15 brigades in Jackson's force carried the initial assault. Colquitt slowed the advance on the right, and exposed Doles's flank. That removed any chance of enveloping the Union positions from both sides, and possibly capturing whole units with their artillery. Had Colquitt's brigade not been transferred soon afterward to North Carolina, he would have had to face a court of inquiry. The Federal hero of this skirmish, whose skimpy infantry picket diverted Colquitt and effectively took three brigades out of the Southern attack, was a newly promoted lieutenant, John Lowe of the 55th Ohio.[51]

Out on the other end of the Rebel assault wave, Iverson's North Carolina brigade followed Jackson's orders literally, swinging behind one Union position after another. When Colston's second rank of attackers overran and mingled with Rodes's leading division, there was "great confusion, the two lines rushing forward pell-mell upon the enemy and becoming mingled in almost inextricable confusion, no officer being able to tell what men he commanded," Iverson reported. "The whole affair from the moment of attack was a wild scene of triumph on our part.

Hungry men seized provisions as they passed the camps of the enemy and rushed forward eating, shouting and firing." [52] One of Iverson's men in the 23rd North Carolina said that as soon as the assault started, "Then commenced the second edition of the Bull Run races—I tell you we carried them two miles and a half at 2.40 speed, and would I believe have completely routed the whole army if we had made the attack three hours earlier. Darkness was all that saved them." [53]

North of the Plank Road, between Iverson and Doles, Col. Edward O'Neal's Alabama brigade kept moving, although its right regiments were bloodied by Union artillery fire along the road. To O'Neal, if no one else, the chaos seemed orderly. He reported that he was with the brigade "throughout its brilliant charge," and despite the dense and tangled forest, despite the sporadic cannon fire, "all the regiments were connected and moved in a regular, unbroken line, the officers exhibiting the greatest coolness and daring, cheering on their men by both voice and example." [54] But in his 12th Alabama, for instance, when the troops were getting wobbly from fatigue, Col. Samuel B. Pickens tried to halt the regiment on O'Neal's orders and let the second wave pass through. Pickens could stop only about 30 men; he left them with another officer and chased the rest of his command another half mile. Before he caught up, the 12th without its colonel had helped carry two more Union works and take three cannon. When Pickens joined his men, they were mingled with others from every regiment in the brigade. He formed them all and marched them back to where O'Neal had said to hold up. [55]

By this time, dusk was deepening and every Confederate in the attack waves was exhausted. Their stomachs were snarling; most had had no rations issued them for forty-eight hours. Few soldiers could see their own regimental colors as they plunged ahead, and eventually thousands found themselves fighting beside strangers rather than the messmates with whom they had lived the winter and started the assault more than two miles back.

But on the far right of Jackson's advancing line, his skirmishers slashed on after absorbing the shock of meeting the 8th Pennsylvania Cavalry. Some of Doles's Georgians, moving fast past the empty Union lines where Sickles's divisions would have been, angled south of Jackson's spearhead and approached the high ground of Hazel Grove. They assumed the only Yankees in their front were fleeing remnants. Pushing through the woods, they surprised a contingent of Sickles's artillery waiting along a southward lane, confident the Rebels were still far away. The cannoneers fled, abandoning a gun and two caissons.

Farther down that road, the Georgians came to a clearing seething with

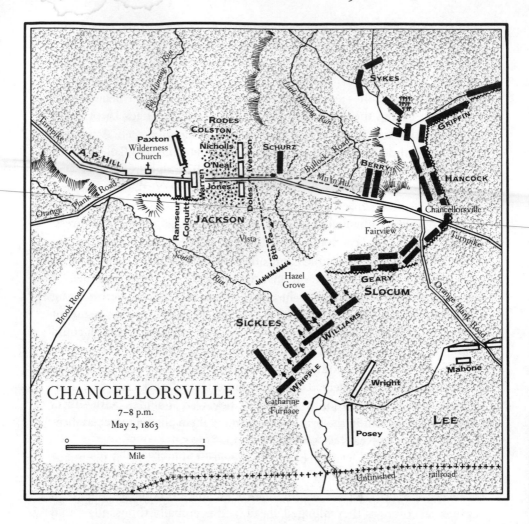

CHANCELLORSVILLE

7–8 p.m.
May 2, 1863

0   1
Mile

9. Out of Control. *By nightfall, Jackson's first two assault waves have become mingled and commanders are losing close control in the thick woods. As Howard's shattered Eleventh Corps falls back, the 8th Pennsylvania Cavalry leaves Hazel Grove and blunders into the flank of Jackson's attackers.*

enemy troops, horses, and guns. Part of Sickles's Third Corps was crossing Hazel Grove, marching northwest, not realizing that the original defensive line it was heading for was already swept by Confederate skirmishers. As this mass of Union troops angled across the field in one direction, streams of Howard's defeated men cut through them toward the rear. Many of those fugitives had ripped the newly sewn Eleventh Corps crescents off their caps so that no one could identify their command. Before them now racketed guns, forges, caissons, and ambulances, many driverless, swept up in the tumult after being left behind by Sickles. This panic infected some of Slocum's Twelfth Corps and Sickles's returning infantrymen, who joined the retreat.[56]

Amid all this, Pleasonton and various artillery officers were trying to assemble a line of guns at Hazel Grove to face the oncoming Rebels. When the crest of this "indescribable confusion" passed, a collection of 22 pieces was more or less ready to fire. As Pleasonton recounted it, he ordered three squadrons of the 17th Pennsylvania Cavalry to charge the Union stragglers to clear the field, which others said just added to the confusion. Then, Pleasonton said, he personally supervised the placement of the cannon as the Rebels approached:

> They came on in line five and six deep, with but one flag—a Union flag dropped by the Eleventh Corps. I suspected deception and was ready for it. They called out not to shoot, they were friends; at the same time they gave us a volley from at least five thousand muskets. As soon as I saw the flash I gave the command to fire, and the whole line of artillery was discharged at once. It fairly swept them from the earth; before they could recover themselves the line of artillery had been loaded and was ready for a second attack. After the second discharge, suspecting that they might play the trick of having their men lie down, draw the fire of the artillery, then jump up and charge before the pieces could be reloaded, I poured in the canister for about twenty minutes, and the affair was over.[57]

Officers around Pleasonton challenged this eloquent first-person account, as they did his tale about the 8th Pennsylvania Cavalry. Capt. James F. Huntington of the 1st Ohio Artillery, the senior cannoneer left at Hazel Grove by Whipple's division, maintained that 18 pieces under his orders were readied while Pleasonton apparently was engrossed in placing one battery of horse artillery.[58] Lt. Joseph Martin, of the 6th New York Light, had started that horse artillery outfit up the road behind the 8th

Pennsylvania and luckily made it back to the clearing by unlimbering his guns on the narrow road and reversing them by hand.

At Hazel Grove, Pleasonton told Martin where to point his cannon. "Not more than 250 yards from the battery there ran a line of fence," Martin reported, "and behind this appeared a line of infantry, but in the fast-increasing darkness it was impossible to tell whether they were our own or the enemy's troops. Lieutenant [Morey] Clark asserts positively that he heard them say, 'Do not fire on your friends,' and these facts, combined with another, that they carried a flag, which if not the American colors was certainly very nearly the same as it, deterred me from opening fire. . . ." Martin said that Pleasonton sent an aide to find out who these troops were, and "he had hardly disappeared in the darkness before a bright line of fire and the sharp rattle of musketry" began. Almost simultaneously, Pleasonton gave the order to fire.[59]

According to Huntington, the Rebels laid down a heavy base of musket fire from the front while some of them slipped between Hazel Grove and the Plank Road, enfilading the Yankee batteries. But soon afterward, Union infantry of Whipple's and Birney's divisions returning from the furnace moved in on both sides of the clearing to help the guns throw back another Confederate push.[60]

The Rebels probing Hazel Grove were led by Lt. Col. D. R. E. Winn of the 4th Georgia, who reported that at Doles's orders, he headed that way with half the regiment and its battle colors. By the time he struggled through the thickets to Hazel Grove, he said, he had not the 5,000 muskets alleged by Pleasonton, but "about 200 men of various commands." As he approached, Winn reported, the Federals were standing in line "exhibiting no purpose to attack." His Southerners tore down the rail fence to make a slight barricade, and saw the apparent commander of the Federals riding forward. "Though I ordered the men not to fire," Winn said, "when he got within 100 yards of me one or two of the men excitedly fired at him, whereupon he rode rapidly back to his command, and immediately a terrible artillery and infantry fire was opened upon us." His men returned the fire until their ammunition ran out, the Georgia officer reported, and when the Federal fire died down, they withdrew to look for their proper regiments.[61]

To Pleasonton, the action at Hazel Grove was the heroic repulse of a major enemy thrust. To the Rebel colonel, it was one last feeler by his exhausted Georgians before they pulled back to reorganize.

Night had fallen. From end to end, Jackson's attacking lines were thoroughly confused, some tangled in abatis, groping in the darkness, searching for their own units. Rodes ordered his troops to hold up to re-form, and sent a request to Jackson to bring A. P. Hill's division forward. In the 44th Georgia, one soldier said that as long as the assault rolled on, the mixup "made no difference, as we never stoped to learn who did this or that. But our watchword was onward. Onward we went untill long after dark." When he halted, he knew only one of the men around him, "though I new that I was with my friends and all was right with me." It took him two hours to find his regiment, and when he did, "my co. had given me up as lost or killed. Just hear let me say to you, that I never seen in all of my life so much rejoicing as we did over the different men and parts of companies as we came up to the reg. Some of the officers and men gave me a good old fashion hug, which was reciprocated by me with all my heart." [62] Thousands of Southern soldiers found their friends and then collapsed in place, hoping to rest and be fed after a glorious victory.

But Jackson was not satisfied.

Chapter Twelve

CHAOS IN THE MOONLIGHT

JACKSON HEARD the firing die down as both armies caught their breath. He was back near Dowdall's, impatient, snapping out orders. He did not fully appreciate how confused things were in the assault lines. But he, more than anyone, understood the meaning of nightfall. He could see total victory slipping away with every darkening minute.

While privates stumbled and called in the thickets looking for their companies, generals looked for their own commands and for the enemy. Rodes's courier brought his request to Jackson to send A. P. Hill's division forward while the assault brigades reorganized. Jackson, displeased at hearing that Rodes was holding up, nodded, nudged Little Sorrel and started quickly toward the front. Just then Hill appeared beside him, ready. Jackson turned and told him to push his division ahead through Rodes's and Colston's lines.

"Press them!" he ordered. "Cut them off from United States Ford, Hill. Press them!" [1]

Rodes himself was riding farther along the Plank Road toward Chancellorsville, to feel out the next Union line of resistance. Surprisingly, it seemed there were no enemy troops between his farthest advance and Fairview, the open plateau with a little country cemetery, half a mile west of the Chancellorsville crossroads. Rodes could not see the organized remains of Schurz's division, which had turned about and dug in across the Bullock Road, behind the woods to the north, or Buschbeck's brigade in the woods to the south. He did not know that Berry's and Williams's divisions were coming up from Chancellorsville and Hazel Grove to form on both sides of the Plank Road. And in the darkness he could not make out the cannon being massed on the crest of Fairview by Capt. Clermont Best, chief of Slocum's Twelfth Corps artillery.

James Lane's North Carolina brigade had trailed the Rebel assault, marching in column along the Plank Road. Harry Heth's and Dorsey Pender's brigades had started as a third line of attack, deployed in the woods, but as the offensive gathered speed they were brought back to the road, marching behind Lane. Now Hill sent Lane first to relieve Rodes's and Colston's lines, waiting crouching in the forest.

Col. Stapleton Crutchfield, Jackson's reserve artillery commander, heard Rodes's report that there apparently were no Yankees immediately ahead. He told Marcellus Moorman's cannoneers to open fire on Fairview to see what was there. A crashing salvo answered Moorman, ripping down the road through the troop column and artillery horses. The Yankees captured in Slocum's log works were being marched back when this "hell broke loose" around them. Sgt. Lucius Swift of the 28th New York recalled how "A rain of shells came sailing over the trees and each one seemed to burst about two feet from the ground and the pieces went in all directions each singing a high note. I had always noticed that only about half of the Confederate shells burst, but our shells were made of good stuff; they burst."[2]

In the resulting panic, Lane waved his men off the road, and they flattened themselves alongside as Union shells tore past. Though heavily outgunned, the Confederate artillery kept up the duel until after Hill sent his adjutant forward to ask what was delaying Lane's advance. Lane told him he had halted because "I do not wish to lose my command. I am unwilling to attempt to form my line in the dark, under such a fire and in such woods." He said he thought the enemy was just trying to quash the Rebel fire, and if the Confederate guns ceased firing, the enemy's probably would, too. Hill's adjutant, Lt. Col. W. H. Palmer, relayed this and in fifteen minutes brought back orders for the Rebel cannon to hold their fire. When they did, the Yankees quickly stopped.[3]

Even with artillery blasting up and down the road, the bedraggled attack lines that had waited in the woods began sifting back toward Dowdall's, where they would reorganize. Along the road, Lane's brigade started forward again, but for a while Moorman and his horse artillery battery were left as the lead element of the Southern advance, out there alone facing who knew how many Yankees. On Hill's orders, Lane deployed his regiments just beyond Slocum's log works. He sent the 33rd North Carolina some 200 yards ahead as skirmishers, put the 7th and 37th North Carolina into line right of the road, and the 18th and 28th to the left. Lane did not know the works were there, but his troops in the woods found them. He moved the regiments left of the road close behind his skirmishers and turned to bring up those on the right.

Before they could advance, an officer of the 7th North Carolina called out—Just a minute, something was happening over on his far right. Out of the darkness, a column of Union infantry appeared through the woods, marching toward the regiment. With no idea the Rebels were so close, it was moving back into the abandoned log works, which angled into the Confederate front. Hearing the Southern troops milling in the underbrush, a Union soldier called, "Who's there?"

"Confederates," answered the Tar Heels.

"Come in, Confederates," said the Union voice—"Whose brigade are you?"

"Lane's," said the Rebels.

"Tell General Lane to come in," the Union officer ordered.[4]

The Gray infantry was aiming into the darkness, about to fire, when a figure emerged waving a white handkerchief tied to a stick. It was Lt. Col. Levi Smith of the 128th Pennsylvania, of Williams's division. He said he came not to surrender, but to find out whether he had blundered into friend or enemy. When he started to return, the Confederates grabbed him, taking him to Lane. Insisting Smith had improperly used a flag of truce, Lane would not let him go. He sent a lieutenant to ask Hill how to handle the situation, and as the debate went on, shouts rose from the Yankees in the dark, asking why their officer did not come back, threatening to open fire. Lane sent Lt. James Emack and four men to find out how many Yankees were there.

Just as this patrol faded into the woods on the right, a Union officer, Brig. Gen. Joseph Knipe, rode into Lane's skirmishers watching the Plank Road. Knipe had been ordered to put his brigade back into the log works, and hailed the figures in the dark, asking who they were.

"Don't come any farther, or we'll fire," the Confederates answered.

"Don't fire, we're friends!" Knipe shouted as he wheeled his horse about.

Lane's skirmishers sent a volley after him, and some of the Federals in the woods fired back. This set off another volley from part of Lane's battle line, which peppered the friendly skirmishers ahead, sending them diving for cover. This rush in turn scared the Federals, who thought Lane had started an all-out charge, and musketry rippled right and left through the woods.[5]

About that time, Lieutenant Emack and his four-man patrol came back to the 7th North Carolina with a whole regiment of Yankee prisoners. Emack had walked right into the 128th Pennsylvania and, thinking fast, raised his sword and said, "Men, Jackson has surrounded you; down with your guns, else we will shoot the last one of you!" In the confusion, the Yankees believed him, threw down their weapons, and trooped meekly into captivity.[6]

THAT CONFUSION—troops of both sides stumbling into each other, battle lines firing into their own skirmishers, generals unsure what lay ahead—put both armies in a state of nerves as they felt their way into position for the next surge of battle.

The Confederates, who had thought the nearest concentrated Union infantry was back of the guns on Fairview, realized now that the enemy was in the woods close ahead and around them. They still did not know that by that time—eight-thirty or after—Union generals Berry and Williams had moved their divisions toward the edge of the open ground at Fairview, Berry north of the Plank Road, Williams to the south. Nor could they know that Captain Best now had 37 Yankee cannon assembled on Fairview, gunners at their pieces, ready to cut loose at the slightest hint of a Rebel advance. As Lane's troops moved up, they passed the carnage left when the 8th Pennsylvania Cavalry blundered into Jackson's attackers less than two hours earlier. Spreading out at right angles to the road, they heard the tale of that cavalry charge, magnified as it passed from soldier to soldier through the Wilderness.

When the artillery quieted, Jackson rode forward again. Nearing the old schoolhouse where a road from Hazel Grove joined the Plank Road, he pulled up to take a message from Jeb Stuart, who was scouting north toward Ely's Ford. Jackson read the message, looked up, and asked the courier, "Do you know all of this country?"

David Kyle, a young cavalryman who had hunted through the Wilderness and lived less than a mile away, was said to know "every hogpath." He assured Jackson that he did.

"Keep along with me," Jackson ordered. With Kyle and his staff, he rode past a jumble of the 8th Pennsylvania's dead horses at roadside. As he passed Rodes's and Colston's men moving back to regroup, and other troops recoiling from the artillery bombardment, he ordered angrily, "Men, get into line! Get into line! Whose regiment is this? Colonel, get your men in line!" Opposite the schoolhouse, Jackson stopped to ask some officers what was happening ahead, then prodded his horse on down the Plank Road. A full moon was just beginning to rise beyond the woods ahead as he passed Harry Heth's brigade, then caught up with Lane's.[7]

Lane's troops were now the only infantry confronting Hooker's flank in the darkness. With Rodes and Colston pulling back, the broad two-mile front on which Jackson had started his attack was shrunk to half a mile—four North Carolina regiments abreast, feeling for their places in the dark. The next brigades of Hill's Light Division were still strung out along the Plank Road, re-forming after scattering into the woods' edge to escape the cannon fire.

Jackson nevertheless wanted to keep the pressure on, to push ahead in a night attack before Hooker could bring order out of panic and organize his defenses. He was keyed up, dispatching one staff officer after another to hurry Hill and his brigadiers. He sent his young brother-in-law Joe Morrison back to tell Brig. Gen. Dorsey Pender to bring his brigade up just behind Lane's, alongside Sam McGowan's, waiting to advance on the Plank Road. Out of the woods then rode Lane, looking for Hill, to ask for orders to move on. He came upon Jackson instead.

"Push right ahead, Lane," said Jackson, shoving his palm forward toward the enemy.[8]

Jackson's staff officers trailed around him as he rode on in that direction. There was his topographical engineer, J. Keith Boswell. Capt. R. E. Wilbourn, his signal officer, caught up to report on Hill's plan of advance. Morrison returned from his errand. Moving left of the artillery in the Plank Road, Jackson reached an opening where the Bullock and Old Mountain roads angled north. Looking back, he called for Kyle, his guide, and asked him where those roads led. The Bullock Road led to a farm "behind Chancellorsville," Kyle said, and the other merely paralleled the Plank Road for about half a mile.

If you know that one, Jackson said, lead the way. Side by side, they rode along Mountain Road 200 yards or so, beyond the Confederate battle line, and stopped again. Jackson wanted to know what was out there; he could have sent any staff officer or nearby lieutenant, but he was impatient. He wanted to find out now, personally, whether he could thrust his men left around the Yankee front, get between Hooker and the river.[9]

One of his worried young officers asked, "General, don't you think this is the wrong place for you?"

Jackson brushed him off. "The danger is all over," he said. "The enemy is routed. Go back and tell A. P. Hill to press right on."

Kyle started ahead again, and Jackson caught up. With Wilbourn, Morrison, and half a dozen orderlies, they rode on toward the unseen Union lines. Hill, joined by Boswell, followed in another cluster of horsemen. Less than 300 yards from the Federals, Jackson halted, listen-

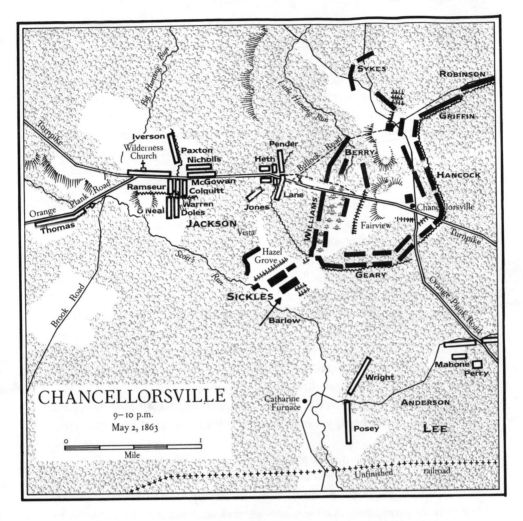

10. Chaos in the Moonlight. *All positions are approximate, because all is confusion. Jackson's first two attack waves sift back to reorganize while Hill's brigades come forward under terrific Union cannon fire from Fairview. Jackson, scouting ahead of Lane, is shot about 9:30 P.M. near position X.*

ing. He could hear officers ordering troops about. Then came the sound of shovels and axes, men digging in and building breastworks.

Jackson sat still, considering what that meant, whether he should push on with a night attack against an alert enemy. By morning his advantage would be gone. The shock of surprise would be over, Hooker would have dug in deeper, the formidable Union reserves would have moved into place. His mind made up, Jackson turned his horse back. After a few yards, his staff fell in around him and the squad of officers and messengers clattered toward its own lines. About halfway back, Jackson turned his horse left, toward the Van Wert house on the Plank Road.

It was almost nine-thirty.

As Jackson crossed the Old Mountain Road, someone fired a single shot. A spatter of other shots followed. Jackson's horse spooked, swinging into the woods. He reined it back with his left hand and fought off overhanging branches with his right. Both groups of horsemen spurred toward safety in the Confederate lines.

The Gray troops on the road had seen the generals ride out, but those in the woods waiting for the order to advance knew nothing of the reconnaissance party. To them, all those horses crashing through the dark brush sounded like a brigade of Union cavalry.[10] This time, they were waiting. A full volley tore through the woods.

A. P. Hill, close in, shouted, "Cease firing, cease firing!" Morrison rode at the Confederate lines, yelling, "Cease firing, you are firing into your own men!"

Out of the dark, someone yelled back. It was Maj. John D. Barry of the 18th North Carolina. "Who gave that order?" he shouted. "It's a lie! Pour it into them, boys!" A long row of kneeling Confederates cut loose at barely 20 paces, their muzzle blasts a streak of flame in the scrubby oaks and pines.

Both parties of horsemen were ripped apart. Horses screamed, men lurched from their saddles. Every horse that was not struck shied and fled away from the musket fire. Morrison saved himself by jumping off, falling painfully to the ground as his mount dashed toward the Union lines.

Jackson was shot three times. His left arm hung loose. He had no grip on his reins as Little Sorrel bolted. The frantic horse plunged between two trees. A low limb struck Jackson's face, tearing off his cap and knocking him backward, almost throwing him to the ground. Groping for the bridle, he found it with his right hand and fought to pull the horse back.

Suddenly someone rode alongside, grabbed the reins, calmed the horse and brought it around. This was Wilbourn. Lt. William T. Wynn came up on the other side, and the two held Jackson in the saddle. Wilbourn, unaware of how badly Jackson was hurt, said, "They certainly must be our troops." Jackson could only nod. In shock, he had trouble understanding that his own soldiers could have fired on him.[11]

Wilbourn asked, "How do you feel, General? Can you move your fingers?" Jackson said he could not, that his arm was broken. When Wilbourn tried to straighten it, Jackson moaned, "You had better take me down," and toppled toward the aide in a near faint.

For a moment, Jackson's feet were caught in the stirrups. Then he got both feet on the ground, but could hardly stand. Little Sorrel ran away into the enemy lines, and was recaptured weeks later by Stuart's cavalry. The two officers helped Jackson into the edge of the woods on the north side of the Plank Road and eased him down beneath a tree. Wilbourn sent Wynn to find Hunter McGuire, the corps medical director and Jackson's personal physician, or some other surgeon. He cautioned Wynn not to tell anyone else who was wounded.[12]

Hill, unhurt, leaped off his horse and hugged the ground beneath the crashing gunfire. Jackson's engineer, Boswell, riding with Hill, was killed and his horse ran off, dragging him toward the Union lines. Afterward his body was found beyond those of fourteen horses killed between the lines.

When the firing let up, Hill remounted and raced furiously toward Lane's brigade, crying, "You have shot my friends! You have destroyed my staff!" He saw his young aide, Murray Forbes Taylor, whose horse was shot dead, pinning him to the ground. He stopped and tried to free him until another aide ran up to say Jackson was down. Half-apologizing, Hill said to Taylor, "Help yourself. I must go to General Jackson. Don't tell the troops."[13]

Wilbourn was bending over the general. With a penknife, he had slit the left sleeves of Jackson's raincoat, jacket, and two shirts. One musket ball had struck Jackson's right hand, another his left forearm. A third had shattered his left arm three inches below the shoulder.

Hill dismounted and knelt by Jackson. His voice almost broke as he said, "I have been trying to make the men stop firing." Tenderly, he leaned over the man he had defied and cursed, the "crazy old Presbyterian fool" who had put him under arrest and refused to back down. For these moments, all that had never happened. Hill tried to stanch the bleeding with his handkerchief. "Is the wound painful?" he asked.

"Very painful. My arm is broken," said Jackson.

Hill slipped off the wounded man's bloody gauntlets and sat to cushion Jackson's head on his lap. Somebody asked if the general would take some whiskey. Jackson hesitated, but Wilbourn insisted. Jackson took a mouthful, then a drink of water, and soon seemed to feel stronger. Hill sent Maj. Benjamin Watkins Leigh to find a surgeon and ambulance. Jackson's aide James Power Smith helped Wilbourn tie the handkerchief as a tourniquet around the broken left arm and tried to make a sling. The blood was clotting, the bleeding slowed. Wilbourn asked where the other wound was. Jackson said, "In my right hand, but never mind that, it's a mere trifle." Leigh came back with Dr. Richard R. Barr, assistant surgeon of Pender's brigade. Jackson asked Hill in a whisper if Barr was a skilled surgeon. Hill said yes, but he would do nothing drastic. McGuire would be there soon.[14]

These urgent ministrations, comings and goings were still in no-man's-land, beyond the Confederate lines. Suddenly, two Federal pickets appeared out of the dark a few yards away, muskets pointed toward the bending figures. Someone sounded out, "Halt! Surrender! Fire on them if they don't surrender!" Hill looked up and quietly told two soldiers to arrest the intruders. The surprised Yankee privates had no idea they were so close to the enemy.

Morrison, shaky from his fall, had momentarily broken down on seeing his sister's beloved husband on the ground. Now he wondered if more Union troops were coming behind the captured pickets. He walked out the Plank Road and looked toward the Union lines. In the moonlight, he could see a brass cannon being manhandled into place, and hear officers ordering it ready to fire. This was Capt. Justin Dimick's battery of New York artillery, sent forward with infantry pickets to watch for signs of Rebel action. Morrison ran back and shouted, "The enemy is within fifty yards and advancing. Take the general away!"

Hill gently lowered Jackson's head and told him he would try to keep news of his wounding from the troops. "Thank you," whispered Jackson. Those were the last words between two stubborn Virginians, fierce fighters, whose pride kept them apart except in the fever of battle.[15]

There was still no stretcher. Wilbourn said they would have to carry Jackson to safety in their arms. "No," Jackson murmured. "If you can help me, I can walk."

They raised him painfully to his feet. At their first step together, the night exploded briefly with Dimick's cannon fire, sweeping down the road and through the woods alongside. Leigh's horse was wounded, and when it started to panic he jumped off to hold it. Jackson, beside him, flung his arm over Leigh's shoulder and, half walking, half dragged, took another few steps toward the Confederate lines.

Wilbourn, struggling with the reins of three scared horses, tried to keep them between Lane's troops and Jackson, so the soldiers could not see who was wounded. As they came abreast of the battle line, troops kept asking, "Who is that?" And Wilbourn and Leigh said, "Oh, only a friend of ours." But the soldiers knew no ordinary casualty would be surrounded by so much attention. They persisted.

Jackson told his helpers, "Just say it is a Confederate officer." One of the Carolina infantrymen slipped between Wilbourn's horses and got a closer look. "Great God!" he said as if stabbed. "That's General Jackson!" [16]

Jackson could walk no more than 20 paces. Leigh called again for a litter, and when it came he urged the general to lie on it and be carried. Leigh, Smith, and two enlisted litter-bearers each took a handle and started again. Within seconds, another, more terrible Federal cannonade opened. The Union gunners at Fairview thought the fire by Dimick's guns on picket down the slope meant the Confederates were about to attack. Over the heads of their own infantry, they let fly "a storm of grape [that] tore through the trees and along the road, mowing down the boughs. . . . Great broadsides thundered over the woods. Hissing shells searched the dark thickets through, and shrapnel swept the road. . . ."

In another few steps, a litter-bearer was hit and fell, but Leigh managed to catch his corner. The cannon kept roaring, and when one of the bearers eased his corner down and scuttled into the woods, the officers had to ground the litter. Smith lay beside Jackson and forcefully held him down as he tried to sit up. Smith, Leigh, and Morrison stretched prone around the general, trying to protect him as he lay with his feet toward the enemy guns. "Over us swept the rapid fire of shot and shell," Smith said, "grape-shot striking fire upon the flinty rock of the road all around us, and sweeping from their feet horses and men of the artillery just moved to the front." [17]

When the firing seemed to turn toward the south side of the road, Jackson again insisted, "I can walk." Smith stood, helped him up, and put his arm about his waist. Carrying most of Jackson's weight, he took him into the edge of the woods, where Jackson sank down again. Leigh asked several soldiers lying flat beneath the cannon fire to help with the litter; they looked away. Finally he realized that pretending Jackson was just another officer could cost the general his life. Leigh told the next group of troops who was wounded and said he needed help to get him to safety. At that, soldiers quickly volunteered.

Just before they started rearward again, Dorsey Pender rode up. He himself had been hit as he brought his brigade in behind Lane. He asked who was wounded. "A Confederate officer," Smith said dutifully. But Pender recognized Jackson. Stepping down, he said, "Ah, General, I hope you are not seriously hurt. I will have to retire my troops to re-form them, they are so much broken by this fire."

Jackson raised his head. For a moment, his voice was strong again: "You must hold your ground, General Pender. You must hold your ground, sir!"[18]

It was his last order on the field.

He slumped back, and with Federal cannon still blasting, his aides struggled with the litter through the bushes along the left of the Plank Road. In the thickets, one of the bearers tripped and went down head first. Jackson was dumped to the ground, falling heavily on his damaged arm and side. He groaned, but then seemed calm. Later he would say he had believed several times in that hour that he was about to die, and this fall convinced him of it. He said a great peace came over him. Smith broke in with a gentle question: "General, are you much hurt?"

"No, Mr. Smith," said Jackson. "Don't trouble yourself about me." He murmured something about winning the battle first, then worrying about the wounded.

Lifting the litter again, the men continued along the Plank Road, then turned south into a woods road, about half a mile from where they had started. There at last they found an ambulance.[19]

WITH JACKSON out of action, shortly before ten o'clock command of his corps passed to A. P. Hill, his senior major general. But Hill was not in charge long, for the same broadside that wounded Jackson's litter-bearer also struck him.

Pistol in hand, he had hurried back, yelling to ready Lane's men after Morrison saw the Union cannon preparing to fire. As he started forward toward Jackson again, a shell fragment slashed across the back of both his legs, tearing off his boot tops. Though he felt no blood, he could hardly walk. After a few steps, he sat on a stump, took off a boot, and examined his wound.

Then Hill painfully pulled himself onto his horse, and rode forward with one foot sidewise out of its stirrup. Despite his wounds, he saw to Pender's move through the woods to Lane's left. Later E. L. Thomas's brigade, catching up after it had turned back to Catharine Furnace during the flank march, was sent to Pender's left. Capt. Murray Taylor found Hill and asked if he was hurt. Yes, said Hill, he had been hit in the calf. He realized the pain was too great for him to ride; he could not do his duty as commander.[20]

There was no other major general to take over. Robert Rodes was the senior brigadier, but his brilliant performance that day was the first time he had handled anything as big as a division in battle. Now, by protocol, he should take charge of Jackson's corps. Hill decided to advise Rodes that the command fell on him, but at the same time to send for Jeb Stuart, who was a major general with both seniority and combat experience. Though a cavalryman who had never commanded infantry, Stuart was much better known than Rodes, adored by all the Confederacy, and would have the confidence of the army at a critical moment. Hill dispatched his signal officer, Capt. R. H. T. Adams, toward Ely's Ford to find Stuart. Murray Taylor was sent to loop south around the enemy and advise Lee, in case he wanted a different arrangement.

Rodes conferred with Colston and Heth, who as senior brigade commander took over Hill's division. In the chaos of the artillery pounding, some troops had panicked back along the Plank Road. The generals were concerned about their right, where Union forces still held Hazel Grove and unidentified units had milled about all evening. The loss of Jackson and the shift of command added to the disorder. Jackson had told Hill, but none of these generals, about his aim of getting at Hooker from the north, between Chancellorsville and the fords. To the generals, all this confusion meant that a night attack risked disaster. Rodes ordered the divisions to be ready to attack in the morning, straight toward Chancellorsville.[21]

Rodes was not eager to give up his brief command of the corps, but he was noble about it. He yielded to Stuart, he reported, "not because I thought him entitled to it, belonging as he does to a different arm of the service, nor because I was unwilling to assume the responsibility of carrying on the attack. . . ." He went along, Rodes wrote, because he assumed either Jackson or Hill had made the decision—"and for the still stronger reason that I feared that the information that the command had devolved on me, unknown except to my own immediate troops, would, in their shaken condition, be likely to increase the demoralization of the corps." Considering Stuart's high reputation, he said, "I yielded because I was satisfied the good of the service demanded it."[22]

AT NIGHTFALL, Stuart had asked Jackson's permission to take some cavalry and an infantry regiment to set up a blocking force against any enemy coming or going by Ely's Ford. Jackson approved, and Stuart took the 16th North Carolina Infantry, from Pender's brigade, to work with the 2nd Virginia Cavalry. As Stuart and von Borcke mounted a rise in the road, they saw the campfires of a sprawling Union bivouac across the Rapidan. Halting their force, they rode close enough to hear the Yankees talking, totally unsuspecting. Stuart realized that he did not have enough men to challenge them head-on, but decided to surprise them with a hit-and-run attack.

Just as Stuart's force lined up along the bluff above the river, Captain Adams arrived with the news about Jackson. Cavalryman Marshall Decker, guiding Stuart, lit a candle, and the general read the message. Quickly, without explanation, Stuart told his infantry to fire three rounds at the camp, then pull back. He gave von Borcke command of the Rebel horsemen, telling him to "act on your own responsibility." Then he raced away. Von Borcke had no idea why Stuart had left so quickly, but went ahead with the raid. Sneaking closer, the Carolina infantry opened fire and sent the enemy flying.

The surprised Yankees were Averell's cavalry, 3,400 sabers and six guns, brought back by Hooker's order after failing to carry out their assignment upriver. They were settling in to spend the night at Ely's Ford when Stuart's raiders attacked. "Soldiers and officers could be plainly seen by the light of the fires rushing helplessly about, horses were galloping wildly in all directions, and the sound of bugles and drums mingled with the cries of the wounded and flying," von Borcke recalled. A Yankee cavalryman admitted that "All was confusion for a short time," and Lt. Col. Lorenzo Rogers of the 16th Pennsylvania "is said to have run behind a barn, and called for the men to 'rally on the barn.' " When some of Averell's horsemen recovered enough to fire back, von Borcke told the Gray raiders to withdraw while he galloped to rejoin Stuart. (According to Averell's report, the attackers were "quickly repulsed.")[23]

OFF TO THE SOUTH, most of the Union infantry that Dan Sickles had taken toward Catharine Furnace reassembled around the artillery at Hazel Grove. During the lull after Rodes held up the Southern advance, the ever-aggressive Sickles asked Hooker's permission to make a night attack. He wanted to retake the cannon that the 4th Georgia had captured but then left in the woods when it withdrew. He also thought that if supported by Williams's and Berry's divisions at Fairview, he could retake the original line along the Plank Road. About eleven o'clock, he got permission to try, and ordered Birney's division ready to go forward with bayonets fixed.[24]

Sickles and his officers gave their troops a pep talk about how vital their mission was. Theodore Castor of the 3rd Michigan recalled how his general went from regiment to regiment explaining the situation—"that we were cut off from the main body of our army, that the breastworks we had built and had left in charge of the Eleventh Corps were now in possession of the Rebels and that there were two things for us to do— either go to Richmond as prisoners or charge them breastworks, drive the Rebels back and join our army We all said charge. . . ."

Close to midnight, "the whole corps started on a charge right in the woods and dark as pitch, with everybody hollowing as loud as he could and making all the noise and firing as often as he could get loaded, right to the direction where we supposed them breastworks were, the cannons on both sides firing and downing shot and shell in between us. We took the breastworks but got badly messed up."[25]

That understates it.

By midnight, the moon was high. Confederate Harry Heth, commanding Hill's division, had broadened his front by putting Pender's troops and Thomas's late-arriving brigade on line north of the Plank Road and shifting Lane's to the south. Now Lane's rightmost regiments were the 18th and 28th North Carolina. Birney's Federals, guiding on the approach road called the Vista, headed their way from Hazel Grove. His lead element, the 40th New York "Mozart" regiment, bumped into the waiting Rebels about 500 yards south of the Plank Road. The Tar Heels let go a tremendous volley that threw the Mozarts back into Birney's next trailing regiment, the 17th Maine. That resistance turned away the left prong of Sickles's advance.

Along the right of the Vista, the 3rd Maine led the attack. The thick forest scattered the moonlight, and the Yankees stumbled upon the 18th North Carolina before they knew it. In the melee the Maine regiment was knocked reeling, losing its flag and a handful of prisoners. This clash forced the rest of Sickles's attack farther to its right, between the Union and Confederate lines. Suddenly the advancing Yankees were caught in a crossfire, from enemy on the left and friend on the right. Williams's troops had no word of Sickles's approach. Expecting a Confederate night attack, they opened up with muskets and artillery.

Some Union regiments, including Castor and his fellows in the 3rd Michigan, turned obliquely to their right, "dashed over a breastwork, and received a fire of musketry and grape from the right. Still they dashed on to within a few yards of the battery, when it was discovered that we were charging the Twelfth Army Corps, of our own troops." Other Yankees angled toward Lane's line. At all this excitement the massed Union guns on Fairview cut loose again, sweeping the Plank Road and the woods on both sides.[26]

A few of Sickles's men between the lines actually reached the Plank Road, but promptly fell back. The whole effort had turned into a "mixed-up mess." Expert narrators afterward called it "one of the most comical episodes in the history of the Army of the Potomac." But there was nothing comical about it to the men in the fire-slashed woods. Williams, who looked on from Fairview, later said, "Human language can give no idea of such a scene—such an infernal and yet sublime combination of sound and flame and smoke, and dreadful yells of rage, of pain, of triumph, or of defiance." Some of Sickles's men fled the chaos, out of control, and had to be turned back at bayonet point.[27]

Had Sickles's attack thrust more to its left, northwest instead of northeast, it might have gotten behind Lane onto the open Confederate flank. By that time there was no Southern force on line between Lane's right and Colston's division, reorganizing almost half a mile back. Lane asked Heth for help to close that gap. When the artillery let up, he guided Sam McGowan's South Carolina brigade in on his right flank. McGowan immediately put out skirmishers who exchanged a few shots with pickets of the 17th Maine, but after that the Confederates settled in for the night, heads down, trying to rest before jumping off in the morning.[28]

True to form, Sickles officially reported this adventure as a great success. "It is difficult to do justice to the brilliant execution of this movement by Birney and his splendid command," he wrote. He asserted that his troops had advanced against terrific fire from 20 Rebel cannon at Dowdall's, regained the Plank Road line, and reoccupied the old breastworks. He maintained that the Confederates had been "thrown into hopeless confusion" on their right, and mounted an attack along the Plank Road that was repulsed by Berry and the artillery. Like several other Union officers, he gave his men credit for putting Stonewall Jackson out of action.

Still, Sickles's night attack was a failure only by contrast with his claims. As he said, his troops recaptured the one gun and three caissons taken and then abandoned by the Confederates near Hazel Grove—though even on that point, Sickles overreached by claiming also to have captured two Rebel pieces. Most important, he succeeded in tying in his right firmly with the main Union position at Fairview and Chancellorsville. And this final eruption in a long day and night of surprise and confusion squelched any remaining chance that the Rebel generals might renew their advance in the dark. Beyond that—and the casualties—its main effect was to postpone sleep in both armies, keeping them on edge, not knowing who might come crashing through the night from what direction.[29]

JEB STUART RODE hard from Ely's Ford, in and out of moonlight, five miles down unfamiliar byroads. On the way he was "determined to press the pursuit already so gloriously begun." He got to the battleground just after Sickles's attack had dwindled out. Replacing Hill, Stuart immediately sent an officer to find Jackson and say he was ready "cheerfully" to carry out his instructions. Then he rode to the front to see how his troops were deployed. Heth had Pender and Thomas left of the Plank Road, Lane and McGowan on the right. When the fighting stopped, James Archer's brigade had come up. Both it and Heth's brigade—now commanded by Col. J. M. Brockenbrough—were put in farther right, bending the line to close the dangerous gap behind Lane.

Told of Sickles's attack, of how artillery had ripped Rebel regiments and friendly troops had fired on each other in the dark, Stuart confirmed the decision of Rodes and Heth not to advance until first light. He sent that word by the roundabout route to Lee. He ordered Col. E. P. Alexander, who had assumed artillery command from the wounded Crutchfield, to pick sites and move up his guns, ready for all-out attack. Then, far past midnight, Stuart set out along the lines to buck up his soldiers, keep them quiet, and prepare them for morning.[30] After the elation of victory, those troops were exhausted, hungry, and then shaken by the storm of artillery fire from Fairview. Not only Rodes's and Colston's men in the attack but some of Hill's moving up the road were panicked and scattered. Brig. Gen. Francis Nicholls, who already had lost his left arm at Winchester, was trying to control his Louisiana brigade when a solid shot slammed through his horse and tore off his left foot.[31]

Later, amid Sickles's attack, one of McGowan's South Carolinians lay flat in terror as soldiers' shouts and curses rang and cannon roared. "We knew nothing, could see nothing, hedged in by the matted mass of trees," he recalled. "Night engagements are always dreadful, but this was the worst I ever knew. To see your danger is bad enough, but to hear shells whizzing and bursting over you, to hear shrapnell and iron fragments slapping the trees and cracking off limbs, and not know from whence death comes to you, is trying beyond all things. And here it looked so incongruous—below raged thunder, shout, shriek, slaughter—above soft, silent, smiling moonlight, peace."[32]

George W. Hall of the 14th Georgia, in Thomas's brigade, remembered how the brightness of the moon, the booming and bursting of shells, "the shrieks and groans of the wounded and dying as I lay nearly insenceable around me that night, displayed all the horrors of war and put feelings and imaginations through the mind that I never wish to experience again. There scattered over the fields and emence forest the Battle field encompassed lay thousands of poor wounded and dying soldiers far away from home and friends, writhing in the agonies of death with no one to speak a soothing word to their ears. . . ."[33]

In the dark woods, those of Stuart's men unhurt except by fear, fatigue, and hunger huddled talking in hushed voices, listening to the whippoorwills' chant. "We could not sleep," Francis Johnson of the 45th Georgia wrote. "The enemy could be heard very plainly in front throwing up breastworks and we knew we had to run them out in the morning."[34] As in battle after battle, they had one another for comfort—and after this midnight, they shared something new, the knowledge that the man who had led them so far, made them believe they were superior to any other soldiers, had fallen. They did not know how badly Jackson was hurt, but most knew who had done it. As they settled down, they tried to make sense of it, to rationalize what had happened.

Major Barry of the 18th North Carolina, who had ordered his regiment to open fire on Jackson's party, insisted to Lane that he had no idea the generals had ridden out front; when he gave the order, all he heard was the noise of horsemen coming fast.[35]

The Tar Heels assured themselves that they had done only what they were told to do. Richard Martin Van Buren Reeves of the 18th maintained later that "I was standing under a large oak tree, Jackson came riding up. He told us the enemy was very near us and we must watch and listen and at the least noise, *Fire,* as it would be the foe. He rode away looking the gallant soldier he was. . . ."[36] By one account, the 18th did not realize its error until Private Arthur Smith of Company K knocked one of the riders in Jackson's party down with the butt of his musket.[37] As some of Reeves's comrades remembered it, Jackson had lifted his cap to the 18th as he passed its lines going forward, just the way he had saluted the regiment on the field after its brave charge at Cedar Mountain the summer before.[38]

The men of the 18th would never forget what they did that night, but when the chaos of the moment faded, their brothers did not blame them. For the rest of their lives, their identity with the 18th North Carolina was a sad distinction.

WHEN JACKSON's litter-bearers found the ambulance half a mile back, two wounded artillery officers were already aboard—Colonel Crutchfield and his assistant, Maj. Arthur L. Rogers. The ambulance belonged to Marcellus Moorman's horse artillery. Moorman, withdrawing his guns, was alongside when the Jackson party appeared. He asked who was coming. Jackson's low voice said, "Tell him it is an officer." Moorman recognized it and held the ambulance. Rogers, less seriously hurt, was taken out to make room for the general. Young Joe Morrison climbed in beside his brother-in-law to hold his arm steady so the jolting would not worsen the pain and bleeding.[39]

As the hard-floored, weak-springed ambulance rumbled along the Plank Road and approached Dowdall's, it was met by Hunter McGuire, the surgeon and close friend Jackson trusted so. McGuire, who left the most detailed and eloquent description of those hours, said, "I hope you are not badly hurt, General."

After the rough handling and loss of blood, Jackson sounded feeble: "I am badly injured, Doctor. I fear I am dying." He paused. "I am glad you have come. I think the wound in my shoulder is still bleeding."

Jackson was dripping blood. The brachial artery was hemorrhaging. McGuire stopped it with a finger while someone brought a light. The tourniquet had slipped; he readjusted it. He found Jackson's calm courtesy and presence of mind remarkable, since "his suffering at this time was intense; his hands were cold, his skin clammy, his face pale, and his lips compressed and bloodless." Jackson's brow was corrugated, his face fixed and rigid, and his thin lips so tight that the impression of his teeth behind them could be seen. McGuire gave him morphine and whiskey, and when Jackson seemed to relax, the ambulance ground to the rear. Well beyond enemy fire, the drivers used torches to light the way and help them avoid potholes. McGuire sat up front and kept a finger above the tourniquet to prevent more bleeding.

Soldiers who recognized McGuire came alongside to ask who was wounded, and repeatedly Jackson told him to say, "A Confederate offi-cer." Reaching up, the general pulled McGuire close to ask if Crutchfield was seriously hurt. Shortly afterward Crutchfield asked the same thing about Jackson, and when told he was grievously wounded, gasped, "Oh, my God!" Jackson, thinking Crutchfield had cried out in pain, insisted that McGuire stop the ambulance and try to ease his friend's suffering.

The three-and-a-half-mile trip to the corps hospital near Wilderness Tavern took till almost 11:30. Dr. Harvey Black, the surgeon in charge, had readied a tent for Jackson in the field north of Wilderness Tavern. There the general was put in bed, covered, and given another whiskey and water. McGuire let him rest until 2:00 A.M., then told him he was ready to give him chloroform and examine his wounds. The surgeon asked whether, if amputation seemed necessary, he should go ahead with it. Jackson said, "Yes, certainly. Do for me whatever you think best." [40]

Assisting McGuire were Doctors Black, R. T. Coleman, and Walls. Coleman rubbed salve over Jackson's face, then made a cone of cloth, soaked it with chloroform, and held it close to Jackson's nose and mouth. At McGuire's bidding, Jackson breathed deeply. As he faded, he whispered, "What an infinite blessing . . . blessing . . . blessing."

Jackson's aide James Power Smith held a lantern as McGuire inspected the wounds. First the surgeon cut out of the right hand a round ball, obviously from a smooth-bore musket—an outdated weapon no longer used by Federal troops, but still common in Southern regiments. This ball had hit the right palm, broken two bones, and slipped around to the back of the hand. Another ball had struck the outside of the left forearm just below the elbow and come out the opposite side above the wrist. The most serious wound was about three inches below that shoulder; the ball had severed the artery and broken the bone. Seeing the damage, McGuire without hesitation made a circular cut and amputated the arm an inch above the break. Then he dressed the wounds and the facial scrapes made when Jackson's horse plunged through the woods.

About 3:30 A.M., Sandie Pendleton, Jackson's adjutant, rode up to the hospital tent, asked to speak to the general, then crumpled off his horse in a faint of exhaustion and hunger. Recovered, he told McGuire that Hill was wounded, Stuart was in command, and the troops were "in great disorder." When McGuire tried to keep the young officer away from Jackson, Pendleton insisted that the fate of the battle, the army, perhaps the Confederacy, depended on his talking to the general.

Jackson had been in and out of consciousness, eventually taking a cup of coffee. When Pendleton went in, Jackson said calmly, "Well, Major, I'm glad to see you. I thought you were killed." Pendleton briefed him and asked for instructions. Jackson came alert, asking quick questions, then stopped as if to consider the next tactical moves. He frowned, pursed his lips, seeming about to give an order. Then his face relaxed and he slumped back.

"I don't know," he said weakly. "I can't say. Tell General Stuart he must do what he thinks best."[41]

CAPTAIN WILBOURN had to loop through the night south of Hazel Grove to carry news of Jackson to Lee on the other side of Hooker's army. The Confederate commander was asleep under an oilcloth lean-to when Wilbourn awoke him. At the young captain's first words, Lee motioned for him to sit beside him on the cot.

When Wilbourn told him Jackson had been shot by his own troops, Lee "seemed ready to burst into tears, and gave a moan." Wilbourn started to describe what had happened, but Lee broke in, saying, "Ah, Captain, don't let us say anything more about it. It is too painful to talk about. . . . Any victory is dearly bought which deprives us of the services of General Jackson, even for a short time."

Wilbourn called it "the saddest night I ever passed in my life, and when I saw this great man so much moved, and look as if he could weep, my cup of sadness was filled to overflowing." Lee was silent until Wilbourn rose, then he held him back to ask about how Jackson's corps was deployed and who was in command. Wilbourn told of the transfer from Jackson to Hill to Rodes to Stuart. "Rodes is a gallant, energetic, and courageous officer," Lee declared, as if he might have made a different decision.

Wilbourn told him the generals on that flank hoped Lee would come there himself. Lee asked where Stuart and Jackson were, so he could send them messages. The young captain said he thought Jackson had intended to cut the road from Chancellorsville to U.S. Ford.

Lee stood abruptly. "These people must be pressed today," he said.[42]

At 3:00 A.M., he wrote to Stuart:

> It is necessary that the glorious victory thus far achieved be prosecuted with the utmost vigor, and the enemy given no time to rally. As soon, therefore, as it is possible, they must be pressed, so that we may unite the two wings of the army.
>
> Endeavor, therefore, to dispossess them of Chancellorsville, which will permit the union of the whole army.
>
> I shall myself proceed to join you as soon as I can make arrangements on this side, but let nothing delay the completion of the plan of driving the enemy from his rear and from his positions.

I shall give orders that every effort be made on this side at daylight
to aid in the junction.[43]

In minutes, Lee was fully dressed, booted and spurred, ordering his
horse and staff ready to ride. He beckoned Wilbourn to his shelter and
spread for him a ham-and-cracker breakfast, from a basket sent by a farm
lady nearby. As Wilbourn finished eating, Lee swung into his saddle.

Just then, Jackson's mapmaker Jed Hotchkiss came in after a four-hour
ride through the Wilderness. He briefed the general on the flank battle and
how the troops were deployed for morning. But when he started to
describe how Jackson was shot, Lee interrupted him, saying, "I know all
about it, and do not wish to hear any more—it is too painful a subject."
He told Hotchkiss he would a thousand times rather have been wounded
instead.[44]

There had not been time, only a half hour, for Stuart to get Lee's 3:00
A.M. message and send back a query. Apparently reacting to what Hotchkiss said about Stuart's deployment and plans, Lee wrote another order
reinforcing his instructions, repeating his aim of linking his wing with
Stuart's.

After sharing Wilbourn's breakfast, Hotchkiss rode off with the
message.

AS DAWN APPROACHED, the 12,000 troops in Lee's wing of the Southern army were holding a broken line anchored at its right on the Turnpike,
just over a mile and a quarter east of Chancellorsville. Wofford's,
Semmes's, and Kershaw's brigades of McLaws's division occupied a mile
of field fortifications between there and the Plank Road. Anderson's
division ran to their left, beginning with Mahone's brigade facing north,
up the Plank Road. There was a half-mile gap between Mahone's left and
the brigades of Wright and Posey, which still looked over Scott's Run and
Catharine Furnace, where they had fought off Sickles's probe Saturday
afternoon.

Stuart's wing, 26,000 infantry minus the casualties of the night before,
was more or less reorganized before sunrise. Confronting Hooker from

11. Stuart Takes Over. *The bend in the Confederate front line confuses the initial
Southern attack early Sunday, separating brigades and exposing their flanks. Hooker has
not yet made the mistake of withdrawing Sickles from the crucial position at Hazel Grove.*

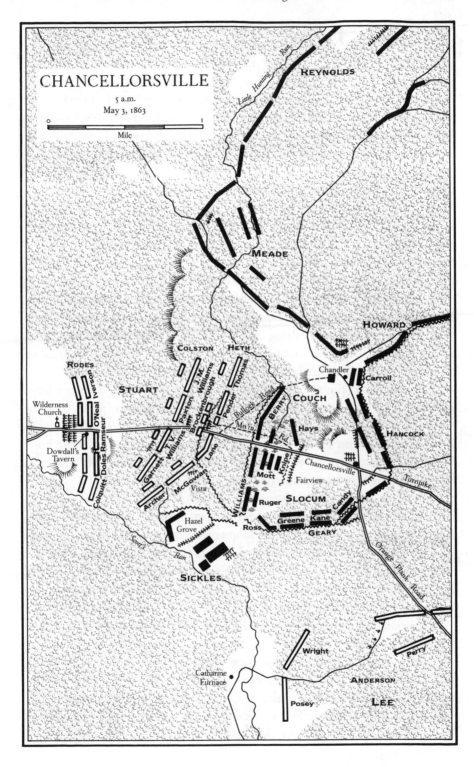

CHANCELLORSVILLE

5 a.m.
May 3, 1863

0   1
Mile

the west, Heth was on the first line, commanding A. P. Hill's division. Behind him was Colston, and farther back the bone-tired regiments of Rodes's division—the reverse of the sequence in which they had advanced the evening before. Heth's front ran from about three-quarters of a mile north of the Plank Road to a mile and a quarter south of it. From left to right, north to south, Heth had the brigades of Thomas, Pender, Lane, McGowan, and Archer. His own brigade, now commanded by Col. J. M. Brockenbrough, straddled the Plank Road close behind this front line.

At their nearest point to each other, across the neck of the Union position at Hazel Grove, Stuart's and Lee's wings of the Rebel army were about a mile and a quarter apart; their pickets were closer than that. But while Jackson's broad front of attack had overlapped Hooker's battle lines the night before, now Hooker's reinforced lines reached just beyond Stuart's on the south. On the north, they ran far beyond the Confederate positions, all the way to the Rappahannock.

Hooker now had six corps on hand. After a 23-mile march from below Fredericksburg, Reynolds's bedraggled First Corps was starting to dig in from the Rappahannock along Hunting Run to the Ely's Ford Road. Meade's Fifth Corps tied in with it there, angling southeast along the road to a point near Chandler's house.

Chandler's was the apex of a heavily fortified fallback position ordered by Hooker. It had Reynolds and Meade behind Little Hunting Run on the west and the collected remnants of Howard's Eleventh Corps behind Mineral Spring Run on the east. Using advantageous ground, these inner lines ran back to protect the Rappahannock fords. After inspecting them later, Confederate artilleryman Porter Alexander called them "probably the strongest field intrenchment ever built in Virginia."

Hooker's forward line enclosed Fairview and Chancellorsville itself. Looking west, near the foot of the slope down from Fairview, Berry's and Williams's divisions still confronted Stuart on the right and left of the Plank Road. Slocum's other division, under Brig. Gen. John W. Geary, faced south along the Twelfth Corps' original line. Looking east toward Lee and Fredericksburg, Darius Couch's Second Corps line ran from the Plank Road up to Chandler's. All of these commands deepened their fortifications during the night.

Still protruding toward the southwest was an oval surrounding Hazel Grove. This was Sickles, with two of his Third Corps divisions plus another infantry brigade, cavalry, and a formidable array of artillery. He was linked with Fairview by two regiments posted along the narrow neck strengthened by his night attack.

Lee, when he instructed Stuart to keep pressing right, to turn Hooker's fortifications if possible, did not realize that Stuart no longer overlapped Hooker's lines. Stuart could not merely slip to his right to unite with Lee; he would have to fight his way. The main obstacle was Hazel Grove, from which Sickles's guns could enfilade Stuart's advance toward Chancellorsville. With more of the boldness Sickles had shown, it might even become the route for a Federal offensive, to keep Stuart and Lee apart and use superior manpower to crush each Confederate wing separately. Conversely, should the Rebels take Hazel Grove, they could pour artillery fire from it onto Fairview and Chancellorsville.

Hooker was sleeping when a messenger from Sickles came to Chancellorsville to urge that the army wrap Hazel Grove into its main lines. Hooker's acting chief of staff, James Van Alen, refused to wake the general until near morning.[45] Neither commander quite realized the potential of Hazel Grove in the darkness before dawn, before the brutal climax of the battle of Chancellorsville.

Chapter Thirteen

So Perfect a Slaughter

JAMES EWELL BROWN STUART was used to riding hard, surprising the enemy, dashing in and out waving his plumed hat, laughing all the way as he circled the whole Yankee army. He was superb at scouting, gathering intelligence, and screening the movements of Lee's army. But he had never been responsible for a mass of infantry struggling through a wilderness where the enemy waited alert and fortified, a situation opposite every glorious legend about the fast-moving cavalry. He had never commanded a corps before, never taken over any such command in the middle of the night in the middle of a battle.

That night, he had not heard first-hand Jackson's intention to thrust north and cut Hooker off from the Rappahannock fords; his only instruction from the wounded Jackson was to "do what he thinks best." It is also uncertain whether he received Lee's orders before morning to reach south and join the other Confederate divisions, to come at Hooker that way. These were ample reasons for Stuart to hesitate, to probe to find Hooker's lines, to await reassurance from Lee or detailed consultation with his infantry commanders before committing himself.

But one principle common to infantry and cavalry alike was reflexive with Lee, Jackson, and Stuart: Strike the enemy before he strikes you. As Stuart rode from Ely's Ford to take command, he intended to pursue the attack as soon as he arrived. But then he saw the disarray along the front during the night fighting. "Knowing that an advance under such circumstances would be extremely hazardous, much against my inclination I felt bound to wait for daylight," he wrote. With or without precise instructions, he had no doubt at all that he was doing the right thing in attacking at first light. Had he been less certain, more cautious, hundreds of Southern soldiers who died would have lived through that warm, clear Sunday morning, perhaps to praise him in their old age for his prudence.[1]

Before dawn, Stuart ordered his entire force to be ready to advance. Most of his troops had only two or three hours' rest, and though some cooked rations, only a few of the regiments to the rear got a chance to eat. Stuart's plan was for his front-line brigades south of the Plank Road—Lane, McGowan, and Archer—to start by pivoting, to align with the troops to their left. Then the whole battle line would move forward at right angles to the road. When the attack began, Colston's division would follow Heth's in support, and behind it Rodes would come on as the third wave.

But at about 5:30, as soon as Lane's, Archer's, and McGowan's men had taken their first steps, Stuart sent orders for a general advance. He explained later that his directions for alignment had been misunderstood. Lane was able to swing on line, but as soon as Archer's men started moving, they struck resistance. After a night that ended in confusion, Sunday morning began that way.

Archer and McGowan moved directly ahead from their overnight positions, sending their skirmishers southeast rather than pivoting to straighten the line. Pushing through dense pines, Archer promptly lost contact with McGowan on his left. His Alabamians and Tennesseeans drove in Union pickets and in less than a quarter mile came to "the open field in front of a battery, which was placed on an abrupt hill near a spring-house."[2]

This was Hazel Grove.

In the fading moonlight before dawn, Confederate artilleryman Porter Alexander had scouted the front for forward positions, to ready his guns for action at daybreak. Besides the Plank Road, the only firing lane through the forest was the Vista along which the 8th Pennsylvania Cavalry had begun its ill-fated ride the evening before, and Sickles's troops had attacked near midnight. At its southern end was Hazel Grove, which Alexander recognized as an ideal artillery position on Hooker's flank. He brought up several batteries, ready to move down the Vista onto the plateau as soon as the way was clear, and alerted Stuart to the tactical potential of Hazel Grove.

Sickles, still holding that plateau with two divisions, a separate brigade, and five batteries of cannon, realized its potential, too, when he urged Hooker to wrap Hazel Grove into his main lines. But Hooker, once he arose before sunup and came down to talk with Sickles, thought defensively. He did not want to leave Sickles dangling out there. He wanted to make the Federal lines more compact. He ordered Sickles to abandon Hazel Grove and move into the Union defenses around Chancellorsville.

As Alexander wrote later, "There has rarely been a more gratuitous gift of a battlefield."[3]

Thus when Archer's Rebel brigade came slashing through the pines to the clearing, it did not collide with all of Sickles's defensive force, but only its rearguard. This was Brig. Gen. Charles K. Graham's Pennsylvania brigade. Before Graham's force could get away, it was struck by "a galling fire from the rapid advance of the enemy." Capt. James F. Huntington, commanding the last battery of Union artillery there, needed more canister at such close range, but had used it up the night before. In an instant he decided to use fuse shrapnel, in which a lit fuse normally would explode the shell on its target—but to leave the fuse hole open, so the propellant charge would ignite the powder and burst the shell in the gun, spewing shrapnel from the muzzle. It was a daring technique; if the gun itself blew open, it could wipe out its crew. Firing this way, Huntington's guns held back the attackers until Rebel musketry drove away his supporting infantry.[4] Then Archer's Confederates came on at the double-quick, taking a hundred prisoners and sweeping the plateau clean.

Suddenly, as his brigade regrouped in the clearing, Archer realized it was out front all alone. Looking northeast, he saw Union troops packed on the rise of Fairview and in the woods between. Nevertheless he attacked into those woods and got within 70 yards of the main Federal line before his thinning regiments lost momentum. Falling back, they reformed, then went in again and got cut up again. About 6:30, Archer brought them back to the clearing. As he waited for infantry reinforcement to carry on, Maj. William J. Pegram hurried up with three batteries of Virginia artillery, the first Rebel guns to reach Hazel Grove.[5]

The exact sequence in which Stuart's brigades advanced, retreated, then advanced again was impossible for the officers involved to sort out, even immediately after the battle. But especially south of the Plank Road, those brigades slammed ahead not in one broad battle line but almost independently, separated by the thickets and then by the varied angles of the Union works before them.

By morning, those works were formidable, with trenches deepened and log breastworks above. Here and there a dead horse was dragged in to fill a gap. To cross the 250 or so yards between their own and Berry's and Williams's line, Rebel infantrymen near the Plank Road had to work their way through the woods, past where Jackson was shot, until they came to a cleared strip 50 to 100 yards wide. There, trees had been felled to provide logs for breastworks and a thick abatis of intertwined treetops pointing toward the advancing Confederates. This was intended to slow them while Federal infantry and artillery opened at close range.

Behind that front line, back of the little creek where ferns and holly bushes grew, was another along the edge of the woods. Up the slope behind it, the artillery had been dug in deeper during the night, making a third line along the brow of the Fairview plateau. Sickles's two infantry divisions and four batteries from Hazel Grove filled in behind this, making Hooker's central position four lines deep as it faced west. However, the mass of Union guns on Fairview could not risk firing downhill over friendly troops to repel attackers close to the first Union line, so in the early going it concentrated on Rebels moving toward the front through the woods.[6]

While Archer was attacking through Hazel Grove, McGowan's regiments got separated from each other as they drove over the first Union works and scattered the 37th New York. They pushed another 100 yards before bogging down in a stationary half-hour musket duel with Williams's Federals in the second line. One of those killed in the charge was sixteen-year-old Jimmie Hunter of the 1st South Carolina, who had kept his comrades' spirits up many a day on the road. As they marched around Hooker's flank the day before, he kept saying he was "going to a May ball," and when he spotted one of Professor Lowe's balloons aloft, he laughed and said, "Mr. Hooker, you've looked at my hand, and I won't play."[7] McGowan himself was wounded shortly after his broad form mounted the Union breastworks.

Federal General Williams, overseeing his line on the Fairview slope, remembered "the thunder . . . sharp bursting . . . peculiar whizzing . . . shriek . . . crash . . . thug . . . phiz" of shells and Minié balls tearing through the woods and human flesh. Thousands of voices screamed, cheered, and cursed in the gunsmoke; wounded men, riderless horses, and skulkers headed for the rear. Despite the horrors, Williams wrote, anyone there had to feel it both terrible and grand.[8]

When Archer regrouped at Hazel Grove, this exposed McGowan's right flank to counterattack by Brig. Gen. Thomas Ruger's Yankee brigade, which threw McGowan's South Carolinians back to the first Federal line.[9] That fallback in turn opened the right flank of Lane's brigade, which suffered more killed and more casualties overall than any other brigade in either army at Chancellorsville. Yelling as they charged, Lane's Tar Heels had carried the first Yankee line, sending the green Union 3rd Maryland to the rear in panic. They flowed around J. E. Dimick's gun section, which had given them so much trouble the night before. Capturing one cannon, they mortally wounded the brave Yankee lieutenant. But then, advancing along the Plank Road where the Federal guns beyond were sighted in, Lane's men were blasted by "concentrated murderous artillery fire." Fresh Union infantry came up; in the seesaw struggle Lane lost twelve of his thirteen field officers. Before the battle was over, his 7th North Carolina had four commanders, the 18th three, and the 28th and 33rd two each.[10]

As Dorsey Pender's brigade attacked Berry's Federals just north of the Plank Road, the thirty-eight-year-old Berry was up front with his men. He was a State of Maine citizen-soldier, formerly a carpenter, navigator, and mayor of Rockland. He believed in managing battle first-hand. Early that morning, he had been astonished to find troops of his 1st Massachusetts and 74th New York falling back. He stopped them and asked why they were retreating. Someone said a staff officer had given the order. As some nearby later recalled it, Berry demanded that the officer be brought to him. Furious, he reached to rip off the man's shoulder straps and pulled open the coat itself. Beneath it was a gray uniform. Berry arrested the man as a spy and sent him to the rear, then ordered his troops back into their defense line.[11]

There Berry's troops held against the first waves of Confederate attackers. In the 1st Massachusetts, Daniel Macomber watched the Rebels "come up in close column, close to our entrenchments . . . our whole line poured the shot into them. You could see them drop all around but as soon as one man fell another stepped into his place. They fight like the Devil there is no rubbing that out. But our line stood firm"—until its flanks were turned.[12] One of Sickles's artillerymen nearby wrote home that "The fighting here was the most desperate of the war. I never before conceived of such a fire. It was terrible, men seemed to fall like blades of grass as the scythe goes through them and artillery horses fell by the scores, it was dreadful, horrible, appalling."[13]

Berry, looking right and left, realized the Rebels were coming on both sides despite their terrible losses. He sent a captain to ask Hooker whether he should hold there or fall back to the next line. Then he started to cross the fire-swept road to speak with Brig. Gen. Gershom Mott. Staff officers tried to hold him back, but he brushed them off. Berry made it across, but as he returned, one well-aimed round from a Rebel sharpshooter struck him down. Carried out of the line of fire, he died within minutes. A knot of grieving officers gathered around him. Hooker, checking on his old division, rode up later and asked who the dead officer was. Told it was Berry, the Union commander leaped off his horse with tears in his eyes, kissed the dead general's forehead, and asked, "My God, Berry, why did this have to happen? Why does the man I relied on so have to be taken away in this manner?" [14]

Brig. Gen. Joseph B. Carr took over Berry's division as Pender and Thomas, on the Confederate left, hammered it back. A series of Union regiments on that side of the Plank Road broke off and retreated toward the fallback line at Chandler's. At the northern end of the attacking line, where Yankee artillery was less a factor, Thomas's Georgians kept going, with the 13th North Carolina of Pender's brigade alongside. The 13th charged so fast that Lt. John R. Ireland ran ahead and captured Union Brig. Gen. William Hays and his staff before they could get away. Cpl. Monroe Robinson chased a Union color-bearer so closely that the Yankee ripped off the flag and threw down the staff, which distracted his pursuer long enough for him to escape. [15]

This pellmell advance by the Rebel left threatened to turn the Union artillery position at Fairview before Hooker's reinforcements could come up. Col. Emlen Franklin's brigade of Whipple's division, back from Hazel Grove, was rushed into line to protect the guns. Later, Maj. Gen. William H. French about-faced his division of Couch's corps from the other side of the Union position and formed almost two brigades at an oblique angle toward the Confederates north of the Plank Road. When Hooker saw this, he ordered French to counterattack and drive the Rebels through the woods. French's men—Ohioans, West Virginians, Indianans—threw off their heavy marching order and lit into Thomas's flank and rear. This sent Thomas's troops fleeing, and their retreat carried Pender's along, both Southern brigades withdrawing over one line of fortifications back to the first Yankee works. [16]

Just south of the road, Mott's and Ruger's Federal brigades converged on Lane's battered troops and drove them back over their own dead and wounded. In this counterattack, Ruger's 27th Indiana charged with fixed bayonets and reported that "the rebels fled before us like sheep" before making a stand at the first Federal line. In hand-to-hand struggle, the Indianans threw the Tar Heels on their left back into the tangled abatis. There, Col. Silas Colgrove reported, the Rebels "became mixed up in a perfect jam, our men all the time pouring in the most deadly fire. I can safely say that I have never witnessed on any other occasion so perfect a slaughter." [17] Only one of Lane's regiments, the 28th North Carolina, managed to hold on behind the first Union breastworks. For the moment the others ceased to exist, until their survivors rallied farther back.

These Southern brigades closest to the Plank Road, where the Union artillery had concentrated its aim, suffered most: Pender's was cut up nearly as badly as Lane's. Behind it in Brockenbrough's, which came on in support, the 55th Virginia had five commanders before the fight was over. But there was desperation and frustration enough to go around. After three Rebel charges against Williams's line, the defenders had fired more than 40 rounds each, and taken heavy casualties. Corps commander Slocum sent one officer after another to ask Hooker for help. Hooker answered: "I can't make men or ammunition for General Slocum." [18]

JEB STUART seemed everywhere. In the first half hour, his horse was wounded under him. Here, he was singing "Old Joe Hooker, won't you come out the Wilderness," to the tune of the "The Old Gray Mare," and his soldiers were joining in. There, he rode shouting "Remember Jackson!" as he urged the fallen general's troops ahead.

When Lane's brigade was driven back, Stuart came dashing along the first Union line, where the 28th North Carolina was doing its best to hold on. He ordered the regiment up and into a second charge. Challenged by Stuart, the Carolinians moved out, though artillery and musketry cut them down as they advanced. Suddenly Yankees came at the regiment's open flank, and it fell back on the Union works again. When the colonel of the 28th, Samuel D. Lowe, went to find Lane for instructions, Stuart appeared in his absence and sent the regiment forward yet again. This third charge "through the same terrible artillery firing" was ordered to support newly advanced Confederate batteries. [19]

Though his horse was wounded, Stuart kept riding back and forth, waving his hat, cheering. He hailed a Virginia battery on the Plank Road and ordered it to fire on counterattacking Yankees in the woods ahead. After a salvo, the gunners adjusted their fire, and Stuart, with an artillery officer beside him, yelled, "You've got it, kid! Give it to them!" [20]

At another point, Col. Abner Perrin of the 14th South Carolina had taken over McGowan's brigade and was swinging it forward behind a rise that shielded it from the devastating Union artillery. But, he reported, he "was prevented from doing so, and ordered to move straight ahead by a general officer, whom I afterward learned was General Stuart." Thus, "The brigade moved up with great spirit and determination, under a terrific fire of grape and shell from a battery in the open field. . . ." [21]

The first Confederate wave, 10,000 men strong, with little artillery support, had attacked and kept attacking. Taking heavy casualties, it had driven over one line of enemy works, then in places over another before Union artillery and infantry counterattacks hammered it back. But a single Confederate division, even with Stuart out front, could not drive head-on through four solidly packed lines of defense. Stuart now realized this. With the wreckage of his first wave huddled along the initial Yankee breastworks, he called forward his second and third lines, both Colston's and Rodes's divisions. He would throw all his reserves into the attack.

At the same time, he ordered 30 more cannon onto Hazel Grove. The new system of artillery battalions was working exactly as intended, as the Confederate guns quickly massed for their finest day of the entire war. On no other field did either side's artillery work so successfully in the attack; the most memorable moments for cannon—at Malvern Hill, Fredericksburg, Gettysburg—were usually on the defensive. On Hazel Grove, battery after battery wheeled into position to fire into Hooker's southern flank. The artillerymen knew they were having a field day; one boy who looked no more than twelve did a backflip each time he jerked the lanyard, to the high amusement of his fellow gunners.[22]

Raleigh Colston, leading Jackson's old division, was new at command on this level. That morning, only one of his four brigades, Stonewall's former outfit now under E. F. Paxton, was led by a general. One of Colston's brigadiers, John R. Jones, had taken himself to the rear with an ulcerated leg, being relieved by Col. Thomas S. Garnett. When Colston himself assumed command of the division, his brigade was taken by Col. E. T. H. Warren, who had been wounded in the assault the night before and in turn succeeded by Col. Titus V. Williams. Francis Nicholls's foot had been shot off by the furious Yankee cannonade that same night, and his Louisianans were now led by Col. Jesse M. Williams. All these changes, the chaos of the night before, and the carnage plain before them unnerved Colston's troops, coming up as the second wave of Stuart's attack. Colston brought them in behind A. P. Hill's front line with J. M. Williams and Paxton left of the Plank Road, Garnett and T. V. Williams to the right. But when they got to the works where Hill's division was holding on under heavy fire, Colston's men—Jackson's old division— dived for cover, and for a while he could not drive them forward.[23]

Col. D. H. Hamilton of the 1st South Carolina took over McGowan's brigade after the general and two other colonels were wounded. He reported that as his command held against a flanking counterattack, "we were re-enforced, or rather encumbered, by a portion of General Colston's command, for instead of pushing rapidly to the right . . . they took refuge (many of them) in the rear of my line, and annoyed my regiment much by firing over their heads, in some instances wounding my men, and in one instance killing one of my best subalterns. . . ."[24]

Colston's officers did their best to move their troops into the attack. T. V. Williams was hit, Lt. Col. Samuel T. Walker was killed and Lt. Col. Stephen D. Thruston was wounded before Lt. Col. Hamilton A. Brown finally assumed command of Warren's brigade. As these and other field officers were cut down, Pender's and McGowan's troops in the works ahead were running low on ammunition, and just then Ruger's Yankee brigade drove onto the Rebel right flank. "This was a most critical moment," Colston wrote. The troops in the works, huddling six or eight deep, were a mixed lot of regiments scrambled as they attacked and fell back. Colston sent for Paxton to rush the Stonewall Brigade from north of the Plank Road to meet the threat on his right. He also called for Garnett to swing his reserve brigade toward the right.[25]

Elisha Franklin Paxton had risen in two years from lieutenant in the Rockbridge (Virginia) Rifles to major on Jackson's staff to brigadier general heading Jackson's old command. Well educated at Washington College and Yale, top of his law class at the University of Virginia, he might not seem the type to speak of premonitions. But he had the night before, after Jackson was wounded, and his friend Henry Kyd Douglas took him seriously. Paxton, depressed for days, told Douglas he was sure he would not survive Sunday's fighting. He told where his papers were, and asked that they be sent home to Lexington. He kept his Bible and a picture of his wife with him. He asked Douglas to write to his wife as soon as he was killed, and see that his body was sent home. "When he finished," Douglas recalled, "I had no doubt of his sincerity and of his awful prescience."

Sunday morning, as Union artillery pounded the woods, Douglas found Paxton sitting against a tree, reading his Bible as he waited for orders. Word came to move up. Paxton stood and reminded his friend of their talk the night before. When I fall, Paxton said, J. H. S. Funk will take over the brigade as senior colonel. Help him all you can, he asked, then started the Stonewall Brigade across the Plank Road.

There it came upon Lane's and McGowan's shredded regiments huddling behind the first Union works—"a large number of men of whom fear had taken the most absolute possession," reported Funk. "We endeavored to persuade them to go forward, but all we could say was of but little avail." Marching over them, some of Paxton's men cracked to the shell-shocked Carolinians, "We'll show you how to clear away a Federal line."[26]

Paxton took the Stonewall Brigade ahead into swampy underbrush with the 2nd Virginia on its right. Pressing on rightward, the regiment gained high ground on the Union flank and enfiladed the enemy line. But in reaching so far that way, it opened a gap of 80 to 100 yards between itself and the 4th Virginia. When Yankee reinforcements moved up, they poured fire into this opening and across the Rebel front. In ten minutes, 140 of the 355 soldiers in the 4th Virginia were killed or wounded. Col. James K. Edmondson of the 27th was shot out of his saddle. And Frank Paxton, trying to coordinate the Stonewall Brigade in the tangled bottomland, was hit as he ran between regiments. A lieutenant rolled him over. Paxton reached up, put his hand over the pocket where he kept his wife's photograph and his Bible, and died.

After being pinned down in a furious firefight, the Stonewall Brigade, like the troops who had attacked before, fell back bleeding behind the first Union line. With some grim pleasure, McGowan's South Carolinians taunted the Virginians as they returned.[27]

Colonel Garnett, bringing his brigade up in support of Paxton, also was mortally wounded. It was a devastating morning for the leadership of the Army of Northern Virginia, as brigadiers and field officers all across Stuart's line exhorted their charges from the front like platoon leaders. Despite their sacrificial courage and the high zeal with which their troops went in yelling at daybreak, despite Stuart's jaunty inspiration, his first wave, then his second, had been slammed back after their opening successes. Now, if Hooker's position was to be carried by assault from the west, it was up to Stuart's third line—Rodes's division, which had been out front the evening before.

While the massed Rebel artillery at Hazel Grove blasted away at Hooker from the southwest, fewer guns could squeeze into position for direct support of Stuart's infantry attack. Firing canister along the Plank Road, Lt. Col. Hilary P. Jones stopped a Federal counterattack as it drove Pender's and Thomas's men backward. When Union general Williams's division was forced away from its first line, the Rebel guns rushed forward with Stuart's foot soldiers and dueled with the artillery on Fairview. One Federal officer later saluted his enemy's work: "I never before saw anything so fine as the attack on that battery; the air was full of missiles, solid shot, shells and musket balls. I saw one solid shot kill three horses and a man, another took a leg off one of the captains of the batteries." Union

Lt. Franklin B. Crosby was working his guns furiously as the Rebels charged, when a musket ball found his heart. He lived just long enough to say to his captain, "Tell Father I died happy."[28]

As Rodes's brigades came up, they passed through the second wave of Stuart's assault troops, most of them now fought out and unwilling to go in again. Col. Edward O'Neal was shot as he brought his brigade along the left of the road, and succeeded by Col. J. M. Hall.

Nick Weekes of the 3rd Alabama recalled how the Federal artillery greeted his regiment: "There must have been 50 guns. . . . The biggest tree offered no protection. One might as well have been in front as behind it. Limbs and the tops were falling about us as if torn by a cyclone." Then shells came screaming close overhead from Confederate artillery back along the road. "We were enveloped, as it were, in dense fog, the flashing of guns could be seen only a few feet away. . . . At every breath we were inhaling sulphurous vapor. . . . What a din. What a variety of hideous noises. The ping of the minnie ball, the splutter of canister, the whistling of grape, the 'where are you,' 'where are you' of screaming shells. . . ."

Weekes saw "an arm and shoulder fly from the man just in front, exposing his throbbing heart. Another's foot flew up and kicked him in the face as a shell struck his leg. Another, disemboweled, crawled along on all fours, his entrails trailing behind, and still another held up his tongue with his hand, a piece of shell having carried away his lower jaw. I had just about made up my mind that 'this is hell sure enough' when one, two, three and the fourth shell dropped almost in the same spot as fast as one could count, exploding as they struck the ground—and all was dark around me. I should say blackness, so black and thick I could feel it, and my feet seemed to rest on a sheet of flame." In seconds he recovered to find himself standing alone while fourteen other troops lay wounded within a few feet.

Rodes dashed up and ordered Capt. M. F. Bonham, leading the 3rd Alabama, to charge regardless of the other commands in front of him. When Bonham started forward, the adjacent commanders tried to stop him, thinking he had "gone wild." Told his left was exposed to a cross fire, Bonham ignored the warning and shouted, "Forward, Third Alabama! The order is forward! Follow me!" The regiments alongside went with him as he started up the slope of Fairview.

"The very air seemed black with shot," said Weekes. "Our line melted away as if swallowed up by the earth." Weekes's friend Cecil Carter was shot, and with another soldier Weekes dragged him behind a tree. Carter opened his eyes, said, "What are you fellows doing?" "Nothing, Cecil,"

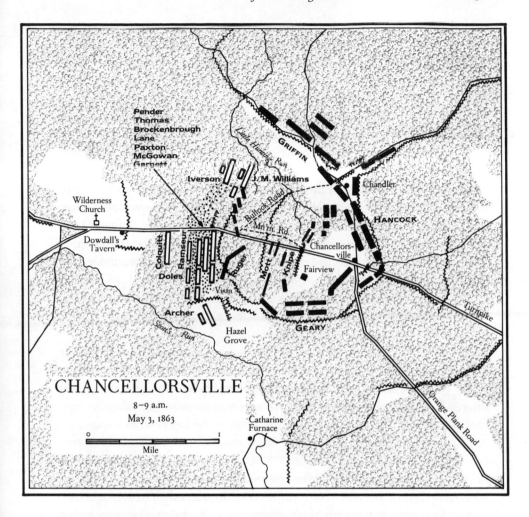

CHANCELLORSVILLE
8–9 a.m.
May 3, 1863

0 _____ 1
Mile

12. Attack and Counterattack. *Stuart's first waves have charged, retreated, charged, retreated, and taken cover six deep along "Slocum's log works." After beating off Union counterattacks, they advance again at Stuart's urging. Hooker, at his Chancellorsville headquarters, is knocked down by a shell shortly after 9 o'clock.*

said Weekes. "You are wounded. Don't try to get up." Carter said, "No, I'm not shot. Where?" "In the breast," said his friends. Carter stuck his finger in the hole. "The bullet must have bounced out," he said. "I can't feel it." Blood gushed from the wound, and Carter fell back. Weekes ran on up the slope, sure his friend was dead.

The Alabamians struck the Yankee abatis, "which destroyed everything like order in our ranks and every man went on his own hook, crawling over and under the felled trees, not stopping to fire a shot till we struck the infantry and drove it back. . . ." Now the woods were afire. To escape the flames and smoke, the attackers rushed into the road, and canister drove them back into the woods. They were upon the enemy cannon when musket fire struck them from behind. They thought it was from their own troops. But beneath the smoke, Weekes saw blue uniforms coming— Yankees in their rear. He and a friend took off. "To have to die is bad enough, but being captured was out of the question," he said. "I think if a rabbit had jumped in front of us we would have originated that saying, 'Get out of my way, Mr. Rabbit, and let somebody run who knows how.' "[29]

That was the pattern—costly advance and then retreat from crushing Union artillery fire and infantry, straight ahead and on every flank. Right of the road, Stephen Dodson Ramseur moved his North Carolina brigade forward and found troops of the first two waves, who had already been through this experience, still huddling behind the breastworks.

"Knowing that a general advance had been ordered, I told these troops to move forward," Ramseur wrote. "Not a man moved." He reported this to Stuart, who told him to take command there "and compel them to advance." Ramseur tried. He pleaded. He threatened. They would not move. Furiously asking for their commander, Ramseur discovered that General Jones was not there and Garnett had been killed, and he could not find Col. Alexander S. Vandeventer, who had taken over after Garnett fell. Riding back to Stuart, Ramseur asked for permission to run over the balky troops before him. Permission "was cheerfully granted," he reported.

Lane, told that Ramseur was about to attack, begged him not to take fresh troops over that ground. Lane's own brigade had been shattered, his brother killed. He urged Ramseur to swing right and enfilade the Union line.[30] In reply, Ramseur turned, raised his sword, and shouted, "Attention!" His men stood, muskets ready. "Forward, boys!" he ordered. "Walk right over them! Forward!"

His Carolinians stepped through and over the shaken soldiers behind the breastworks. Col. Bryan Grimes, leading his 4th North Carolina, was so outraged by the sight of one officer hugging the earth that he pushed his face into the dirt with his boot. William Calder of the 2nd North Carolina said, "The brave, chivalric Virginians lay flat on the ground and the tar-heels whom they so often ridicule walked over them to glory and to victory." But it was not glorious for long. From the motionless troops, a voice called to Grimes: "You may double-quick, but you'll come back faster than you go!" [31]

With a yell, Ramseur's brigade charged into a storm of artillery. "I have never in my life heard the missiles of death whistle so thick and fast around me," said Lt. William Norman of the 2nd North Carolina. "I was very nearly covered in the earth many times by bombshells. The bark from the trees often made my face sting, and splinters knocked from the neighboring trees or saplings were stuck in my clothes." [32]

Ruger's battered Yankee brigade, after driving back three Confederate charges, had pulled away toward Chancellorsville. The right of Ramseur's advance struck the right of Graham's Pennsylvanians, coming in where Ruger had moved out. Thus, while Ramseur's left regiments drove on across the second Union line, those on his right had to hold back to defend their flank. Doles's Georgia brigade, assigned to advance alongside, had been thrown off course by the deep thickets and wandered past the other end of Graham's defenders. Ramseur started taking "a horrible enfilade fire" through a 500-yard gap on his right. Seeing the danger, he sent back repeatedly for Jones's brigade, now under Vandeventer, to come up beside him. Nothing happened. He ran the gantlet of fire twice to plead with officers and men of Vandeventer's command, "but all in vain." Ramseur sent word to Rodes that without help he would have to withdraw. Rodes himself, a powerful presence, rode up and tried, but could not stir the dispirited men.

Stuart, hearing of Ramseur's desperation, raced to where the Stonewall Brigade crouched under cover. Because it was Stuart, singing, taunting Old Joe Hooker, telling his troops they must avenge Jackson, he succeeded where Ramseur and Rodes had failed. The Stonewall Brigade moved out across the breastworks again. The 12th Georgia, slipped loose from Doles's brigade, advanced on its right. Suddenly the 30th North Carolina, which had been detached from Ramseur to protect the guns at Hazel Grove, rejoined alongside. It struck the threatening Yankee envelopment by the flank, taking several hundred prisoners. The Stonewall Brigade pushed on, its soldiers shouting "Remember Jackson!" Funk reported that it drove the enemy three-fourths of a mile, "pell-mell around the Chancellor house," though in this surge it could not have reached that far. But under cover of murderous, converging artillery and musket fire, still more Union troops crowded up the ravine on the right of the attacking regiments. Low on ammunition, Ramseur's and Paxton's brigades withdrew to the breastworks, joining the others who had charged shouting and fallen back bleeding over that same ground.[33]

Seeing troops coming back, Stuart thought for a moment they were withdrawing without orders. He asked whose brigade it was. Ramseur's, he was told. Stuart's face changed immediately. Waving his hat over his head, he yelled, "Three cheers for Ramseur's brigade! Men, you have done your duty!"

As the brigade regrouped, Ramseur came down the line to the 2nd North Carolina, stopped and asked, "Is that all that's left?"

"This is all, sir," said an officer.

Ramseur burst into tears. "Men," he cried, "I love you."

Out of 340 men, the 2nd North Carolina lost 214 killed and wounded; out of about 1,400, Ramseur's brigade lost 623. Lieutenant Norman, searching for the remains of Company A between attacks, found his captain mortally wounded. Of those in the charge, only one private could be found. Later Norman turned up one lieutenant and two more privates who had been assigned to the rear: altogether, his surviving company consisted of two junior officers and three privates. After the battle, the regiment's ten companies were merged into four.*[34]

WHILE BRIGADE after brigade battered against Hooker's lines near the Plank Road, farther right and left the troops who had swept ahead so triumphantly on each end of Jackson's attack the night before tried to do it again. About half of Doles's Georgians, after losing contact with Ramseur, charged across the second line of Yankee works and kept going up a creek bottom between the west and south faces of Hooker's position. Doles was deep within the Yankee lines, far beyond other Southern forces

---

*After the battle, Funk heard that Ramseur was saying that the Stonewall Brigade had "disgraced itself" by refusing to go forward, and by allowing other troops to run over it. He wrote to Ramseur, demanding an explanation. Ramseur answered that he had mentioned "only part" of the Stonewall Brigade. Said North Carolinian Ramseur to Virginian Funk, "I have always deprecated all miserable jealousies between troops from Sister States contending for a common and glorious cause, and this matter has been spoken of by me with caution & regret." Ramseur added a postscript explaining that he would have responded to Funk sooner, but he was absent on account of wounds. Yet in his official report filed the day after this letter, he still did not credit the Stonewall Brigade with coming to his aid that bloody morning.[35]

in that sector. He charged two Union brigades from their rear, sending back a flock of surprised prisoners. Then, protected by the slope of Fairview hill, he pushed past the flank of the artillery position there, chasing the gunners away from seven pieces. His brigade fought off one infantry counterattack, but then Union cannon back at the Chancellor house found and flailed his line with bursting shells and canister.

In Doles's 44th Georgia, Sgt. George W. Beavers of Company D carried the regimental colors, with orders from Col. John B. Estes to head straight for a tall chimney at Chancellorsville. "I set out across a field of old brown sedge intent upon doing my full duty," Beavers recalled. After a flurry of shells burst around him, he looked back. "Instead of my advancing regiment, not a man was in sight." Turning and running back, he was hit in the right shoulder by a Minié ball that ranged down through his body. "Shot like a hog," he said to himself, then thought of his wife and children and passed out. When he awoke, he started crawling to a nearby rifle pit to die.

His captain called out, "Stop, George, you'll be killed!"

"I'm already killed!" Beavers yelled.

The captain helped him drink from one of his two canteens, then suggested giving the rest of the water to dying soldiers a few feet away. Beavers objected—"Why, they're Yankees!" "That's all right," said the captain. "I bear them no malice. We'll do what we can for them." Beavers was taken off the field when the Georgians, without support, pulled back down the creek bottom after coming within yards of the main Federal batteries.[36]

Left of the Plank Road, Col. J. M. Williams led the wounded Nicholls's Louisiana brigade out the Bullock Road against Union general French. Col. J. M. Hall had taken over O'Neal's Alabama brigade. With Iverson's North Carolinians, it moved to outflank Fairview from the north. As the Federal batteries there gradually ran out of ammunition, some had departed to the rear, leaving 20 to 30 guns still in position, firing westward with their right anchored on the road. First Lt. George B. Winslow, commanding a New York battery, told how the Rebel infantry "came down the hill in almost solid masses, and our artillery greeted them with shot and shell, causing a fearful destruction in their ranks." Beaten back, the Confederates came again and again, "covering, as it were, the whole ground in front of our lines, with at least a dozen stand of colors flying in their midst." When his protecting infantry faded away, Winslow ordered his gunners to load solid shot and fire at 1½ degrees elevation, like huge pistols at close range. "The effect was most terrible," he said.

Still the Rebels came on. Charging out of the woods, they planted their flag beside the road and proceeded to pick off Winslow's gunners and horses. These Confederates were skirmishers of Col. Daniel H. Christie's 23rd North Carolina. After fighting across the Union works and enduring "a hard tug for about a half hour," they emerged only 60 yards from the heavy battery that had done so much damage to troops attacking earlier alongside the road. Christie reported that his soldiers' musketry quieted the guns, and when the Yankees started to pull them out, he ordered a charge that reached the enemy cannon. Winslow's version was that once the Confederates clustered thickly around their colors, he ordered his gunners to reload with canister and blew the attackers back repeatedly. But when they got within 25 or 30 yards he was out of ammunition, so unlimbered and departed in an orderly way.[37]

"There I reckon the hardest fight of the war took place," Confederate John C. Ussery said. "This [23rd] regiment never saw anything equal to it. The enemy flanked this regiment completely, and cut us up terribly. . . . the only chance to escape was running down to the right between their lines. . . . only one of my company was left. I turned to him and told him that we must try and get away from there . . . how I can't see, for it looked like nothing human could pass through such a shower and come out unhurt." An enemy force flanked the Carolinians there on both sides, but then Rebel reserves "came up just at the right time and cut them all to pieces, in fact I never saw such a slaughter in my life. It looked like a regiment had been formed and a cannon placed at one end and fired down the line, killing every man." Over and over, in their letters and diaries, veteran troops, men of both armies who had been through the horror of Bull Run and Antietam, used the word "slaughter" to describe Chancellorsville as the worst they had ever seen.[38]

As the Rebels kept pressing left, George Meade sent Brig. Gen. Erastus Tyler's Pennsylvania brigade to support French's position on the northern flank. Tyler filled in beside French and held for more than an hour in a struggle so fierce that ten color-bearers of the attacking 10th Louisiana were cut down in succession. Eventually Colquitt's brigade came around on the Louisiana brigade's left and rolled up the Pennsylvanians. The turn of the struggle there on the Union right, along Little Hunting Run, produced a vivid account of one man's thoughts and fears at Chancellorsville. On the way to the front, Lt. Clay MacCauley, a ministerial student from Chambersburg, five days short of his twentieth birthday, was learning as much about himself as about battle.

His regiment, the 126th Pennsylvania, was halted amid dozens of dead and wounded, and to him it was "most trying—with nothing to do and with mutilation and death visible at our very feet, and with peril to ourselves increasing, rather large drafts were made on our moral forces." But they marched on, turning through mud, underbrush, and briers toward the enemy.

There in a thicket, they lay and began firing. "It was an ugly give and take," he recalled. "We could not see the enemy, but the whizz and ting of bullets proved that they were not far away." In the excitement some of his troops stood to load and shoot, and kept standing despite the enemy fire. (The drill manual described seventeen separate movements to ready each shot from a muzzle-loader, and standing was the only practical way to do it. Frequently, soldiers in the excitement of battle loaded their muskets two or more times, forgetting whether they had fired. After Gettysburg, some captured Confederate muskets were found with up to twenty-three rounds rammed into their barrels.)[39]

One of MacCauley's men forgot to pull his ramrod. He fired and it went whanging off through the leaves. To get him another, MacCauley slipped back to where he had seen a musket lying. He had gone only a few feet when "an irresistible sense of loneliness and dread seized me. . . . Soon I was practically panic-stricken." Running, he picked up the lost musket and rushed back to the line. "I never felt more alone or helpless than in those few moments of isolation from my comrades," he wrote. "I was sure that each next moment would bring death."

Bullets cut the brush around him to waist height. Ammunition was dwindling. One after another, MacCauley's men stopped firing. "Something had gone wrong. The men began to feel it. As our firing slackened I noticed a foreboding disorder on our right . . . a feeling of suspense and doubt seemed to thrill along the line." A spent bullet painfully bruised his ribs. "The disorder, changing into tumult, came near and nearer. At last it swept in upon the company next to mine. Then it struck my own company's right. The companies, rising in successive ranks from the ground, the men with questioning looks at one another, started at first slowly and then rapidly backward." It was not panic, MacCauley said, but "a rather disorderly falling back of almost helpless men, from a coming danger they felt themselves powerless to resist."

These men were not rookies. They had been at Fredericksburg in December; MacCauley had been wounded in the knee there. But now they had no ammunition. "A wave rolling backward on a curving beach does not more steadily sweep broken on its way than did the retreat of our battle line from right to left," MacCauley wrote. The Rebels, seeing this, charged along the Union line.

Suddenly, MacCauley was alone. He started to run, but his legs got tangled with his sword and he tripped. Getting up, he tried to force his way through the thicket as bullets slashed around him. He fell again, too exhausted to get up. He crawled beside a badly mangled man and started to give him water from his canteen. Looking up, he saw Confederates coming. It was like "some dreadful dream," he said. He tried to run, but an advancing Rebel pointed his musket straight at him. Half-risen, MacCauley stared for what seemed minutes into the muzzle of the oncoming weapon. Everything else around him, men rushing through the woods, seemed in a faraway mist—"my brain was concentrated on that one advancing figure." When the Rebel came close, he lowered his bayonet at MacCauley's chest and yelled, "You — — — of a ———, give me that sword!" (After the war, preacher MacCauley recorded it that way.) The attacker was a big, tawny-bearded Alabamian. Then, seeing how young MacCauley was, he leaned over and asked if he was hurt. "I don't know," said the scared lieutenant. "Get me out of this."

MacCauley realized the Yankee cannon would tear the woods apart as soon as the Rebels showed their colors. "I had no desire to be killed by grape, canister, shell or anything else from our own guns," he said. He urged the Alabamian to run with him, fast, and his captor put an arm under his shoulders, half carrying him to the Rebel rear. Barely a hundred yards back, "the expected happened. It seemed as if a tornado out of a clear sky had all at once burst upon that forest." The two men dived into a hole. For ten minutes, "a roaring torrent of iron plunged through the air above us. We were almost covered by fallen tree limbs and branches. The noise was horrible."

When the shelling lifted, bleeding survivors of the 5th and 6th Alabama came streaming back. MacCauley and his Rebel friend ran with them until their flight was halted by officers in the next battle line. MacCauley was taken farther back, where he formally surrendered his sword to General Rodes. Rodes sent him to the rear, past scores of Union and Confederate dead. Twice, MacCauley said, batteries racing to the front along the Plank Road ran over these fallen soldiers, "the hoofs of the horses and the carriage wheels crushing and mutilating the bodies of friend and foe." Hundreds of wounded lay by the road, sheltered from the sun by blankets held up by muskets, each weapon with its bayonet stuck in the ground and its hammer closed on a blanket corner. Despite the uncaring cruelty of the artillery drivers, MacCauley got "nothing but kind words and treatment" from the Rebels on the battlefield.[40]

On the slope of Fairview, a Union major told a friend that "the Rebs seemed drunk," the way they kept charging in solid waves, three deep. Wounded Confederate prisoners told their captors that Jackson had intended to break through their lines "if he had but two men left." As one captured Confederate limped past a Massachusetts battery, a friendly Yankee asked, "How are you, John Reb?" "That's my name and I'm happy to own it," said the Southerner. "How are you, you damn Lincolnite?" A Confederate captain held by the Yankees, hearing heavy firing back at the lines, told his captors, "I'd give my right arm to be with my company in that fight."[41]

About the time Clay MacCauley was captured, Hooker's chief quartermaster, Col. Rufus Ingalls, sent a telegram from U.S. Ford to Chief of Staff Butterfield at Falmouth:

> A most terrible bloody conflict has raged since daylight. Enemy in great force in our front and on the right, but at this moment we are repulsing him on all sides. Carnage is fearful. General Hooker is safe so far. Berry is killed. I return to the front, but will keep you advised when in my power. Our trains are all safe, and we shall be victorious. Our cavalry has not come up.[42]

It was only 8:50 A.M., five minutes later, when Butterfield sent Lincoln one of the war's great understatements:

> Though not directed or specially authorized to do so by General Hooker, I think it not improper that I should advise you that a battle is in progress.[43]

Chapter Fourteen

LEE'S SUPREME MOMENT

JOE HOOKER, "safe so far," was commanding his army from the south porch of the Chancellor house, waiting and hoping to hear that Sedgwick's Sixth Corps was coming up behind Lee at last.

Inside the house, surgeons worked without letup on casualties who streamed away from the approaching battlefront. In the cellar, the Chancellor women huddled as Rebel cannon "made splendid practice" upon the house and everything around it. "O the horror of that day!" Sue Chancellor remembered. "The piles of legs and arms outside the sitting room window and the rows and rows of dead bodies covered with canvas!" As the fighting converged on Chancellorsville, scared soldiers crowded into the cellar to hide from Confederate fire until an officer ordered them out, telling them not to intrude on the terror-stricken women.[1]

Couriers raced up; Hooker seemed impatient for their messages, though his brigade and division commanders were making most of the morning's tactical decisions. Not long after nine o'clock, Dan Sickles dispatched his aide, Maj. H. E. Tremain, to tell Hooker he needed help, right away. Hooker saw Tremain coming and leaned over the porch rail toward him, next to one of the building's white columns. Just then a solid shot from a Confederate cannon hit the column and split it lengthwise, throwing half of it against Hooker. The stunning blow to the head and right side of his body knocked him to the ground.[2]

As Hooker recalled it, "For a few moments I was senseless, and the report spread that I had been killed. But I soon revived, and to correct the misapprehension I insisted on being lifted upon my horse, and rode back toward the white house [Chandler's], which subsequently became the center of my new position. Just before reaching it, the pain from my hurt became so intense that I was likely to fall, when I was assisted to dismount and was laid upon a blanket spread out upon the ground, and was given some brandy. This revived me, and I was assisted to remount. Scarcely was I off the blanket when a solid shot fired by the enemy at Hazel Grove struck in the very center of that blanket, where I had a moment before been lying, and tore up the earth in a savage way." [3]

Gen. Darius Couch was close by when the shell stunned Hooker and the rumor sprang up that the commander was dead. Galloping to the porch, Couch leaped off his horse and ran through the house looking for Hooker, thinking, "If he is killed, what shall I do with this disjointed army?" Back of the house, to his "great joy," he found him in the saddle. "Briefly congratulating him on his escape—it was no time to blubber or use soft expressions—I went about my business," Couch recalled. "This was the last I saw of my commanding general in front."

Couch was senior corps commander, but Hooker neither notified him of his departure from the field nor gave him any orders. By this time, Couch realized that with Sickles's and Slocum's Union lines collapsing on the west and south, "the last stand would be about the Chancellor house." He asked for more cannon; his Second Corps artillery to the rear could not get forward over the jammed roads. Stuart had crowded 40 pieces onto Hazel Grove. As they slammed shells into and around the Chancellor house, some of this cannonade also rained onto Hancock's division, in breastworks facing the other way, toward Fredericksburg. As Couch said, "Lee by this time knew well enough, if he had not known before, that the game was sure to fall into his hands, and accordingly plied every gun and rifle that could be brought to bear on us."

But that was Couch's judgment afterward; at the time, he thought he still could save the day. At about nine o'clock, the Union artillery commanded by Captain Best on Fairview had been overrun on its right, threatened on its left, and was almost out of ammunition. As his infantry protection thinned away, Best pulled all the cannon out of the main Fairview line. Those guns had done more to hold back Jackson's attack, then Stuart's, than any other one element of Hooker's defense. Most of them were repositioned in the clearing near the Chancellor house. Despite the pullback, Couch believed that 40 or 50 Union pieces firing from Chancellorsville could repel the Confederates then pressing Geary at the southwest corner of the Federal position, as well as neutralize the guns at Hazel Grove. [4]

But Hooker, his force far outnumbering Stuart and Lee combined, was still looking for salvation from Sedgwick downriver rather than the troops at hand. At 6:45 A.M., Butterfield had advised him that Sedgwick was still not out of Fredericksburg. Nevertheless Hooker, at 9:15, immediately before he was knocked down, wired Sedgwick: "You will hurry up your column. The enemy's right flank now rests near the Plank road at Chancellorsville. You will attack at once." To Butterfield, Hooker ordered: "Communicate with Sedgwick. We are driving the enemy and only need him to complete the job." The state of communications and assumptions between wings of the Union army was as bad as Hooker's assessment of what was going on directly around him. At 9:50, Butterfield at Falmouth informed his artillery chief, Brig. Gen. Henry J. Hunt, that Hooker was attacking down Chancellorsville road, "probably, from the sound, pushing this way." Ten minutes later, Hooker urgently forwarded a question for Sedgwick: "Where is he?" [5]

Before and during that flurry of messages, Hooker was telling his officers to do everything but drive the enemy. For a few minutes after he was knocked down, he mounted and rode in pain and shock around his shrinking lines, to show himself to his troops. Sickles, ever combative, may have gotten the wrong impression from Hooker's display of spirit. He wanted to take back his lost ground with a bayonet charge, but Couch restrained him. Meade sent a colonel to scout possibilities on the Union right, and saw the opportunity to swing down on the north flank of Stuart's attacking line. He asked Hooker for permission, but Hooker said no. Reynolds, farther up the Union right, spotted the same chance, but Hooker said no again. Meade sent a brigade to support the right, but Hooker told him he shouldn't have. Whether because the falling pillar had knocked the fight out of him or because he was fixed on Sedgwick as the key to success, Hooker could not break his defensive mindset. [6]

From a tent half a mile back of Chancellorsville, he sent for Couch. Meade, other generals, and staff officers clustered about. Hooker was lying down when Couch stepped in. Couch said that "he seemed rather dull, but possessed of his mental faculties." Pushing up to lean on an elbow, Hooker told Couch, "I turn the command of the army over to you. You will withdraw it and place it in the position designated on this map." The surge of hope in Couch at Hooker's first words lasted less than five seconds: Given command, in the next sentence he was told what to do, making command meaningless. Couch nodded and stepped outside the tent. Meade looked at him, expecting the order to attack. One of Hooker's colonels exulted, "We'll have some fighting now!"

Couch disappointed them. Grimly, he dispatched an officer to tell Sickles to start pulling out of his works on Fairview. When Sickles had withdrawn, Geary and Hancock would follow to the fallback line anchored on the Chandler house. [7]

· · ·

WHILE STUART'S CONFEDERATE brigades ground themselves down in repeated attacks from the west, on the other flank Lee had ordered R. H. Anderson's troops to pivot and come up from the south. In the early going, they fought the thickets and terrain more than the Yankees. Just after daybreak, E. A. Perry's three-regiment brigade of Floridians swept from the Plank Road southeast of Chancellorsville toward Catharine Furnace. Continuing past the abandoned furnace, Perry lined up to the left of Carnot Posey, A. R. Wright, and William Mahone as Lee swung north toward Geary's Union breastworks.

After a brisk firefight, Perry's men drove through the skirmishers protecting Hooker's south-facing line. In the brush, they could not tell which way to go on to the main Union position; the Minié balls buzzing past soon told them. Charging through the woods, the Floridians chased Geary's troops out of the corner of their works, but were hit immediately by canister. Flattening themselves behind a rise of ground, the Confederates ducked the worst of this shelling.[8]

Right of Perry, Posey's Mississippians made what he called a "gallant and daring and irresistible charge," driving half a mile and over the Yankee works. As Company F of the 16th Mississippi spilled over the Union line, a boy named Willis Hawkins was out front. He raised his musket to fire point-blank at a blue uniform when the Federal screamed, "Hello, Hawkins! Don't shoot me!" Hawkins paused and lowered his weapon, his jaw open. "Great God, old fellow! I wouldn't shoot you for nothing in the world," he said. The lucky Yankee was one of those who had captured Hawkins at Sharpsburg the September before, and treated him decently before he was sent away for exchange. "Get back to the rear," Hawkins told him. "I ain't got time to tend to you now." The Union soldier, whose earlier kindness had saved his life, gladly ran back as Hawkins charged on.[9]

But to Posey's right, Wright's Georgians were held up by determined skirmishers, then blasted as they approached the Union line by "the most terrible fire of artillery and musketry" Wright had ever witnessed. For terrifying minutes, they also were targeted by friendly cannon at Hazel Grove, but when the 22nd Georgia showed its colors, those guns lifted their fire onto the Federal works. At a break in the shelling, Wright ordered a captain to climb a tree to spy out the Union position. The captain refused and was reprimanded. But Pvt. John Miller of Company G of the 22nd shinnied up the tree and shouted down a description of the enemy line, and later was formally commended by the general.[10]

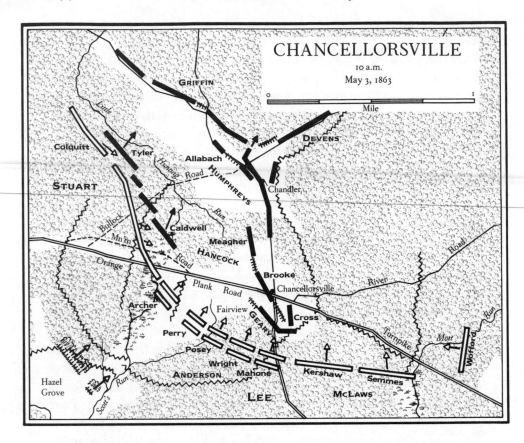

CHANCELLORSVILLE
10 a.m.
May 3, 1863

13. The Brutal Climax. *After Stuart's divisions attacking from the west have been terribly mauled in repeated assaults, Lee brings his force against Chancellorsville from the south. Confederate artillery firing from Hazel Grove pounds Fairview and Chancellorsville.*

Looking farther right for support, Wright was unable to find Mahone, who had advanced beside the Plank Road but lagged behind. Interestingly, Mahone in his official report says nothing at all about what his brigade did Sunday morning.[11]

Progress was slow there on the Confederate far right largely because of one superbly skilled Yankee officer, twenty-four-year-old Col. Nelson A. Miles, of the 61st New York. Miles commanded the reinforced skirmish line in front of Hancock's works both Saturday and Sunday, defying probes and demonstrations by infantry and artillery. As Rebel pressure mounted, Miles was shot in the abdomen at about nine-fifteen, shortly before Hooker was knocked down. When Miles was carried in one door of the Chancellorsville house, he saw the dust-covered commander going out the other. This near-fatal injury was Miles's third wound of the war; at Petersburg, there would be yet another. Although a prewar store clerk, a nonprofessional soldier, he survived to become a general, commander-in-chief of the army during the Spanish-American War. His performance at Chancellorsville was the most spectacular of his career; for it he was awarded the Medal of Honor many years later.[12]

Lee himself rode to the left behind his thinly stretched brigades as they charged yelling and charged again, going on even when their flanks were blasted by artillery, sensing that this was the decisive hour of the battle. Their sacrifice must have weighed upon Lee as he stopped briefly, watching and talking with Capt. Justus Scheibert, a German observer. For those few moments, the conversation was not about tactics; Lee spoke instead of his concern for how young Southerners would be educated after the war. What he saw and thought there that morning may have helped him decide what he himself would do when the guns finally fell silent.[13]

Snapping back to business, Lee continued left and arrived close to ten o'clock at the Hazel Grove plateau. Confederate guns there were hammering Hooker without letup. After earlier probes toward Fairview, Archer's brigade was protecting the artillery. Now Lee sent Archer ahead again. At his orders the Alabamians and Tennesseeans stepped out with fresh spirit, accompanied by three regiments of Doles's Georgians. Halting after a quarter mile for a resupply of ammunition, they moved on again, splitting into the woods on both sides of the clearing before Fairview. This move brought Archer's right in touch with Perry's brigade, achieving the critical juncture between Lee and Stuart. From that point, the Southern line was continuous to left and right, around three sides of Hooker's shrinking position at Chancellorsville.[14]

Amid the blasting, smoking cannon and Federal return fire, Lee sat calmly aboard Traveller and dispatched word to Stuart that their commands had connected. Stuart by then was re-forming, sending rations forward to his dazed troops. Before the Union guns were pulled off Fairview, he faced the fact that his attack was spent; for more than four hours he had thrown all he could muster at Hooker's lines without a decisive breakthrough. Regiment after regiment was wrecked as his brigades made essentially separate attacks, pulled apart by the wilderness and the confusing angles of terrain and enemy positions.

Had Stuart delayed his offensive that morning only briefly, until Hooker's withdrawal from Hazel Grove, the infantry bloodbath on the west front might not have been necessary. Once the attack was launched, had he merged all three of his battle lines into one concentrated assault, he might—*might*—have driven through Hooker's deep defenses without such heavy casualties. When Stuart heard the good news of the linkup with Lee, he sent back for orders. Lee told him to attack yet again, with his whole command, toward Chancellorsville. Anderson and McLaws would do the same from south and east.[15]

Stuart's troops, brightened by the knowledge that Lee was close by, stood up and went forward one more time. Anderson's fresher men moved faster, pushing across Geary's works. Earlier, one of Geary's men, James T. Miller of the 111th Pennsylvania, had been inspired by seeing Hooker, "riding bearheaded rite into the thickest of the fight and cheering his men by his voice steadying them by his example and at that point our men did fight more like devils incarnate than men for they clubed their muskets and drove the foe back for some distance by clean hard pounding."[16]

But now the Rebels kept coming. As Geary's line gave way, Sgt. Sam Lusk of the 137th New York thought that "happily never in the history of the world was so much life destroyed in so short a time or so much human suffering. The scene . . . was enough to break a tyrant's heart. Men with part of their head blowed off trying to get off the field. Some with their legs partly shot off hobbling along to get out of reach of the enemy. . . . I saw men by the side of the road with their legs shot off with the bones sticking out & they still alive. Some with their heads blown off, wounded every way you can immagin. . . . As we retreated the enemy pursued us clostly, as we passed our batteries they fired on the rebs which were following us in mass & mowed them down. . . ."[17]

Behind Anderson's men, Confederate cannon came jolting onto the Fairview clearing. Lt. Col. Thomas H. Carter, commanding Rodes's division artillery, had divided his guns, sending his smooth-bores to Hazel Grove and firing ten rifled pieces in relays along the Plank Road. This cross fire had helped drive the Federal cannon away. Now, at Lee's urging, Carter rushed the batteries from Hazel Grove onto Fairview. More than 40 guns assembled there and opened on Chancellorsville from the west while Anderson's artillery, under Maj. Robert Hardaway, joined in from the southeast.[18]

This fire focused on the Chancellor house, an irresistible target. The gunners did not know it was overflowing with wounded as surgeons tried in vain to keep up with the battle. Union cannon were assembled around it, firing back. As the gunners of one broken Federal battery started to pull away, the slim figure of Sgt. Anne Etheridge appeared and urged them to stay. Annie, the idol of the 3rd Michigan, had been tending wounded and bringing coffee and hardtack to the front all morning. As the gun crew turned around for one more salvo, she yelled, "That's it, boys, now you've got good range, keep it up and you'll soon silence those guns!" [19]

But nothing would quiet those Rebel guns; at that moment, they were deciding the fight. With solid shot, they knocked down the chimneys of the Chancellorsville house, raining brick on those below, and smacked holes in the upstairs walls. Exploding rounds set the building afire. The Confederate women in the cellar were terrified when an officer shouted down and told them to come out, he would take them to safety. "Cannon were booming and missiles of death were flying in every direction," Sue Chancellor remembered. "If anybody thinks that a battle is an orderly attack of rows of men, I can tell them differently, for I have been there."

When the Chancellor family came up from its dark cellar, "The woods around the house were a sheet of fire, the air was filled with shot and shell, horses were running, rearing and screaming, the men a mass of confusion, moaning, cursing and praying." Federal troops and Rebel captives worked together carrying wounded of both sides out of the flaming mansion. The officer who had come for the women was Hooker's adjutant, Joe Dickinson. He rode slowly, leading the stumbling group back across the bloody field with Sue's mother walking beside him, her hand on his knee. A half mile along U.S. Ford Road, Sue's sickly sister began to cough blood, and Dickinson stopped a soldier and made him give her his horse. Farther along, another officer reined up indignantly and asked Dickinson why he was not at his post of duty. "If here is not the post of duty looking after the safety of these helpless women and children, then I don't know what you call duty!" Dickinson shot back, and took the Chancellors on to the ford. Sue insisted years later that "a nobler, braver, kindlier gentleman never lived" than Joseph Dickinson, a Yankee from Pennsylvania.[20]

The simultaneous Confederate charge from west and south was the fourth of the day for Stuart's troops, the second for Anderson's men under Lee. This time they kept moving over the outer works onto Fairview, but as the Gray infantry closed in on Chancellorsville itself, it ran into a hurricane of canister.

With 18 pieces clustered around the mansion, Federal gunners fought a reckless rearguard action to protect the army retreating into Hooker's fallback line, three-fourths of a mile north. Lt. Francis B. Seeley's battery was cut up by galling Rebel musket fire as it repositioned from Fairview. Wheeling his cannon about, he ordered his gunners to hold their fire until the oncoming Southerners were within 350 yards, then rip them with canister. Out of canister, Seeley's men kept firing solid shot until their ammunition was gone, then drew off their guns, cheering as they departed under heavy fire.[21] A Rebel shell exploded a caisson of ammunition, throwing fragments of shot and wood into the batteries still working. Furiously, crazily amid the mounting chaos, the Yankee gunners around the mansion blasted away as the determined Rebels came on.

Behind Chancellorsville, as the Federals fell back on their far right, Meade told Brig. Gen. Charles Griffin to send help that way. Griffin, who had practiced gunnery in Mexico and taught it at West Point, said, "Let me have the spare artillery that's lying around here and I'll make them think hell isn't half a mile off."

Meade approved, scattered batteries were rushed up, and Griffin told the gunners, "Double-shot your pieces with grape and canister and let the Rebs come within fifty yards." Leaning and swinging his arm like a bowler, he said, "Roll them [the bursts] along the ground." Three batteries took turns with six-gun salvos, slowing the Rebel advance but also killing some friendly infantrymen who did not have time to clear the front.[22]

With Hooker down, the short, fiery Couch was in charge on the field. Sickles had withdrawn under orders. Couch rode back and forth, shouting commands. He was hit. His horse was killed under him. He was hit again. Only Hancock's and Geary's divisions were left. Confederate shells came from three directions. Some fired from one side of the Union line whooshed over and crashed into the other side; some passed entirely over both sides and into Rebel positions beyond.

Couch gave Hancock command of the final defense around what was left of the Chancellorsville house. Lee's men drove Geary back. The tall, angry Geary called to Hancock's troops to cover his retreat. "Charge, you cowards, charge!" he yelled. Two of Hancock's men were so insulted they lowered their bayonets toward Geary until an adjutant stepped in. Geary ran to Hancock, who told him, "General Geary, I command here!"

Hancock rode behind his fragmented defenses, saying calmly, "Gentlemen, we are left to keep them in check until the second line is formed." As one private said, "I became a hero by that man's influence."

A solid shell hit Hancock's horse, leaving one leg dangling by a piece of skin. Hancock jumped off, hugged the horse's neck and told an aide to shoot it. He waved one brigadier into position and told him, "General, whatever happens, I want you to hold this ground."

Looking around, the brigadier asked, "Where are my reserves?"

"None of your business," said Hancock, who would perform the same way at Gettysburg. "That's my business. I have placed you here to hold this ground, and that's all you are required to do, and I want it done, sir." Couch at last ordered him to pull back, but Hancock still wanted to save his artillery.[23]

Rebel fire had knocked down all the officers, gunners, and horses of the battery commanded by Lt. Edmund F. Kirby. Hancock sent a detail of Pennsylvania infantry to drag the guns away. "That was the hottest place I ever saw or ever will," said a man in the 140th. When troops started to lift Kirby, who lay with his thigh shattered, the lieutenant waved them away, shouting, "No, take off that gun first!" He was rescued despite this brave refusal, but died before the month was out. Companies D and E of the 140th pulled the cannon away by hand as the charging Rebels came within a hundred yards.[24]

About ten-thirty, the last Federals left Chancellorsville, past woods set aflame by Rebel artillery. Confederate troops swarmed across the clearing, around the mansion, and caught and captured the 27th Connecticut before it got away. A brigade of Yankees was positioned south of Chandler's to cover the road into the new Federal line.

Lee had watched with his binoculars from Hazel Grove. When a courier galloped back with word that Chancellorsville had been taken, he mounted Traveller and rode north to the Plank Road, then east to Fairview. Rebel cannon there were throwing shells after the retreating enemy. The wreckage of regiments and batteries was strewn along both sides of the road and through the shattered woods. Discarded guns, packs, broken wagons, caissons, dead horses were everywhere. Here and there Confederate troops held up a prize of Yankee bacon, snatched from an abandoned knapsack, gnawing on it as they kept going. Dead men, wounded men, fragments of men lay uncounted.

Between Lee's and Hooker's scrambled lines, pickets of both armies could do little as one more trauma was added to their memories of the past eighteen hours. Fires started by bursting Confederate shells spread through the woods where lay dozens, some said hundreds, of dead and wounded. The fire raced through the carpet of leaves. Occasionally it would set off a handful of cartridges in a fallen soldier's pocket. Helpless men lying in its path turned their faces away, swept their arms in arcs trying to brush away the burning leaves, covered their heads, screamed weakly, and died. In their suffering they were no longer Yankees or Rebels; on both sides there were rescue efforts along the fire's edge. But few were saved. Describing the Chancellorsville scene to his wife, Lt. Col. David Winn of the 4th Georgia wrote, "This will not give you even a faint idea of the horrible reality."[25]

When Lee rode from Fairview into the Chancellorsville clearing, the Confederate survivors of that horror rushed around him, waving their hats in celebration. Some were in tears of worship, reaching out to touch him and his horse. Lee's aide, Maj. Charles Marshall, described it: "The fierce soldiers with their faces blackened with the smoke of battle, the wounded crawling with feeble limbs from the fury of the devouring flames, all seemed possessed with a common impulse. One long, unbroken cheer, in which the feeble cry of those who lay helpless on the earth blended with the strong voices of those who still fought, rose high above the roar of battle, and hailed the presence of the victorious chief. He sat in the full realization of all that soldiers dream of—triumph; and as I looked upon him, in the complete fruition of the success which his genius, courage, and confidence in his army had won, I thought that it must have been from such a scene that men in ancient times rose to the dignity of gods." [26]

Lee's biographer Douglas Southall Freeman called it "the supreme moment of his life as a soldier." [27]

At that high point, Lee's heart must have knotted with both pride and grief. His boldness had done it; no other general in either army would ever calculate or improvise a masterpiece so striking. But whatever his brilliance, his daring, none of it would have meant anything without those troops, those ragged, famished, exhausted, brave men, so many of them dead, the others cheering him as if he had fought the battle while they looked on. And he would not have dared as he did, they would not have marched as they did, the battle would not have turned as it did without Jackson, who lay wounded four and a half miles away.

IN THE HOSPITAL tent across the road from Wilderness Tavern, Jackson had rested in and out of sleep for half an hour after his arm was amputated. Then, by doctor's orders, young Lieutenant Smith roused him to offer strong coffee. Jackson liked it; it was his first nourishment in more than twenty-four hours. Looking down at the stump of his arm, he asked Smith, "Were you here?" Smith nodded. Jackson thought a minute and asked whether he had said anything under the anesthetic. He said he had always thought it was wrong to use chloroform if death seemed imminent. But, he said, "it was the most delightful physical sensation I ever enjoyed . . . at one time I thought I heard the most delightful music that ever greeted my ears. I believe it was the sawing of the bone." But, he said, "I should dislike above all things to enter eternity in such a condition." [28]

Smith urged him to sleep, and for nearly six hours he did. About 9:00

A.M., he awoke to the rumble of cannon from the east. Though eager for news from the battle, he was still subdued. After a taste of refreshment, he asked Lieutenant Morrison to go to Richmond to fetch Mrs. Jackson, Morrison's sister. He dictated a note to Lee, telling him of his wounding and saying he had turned command of the corps over to A. P. Hill. Then the Reverend Mr. Lacy hurried in, distraught.

"Oh, General, what a calamity!" the minister said. Jackson tried to soothe him. What has been passed on about their conversation was written by Lacy soon afterward. Like much of the dialogue in the days after Jackson was wounded, it is embellished in the telling, like a prayer or sermon. As a minister, Lacy would want it that way to glorify Jackson as an example for the righteous. But while we can doubt that a weakened Jackson would have gone on so elaborately, he did indeed speak and conduct himself in reverent tones, especially in discussion with men of God. And as we know from their letters, that is the way ordinary soldiers of the time often expressed themselves, too.

"You see me severely wounded, but not depressed, not unhappy," Jackson said. "I believe that it has been done according to God's holy will, and I acquiesce entirely in it. You may think it strange, but you never saw me more perfectly contented than I am today, for I am sure that my Heavenly Father designs this affliction for my good. . . . If it were in my power to replace my arm, I would not dare do it, unless I could know it was the will of my Heavenly Father." He told of his belief that he was dying when he fell from the litter the night before, and the peace he felt confronting death. He went on, until the doctor said he should rest.[29]

Near eleven o'clock, his young staff officer Kyd Douglas arrived with news of the victory at Chancellorsville. Jackson was alert, asking for details. He was delighted that Stuart had led the corps so bravely. Told of Paxton's death, Jackson turned away for a moment in grief. Douglas told how Paxton had been reading his Bible when ordered to move up. He told how the Stonewall Brigade had charged, been thrown back, and then at Stuart's urging charged again, shouting, "Remember Jackson!"

Jackson's eyes watered. "It was just like them," he said, "just like them. They are a noble set of men. The name of Stonewall belongs to that brigade, not to me."[30]

He closed his eyes to rest again.

AT ABOUT THAT TIME, Jackson's messenger rode into the Chancellorsville clearing looking for Lee. The general was directing the rescue of the wounded from in and around the burning mansion when the rider found him and thrust the dispatch into his hand. With his gauntlets on, Lee could not open it. He handed it to Marshall, who read it to him. Only then did Lee realize that Jackson's wounds were so serious, and that his arm had been amputated. His voice husky, he dictated a reply:

> I have just received your note, informing me that you were wounded. I cannot express my regret at the occurrence. Could I have directed events, I would have chosen for the good of the country to be disabled in your stead.
> I congratulate you upon the victory, which is due to your skill and energy.[31]

Lee also sent a brief report to Jefferson Davis, saying that Hooker had been "dislodged from all his positions around Chancellorsville, and driven back toward the Rappahannock, over which he is now retreating. . . . We have again to thank Almighty God for a great victory. . . ."[32]

His report was premature.

Lee did not realize the strength of the deep, laboriously prepared fortifications behind which Hooker's six corps now waited. Sickles was dug in at the southern point of the Union position, near Chandler's. Meade and Reynolds were along the Ely's Ford Road, and Couch, Howard, and Slocum along the Mineral Spring Road. Although four of those corps had been mauled by the Confederate onslaught, Meade's was little damaged and Reynolds's had hardly been engaged at all. Hooker's force still outnumbered Lee's by about 77,000 to 34,000 on the scene. Downriver, Sedgwick's corps outnumbered Early's holding force almost three to one. Recognizing these figures, the roughness of the ground, and the "arduous and sanguinary conflict" his troops had just gone through, Lee conceded that "great caution" was necessary. Nevertheless, he thought of nothing but attack.

He gave his disorganized regiments a short rest, then re-formed along the Plank Road in a line not quite two miles long, with Rodes's division centered on Chancellorsville. Heth (A. P. Hill's division) was on his left, and on his right, Colston's line curled north just back of River Road. Later, Anderson's division was sent up that road to the right, blocking its junction with Mountain Road and ready to advance on Hooker's flank. Although Lee was careful in preparing his plan, there was nothing complicated or diversionary about it; he intended to attack head-on and drive Hooker into the Rappahannock.

But, for Lee and his outnumbered army, no victory, no moment of triumph, was ever to be complete. At about twelve-thirty, as Lee prepared to send his ragged but willing troops ahead, Lt. Andrew L. Pitzer arrived on a frothing horse from near Fredericksburg. He was one of Early's aides, but Early had not sent him. From a hill overlooking the lines, Pitzer had watched that morning as Early's men threw back repeated attacks by Sedgwick. But then, shortly before noon, the lieutenant saw Yankees flood over the high ground above the town. On his own, he rode off to bring the news to Chancellorsville:

Sedgwick and a reinforced corps of Union infantry were headed for Lee's rear.

Chapter Fifteen

We're Going to Cut Our Way Through

JOHN SEDGWICK was all soldier.

He had graduated from West Point in 1837, six numbers behind Jubal Early, the classmate who now faced him on the heights behind Fredericksburg. A forty-nine-year-old Connecticut Yankee, bachelor, grandson of a Revolutionary officer, Sedgwick had fought in Florida, Mexico, and the West, and since Sumter had been wounded on the Peninsula and at Antietam. His troops called him "Uncle John." Some thought him the best loved of all Union generals, a tribute others paid to McClellan. He was a hard fighter and a solid, reassuring presence to his men. The army was his life—and death: he would be killed a few miles away at Spotsylvania Court House, a year later. Before then he would be praised for leading his corps on one of the fastest marches of the war, to make a timely arrival at Gettysburg. But on the first weekend in May 1863, Sedgwick was afflicted with another trait Lincoln had found in McClellan: "the slows."

Late Saturday, as Jackson smashed in the far flank of the Union army, a blizzard of messages from both Hooker and Chief of Staff Butterfield still had not persuaded Sedgwick of the new urgency of his role—that even with six of seven corps upriver, Hooker was counting on Sedgwick's single corps to turn defeat into victory. All evening, Butterfield kept prodding Sedgwick. At 8:00 P.M., he said, "They cannot but be panic-stricken if you give them a sharp blow in the night. Your opportunities are grand beyond question." At 8:25, his tone was almost pleading: "Can't you take Fredericksburg tonight?" About the time that Jackson was starting forward of the Southern lines to scout a way behind Chancellorsville, Hooker made the question another order, sent through Butterfield:

> The major-general commanding directs that General Sedgwick crosses the Rappahannock at Fredericksburg on the receipt of this

order, and at once take up his line of march on the Chancellorsville
road until [he] connect with us, and he will attack and destroy any
force he may fall in with on the road. . . . He will probably fall upon
the rear of the forces commanded by General Lee, and between us we
will use him up. Send word to General Gibbon to take possession of
Fredericksburg. Be sure not to fail. Deliver this by your swiftest
messenger. . . .[1]

A dispatch from Sedgwick crossed this one en route, saying he was
proceeding along the Bowling Green Road, and his whole corps would be
in motion at daylight—by which time his orders told him to be approaching Chancellorsville. Hooker roared back that his instructions "must be
fully carried out to the very letter. This is vitally important." But once
again, the leisurely pace of communications took the edge off the aggressive orders that Hooker—or his aide, Brig. Gen. James Van Alen—found
so easy to issue to the disconnected wing of his army. Sedgwick got his
imperative instructions only at 11:00 P.M.[2]

He had excuses for delay, but their weakness is obvious in one muddy
sentence from his official report:

> I had been informed repeatedly by Major-General Butterfield, chief
> of staff, that the force in front of me was very small, and the whole
> tenor of his many dispatches would have created the impression that
> the enemy had abandoned my front and retired from the city and its
> defenses had there not been more tangible evidence than the dispatches
> in question that the chief of staff was misinformed.[3]

That "more tangible evidence" was in part manufactured by Jubal
Early. He had repeatedly ordered demonstrations to convince the Federals
that his command was much stronger than it really was. His regiments
were busiest at this make-believe late Saturday, when on those miscarried
orders from Lee, he had marched most of his division toward Chancellorsville, then turned around and reoccupied his works on the heights about
Fredericksburg. To cover his absence, Early had the troops left behind
show themselves along their lines from Hamilton's Crossing up past the
town. That night, as the rest headed back in, details were ordered to make
fires and "holler and hoop," wrote Urbanus Dart of the 26th Georgia.
"Even the noise, without any other show of numbers, seems to have been
sufficient. The yells would commence on one end of the line and it would
go as fast as men could hoop along the lines till it would reach the other
end and thus we kept at bay such a force for that length of time. The boys

did not know what to think of the officers when they were told they were on a hollering detail, but appeared to be quite fond of it."[4]

Sedgwick's pickets had been watching Early at close range since the first crossing; he should have known as well as Butterfield that the force confronting him was indeed small. But he, like the rest of the Union army, also knew that Burnside's force had outnumbered Lee's in December, and remembered what had happened on the same ground then. He was understandably reluctant to test Early by attacking head-on.

Sedgwick also dithered over how his other orders were worded, directing him to "cross at Fredericksburg." With his corps already over the river, to take this literally would mean recrossing and crossing again into the town, where there were yet no bridges, an operation he said would have taken till long after daylight. Thus, eventually, he started to move by his right flank, up the Bowling Green (Old Richmond) Road.[5]

Since the operation began, John Gibbon had been standing by opposite the town with two-thirds of his division from the Second Corps. The way he put down what he called mutiny by short-timers in Sully's brigade on May 1 may have been harsher because of his frustration at watching other divisions move into action while his own stood and waited. Late Saturday evening, he got orders to cross and take Fredericksburg. There, he was to link up with Sedgwick's corps coming from his left, and together they would head for Chancellorsville.

Gibbon called for 100 volunteers for a storming party to cross the river first and cover the laying of pontoon bridges. Of the 25 who stepped forward from the 34th New York, 18 were men who had risked execution less than two days before by defying their officers, maintaining their hitches were over. Byron Laflin, who began the campaign as colonel of the 34th and later took over the brigade, proudly noted this in his report. (While those of Gibbon's men persuaded back to duty left the army with clean records, some such mutineers in other commands were court-martialed and spent two years in the hell-hole of Fort Jefferson, on the Dry Tortugas.) When Gibbon's men put their first pontoons in the water at 2:40 A.M., Mississippi pickets across the river let fly until Union artillery quieted them with a burst of canister. After that, sporadic Confederate musketry held up bridging until after dawn, and then the first boats made it across without serious losses.[6]

By that time, the importance Hooker placed on Sedgwick's advance finally had sunk in on "Uncle John." Butterfield had told him at 2:35 that "Everything in the world depends on the rapidity and promptness of your movement. Push everything." Brig. Gen. Gouverneur Warren delivered

Hooker's latest orders to Sedgwick by hand, and described the situation upriver more frankly than anybody had thought it wise to do on paper.[7]

Confederate skirmishers slowed Sedgwick as he moved north up the Bowling Green Road, so lead elements of John Newton's division did not strike the outskirts of Fredericksburg until about 2:00 A.M.. As they approached, a staff officer brought orders to Col. Henry Eustis, and Eustis seemed exultant as he turned to tell adjutant Charles Brewster of the 10th Massachusetts, "We're going to cut our way through and join Hooker!"

At this, Brewster said to himself that "some of us must sleep our last sleep before night."[8]

AS DAYLIGHT APPROACHED, Newton marched his division into the streets of devastated Fredericksburg. The few townspeople left were hiding behind their shuttered windows. Newton faced his troops left, toward the heights. Federal artillery on both sides of the river opened fire on the Rebels behind the town. "Never was a calm waked up so fearfully on a quiet Sabbath morn before," Brewster said.[9] Just after dawn, Newton sent four regiments against the Confederate works. When the Yankees came close, Barksdale's Mississippians at the foot of the hill and cannon above cut down 64 soldiers of the 62nd New York and 102nd Pennsylvania in about as many seconds; the flag of the 62nd was shredded by 30 musket balls.[10] One Federal officer said sadly, "It was at once felt that a desperate encounter was to follow, and the recollections of the previous disaster were by no means inspiriting." Sedgwick himself was watching from a point so far forward that Rebel sharpshooters picked him out as an inviting target. An aide urged him back.

"By heaven, sir, this must not delay us!" Sedgwick declared. Rather than attacking straight on, he would go after the heights from both flanks.[11]

After daylight the pontoon bridge just above the Lacy house was finally complete, and Gibbon had his two brigades across by about seven o'clock. Sedgwick ordered him beyond the town to the right. Thus, Sedgwick's divisions faced the waiting Confederates along almost a four-mile front: Gibbon on the right, Newton in Fredericksburg, Albion Howe from Hazel Run to Deep Run, and William T. H. Brooks beyond him on the left. Sedgwick's plan now was for Gibbon to swing around the right while Howe turned the other flank of the key Southern strongpoint at Marye's Heights. Newton would demonstrate to keep the defenders busy in between.

Under fire, Gibbon marched his troops north out of Fredericksburg.

They crossed one bridge spanning a millrace canal, onto the flats below the westward bend in the Rappahannock, and faced left toward the enemy. But halfway from the river to the Rebel line, they discovered another canal across their front, six feet deep and 30 feet wide. General Warren, the engineer, rode out and found the skeleton of a bridge torn up by the Rebels. Troops of the 19th Massachusetts were ordered to plank it with siding from a nearby house. As they went to work, two Confederate cannon started to enfilade Gibbon's stalled force. Shell fragments hit more than 50 men before Col. Norman J. Hall, commanding one of the brigades, could move them to cover behind a roadside fence.[12]

On the other side of Marye's Heights, Howe advanced just left of Hazel Run. Probing Rebel lines, he found that "the character of the stream" between his and Newton's divisions blocked any move across it onto the flank of Marye's Heights. To turn that way also would expose his own flank to the Confederates along the crest. Pummeled by Early's cannon, he pulled back.

With both these turning movements frustrated, Sedgwick reluctantly concluded that "Nothing remained but to carry the works by direct assault."[13]

EARLY'S DEFENDING FORCE, his one division plus Barksdale's brigade, was tautly stretched at dawn from north of the Orange Plank Road near Marye's Heights all the way down to Hamilton's Crossing. Most of it was below the town, facing Sedgwick's original bridgeheads. Early realized that that had been the Confederates' most vulnerable sector in the December battle. At first, he was concerned that a strong enemy thrust up Deep Run could cut his force in two, and Brooks's Union division brought on an artillery duel when it moved across that creek toward the R.F.&P. Railroad in early morning.

The railroad cut, with Rebel works along the slope behind it, looked formidable to Brooks. He assigned Brig. Gen. Joseph J. Bartlett to take it, and Bartlett ordered the 96th Pennsylvania to lead the charge. As Brooks watched, he said quietly to the brigadier, "Goodbye Ninety-sixth, that's the last you'll see of them."[14]

When Brooks's troops came under heavy shelling, he climbed atop a roadside fence, stood tall to watch one of his own shells strike, and yelled to the artillery lieutenant, "Lower the range of that piece!" At the next impact, he clapped his hands and shouted, "Keep her there, you've dismounted one of their guns!" As the batteries swapped fire, Brooks's troops crouched watching incoming artillery rounds plunge lazily toward them. A captain in the 15th New Jersey shouted, "Look out, here comes a shell!" and saw it plow beneath a sitting private, lifting him unhurt off the ground and knocking his knapsack 50 feet away. Capt. Lewis Van Blarcom of the 15th was paying close attention. Solid shot or shell, he noted, "has the peculiarity, after striking the ground, of moving without much running speed, end over end, for some distance and then flying in the air at a great height and distance." The 96th Pennsylvania took the railroad cut at a cost of five killed and 18 wounded, held it an hour, then was withdrawn.[15]

Sedgwick's objective was now the road to Chancellorsville, not the one to Richmond. Thus the key Rebel position was Marye's Heights and the trenches immediately around it, near the north end of Early's line. It was held by Barksdale's Mississippians, with a company of the Washington Artillery from New Orleans. Except for pickets, at dawn there were no defenders at all north of the Plank Road overlooking the canal.

Just before dawn, as Barksdale heard reports of his pickets falling back through Fredericksburg, Col. B. G. Humphreys of the 21st Mississippi came to his headquarters and asked if he were sleeping. "No sir!" growled Barksdale. "Who could sleep with a million of armed Yankees around him?" Knowing the Federals had been trying to put a bridge across at Fredericksburg, he assumed that the flow of Blue troops into the town meant they already had succeeded, so he galloped to Early to ask for reinforcements. Early ordered Brig. Gen. Harry T. Hays's Louisiana brigade to displace more than five miles from the far right to the far left of his line.[16]

Hays's hard-marching Louisianans arrived there "utterly fagged-out," just in time to keep Gibbon from repairing the bridge across the canal. Before the main Union attack, that flank also was bolstered by part of Cadmus Wilcox's brigade, which had been posted upstream guarding Banks' Ford.

At daybreak, Wilcox had checked his pickets, and noted that the enemy force across the river was much thinner than the night before. With his binoculars, he saw that the Yankees remaining were wearing haversacks, as if ready to move on. Lee had told Wilcox that if he was confident the Union army was not going to cross there, he should leave a detail to watch the ford and bring his brigade to Chancellorsville. Thus Wilcox ordered his troops to load up to march west. But just before they set out, one of his far-spread lookouts came running to report that Gibbon was moving upstream between the river and the canal. Wilcox turned his brigade back along the River Road to Taylor's and Stansbury's hills, overlooking the

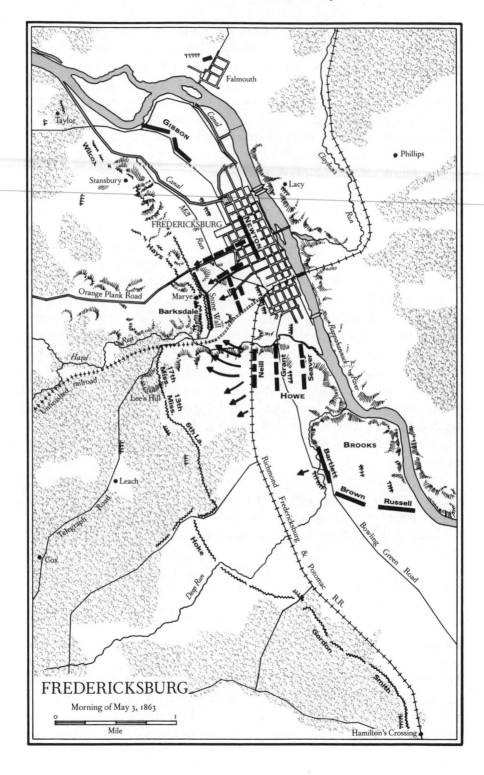

FREDERICKSBURG

Morning of May 3, 1863

0   1

Mile

canal. Only when he went looking for Barksdale near Marye's house did he realize that the Federals had moved into Fredericksburg. Soon afterward Barksdale asked for help, and Wilcox sent him the 10th Alabama. But by then it was too late.[17]

This time, Early had fewer than one-sixth as many defenders as Lee had used so effectively in December. Wilcox's arrival gave Early some 12,000 troops to Sedgwick's 27,000. Deployed along a seven-mile front, for most of that distance the Confederates were only one line deep. Wilcox plus four regiments from Hays watched the left, above the Plank Road. More than half of Early's force—Hoke's, Gordon's, and Smith's brigades—was well to the right, south of Howison's Hill.

The critical section in between, at and around Marye's Heights, was held by only Barksdale's four regiments and one from Hays. The 13th and 17th Mississippi, with the 6th Louisiana, spread along the crest to the right, on and beyond Lee's Hill. The 21st Mississippi was on the crest to the left, toward the Plank Road. Three of its companies were with the 18th Mississippi, behind the stone wall below.

Sedgwick's superiority in numbers kept Early guessing, unable to concentrate his meager defenses at any one point. When the Union general decided he had to make a direct assault, he aimed at the section that had been impenetrable in December, but now the defenders there were thin on the ground. Sedgwick ordered two storming columns from Newton's division to lead his attack: one column of fours under Col. George C. Spear would follow the Plank Road, the other under Col. Thomas D. Johns would take the Telegraph Road. A broad battle line under Col. Hiram Burnham would follow, extending to their left. Meanwhile Howe would send forward three assault lines of his own, moving again along the left of Hazel Run, aiming at Lee's Hill. The first wave of attackers would converge on Marye's Heights.

Newton ordered ten regiments to drop their heavy marching gear in the streets of Fredericksburg before making the main assault. To their left, Howe assigned nine regiments to his attack. Soon after 10:30, they moved to their line of departure.[18]

Only 140 feet above sea level, Marye's Heights was the lowest of the

14. Sedgwick Storms the Heights. *After failing twice to take Marye's Heights, Sedgwick succeeds by ordering direct assaults against the thinly manned stone wall and along Hazel Run. The Confederate defenders are split; Early regroups to the south, Wilcox delays Sedgwick's move west.*

knolls along the Confederates' defensive ridge, but from a bend in the ridge it looked down north, east, and south. That view allowed it to dominate the gently sloping mile of ground leading up from the Rappahannock. Atop the hill was the Marye family mansion; along the foot was the sunken road and stone wall behind which the Southerners had crouched to shred Burnside's army less than five months before.[19] Approaching it, Newton's troops followed orders not to fire a shot—to double-time forward at trail arms, then use the bayonet against the waiting Rebels.

The crunch of boots, the clink of weapons, the shouts of officers dressing the line were the only sounds from the advancing regiments. Ahead of them, Southern officers behind the stone wall told their riflemen to Hold steady, don't fire . . . wait . . . wait . . . wait till the right moment.

Though the infantry waited, Confederate howitzers on line with the stone wall opened on the attackers. Those on the hill could not depress far enough to be effective so close in, but the guns at the bottom of the slope cut loose with canister and blew away the head of the right Yankee column, killing Colonel Spear. The other column marched on toward the wall. The Rebel artillery "had perfect range of us, but the boys never wavered a particle," wrote Charles Brewster, watching from the town. The cannon were firing spherical case, he said, "a hollow iron ball filled with musket bullets and when it bursts it throws a perfect shower of fragments of iron and lead and these balls it is just like taking a handful of beans or shot and throwing them all at once only the effect is much more serious if they hit you."[20]

The Rebel infantry behind the wall was quiet, taking aim, holding fire. The disciplined Federals came on, still on, through the artillery fire, bayoneted muskets at the ready. When they were less than 40 yards from the stone wall, one Rebel musket popped. Finally a voice yelled "Fire," and around the attacking troops, the very air exploded.

Both columns were broken. Burnham's line behind them hesitated; in six minutes, Rebel bullets cut down almost a third of the 5th Wisconsin and 6th Maine. Troops dived into shallow wrinkles in the earth, trying to escape the "blinding rain of shot" that swept the field, "more than human nature could face." Some officers caught in it shouted "Retreat, retreat!" while from the rear, staff officers galloped up waving their swords, trying to cheer the attackers on. Sedgwick and Newton, watching from the garden of a brick house beside the Telegraph Road, looked in each other's face and read disaster. The second battle of Fredericksburg was about to end like the first.

In the tumult before the wall, an enlisted soldier yelled, "Forward, don't retreat! We'll never get this close again!" Colonel Johns restarted some of his column, and again it was shattered. He tried yet again, was hit and badly wounded. Burnham was shot off his horse. The attack dwindled and fell back.

Survivors of the 7th Massachusetts, which took almost 40 percent casualties leading Johns's column, found cover behind a house with a high board fence. Morton Hayward recalled what he thought as he lay there: "One man was killed right by my side and several wounded. But one does not seem to think anything of it while in action. You have something else to take up your mind with the bullets whistling by your ears and the shell with awful shriek rushing through the air. It is true that I felt kind of a queer feeling steal over me when I knew that I had got to go where the Angel of death would be fast thrusting in his sickle but no sooner were we engaged than this feeling vanished and I had no more thought of being suddenly struck down by the showers of bullets that went hissing on all sides of me.

"The enemy were giving vent to their yells and we were yelling back to them in earnest loading and firing till it became our destiny to be killed or wounded everything is all excitement the men dropping by your side telling you in their last gasp to give it to them boys dont spare the pills the enemy advancing or retreating the shouts of the foe the cryes of the wounded and the roar of the artilery and rattle of muskets all combined to gether do not give one chance to take a sober thought of anything. I was more afraid of being hit when I left the rank than anytime before for when I was firing I did not notice much about the balls but when you see them go zipping into the dirt beside you begin to think that before you get out of range that some stray ball may overtake you and that is not very pleasant to think of getting hit in the back." Soon afterward, Hayward's finger was ripped open when his weapon fired accidentally as he was loading it, jabbing the ramrod into his hand.[21]

Hidden behind the house, some of the Yankees poked about and saw through a crack in the fence that the Rebel flank, seemingly anchored there, was wide open. One of the Federal officers sent forward a flag of truce, to ask if he could retrieve his wounded lying in front of the wall. Trustfully and unwisely, Col. Thomas M. Griffin of the 18th Mississippi gave permission. The Yankee collecting party worked up toward the wall, close enough to see how thinly it was held. These discoveries were passed up the Union chain of command.

Within minutes, someone roared, "Massachusetts colors to the front!"

Lt. Col. Franklin P. Harlow ordered the 7th to its feet. The flag went forward; following it, what was left of the regiment crashed through the board fence onto the Rebel flank. The Confederates behind the stone wall were totally surprised at the Yankee charge from that direction. As they turned to meet it, the attackers fired into them point-blank, without aiming. Then bayonets, rifle butts, fists, and curses replaced musketry as soldiers of Mississippi and Massachusetts tangled hand to hand.

Col. Thomas S. Allen of the 5th Wisconsin took over Burnham's assault line and rallied it with words his men remembered long after: "When the signal *forward* is given, you will start at double-quick, you will not fire a gun, and you will not stop until you get the order to halt. You will never get that order!"

The bugle sounded *Charge!* Allen's men stood and surged forward in three waves, up to and over the stone wall that had been tried so many times before.

Simultaneously flanked and assaulted straight on, the Rebels at the foot of Marye's Heights struggled for a few desperate minutes, swinging their muskets like clubs. Then those who could get away scattered up the hillside, leaving behind empty weapons leaning against the once impregnable wall, packs and canteens and dead comrades in the roadside ditch where they had knelt to fire. The Federals, after catching their breath and re-forming into line, climbed the hill as the storming columns on their right pushed up alongside. The first Union colors spotted on the heights were those of the 6th Maine.[22]

To the left of Marye's Heights, Howe's columns waited for Newton's attack as their signal to move forward. After his troops flushed Rebels out of the railroad cut, Howe sent cannon ahead to pound the high ground. When they joined in, that made 60 Union guns in action against the Rebel works, plus long-range batteries firing from across the river. As shells burst along the ridge, Howe's first two ranks, under Brig. Gen. Thomas A. Neill and Col. Lewis A. Grant, charged ahead. Confederate artillery ripped the 26th New Jersey, leading Grant's attack. The regiment took cover in the deep ravine of Hazel Run, where Grant's winded troops rested a moment before angling onto Marye's. Howe's third line, led by Col. T. O. Seaver, kept going straight at Lee's Hill.

The momentum of these attacks converging in quick order at last drove the Confederates off Marye's Heights, but the Rebels there made it a near thing: although the Federals outnumbered the Confederates by about 7,500 to 1,000 in that sector, Newton said later that if there had been another 100 defenders on the hill, he never could have taken it. Neill's troops grabbed the colors of the battered 18th Mississippi, whose survivors had fallen back from the stone wall. A fraction of the 6th Louisiana was caught. And before the gunners could rescue their pieces, Capt. C. W. Squires's company of the proud Washington Artillery was captured.[23]

The cannoneers from New Orleans probably had killed and wounded more Federals on that field than any other like-sized command. When Yankee troops swarmed up the slope around them, their infantry support dropped back and only officers and gunners hung on beside the cannon. For Howe's division, which did not have to contend with the stone wall along the foot of the heights, the hardest fighting was against the Rebels working those guns atop the hill. "I must say that their artillery men was gritty," wrote William Stowe of the 2nd Vermont. "They did not abandon their guns untill our men had shot nearly all of them down and when they was a loading it the last time our men shot the one from his gun before he could have time to fire. The rammer was left in the gun."[24]

That last defiant Rebel gunner was someone like Cpl. Thomas J. Lutman of New Orleans, who had been keeping a diary in the first days of battle, sometimes in pig Latin, his own version of a secret code. His entry for May 2 ended, "Slept in the road all night." Sunday morning, even after the 6th Maine had planted the Stars and Stripes on the works before Lutman's piece, he doggedly kept firing. Told to stop, he fired again, "and had his brains blown out as a consequence of his willfulness." That was the postscript added to his diary by the Yankee who took it off his dead body.[25]

Desperately trying to pull their guns away, the artillerists were overrun because they had moved many of their horses back behind the crest for protection. One gunner asked as the panting Union troops reached the summit, "What troops are you?"

"We're Yankees!" the attacker shouted. "Do you think we'll fight now?"

Stepping up to surrender his sword to Colonel Allen, the artillery commander said, "Boys, you've captured the best battery in the Confederate service."[26]

The fall of Marye's Heights exposed other defenders along the ridge in both directions. Although outflanked Rebel cannon kept firing till the last minute, this penetration collapsed the whole Confederate position there. The defenders were split, some falling back to the north, some to the south. A Union officer, Huntington W. Jackson, rushed to find Sedgwick, who was giving Brooks and Howe orders to move up. This is a rare chance for cavalry, Jackson said excitedly. A regiment of horsemen could slice between those defeated Rebels, reap a harvest of prisoners and munitions, and clear the way toward Lee's rear at Chancellorsville. Maybe so, Sedgwick shrugged, but there was not a cavalryman to be had.[27]

After trying since dawn, the Federals had finally overwhelmed Marye's Heights so quickly that neither Early, to the south, nor Wilcox, to the north, realized at first what had happened. The Mississippi soldiers taken on top told their captors "they never was whipt," said William Stowe, "but they got a handsome whipping this time . . . but our regiment had to fight like mad men. . . . we green mountain boys are good for it as long as we are alive."[28]

Early, after satisfying himself that the Union jabs at the Confederate right were not serious, rode to inspect the situation at Marye's. Before he got there, a staff lieutenant galloped back with news that the hill had been taken. Early sent him with orders for John B. Gordon to bring his brigade up the ridge. Then he hurried to the Telegraph Road, along which some of his reserve batteries were dashing for the rear. "Old Jube" stopped them with a barrage of country cussing and rode on to find Barksdale. Despite being driven off the key position, Barksdale was calm.

One of the artillerists who had been at Marye's Heights, asked where his guns were, roared, "Guns be damned! I reckon now the people of the Southern Confederacy are satisfied that Barksdale's brigade and the Washington Artillery can't whip the whole damned Yankee army!"

But Barksdale could see that the fight was not over. "Our center has been pierced," he said. "That's all. We'll be all right in a little while."[29]

With Early, he formed a thin new defense near Leach's house, along the first rise on the plateau behind Lee's Hill. The core of it was the 6th Louisiana, which had come back in better shape than the regiments around it. The Federals braked when they saw this line of defenders, and brought up guns to spray the Rebels with canister. Early pulled away a few hundred yards along the Telegraph Road. There he stopped and spread out to slow the Yankees again. Then he brought his brigades together to make a stand along the high ground near Cox's house, almost three miles south of Marye's Heights.

Cadmus Wilcox was not there. Earlier, when Barksdale sent to him for help at Marye's, Wilcox had ridden ahead of his 10th Alabama to guide it into position. En route, he saw Hays's Louisianans pulling back and assumed they too were going to reinforce Barksdale. Only then did he find out the key hill had fallen, and that Hays was retreating south to the Telegraph Road. Wilcox told him that the two brigades together could hold off the enemy and at least slow Sedgwick's advance toward Chancellorsville. Hays agreed, but insisted that his orders were to follow the Telegraph Road instead. Then a courier arrived with Barksdale's suggestion that Wilcox come that way, too. But it was just a suggestion, not an order, because Wilcox outranked Barksdale. Once again daring independent judgment, Wilcox decided to try with his single brigade what he had wanted Hays to do with him—block the way to Chancellorsville. Thus, when the rest of Early's command fell back southward, Wilcox's brigade alone was between Sedgwick and Lee's rear.[30]

Sedgwick, with his superior numbers, might have curled back over these divided Confederate forces, shattered them, and broken up Lee's supply base at Hamilton's Crossing. But his orders pointed him west, toward Chancellorsville. At first, like a hunter chasing a partridge fluttering away from her chicks, he started along the Telegraph Road after Early. By the time he turned back toward Lee's rear, minutes were slipping away. When Newton's lead regiments started west out the Plank Road, a thin string of Wilcox's Alabamians slowed them along the ridge behind Marye's. After Federal cannon bombarded this line and infantry started to outflank it, Wilcox dropped back.[31] In fits and starts, Newton's troops approached Guest's house, two miles beyond Marye's. There Sedgwick halted them and gave them a break while he brought up his other divisions.

Some Union soldiers slept, others cooked their first meal of the day. Wounded men poured into hospitals set up in Fredericksburg and around the mansion on Marye's Heights. As Brooks's division marched through Fredericksburg, the scene was to one Pennsylvanian like "the destruction of Jerusalem."[32] Brooks's men had had an easier morning than the troops who charged the heights. Some thought the rest of the contest would be a sure thing, that "now all we had to do was to move down toward Richmond and pick up prisoners." Because this was Sedgwick's freshest division, when it caught up he assigned it to take the lead toward Chancellorsville. Newton and Howe would follow. Gibbon's two brigades were left to guard Fredericksburg. Fenced off by the canal across their front, they had done little at the peak of the battle but watch and cheer the storming of Marye's Heights, the brightest Federal victory in many a month.

WHATEVER SURGED inside Lee, he was outwardly calm as Lieutenant Pitzer gasped out the news from Fredericksburg. Unconsciously, he may have remembered Zachary Taylor's example the day the old general so gently deflated another young officer's excited warning about a dangerous enemy approaching, years before in Mexico. But in 1863 at Chancellorsville, Lieutenant Pitzer's message was not farfetched, it was all too believable. Lee could hope that luck would govern, that Sedgwick would remain passive and never move to squeeze him. But the true question was not whether, it was when, Sedgwick finally would do the obvious.

Lee's response was quick. His choices were few. As he considered them, another rider came up the road at full speed, without a saddle on his harshly puffing horse. It was the chaplain of Barksdale's brigade, with the same news that Lieutenant Pitzer had brought. Panting, he almost flung himself on Lee to tell of disaster at Fredericksburg. Lee started to smile, controlled it, and gently raised a hand to stop the chaplain. "Thank you very much," he said, "but both you and your horse are overheated. Take him to that shady tree yonder and rest a little. I'll call you as soon as we are through"—and then he turned back to business.[33]

Lee had to deal with Sedgwick, but he could not leave Hooker unguarded. Based on three days' fighting around Chancellorsville, he was willing to gamble that he could keep Hooker in his works. Once again, Lee decided to divide his army in the face of the odds. Leaving most of it to demonstrate and hold Hooker in place, he would send the rest to meet Sedgwick. That would be McLaws's command, which was closest to the threat and had not been so terribly bloodied in the morning's fighting.

Through the smoldering woods, Lee rode to McLaws and told him to send two brigades—Mahone (of Anderson's division) and Kershaw—immediately toward Fredericksburg. After their conversation, Lee spoke up so the troops nearby could hear: "Now, General, there is a chance for your young men to distinguish themselves!"

As he moved by with his staff, Union prisoners in the road stepped aside to let him pass. "That's him, that's Lee!" they told one another. "Hats off, boys!" To a man, they faced him and uncovered as he rode by. He looked at them solemnly, raised his hat, and nodded. At this the watching Rebels cheered both their prisoners and their general. Then they fell in for a quick inspection, filled their cartridge boxes, and headed toward Fredericksburg. When the first two units were well on the way, Lee ordered McLaws himself to follow with his remaining brigades, Wofford and Semmes.[34]

FROM THE FAST-RIDING Pitzer, Lee learned about the fall of Marye's Heights before Hooker did from his erratic telegraph service. But there was a chance that that good news would jump-start Hooker when he got it. Since the battle's opening moves, this was his best opportunity; if Hooker was ever to retake the offensive, he would do it when he found out that Sedgwick was about to clamp Lee between the wings of the Union army.

Thus Lee, headquartered in a tent beside the Plank Road, busied his troops to discourage Hooker from any such rashness. He called in Colston, who remembered that Lee spoke quietly, and "His plain gray sack-coat, with only three stars on the rolling collar, was, like his face, well sprinkled with the dust of the battlefield." Without explanation, Lee ordered Colston to take his division from Chancellorsville up the U.S. Ford Road. Expect to meet resistance before the bend in the road, Lee said. Do not attack, but feel out the enemy, keep him from advancing. Most important, he said, "Move at once." Colston, who still did not know what had happened at Fredericksburg, was "more than a little puzzled," but he moved immediately.[35]

It was three o'clock. After issuing his orders to Colston, Lee rode to find Dick Anderson. He directed Anderson to march his division north out the River Road, to block its junction with Mine Road. There he could threaten Federal communications across the river while preventing Hooker from moving down either road to meet Sedgwick. Anderson took with him a baker's dozen of rifled artillery pieces, which were sited far enough up the River Road to reach across the Rappahannock as well as support the infantry.

Colston had barely started up the road to U.S. Ford when Yankee cannon raked his lead regiments. They flailed the 10th Louisiana, knocking down 50 troops in less than two minutes. With regimental officers, Colston rallied the Louisianans, but his advance was stopped short. Up the road he saw a dozen Union guns along a low rise, with infantry trenches off to both sides. Another line of infantry stretched across their front. The Federal works extended far beyond his own skirmishers. Wisely, Colston decided that to move against them with his battered division "would have been only to insure its destruction." He reported the situation to Stuart, and was ordered to withdraw into the abandoned Federal trench line beside the Turnpike.[36]

This brief collision suggests what would have happened if Lee had not been diverted by Sedgwick, and had gone ahead with his all-out assault on Hooker's elaborate defenses anchored at the Chandler house. He may or may not have carried the Union position; either way, the price could

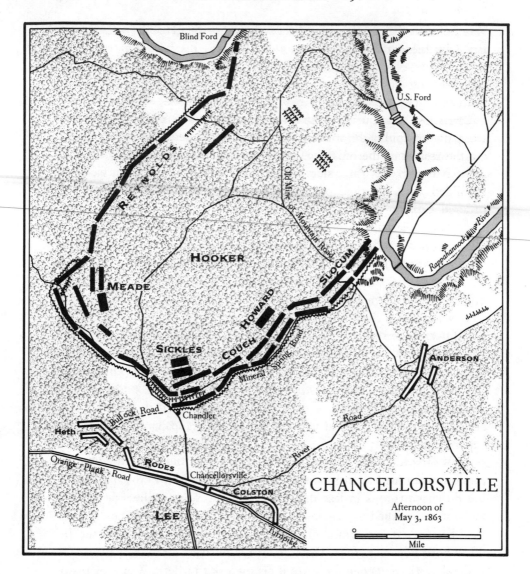

15. Hooker Hunkers Down. *After costly Southern assaults finally drive the Federals away from Chancellorsville, Hooker pulls back into prepared positions anchored at Chandler's house. Meanwhile Lee has sent McLaws east to help Wilcox block Sedgwick at Salem Church.*

have been even higher than what he had paid in the morning for Fairview and Chancellorsville.

AS USUAL IN Hooker's army, events were running well ahead of communications. At 12:45, when troops were starting to move toward their next clash, the left and right arms of the Union army were still trying to find out the results of the morning, and President Lincoln would have been grateful for news from anywhere along the Rappahannock. Quartermaster Ingalls, with Hooker, advised Butterfield at Falmouth:

> I think we have had the most terrible battle ever witnessed on earth. I think our victory will be certain, but the general told me he would say nothing just yet to Washington, except that he is doing well. In an hour or two the matter will be a fixed fact. I believe the enemy is in flight now, but we are not sure.[37]

Butterfield, notified of Hooker's injury, sent his regrets and asked permission to go with Sedgwick. He said he expected the enemy to make a desperate effort about dusk, "if he lasts that long." "I am heartsick at not being permitted to be on the actual field, to share the fate and fortune of this army and my general," the chief of staff added.

A few minutes later, at 1:30, he violated the express wishes of his general by wiring Lincoln that "the battle has been most fierce and terrible," with heavy losses on both sides. He told the president that Hooker had been slightly wounded, and Lincoln thanked him. But the president's anxiety was rising. At four o'clock, he got this delayed telegram from Hooker:

> We have had a most desperate fight yesterday and to-day, which has resulted in no success to us, having lost a position of two lines, which had been selected for our defense. It is now 1:30 o'clock, and there is still some firing of artillery. We may have another turn at it this p.m. I do not despair of success. If Sedgwick could have gotten up, there could have been but one result. As it is impossible for me to know the exact position of Sedgwick as regards his ability to advance and take part in the engagement, I cannot tell when it will end. We will endeavor to do our best. My troops are in good spirits. We have fought desperately to-day. No general ever commanded a more devoted army.[38]

Lincoln read between the lines. He asked Butterfield plaintively: "Where is General Hooker? Where is General Sedgwick? Where is Stoneman?"

Butterfield could answer only two-thirds of his questions:

> General Hooker is at Chancellorsville. General Sedgwick, with 15,000 to 20,000 men, at a point 3 or 4 miles out from Fredericksburg on the road to Chancellorsville. Lee is between. Stoneman has not been heard from. This is the situation at this hour from latest reports, 4:30 p.m.[39]

At that point three or four miles out from Fredericksburg, the situation would change within minutes.

Chapter Sixteen

FIRE IN THE PULPIT

CADMUS MARCELLUS WILCOX was carrying out a classic delay-ing action, forcing Sedgwick's advancing corps to deploy repeatedly, eating up precious time while McLaws force-marched his troops from Chancellorsville.

On the first ridge behind Marye's Heights, Wilcox had spread his brigade across the Plank Road, with two cannon at each end of his line. The artillery held off the advancing Yankees for long minutes, until Newton's division opened fire with a six-gun battery and pushed infantry onto Wilcox's front and right flank. The Federals came in fits and starts; "they seemed reluctant to advance," Wilcox said.

By slowing them, he had done what he meant to do, so he pulled back along the road. He sent Maj. C. R. Collins with 40 or 50 detached troopers of the 15th Virginia Cavalry to dismount in a pine grove near Downman's farmhouse and straddle the Plank Road as skirmishers. With his brigade, Wilcox kept on to Salem Church. But once there, he rode back to inspect a low rise around the tollgate on the Plank Road, half a mile east. He decided to make another short stand abreast the tollhouse before settling in along the gentle ridge at the church.

From First Manassas to Appomattox, Wilcox had other fine days; this was his finest. Born of a Connecticut Yankee father in the North Carolina mountains, he graduated from West Point near the bottom of the class of 1846, below George McClellan and Stonewall Jackson but above George Pickett. As a lieutenant in Mexico, he led a storming party up Chapulte-pec, then risked his life by climbing an aqueduct under fire to signal the American entry into Mexico City. A year later he was a groomsman at U. S. Grant's wedding. Between wars he taught infantry tactics at West Point. He entered Confederate service as colonel of the 9th Alabama, then led his Alabama brigade through every major fight in the East, losing almost 60 percent of his command during the Seven Days' Battles before Richmond. At Banks' Ford this Sunday, his alertness in noting that the Federal pickets were wearing their packs turned out to be one of the keys to the battle. But never would he or any of his classmates practice infantry tactics more skillfully than Wilcox did this afternoon on the road back of Fredericksburg.

Sedgwick, with Brooks's division in the lead, came on until he saw Major Collins's dismounted cavalry. This puny detachment gave the Federals a brief firefight, long enough for Wilcox to be warned, then it retired. When the Union troops approached the brigade waiting at the tollgate, Wilcox ordered two rifled guns in the road to open fire, which halted the advance again. Skirmishers traded shots while the Yankees brought up artillery and began shelling Wilcox's position. Just then an aide from McLaws arrived to tell Wilcox that reinforcements would be there soon, and Wilcox asked that they stop out of sight behind the church.[1]

On the way east, McLaws had deployed his brigades briefly at the junction of the Turnpike and the Mine Road, two miles west of Salem Church. There he sent some troops into the Confederate trenches dug as a blocking position facing the other way three days before, which seemed a year to many of them. But when he rode ahead, he found Wilcox at Salem Church, so moved as fast as possible to fill in beside him.[2]

SALEM CHURCH STANDS on the south side of the Orange Plank Road, five miles west of nineteenth-century Fredericksburg and six miles east of Chancellorsville. It is a picture-book country Baptist church, its red brick walls the color of Virginia clay. In the spring of 1863 it was nineteen years old. Before the war its congregation had been almost half black; there is still a separate entrance to the south balcony, known then as the slaves' gallery. After Fredericksburg was torn apart in December, dozens of refugee townspeople had camped in and around the 38-by-42-foot building, and much of their furniture was left stacked inside. Now Cadmus Wilcox was making the church a fortress.

Dropping back from the tollgate, he spread his brigade across the Plank Road just behind the church, using rifle pits dug by Pickett's division in January as a fallback position behind Fredericksburg. Wilcox put the 11th and 14th Alabama on the left facing east, the 8th and 10th Alabama on the right. On the road between them he positioned four artillery pieces. One company of the 9th Alabama was stationed in the church, another in a

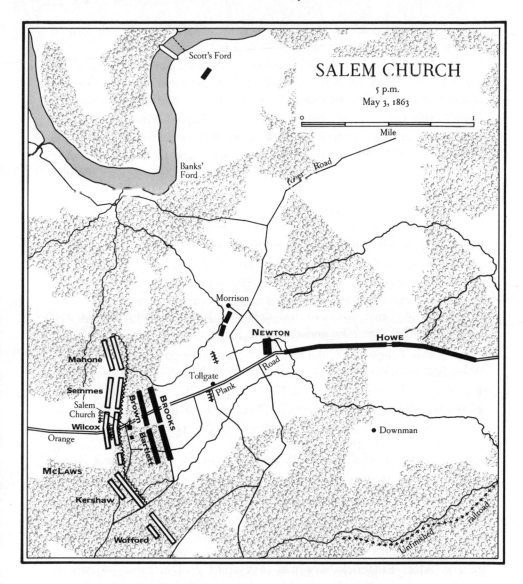

16. Fire in the Pulpit. *After delaying Sedgwick again at the tollgate, Wilcox is reinforced by McLaws. Wilcox's Alabamians and Semmes's Georgians play the major role in throwing back Brooks's advance at Salem Church.*

frame schoolhouse 60 yards to its right front. The rest of the 9th formed behind the 10th, close to the road.

When Mahone and Kershaw arrived ahead of McLaws, they started to fill in left and right of Wilcox. Then McLaws, coming up with Semmes and Wofford, shifted Mahone farther left since he had been in that area before, and sent Semmes between him and Wilcox. Thus from left to right, the Confederates facing Sedgwick were Mahone, Semmes, Wilcox, Kershaw, and Wofford—five brigades, four more than the advancing Federals had met along the road before, enough to make Sedgwick wonder whether he had collided with Lee's whole army.

But before the Rebel reinforcements were in place, Union cannon near the tollgate opened on the Salem Church ridgeline. For 15 or 20 minutes, Southern gunners answered, then withdrew when they were nearly out of ammunition. At five o'clock, Federal artillery fire lifted and Brooks's skirmishers edged forward to clash with Wilcox's for another quarter hour. Then two brigades of Brooks's infantry started up the gradual slope toward the church. There the Confederates waited along the rear edge of a thick belt of timber.

In the 16th New York, the order to fix bayonets passed down the line. A soldier remembered it: "There is a rattling of steel against steel as the bayonets are put on and locked. 'Forward, march.' Slowly and steadily, elbow to elbow, we move forward. There comes a shell. We see the puff of smoke from the gun. It falls harmless. But that next does not; it leaves a gap in the line ahead. *Hum,* that is a rifle ball, almost spent, yet reaching beyond our line. 'Steady.' Shot and shell multiply; the man at my right falls, my tentmate, but I must not stop to help him. Glancing back, I see him limping to the rear. We come to a rail fence and are just about to spring upon it when the order comes, 'Halt and lie down.' We drop behind the fence, my head close to a rail. *Thud,* a bullet strikes the rail, I glance at it and see that it was directly in range and has almost passed through. It is slivered just in front of my head. Saved by a hair's breadth. We lie perhaps two minutes. . . . 'Fall in' and we spring up. 'Right face, march,' and we cross the road, raked by the enemy's artillery. 'By the left flank' and we enter the thicket, from which a regiment has just been driven. We press into it, and catch sight of the hedge beyond, and the church. . . ."[3]

The Confederates poured musket fire into the woods as the attackers pushed through, skewing their formations in the undergrowth. The Federals took minutes to reorganize. Then, with three hurrahs, Sedgwick's infantry charged onto the Southern line.[4] Bartlett's brigade thrust at the church and the rifle pits behind it. Wilcox's Rebels held their fire until the shouting Yankees were within 80 yards, then let loose a volley that thinned the Union line. The Federals wavered but came on.

As the 16th New York shifted to the right of the Plank Road and pushed ahead, everything was hidden by "the cloud of smoke which rises from the muzzles of muskets and cannon, whose leaden and iron hail gives us greeting. Can any man escape? See the twigs drop on all sides; hear the bullets hum, and the grape and canister rattle, and the shells scream. What is life worth here? Nothing; then throw it away by give and take as you may. What is going around? There goes Hank; he was talking of home yesterday. He has his discharge and gone home three days before he expected it. There comes Joe Trompley driving our cowardly adjutant to the front at the point of his bayonet. But he slips down the line and gets to the rear as fast as his long legs will carry him. . . . I see and hear all these things plainly, all the time loading and firing as fast as possible. 'Forward, charge,' and again we rush a little nearer to the enemy. . . . Load, fire, once, twice, three times. . . ."[5]

The Federals kept coming. They flowed around the little isolated schoolhouse and captured the entire company that had been firing from between its logs. Then they focused their fire on the church.* Still pressing, they drove in the 10th Alabama behind the school. But as that regiment stumbled backward, the 8th Alabama opened on the attackers' left. Wilcox spurred forward; four bullets hit his uniform and his horse as he waved in his only reserve. The rest of the 9th Alabama behind the 10th rose up and reversed the tide.

Roaring into the Yankees, the 9th retook the schoolhouse and freed the captured company. Without giving the attackers time to rally, the regiment pushed them back through the timber. From the north gallery of the brick church, Confederate riflemen poured "harassing and deadly fire" into the retreating Yankees. One of the Alabamians inside shooting out felt guilty: "We had literally converted the House of God into a charnel house, had pushed aside the book of Life and were using instruments of death."

Four sharpshooters were in the pulpit, firing through the window at its rear. One of them was an Irishman, quoted as saying, "Captain, I was being after sinding out from that pulpit some of the most forcible argument any one iver sint from it before."[6] As the Rebels pursued, the

---

*Almost 130 years later, with the worst damage long since repaired, the outer walls of Salem Church still show the pockmarks of 168 bullets, 81 of them on the east side, 53 on the north.

disorganized 10th Alabama recovered and joined the counterattack. Capt. Jacob Haas of the 96th Pennsylvania admitted that his company fled in "a terrible skedipper."[7]

North of the road, Union Col. Henry Brown's New Jersey brigade pelted Semmes's Georgians with musketry as the Rebels extended their defensive line behind a long hedgerow of cedars. The tall, ruddy Semmes was with his troops. Heading into battle, he liked to dress for the occasion—red turban, polished boots, elegant uniform with red sash around the shoulders and waist—so his men would know he was there.[8] The Yankees came hard at the 50th and 53rd Georgia on his left, but were thrown back repeatedly. In the 50th, troops fired so fast some of their musket barrels leaded up; they dropped those weapons and grabbed others from the dead and wounded. The regiment had brought 60 rounds of ammunition per man into the fight, but was running out. Litter-bearers scrambled back for more. Lt. Col. Francis Kearse turned to the officer beside him. "I'll have no regiment left if this lasts a half hour longer," he said. "Oh, that the sun should set! Is there no support?" But suddenly up and down his line, troops were shouting, "They're giving way! Let's charge them!"[9]

Hit by fire from the hedgerow ahead and the church on its flank, the 16th New York lost momentum. Out front, the soldier realized the friend at his elbow was shouting at him. "What is Ellsworth saying? 'Well, if they have all gone, we may as well go too.' True enough; we turn around and no one but the dead and wounded is in sight. The rest have received orders which we did not hear to fall back. . . . I followed back by the way I had come in. This I knew for I saw my rubber blanket lying on the ground where it had been shot from my knapsack while we were advancing. I partly stooped to pick it up, but in doing so glanced back and saw several Johnnies close behind me. . . . Shall I run? No use, their bullets will catch me. I stiffen up as straight as a ramrod and walk off. *Zip, zip, zip, zip, zip:* strange I am not hit. . . ."[10]

The 10th and 51st Georgia, close to the road, lunged out of their works with a yell and took up the chase alongside Wilcox's regiments. Col. Mark Collet of the 1st New Jersey was killed as he tried to stem his troops' retreat. Wilcox grumbled over the depleted Rebel artillery: "With a good battery to play upon this retreating mass, the carnage would have been terrific."

Out on the Federal right, Brig. Gen. Frank Wheaton had taken three regiments of Newton's division to probe the defenders' flank. Soon after they crossed a creek near the Morrison house, they were lashed by fire from Rebels who came charging up the ravine. About that time, Sedgwick's first line of attack reeled back from the center. Federal reinforcements double-quicked up the road and spread across it in front of the oncoming Rebels. But the Southerners' momentum kept them going, and this new Union line had barely formed when it broke, too.

Wilcox's and Semmes's troops drove the Federals back to the tollgate, half a mile or more. There they ran into Newton's division, blocking the road. Still they charged on, "waving their old red rag of a battle flag and yelling like demons," until Sedgwick himself directed Union artillery to fire over the heads of the retreating infantry. As the fleeing Yankees filtered past the gun positions, the cannoneers switched to canister. The leg-weary Rebels faltered, took cover, and regrouped. With dusk falling, they pulled back to their line at Salem Church.[11]

Near the tollgate, Union soldiers wandered from cluster to cluster of men, wherever there was a crowd around a flag, looking for their regiments. On the bloody half mile of ground between there and Salem Heights, wounded men and horses cried out in the near-darkness.

Unable to hear this without trying to help, some of the men in the 10th Georgia crawled out between the lines and dragged in as many fallen troops as they could find. When they brought back their comrade William Hudson, apparently mortally wounded, he told of a child moaning at the edge of the swampy ground near the enemy. The rescuers sneaked back and found a Yankee, "not over 15, whose voice was like a child's. He was frightfully wounded. . . . His clothing was literally riddled by bullets and several had pierced his body." Thinking he would surely die, the Georgians sent the boy to the rear on a litter and were surprised to learn later that he had survived.[12]

Nearby in the 50th Georgia, a litter-bearer came to a Scottish-born officer, Capt. Peter A. S. McGlashan, and told him that one of his soldiers wanted to see him before he died. McGlashan went back and found a "plain pine woods farmer" from Colquitt County, whose eyes and nose had been shot out by a ball through his temple. "Is the colonel here?" asked the soldier. When McGlashan answered, the soldier said, "Colonel, take my hand." McGlashan did, kneeling beside the stretcher. "Colonel, have I done my duty?" asked the soldier. McGlashan assured him that he always had.

"Oh, that's all right," said the soldier. "Tell my people, when you return home, that John Culpepper died doing his duty."[13]

·   ·   ·

ONCE AGAIN LEE'S MEN had whipped an overall superior Federal force because the Rebels had more troops at the point of collision. Having more men in the vicinity won nothing for Sedgwick, because the Confederates had more in the fight. The five Southern brigades at Salem Church totaled only about 10,000 men, against more than 20,000 in Sedgwick's Sixth Corps. But Sedgwick sent only eleven regiments, some 5,000 men including artillery, into his initial attack. At Fredericksburg, he had superior force and eventually used it to take the heights, but when the battle began at Salem Church two of his divisions were trailing, a mile or more behind Brooks. While Wilcox fired and fell back in front of Sedgwick, the other four Southern brigades under McLaws had to march more than five miles from near Chancellorsville. Yet they got to Salem Church in time, because of Lee's quick decision to send them—and Wilcox's masterful performance along the road from Fredericksburg. Four brigades, two from each side, did the heaviest fighting Sunday evening at Salem Church. But farther left and right, the attackers could see other Confederates filing in, contributing a few rounds to the defense. They were nervous about who those unexpected regiments might be.

At the height of the battle at Salem Church, Union chief of staff Butterfield was taking seriously what he had heard from Captain Squires of the Washington Artillery, feted and offered his choice of wines after being captured on Marye's Heights: Hood's and Pickett's Confederate divisions were expected soon. A North Carolina prisoner said Lee had telegraphed Early that if he could hold on, reinforcements would arrive that night. Butterfield advised Hooker that "The general impression of the prisoners seems to be that we shall hear from Hood before long." [14] While there was nothing from Union sources to support these recurring reports from captive Rebels, they were credible to Hooker's officers because of the surprises Lee already had sprung. Jackson had appeared with overwhelming force on the far Union flank after dozens of firsthand warnings were ignored. Now Federal generals were jumpy.

If Union cavalry had been operating near the battlefield, doing the scouting and reporting normally expected from their service, Butterfield would have known that Hood and Pickett were still far away south. No serious reconnaissance was done even by the skimpy detachments of horse left behind with Hooker's army. And while the furious battles were going on at Chancellorsville, Fredericksburg, and Salem Church, most of Stoneman's cavalry was off on a lark. The objective of his massive raid was to cut Lee's connection to Richmond, thus scaring the Confederates into retreat. Stoneman's excursion did indeed scare Richmond, but it made little impression on Lee. Instead of scaring, he attacked.

As Stoneman began his mission, he had no guide, and was held up by fog after he took the main body of his troopers across the upper fords of the Rappahannock and Rapidan. In the Saturday morning darkness, Brig. Gen. David Gregg's division eventually reached Louisa Court House and started tearing up the Virginia Central Railroad from there east. Later that morning, Stoneman brought his whole force together at Louisa and dispatched squadrons east and west to destroy bridges. (See Map 2.)

A contingent of the 6th Maine Cavalry headed for Gordonsville, the junction of the Virginia Central and Orange & Alexandria rail lines, because Stoneman, too, thought reinforcements for Lee were arriving from southward. "We knew that six or seven trains had passed up the evening previous, loaded with troops," he reported. The Maine horsemen were slapped back by "Rooney" Lee's 9th Virginia Cavalry, losing one killed, one wounded, and twenty-four prisoners.[15]

Loyal Confederates conceded that the Union raid through the region "was indeed a very bold affair, but accomplished very little with respect to public affairs. Privately, however, they did a great deal—bacon, corn, horses and negroes suffered, and utter desolation with respect to that sphere of property is seen in this tract." Six Yankee riders came to the Rowe farmhouse near Gordonsville, threatened the owner unless he told where his horses were hidden, and broke into his meat house—but then were surprised by Rebel cavalrymen who "captured every one and gave them a free ride to Richmond."[16]

Trotting east from Louisa, a squadron of the 1st U.S. Cavalry reached Frederick's Hall. There, they destroyed a warehouse and depot, and ran into distractions. An officer, Isaac Dunkelberger, came upon a pair of legs sticking out from under a stack of straw. The legs wore blue pants, but he thought they might belong to a Rebel trying to hide. He ordered a trooper to pull the suspect out, and it was not a Rebel at all.

"Bejabers, I found a barrel of apple whiskey!" the hiding Federal explained. He had poked a hole in the barrel and filled a half dozen canteens. Dunkelberger, not wanting to ride with drunken cavalrymen in unfriendly country, confiscated the whiskey and moved on. But that night, on picket, he saw to it that every man in his command got a good slug of applejack.

The next day, they captured another warehouse with a generous supply of chewing tobacco. But then their luck turned. A messenger came asking for help to meet an attack on the head of the long column, so hundreds of pounds of good Virginia leaf were tossed away—all for nothing, because by the time Dunkelberger's horsemen arrived up front the skirmish was over.

Hard riding broke down Stoneman's horses, and his men appropriated all they could find from farms along the way. Mules, too: when one of Dunkelberger's troopers lost his horse, he caught a huge mule and mounted it, but the creature bucked so viciously he was thrown off. The Yankee was afraid to get on again, yet unwilling to let the prize go.

Dunkelberger's man Flaherty solved the problem. "Bejabers!" he said, "I have it! There's a Nager in the fence corner and divil the harm if the mule breaks his neck." Flaherty motioned to the slave—"Nager, mount this mule." Dunkelberger recalled that "He was as fine a specimen of a colored man as I ever saw, but the mule finally got the best of him and bucked him off." But Flaherty persisted. "Nager," he said, "mount that mule and don't dismount till you get orders!" This time the slave wrapped his arms about the mule's neck and "held on like a tick." The mule bucked, but the black man stuck, and finally the mule gave up and moved along as quietly as any horse in the squadron.

"All this time we heard nothing from our army under Hooker," Dunkelberger recalled—nor did Hooker hear anything from his long-riding cavalry.[17]

Late Saturday night, Stoneman's troopers had destroyed 18 miles of track, depots, and water tanks along the Virginia Central, and arrived at Thompson's Crossroads, on the South Anna River. There, he called in his regimental commanders, unfolded his maps and laid out his plan: "I gave them to understand that we had dropped in that region of the country like a shell, and that I intended to burst it in every direction, expecting each piece or fragment would do as much harm and create nearly as much terror as would result from sending the whole shell, and thus magnify our small force into overwhelming numbers. . . ."

Stoneman sent out six separate raiding parties: The 1st New Jersey Cavalry would go after the canal aqueduct over the Rivanna River where it joins the James, at Columbia. The 2nd New York would thrust east to destroy the railroad bridges over the Chickahominy and throw a fright into Richmond. The 12th Illinois would cut the railroads near Ashland. These three expeditions had the option of pushing east past Richmond to Union-held country at the mouth of the York River. The 1st Maine and 1st Maryland would ride along the South Anna, destroying bridges on the way. The 5th U.S. would follow that line, completing the destruction. A detachment of the 1st Maryland would head out to strike targets of opportunity. Stoneman, suffering from painful piles, would stay back with about 500 men as a rallying point after his troopers completed their missions.[18]

Thus, when Lincoln asked where Stoneman was that Sunday afternoon, Hooker could have reported accurately that his cavalry chief was romping about in Lee's rear, tearing up the main links to the Confederate capital. Stoneman could have reported doing lots of damage but finding no major reinforcements on their way to Lee. If any news could have given Hooker the confidence to take the initiative, that pair of reports combined with Sedgwick's move should have done it. But Hooker was not in touch with Stoneman, and vice versa. Despite the excitement that Stoneman's troopers stirred far behind Rebel lines, the fighting along the Rappahannock proceeded as if the Union cavalry did not exist. Lee snatched back the initiative every time it looked as if the battle might tilt the other way.

JUBAL EARLY was driven off the heights above the Rappahannock, but in his mind the fight had just begun.

Although "Old Jube" was forty-six, before Sumter he had spent only two years as an officer on active duty. Graduating from West Point in 1837, he had resigned from the army after a year fighting Seminoles in Florida. He returned briefly during the Mexican War, but missed the action. Thereafter he became a lawyer and Whig politician, and spoke and voted against secession in Virginia's 1861 convention. Entering Confederate service as colonel of the 24th Virginia, he led brigades from First through Second Manassas, then took over his division before Sharpsburg. He worshipped Lee and Jackson. Like them, he was pugnacious on the field. Like them, he wore a beard. But there the superficial resemblance stopped. Though loyal and generous down deep, Early was sarcastic, irreligious, and a virtuoso of hill-country profanity.

As soon as he drew his defensive line across the Telegraph Road south of Fredericksburg, he advised Lee of his situation. Lee, at Chancellorsville, heard the fighting five miles away at Salem Church. After an hour and a half, it still rumbled on. Though the battle there was undecided, Lee already saw it as another opportunity to strike, rather than retreat. He told Early:

> If they are attacking [McLaws] there, and you could come upon
> their left flank, and communicate with General McLaws, I think you

would demolish them. See if you cannot unite with him and, together, destroy him. With his five brigades, and you with your division and the remnants of Barksdale's brigade, I think you ought to be more than a match for the enemy. . . .[19]

Then Lee sent this to McLaws:

> I have just written to Early, who informs me he is on the Telegraph Road . . . to unite with you to attack the enemy on their left flank. Communicate with him, and arrange the junction, if necessary and practicable. It is necessary that you beat the enemy, and I hope you will do it.[20]

Despite approaching darkness, Lee obviously meant to do it immediately, not later. But by the time his messages were delivered, the fighting at Salem Church had broken off. During the evening, Early sent a note to McLaws, saying he would attack in the morning. Rather than linking first with McLaws, he would head north to retake Marye's Heights, cutting Sedgwick's link to Fredericksburg. Then he would turn left and strike Sedgwick from the east while McLaws came at him from the west. McLaws forwarded this version to Lee. At midnight, writing by the light of a candle produced by Stuart's friend von Borcke, Lee approved—but urged McLaws to press the Federals, so they could not concentrate on Early.[21]

Back near Chancellorsville, there were repeated alarms along the lines during the night. These flare-ups occasionally brought a Yankee shell arcing into the trees near Lee's tent, keeping his headquarters awake. Wounded men lost in the thickets cried out for water. The cannon fire hit a barn not far away where some 300 Union casualties were collected, and their wails blended with the monotonous dirge of the whippoorwills.[22]

WHILE LEE WAS BUSY planning for the morning, at 11:00 P.M. Hooker was deep asleep at his headquarters north of Chancellorsville. His engineer and liaison to Sedgwick, Gouverneur Warren, returned and asked if he had orders for Sedgwick. Hooker, apparently still groggy after his injury more than twelve hours earlier, awoke just enough for Warren to "get his ideas." There were no other senior staff officers present; through most of the battle, Butterfield and the rest remained across the river, passing messages back and forth and egging Sedgwick on. Warren, reluctant to leave Sedgwick wondering what to do, took the responsibility of sending

Grounded.   *One of Thaddeus S. C. Lowe's observation bal-*
loons (1) at rest, protected from wind by pine saplings. On the
hilltop are the ruins of the Phillips house (2), which was
Burnside's headquarters during the battle of Fredericksburg.
Lowe's portable hydrogen generator (3) waits beside Claiborne
Run.   BY EDWIN FORBES. LIBRARY OF CONGRESS

The Mud March.   *Burnside's last effort to make up for defeat
at Fredericksburg began in reasonable order, but disintegrated
in the great rainstorm of January 21–22.*

Maj. Gen. Daniel Butterfield. *Hooker's chief of staff, said by some to be his brains.*

LIBRARY OF CONGRESS

LEFT: Maj. Gen. Joseph Hooker. *A photograph by Mathew Brady, taken after Fredericksburg and before Chancellorsville.*

LIBRARY OF CONGRESS

Lincoln tries again. *With the discarded figures of seven generals behind him, the president appoints Hooker to command of the Army of the Potomac. A contemporary cartoon.*

LIBRARY OF CONGRESS

Winter in camp near Stoneman's Switch. *Most troops of both armies slept in tent-roofed log dugouts. Note barrel used as chimney. This scene is dated January 25, 1863; on Washington's Birthday some weeks later there was almost a foot of snow, and five inches fell on Easter morning, April 5.*

Gen. Robert E. Lee, 1863. *The Confederate commander is
seen here at the height of his powers.*

Hooker's infantry. *The 110th Pennsylvania Volunteers of Bowman's brigade, Whipple's division, Sickles's Third Corps, ready for inspection the week before the battle. The regiment was heavily engaged May 3 near the Chancellorsville house.*

Lt. Gen. Thomas J. Jackson.   *Stonewall's last portrait was taken during his wife's visit to the Confederate camp, just before the battle began.*   LIBRARY OF CONGRESS

Maj. Gen. J. E. B. Stuart.   *Waving his plumed hat, Lee's cavalry chief led the attack after Jackson fell at Chancellorsville. His flamboyant career ended at Yellow Tavern in 1864.*   LIBRARY OF CONGRESS

Making ready to fire. *An officer out front gives orders to U.S. Army Regular artillerymen at a position overlooking the Rappahannock and Fredericksburg.* REVIEW OF REVIEWS

Crossing the Rappahannock. *Early on the morning of April 29, Federal infantry of Russell's brigade, Brooks's division, Sedgwick's Sixth Corps, head into the fog toward the Confederate shore.* WAUD. LIBRARY OF CONGRESS

Chancellorsville, May 1. *View from southeast toward Chancellorsville mansion (1), Hooker's headquarters. Federal troops arrive on U.S. Ford Road (3) and Turnpike (4) as others march out Plank Road (5) and Turnpike (6) toward approaching Confederates. Meanwhile artillery deploys across foreground (7).*   FORBES. LIBRARY OF CONGRESS

Maj. Gen. Oliver O. Howard. *He had won the Medal of Honor and lost an arm at Fair Oaks in 1862 before coming back to command the Eleventh Corps at Chancellorsville.*

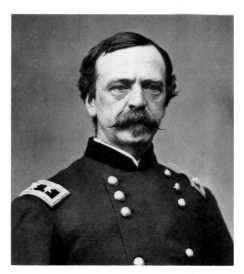

Maj. Gen. Daniel E. Sickles. *Hooker's aggressive and favorite corps commander had behind him a boisterous past in Washington and would lose a leg at Gettysburg.*

Maj. Gen. John Sedgwick. *Loved by his troops, "Uncle John" was faulted by Hooker in congressional hearings after Sedgwick's death at Spotsylvania in 1864.*

LIBRARY OF CONGRESS

Brig. Gen. Robert E. Rodes. *His division led Jackson's flank attack late Saturday. After both Jackson and Hill were wounded, Rodes graciously yielded corps command to cavalryman Stuart. Rodes was killed at Winchester in 1864.*

LIBRARY OF CONGRESS

Maj. Gen. Ambrose Powell Hill. *The fiery Hill's long feud with Jackson ended moments after Stonewall was wounded. Hill was killed at Petersburg a week before the war ended.*

LIBRARY OF CONGRESS

Maj. Gen. Jubal A. Early. *Colorfully profane and unshakably loyal, "Old Jube" loved to fight, and wanted to keep on even after Appomattox.*

LIBRARY OF CONGRESS

Near 3 P.M.
May 2d, 1863

General,

The enemy has made a stand at Chancellor's which is about 2 miles from Chancellorsville. I hope as soon as practicable to attack. I trust that an ever Kind Providence will bless us with great success.

Respectfully
T. J. Jackson
Lt. Genl.

Genl. R. E. Lee.

The leading division is up & the next two appear to be well closed.

T. J. J.

Jackson's most famous message. *This dispatch to Lee was written in the saddle as he was about to launch the flank attack that capped his career.* BATTLES & LEADERS

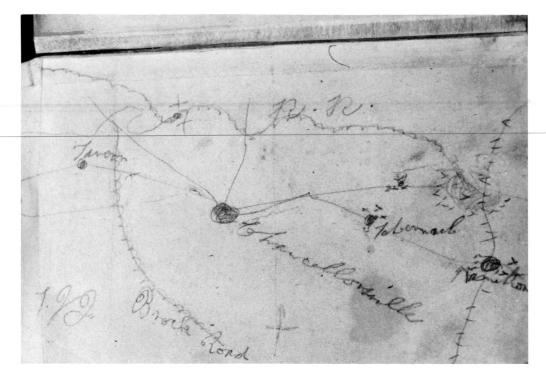

Jackson's crude pocket map.   *Scrawled in his own hand, his map did not show Bullock Road, which cuts northeast behind Chancellorsville. If it had, he might not have felt the need to reconnoiter beyond his lines, seeking a way to drive between Hooker and the river. This map, previously unpublished, was acquired by Lee and pasted inside the cover of his copy of John Esten Cooke's biography of Jackson.*

Stampede of the Eleventh Corps. *Couch's Second Corps,
coming up on the right, tried vainly to halt the frantic retreat
of Howard's command from Jackson's attacking Confederates.*

Chaos in the woods. *Amid gunsmoke and moonlight,
Meagher's Irish brigade was ordered to block the Eleventh
Corps' flight up U.S. Ford Road. It also failed.*

Lee's supreme moment. *At the climax of his greatest victory, Lee's battered soldiers cheer his arrival at Chancellorsville. This idealized drawing catches the feeling, but has none of the raw realism of sketches by Forbes and Waud, artist correspondents with the Union army.*

Behind the stone wall. *This photo was taken by Union Capt. Andrew J. Russell on the morning of May 3, 20 minutes after Sedgwick's troops overran Confederate defenses at the foot of Marye's Heights.* LIBRARY OF CONGRESS

The work of one shell. *During the few hours before Early retook Marye's Heights, Russell made the nearest thing to combat photographs of the battle. Here, Brig. Gen. Herman Haupt, chief of the Bureau of Military Railways, leans against a stump talking to W. W. Wright, superintendent of the military rail line from Aquia Creek. A single shell from Union artillery across the river killed these horses and destroyed the caissons.* LIBRARY OF CONGRESS

After the battle. *Hundreds of soldiers were left where they fell, others were buried in and around the huts of their comrades, as in this Union camp at Stoneman's Switch. Some bodies were retrieved by families for reburial at home; more were brought together later in national cemeteries.*

him instructions.[23] That decision was another seemingly minor but fateful detail in the campaign of Chancellorsville.

Warren wrote to Sedgwick:

> I find everything snug here. We contracted the line a little, and repulsed the assault with ease. General Hooker wishes them to attack him to-morrow. If they will, he does not desire you to attack them again in force unless he attacks at the same time. He says you are too far away for him to direct. Look well to the safety of your corps, and keep up communication with General Benham at Banks Ford and Fredericksburg. You can go to either place, if you think it best. To cross at Banks Ford would bring you in supporting distance of the main body, and would be better than falling back to Fredericksburg.[24]

Warren, an engineer, mathematics professor, and future corps commander who would take a crucial initiative at Gettysburg, was ordinarily precise and realistic. He conceded afterward that this dispatch was a mistake. It was written "at a time when I was exceedingly exhausted," he said—as he must have been, after staying in the saddle for most of the previous twenty-five hours. For him to say "everything snug" was correct as far as it went, since Hooker was safe for the moment behind formidable breastworks. But to tell Sedgwick after the terrible fight at Chancellorsville that the Federals had merely "contracted the line a little" smacked of censoring the news to a corps commander. True, Hooker did still hope Lee would attack him in his strong position, as he had asserted all along. But there was no sign that he intended to attack Lee in concert with Sedgwick. Most significantly, Warren implied Hooker's sanction for Sedgwick to retreat across the newly laid pontoon bridge, which actually was at Scott's Ford, not at Banks' Ford a mile away. While Sedgwick must have been thinking of that contingency, neither Hooker nor Butterfield had previously mentioned it on paper.

Though Warren took responsibility for the dispatch, its euphemisms sounded like Hookerisms. "Contracted the line a little" might have come directly from the commanding general's lips. But Warren never says he was quoting Hooker. Historian John Bigelow, Jr., without offering a source, reports that when Warren asked for orders for Sedgwick, Hooker said only one word: "None."[25] The vagueness about just what Hooker said, and how deeply he slept, suggests that we consider again whether he had turned to the bottle for help when he confronted Lee.

The most widely accepted version is from General Couch, whose words are worth careful examination: ". . . I have always stated that he probably abstained from the use of ardent spirits when it would have been far better for him to have continued in his usual habit in that respect. The shock from being violently thrown to the ground, together with the physical exhaustion resulting from loss of sleep and the anxiety of mind incident to the last six days of the campaign, would tell on any man."[26] Of course that last sentence is true; concussion alone can fog the brain for hours. But Couch never says flatly that Hooker was not drinking, or even that he believes that was the case; he says, "I have always *stated* that he *probably* abstained"—two qualifiers back to back. Couch was outspoken and disgusted with Hooker's performance, but focused his criticism on his military rather than personal conduct.

Engineer officer Washington Roebling arrived at Chancellorsville the morning of May 1 and was told by fellow officers "that Gen. Hooker had been so elated over his wonderful success so far that he had taken a drop too much the previous evening and was still busily sleeping it off at 9 A.M. . . ." That previous evening was when the commander issued his celebratory General Orders No. 47, about how Lee "must ingloriously fly" or "certain destruction awaits him." Roebling served at headquarters, occasionally as a liaison for Hooker. He said that on Sunday morning, "Hooker acted like a jealous drunkard. When he had a drink he felt aggressive for half an hour, then he weakened, countermanded all forward movement, actually withdrawing troops who were driving the enemy!"[27]

Pvt. Robert G. Carter of the 22nd Massachusetts (who went to West Point after the war and won the Medal of Honor as an Indian fighter) wrote that Hooker's tent was within 100 yards of his regiment's right flank, on its route to fetch water. Soldiers of the 22nd "constantly passed his tent, the flaps of which were back, and saw him lying drunk from Sunday noon (May 3) until we withdrew from our works. . . ."

Carter's remarks are in his handwritten annotations to T. A. Dodge's *The Campaign of Chancellorsville:* When Dodge describes Hooker's plan, Carter says, "At this hour he was lying at the White House [Bullock's, or Chandler's] so drunk that he was incapable of executing any plan." When Dodge says that from Thursday noon or at latest Friday morning, Hooker's "enervation was steadily on the increase," Carter insists that "This means his drunkenness," and indeed Dodge's choice of words is rather suggestive. When Dodge says Hooker's inactivity was such a puzzle, Carter retorts, "It was 'no puzzle' to those of us who constantly passed his tent. . . ." When Dodge says that Hooker blamed Sedgwick as scapegoat only after the battle, Carter explains, "This was after he had got over his drunken debauch." When Dodge quotes Warren as saying, "Gen. Hooker appeared very much exhausted," Carter says, "DRUNK!!!" And when Dodge notes how Hooker "lay listlessly expectant" after boasting of what he would do, Carter calls it "a h—l of a case of watchful waiting!" Carter's comments lack scholarly trappings, but they do have a confident first-person vigor.[28]

Col. Charles Albright of the 132nd Pennsylvania, who had taken over a brigade in Couch's corps, told of going to Hooker's headquarters to resolve a conflict of orders at about one o'clock Sunday afternoon. Albright scratched at the tent flap and an officer opened it, saying that "You cannot see General Hooker" and that he would take any communication for the general. Albright pushed past him, "and there lay General Hooker, apparently dead drunk. His face and position gave every indication of that condition, and I turned away sick and disgusted." Only later was Albright told that a shell had disabled Hooker. Maj. Frederick L. Hitchcock of Albright's regiment asked, "If [Hooker] was physically disabled, why was not the fact made known at once to the next officer in rank, whose duty it would have been to have assumed command of the army, and if possible stem the tide of defeat now rapidly overwhelming us?"[29]

Hooker himself admitted that he accepted a slug of brandy just after being knocked down by the shell Sunday morning. If he had taken the pledge and kept it until that moment, his injury apparently made it inoperative. Artillery Col. Charles S. Wainwright recalled coming back exhausted to Hooker's headquarters early Sunday evening: "His spring waggon had just come as I got there, and he had a half bottle of champagne opened. How good it was!" We do not know whether that was the only split of champagne popped during the evening. But at that early point, ten or twelve hours after his injury, Hooker was not groggy. He was as communicative and boastful as in happier times, telling Wainwright he would give Lee the next day to attack him, and "then if he does not, let him look out."[30]

Whatever caused Hooker's condition Sunday night, he kept his army almost as stationary as he was on his cot. As he barely stirred to speak to Warren, his divisions were shifting along the line and digging in even deeper. Wainwright, circulating among Hooker's generals, found them all certain that Lee would send troops to attack Sedgwick, and then Hooker would pile into the weakened Rebel force around Chancellorsville. "The merest tyro" understood this, said Wainwright. But Hooker himself contributed no specifics to such assumptions. In his mind, anything assertive still would have to come from the left wing of his army. And there, the repulse at Salem Church and persistent rumors of Confederate arrivals from Richmond had Sedgwick on edge.

Warren's 11:00 P.M. message to Sedgwick was, as usual, a long time in delivery. At 1:30 A.M., Monday, Sedgwick wrote to Hooker that "I believe the enemy have been reinforcing all night, and will attack me in the morning. How do matters stand with you? Send me instructions." At 6:00 A.M., Hooker was asking Sedgwick for his and the enemy's position, and "Is there any danger of a force coming up in your rear and cutting your communication?" Twenty minutes later, Sedgwick wrote to Butterfield, saying he was "anxious to hear from General Hooker"—that he could not attack the strong force facing him without knowing the rest of the army's intentions, and had not heard from the general since Sunday. Butterfield feared the courier with Warren's dispatch had been captured en route— but at 6:30, seven and a half hours after they were sent, Sedgwick finally got those not very helpful instructions. Apparently the most impressive words to him were "Look well to the safety of your corps. . . ."[31]

By that time, any decision about what to to do was dictated by Jubal Early.

Chapter Seventeen

━━━━━

EVERY HAT RAISED HIGH

EARLY ORDERED John Brown Gordon, a preacher's son with "a voice like a trumpet" and a flare for dramatic rhetoric, to lead a counterattack to retake Lee's Hill and Marye's Heights. Gordon's Georgia brigade had been spared heavy duty on Sunday, and his troops were spoiling to get into the fight.

Before the war was over, Gordon would make himself "the most important military figure in the history of Georgia," but he had entered it with no military education or experience at all.[1] Starting as captain of an Alabama mountaineer company calling itself the "Raccoon Roughs," he learned fast. Gordon in battle was an inspiring sight, "the most prettiest thing you ever did see on a field of fight," said one of his soldiers. "It 'ud put fight into a whipped chicken just to look at him." "Oh, how we love him!" wrote Urbanus Dart of the 26th Georgia.[2]

Every man there remembered how Gordon rode up and down in front of his brigade that Monday morning and told them what lay ahead. Henry C. Walker of the 13th crudely quoted him:

"See, men, yesterday Gen. Lee drove the Yankees 10 miles and taken three thousand prisoners & says if we want any reinforcements we can have them, but I say we have got men enough. Every man that is willing to follow me up them hights today let him raise his hat. . . . I dont want you to hollow, wait until you get up close to the hights. Let every man raise a yell & take those hights. On the 13th day of December you turned the tide of battle and I want you to do so today, will you do it? I ask you to go no father than I am willing to lead."

Every hat was raised high, and the Georgians moved out with a yell.[3]

Early sent Gordon's troops in line of battle astride the Telegraph Road, followed by an array of cannon, then Barksdale's and Smith's brigades. Hays and Hoke would move their brigades to the right, along Hazel Run.

When the heights were taken and Sedgwick's link to Fredericksburg cut, Gordon and Smith would push out the Plank Road and along the river. Barksdale would stay behind to defend the heights and protect the division's rear, holding the same sunken road and stone wall where his troops had fought the day before. Hays and Hoke would then reach left to connect with McLaws, who presumably was stretching his right flank toward Early.

The eager Gordon misunderstood Early's directions and started before the other brigades were ready. That set the whole effort in motion. Gordon drove fast up the Telegraph Road and found Lee's Hill unoccupied, but saw both infantry and artillery ahead. As he pushed north on the ridge behind Marye's Heights, "a considerable force" of Yankees threatened his left flank, but they were driven off by Rebel cannon. His Georgians then dashed along the rolling ridge and collided with a strong line of Federals holding the Plank Road embankment.[4] Adjutant William C. Mathews in the 38th "thought the tug of war had come, for we had to charge down the hill and across a deep mill pond and then up a long slant to dislodge them. They had commenced shelling us also. After a little halt, during which time bayonets were fixed, we commenced the charge. We went down the hill like an avalanche and into that mill pond where the water on the right of the regiment reached to our waist. We were soon across and under the brow of the hill, reformed and started again. Then the bullets commenced their music, but before we could get near the road the Yankees were going like a parcel of sheep through the woods. . . ."[5]

That charge put Sedgwick in a vise. It secured both Lee's and Marye's hills and cut him off from the crossings below Fredericksburg. Early brought Smith's brigade up on Gordon's right and sent Barksdale to man the slope behind the town. If the streets were lightly defended, Barksdale could take the town, too, and capture the bridges and a huge assembly of wagons Early had spotted nearby. But Barksdale promptly ran into a Union force strongly posted—John Gibbon's troops, left behind by Sedgwick to protect the town and the bridges there. Barksdale had approximately 1,600 men, including artillery. They moved into their old defenses to neutralize Gibbon, who had more than twice as many troops, while Early turned toward Sedgwick.

Once on the heights behind the town at about eight o'clock, Early listened for McLaws's guns to the west, but heard nothing. He had surprised the Federals with his quick recapture of the high ground, but hesitated before pushing on against Sedgwick. Gordon's handsome advance had succeeded before the other brigades came abreast. Early was unsure what forces might be hidden in the gullies ahead, as the ground kept rising to where Sedgwick was now cornered. He ordered Smith's Virginia brigade, on Gordon's right, to find out.[6]

"Extra Billy" Smith was old enough to be father to most Civil War generals. Born in 1797, he, like Gordon, had had no prewar military background, and was frank about it. He was a politician—a former congressman, once and future governor of Virginia—and when the current governor offered him a brigadier's commission after Sumter, he turned it down, saying he was "wholly ignorant of drill and tactics." Taking command of the 49th Virginia, he fought with it through major battles while serving in the Confederate Congress between campaigns. He was seriously wounded at Sharpsburg after taking over Early's old brigade, and about to get a quick comeuppance back of Fredericksburg.[7]

Sending his brigade up the ridge near Taylor's Hill, he struck deeply entrenched Yankee regiments. These were troops of Howe's division, which had brought up the rear when Sedgwick marched out the Plank Road the day before. Now they had turned around to protect his back. As the Virginia troops started up, a strong force of defenders appeared along the crest. Union artillery opened from near Taylor's house. The 13th and 58th Virginia, on the right, were most exposed. Early, seeing that a straight-ahead attack could not carry the ridge, ordered the troops back. The 49th and 52nd made it down with little loss, but the other two regiments were caught in the cannonade. Some of the 58th, with their color-bearer, took shelter in a house at the foot of the slope, and would not fall back over open ground swept by cannon fire. They were surrounded, and 71 troops plus the regimental flag were "captured by their own misconduct," Early said.[8]

Stymied at that end, Early sent the trusty Lieutenant Pitzer to urge McLaws to join in hitting Sedgwick simultaneously from both sides. Early would shift two of his brigades left to hook up with McLaws, as they had agreed during the night. He gave his courier time to reach McLaws, then listened impatiently for the noise of an attack. Nothing happened. Soon Pitzer came back with word that McLaws would advance, but only if Early started first. Meanwhile McLaws asked Lee for reinforcement, and Lee promptly responded: the rest of Dick Anderson's division was on its way. At that, McLaws held up his advance till Anderson arrived. McLaws officially explained that he had begun by extending his right toward Early, "but finding my force was insufficient for a front attack, I withdrew to my line of the evening previous, General Early not attacking, as I could hear."[9]

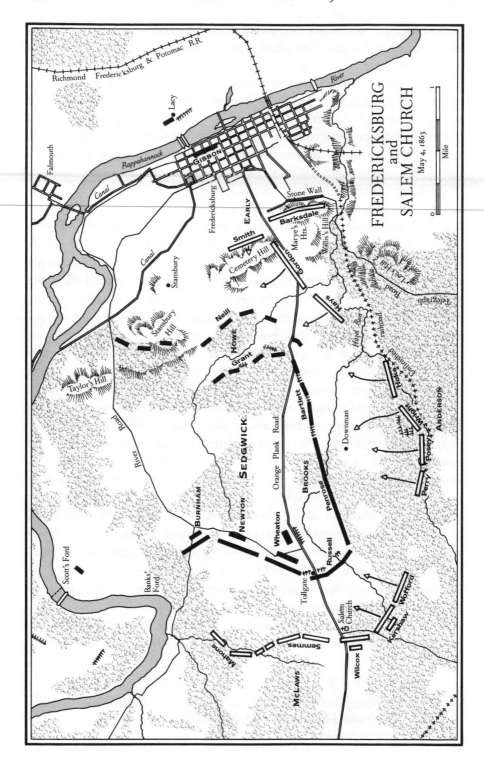

Richmond Fredericksburg & Potomac R.R.

River

Lacy

Falmouth

Rappahannock

Canal

GIBBON

Canal

Fredericksburg

Stansbury

EARLY

Smith

Cemetery Hill

Stone Wall

Barksdale

Marye's Hts.

Wallis's Hill

Sedgwick

FREDERICKSBURG
and
SALEM CHURCH

May 4, 1863

Mile

Stansbury Hill

Neill

Howe

Grant

Taylor's Hill

Bartlett

Hazel Run

railroad

Wright

Mahone

River Road

SEDGWICK

Orange Plank Road

BROOKS

Downman

Telegraph Road

Wilcox

Perry

Posey

ANDERSON

BURNHAM

NEWTON

Wheaton

Penrose

Russell

Tollgate

Salem Church

Wofford

Kershaw

Scott's Ford

Banks' Ford

Semmes

Wilcox

McLAWS

Hays

Goodwin

Whether this was a function of McLaws's hearing or of the breeze and barometer is not clear. The short, square, reliable McLaws had been a professional soldier since finishing West Point in 1842, but he was not a risk-taker. His division had held Marye's Heights in the December battle, mangling the brigades Burnside kept sending against the stone wall. Since seeing hundreds slaughtered that day, McLaws had not been quick to throw his own troops against any firmly positioned enemy. Whatever the cause for his delay on Monday morning—and perhaps wisely—he was waiting for Anderson.

ABOVE CHANCELLORSVILLE, just after dawn, Confederate Maj. Robert A. Hardaway had opened fire with ten guns run forward on the River Road near Anderson's division. From Hayden's farm, they could easily reach an immense camp of Federal wagons across the river. Before the Yankee teamsters were fully awake, Hardaway blasted them with 15 rounds per gun, stampeding the supply train, sending mules and broken wagons crashing into one another, spilling food and munitions. A batch of Rebel prisoners in the camp started cheering for Jeff Davis when the shells started falling, and laughed at the skedaddling Yankees all around them. As Hardaway tugged his batteries back through deep mud, Union skirmishers from Slocum's corps moved out as if to capture the guns. Anderson sent his own skirmishers to discourage the Federals, and they kept going until they hit the strong Union line along the ridge below U.S. Ford.[10]

Before either side made anything of this collision, Anderson got urgent orders from Lee: Form your division and march toward Fredericksburg; report to McLaws. Meanwhile Henry Heth, who had taken over Hill's division, would move into Anderson's line facing Hooker.

Lee did not want merely to block Sedgwick, he wanted to crush him, and to do it he was calmly gambling yet again. He was leaving three Confederate divisions to contain Hooker—the same weary, bloodied divisions that had marched around and attacked his flank Saturday night, and then done the murderous work of driving him away from Chancellorsville Sunday morning. Lee left them, now hardly 20,000 able-bodied

17. Sedgwick Surrounded. *Lee brings Anderson east to join Early and McLaws, converging on Sedgwick from three sides. Lee's night attack dwindles away, but Sedgwick's corps retreats in darkness across the pontoon bridge at Scott's Ford.*

men, to hold Hooker's six army corps. Those six corps, 16 divisions, had more than 75,000 men on duty even after what some of them had been through in the past two days.

This latest gamble suggested that Lee's confidence had grown to contempt for Hooker. As if demonstrating it, Lee turned his own back on the man who had said such a short time earlier, "may God have mercy on General Lee, for I will have none." Hooker's lines above Chancellorsville clearly were even more forbidding than the day before; for Lee to mount an assault with what he had there would sacrifice too many lives. As Lee put it, "the enemy had so strengthened his position . . . that it was deemed inexpedient to assail it with less than our whole force, which could not be concentrated until we were relieved from the danger that menaced our rear. It was accordingly resolved still further to re-enforce the troops in front of General Sedgwick, in order, if possible, to drive him across the Rappahannock." [11] That explanation, written after the battle, may understate what he wanted to do to Sedgwick. Though heavily overmatched near Chancellorsville, on the other front the Confederates were almost Sedgwick's equal. Reinforced, they could outnumber him. Lee saw a chance to destroy Sedgwick, then bring his whole army back to destroy Hooker.

That he would have to take the chance of further dividing his forces, the chance that Hooker's powerful army would come over its breastworks after the inferior Rebel force left around Chancellorsville, did not slow Lee. In fact, it speeded him; if all went well, he could smash Sedgwick and return to Chancellorsville before Hooker reacted. Lee left Heth's, Colston's, and Rodes's divisions to hold the six corps commanded by Reynolds, Couch, Sickles, Meade, Howard, and Slocum. Mounting Traveller, he rode toward Salem Church.

He got there about 11:00 A.M., just ahead of Anderson. He decided to send Anderson off the Plank Road to the right, between McLaws and Early. Anderson was bringing three brigades; Wilcox and Mahone, detached from him earlier, were already at Salem Church. He pointed Wright, Posey, and Perry toward the unfinished railroad cut between the Plank and Telegraph roads, where they would tie in with Hoke's brigade from Early's division. That would enclose Sedgwick with one Rebel division on each of three sides, and the Rappahannock at his back. The only crossing behind him was the pontoon bridge at Scott's Ford.

But all afternoon, Lee's attack was delayed by one of those inexplicable lapses that can bog down the boldest intentions. "Some delay occurred in getting the troops into position, owing to the broken and irregular nature of the ground and the difficulty of ascertaining the disposition of the enemy forces," Lee wrote. His restrained report did not disclose his impatience when he realized that McLaws had not felt out the enemy lines aggressively enough to know just what he faced, and where. That impatience came near anger as Anderson's troops seemed barely to creep along, marching up the Plank Road, assembling back of the church, and filing off to the right. Nor did Lee's report credit Sedgwick with extending his defensive line across the Plank Road, thus blocking the easy way for Anderson to hook up with Early and forcing the Rebels forming for attack to scramble over rough ground.[12]

ANDERSON'S WERE not the only tired soldiers. For a week and more, on both fronts, in both armies, troops had been marching, skirmishing, digging, attacking, defending, retreating, but sleeping and eating very little. Officers and men alike were beginning to think that if the fight was not over, it ought to be. During lulls, they acted as if the war were far away.

Near Chandler's house, at the apex of Hooker's line above Chancellorsville, Union general Amiel Whipple sat on his horse in the morning sun, watching his men improve their breastworks. A Rebel sniper in a tree nearby was annoying them. Whipple started to scratch out an order for some of Berdan's Sharpshooters to rid them of this nuisance. *Thunk.* The Confederate rifleman's next round struck Whipple's belt in front and came out the back between his coat buttons, mortally wounding him. One of Berdan's lieutenants crept past the Union skirmishers, watched for the sniper, and potted him before he could fire again. He brought back a rifle, a fox-skin cap, $1,600 in Confederate money, and $100 in U.S. paper.[13]

That exchange seemed just as capricious as the brief outbreak around a New Jersey private who considerately went well away from his comrades to relieve himself, out front between the zigzags of the line held by Reynolds's corps. When he rose from his haunches, friendly troops thought he was a Rebel and opened fire. At the adjacent zigzag, other Federals thought the Rebels had fired, and blazed back. A full-blown firefight followed, lasting five minutes and killing and wounding several troops, but not "the man whose modesty caused it all."[14]

While others were probing Sedgwick's lines and moving into place near Salem Church, some of McLaws's troops combed Sunday evening's battlefield. Marcus Green of Phillips's Georgia Legion unashamedly wrote the folks at home how "I got some things out of yankees pocket. . . . I taken a pocket knife and looking glass out of ones pocket, a nice needle case out of another, $10.00 in greenbacks out of another, a ladies ambrotype another and taken a gold ring off ones finger." [15]

The whimsy, the innocent callousness of war were there in calm and in tumult. Professor Lowe's balloons drifted silently over the river, and Yankee officers worriedly quizzed captives not about whether, but about how many and when, massive reinforcements were arriving for Lee. In late morning, Butterfield had wired Maj. Gen. John J. Peck, who faced Lee's detached divisions 130 miles away at Suffolk, that "Our cavalry bring information of 15,000 or 20,000 of Longstreet's forces getting off from the cars at Gordonsville." Yet again, Peck responded with descriptions of what Longstreet's two divisions were doing in front of him, but this did not convince Hooker's generals.

Ordinary Union troops, too, thought the force against them had to be bigger than it was. "We knew that the enemy had bin reinforced during the day Monday for some of the prisoners that we took stated that they was just from N.C. and hadent bin off the cars but two hours before they came into the fight," wrote one of the Vermonters with Sedgwick. Lee's most valuable soldiers may have been those who were captured and told the Yankee generals what they wanted to hear. [16]

TO GET INTO position along Sedgwick's south front, Anderson's division had to slide and climb in and out of a series of ravines on the slope beside Hazel Run. Even if they stuck to rough trails and the railroad right-of-way, his lead regiments had to march still farther to reach Early's extended flank. Once there, they lay in the woods waiting for orders, thinking of what might lie ahead. That thinking got to a soldier in the 22nd Georgia, who stuck the muzzle of his weapon against his foot and pulled the trigger, taking himself out of the fight. His major, cursing him as a coward, said the shot should have been through his head. Another man in the 22nd intentionally swallowed a wad of tobacco to make himself sick and miss the battle. [17]

Back of Anderson's line, Lee rode to find Early behind Fredericksburg, and heard him explain how he would push mostly northward and try to turn Sedgwick's left near the river. Lee approved, and told Early to be ready to jump off on signal. Anderson plus McLaws's two rightmost brigades also would push north, against Brooks's side of the Union line that roughly paralleled the Plank Road. The map suggests that McLaws, closest to the river on the Confederate left facing Newton, might have thrust northeast and cut the Federals off from the bridge at Scott's Ford, or at least thrown them into panic in fear of being cut off. But Lee told McLaws to hold his position until Anderson and Early drove Sedgwick's lines back toward him, then swing north alongside.[18]

It was nearly six o'clock when three quick cannon shots signaled the attack.

On Early's front, the former New Orleans lawyer and Whig politician Harry T. Hays looked along his brigade line, drew a deep breath, and yelled, "Charge!" His Louisiana Tigers scrambled up the slope "like a legion of 50-ton locomotives," said one of them; like a pack of dogs turned loose on a fresh track, said another. R. A. Pierson in the 9th Louisiana said that "even the yell of the demon Louisianans as they call us was more than [the Federals] could bear; all the prisoners who were captured said they knew that we were La. boys as soon as we screamed. They say they had rather fight a whole Division of Virginians than one of the La. brigades."[19]

Hays and Hoke quickly closed the distance between Hazel Run and the Plank Road. "It was a splendid sight to see the rapid and orderly advance of these two brigades, with the enemy flying before them," Early wrote. The artillery he had posted to cover a retreat in case of disaster had nothing to do, but it "could not refrain from enthusiastically cheering the infantry, as it so handsomely swept everything in front." The shock of the attack broke Col. Ernst von Vegesack's 20th New York, a German regiment, which fled to the rear.

Early was watching with Lee. When he saw Hays's brigade break through the first Federal lines, he slammed his hat down and shouted, "Those damned Louisiana fellows can steal as much as they please now!" Beside him, Lee passed the credit upward. "Thank God!" he said. "The day is ours." But the day was far from over.[20]

Farthest right, John Gordon rode out in front of his troops again, as he had before the morning's advance. This time, he said he wanted them "to charge some batteries and drive every Yankee into the river." Again, every man waved his hat.

The low hills ahead were so steep that the Georgians climbed them on hands and knees. On top, they were hit by cannon firing from across the river and from their front and left flank.[21] Adjutant Mathews of the 38th Georgia brought six companies out of the ravine where they had taken cover. "We had scarcely got out of the ditch before they fired upon us, and 'Jewhilikens!' I never heard anything in my life till then, at the first fire over 20 men were shot down. We retired at a full run. . . ."[22]

George Bandy in the 60th said, "I never have saw yankees Skeedadle so in all my life. When they hear the Rebels come chargeing and hallowing they cant stand." Then his outfit, too, ran into the Union batteries, not 300 yards away. "But it was so dark we had no chance to charge it. So we just laid as flat to the ground as ever you saw a flying squirl lay to a tree. Hear there was severl mens heds tore off."[23]

When Gordon's troops held up in a stretch of forest, he rode forward again. He said he was proud of them, and told them to fix bayonets to clean out the woods ahead—and they did. The brigade's attack bent back the far left of Sedgwick's line and opened the way toward the river.[24]

Despite the destruction, Early's brigades ground ahead until Robert Hoke, leading his Tar Heels, was knocked off his horse by a musket ball that shattered his arm near the shoulder. He was out of action, and Col. Isaac E. Avery of the 6th North Carolina, who took over his brigade, had not heard Early's instructions. Double-timing across the Plank Road, Hoke's troops ran into Hays's Louisianans in the thickets, and the two commands were thrown into confusion. Mingling, they pushed on until they reached a second line of Yankees, behind a swell of ground where those fleeing had rallied. There the Confederates struck a wall of musket and cannon fire, converging from three directions.

On that second line, Lewis Grant's Green Mountain Boys cut down so many Rebels that William Stowe of the 2nd Vermont wrote, "their dead covered the ground as grey as a badger in front of us. After they found they couldn't break our lines they tried to flank us but in that movement they found a bloody bath for our Artilery was got into position on our left and it put the grape and canister into their ranks. . . . The air was full of arms and pieces of men blown to pieces. . . . They fairly melted like dew on the grass in the noon day sun." When the Vermonters enticed the Confederates ahead by withdrawing back of an open field, the attackers "came on mad with joy till the field in our front was literally covered with them. Our brigade was a support for a battery of brass Napolean guns that opened on them again with grape and canister that piled the dead and wounded knee deep to the horses. . . ."[25]

In this explosion of fire, one soldier said a single shell cut down 17 men of the 9th Louisiana. Disorganized, the Confederates recoiled; Colonels Leroy A. Stafford of the 9th and Davidson B. Penn of the 7th Louisiana were captured along with other attackers so winded they could not get away. To their right, Hoke's and Hays's men heard Gordon's attack and thought they were being flanked by the enemy. At this, they fell back and re-formed along the Plank Road.[26]

Anderson's troops, coming at Brooks's Federal division from the south, got snarled early in the attack. On Anderson's right, closest to Early, A. R. Wright's Georgians sneaked along a ravine to flank Yankee sharp-shooters behind the fences around Downman's house. They emerged onto a field behind the house and started taking cannon fire, some of it from their front, some enfilading their line from the right. Sgt. Micajah Martin of the 2nd Georgia Battalion wrote, "We could distinctly hear the commander of the battery halloo to his men, 'G—d d—n them, pour the grape into them!' and they did pour grape into us with severity." But the Rebels kept going, striking the infantry line behind Downman's and "driving the enemy like chaff," Wright said. Reaching woods beyond the field, he held up his brigade lest he bump into Wofford, whom he expected to be advancing from McLaws on his left.[27]

Instead of that, in flanking the Federals at Downman's, Wright's own troops had crossed in front of the Southern brigades to his left. While Carnot Posey reported that his Mississippi regiments advanced through heavy fire to the Plank Road, E. A. Perry complained that Wright's move had kept his Floridians from attacking and capturing fleeing Yankee guns and infantry.[28]

At the southwest corner of Sedgwick's defensive rectangle, Kershaw's and Wofford's Confederates beat through thick woods to the Plank Road, with Porter Alexander's artillery in support. But by then, dusk was deepening. All three Confederate divisions had driven Sedgwick into closer quarters, but when night compounded the confusion of attack, they stopped to hold what they had taken.[29]

Lee was unhappy. He had not done what he had come to do. Although his cordon around Sedgwick had been tightened, coordination through the ravines and thickets was still nearly impossible. Yet he determined on something every textbook advised against. Its dangers had been proven less than forty-eight hours earlier on the other side of Chancellorsville. Now, as fog eased up the hollows from the river, Sedgwick was shrinking his lines. Lee assumed that once pulled in, they would be denser and harder to break in the morning. By then, Hooker might begin to stir. But what Lee heard from his brigadiers made him believe that if he went all-out tonight, he could push Sedgwick across the Rappahannock. For the first time, he ordered a night attack.[30]

Lee did not know that during the fighting at dusk, Sedgwick had ordered a general withdrawal toward Scott's Ford. Along the Federal line, orders were passed to fall back gradually, holding the Confederates in check. The 16th and 27th New York were out as skirmishers at the southeast corner of Sedgwick's lines, and retreated in two ranks that took turns firing into the darkness toward the enemy, then sifting back, one behind the other. One soldier of the 16th said his outfit would have been captured, sacrificed that the main force might escape, if the colonel had not ridden up and called out, "Where are my men?" When the troops answered, the colonel said, "Well, get out of this as quick as you can!" and spurred away. Starting at an orderly march, the New Yorkers soon were crashing through the woods to outrun Rebel skirmishers close behind.[31]

Southern pickets in McLaws's division shouted, "Surrender! Lay down your arms!" as they heard the Federals pulling out. But, wrote Luther Furst of the 139th Pennsylvania, "our men would sing out 'Go to hell,' give them a volley & fall back." Furst was a messenger to and from Sedgwick, and said that when he delivered his last dispatch at dark he heard the general sigh to no one, "Oh dear! What will become of us if they break our lines?"[32]

As the Federal withdrawal gathered speed, Mahone heard wagons rumbling over the Union pontoon bridge at Scott's Ford. McLaws ordered Alexander to lob shells onto them. After Kershaw reached the Plank Road, McLaws told Wilcox, who was familiar with the land around Banks' Ford, to take Kershaw's brigade and part of his own and press on toward the river. They grabbed high ground where more guns could pound the crossing. Only later did McLaws get a 10:00 P.M. message from Lee at Downman's house, saying he wanted the Yankees pushed over the Rappahannock during the night.

In response, McLaws brought Wofford up to advance with Wilcox and Kershaw. Together they kept going north to the River Road, taking prisoners and the approaches to Banks' Ford. They were so close in pursuit that McLaws told Porter Alexander to aim his artillery fire at the far bank only, to avoid shelling friendly troops. As McLaws told it, "the enemy, throwing away their arms and breaking ranks, fled across the river in the greatest disorder. . . ." But according to Lee, "darkness prevented General McLaws from perceiving the success of the attack until the enemy began to recross the river a short distance below Banks Ford." Lee said, "A dense fog settled over the field, increasing the obscurity, and rendering great caution necessary to avoid collision between our own troops."[33]

Thus his risky night attack dwindled away, seemingly short of its goal, and a tired, frustrated Lee resolved to push on at dawn.

. . .

HAD LEE BEEN TAPPING Federal telegraph lines, he would have rested easier.

Soon after Early's morning attack, Sedgwick had advised Hooker that "The enemy are pressing me. I am taking position to cross the river whenever necessary." Hooker replied at 10:30 A.M., saying that "in the event you fall back, you [should] reserve, if practicable, a position on the Fredericksburg side of the Rappahannock, which you can hold securely until tomorrow p.m. [May 5]. . . ." Half an hour later, he said he did not want Sedgwick to cross the river "unless you are compelled to do so." At that moment, Sedgwick was sending Hooker a message based on what Warren's dispatch had said the night before. "If I can hold until tonight," he said, "I shall cross at Banks Ford, under instructions from General Hooker, given by Brigadier-General Warren." Only fifteen minutes after that, Sedgwick said he was threatened on two fronts, that he had positioned his corps to attack and not defend, that his bridges might be lost, and asked for strong help if he was attacked.[34] This produced a vague explanation from Hooker's headquarters:

> If the necessary information shall be obtained to-day, and if it should be of the character he [Hooker] anticipates, it is the intention of the general to advance tomorrow. In this event the position of your corps on the south bank of the Rappahannock will be as favorable as the general could desire. It is for this reason he desires that your troops may not cross the Rappahannock.[35]

In early afternoon, Hooker—or one of the headquarters staff acting in his name—sent Sedgwick another, stiffer message. This one asserted that "It is of vital importance that you should take a commanding position near Fredericksburg, which you can hold to a certainty till tomorrow." But he enclosed a not quite exact copy of Warren's dispatch, saying in part, "Look to the safety of your corps," and "You can retire, if necessary, by way of Fredericksburg or Banks Ford." Those suggestions, Hooker said, "meet my full approval."[36] Poor Sedgwick had more than merely Lee to puzzle over.

Some of Hooker's messages were signed with his name, others with the names of his staff officers. It is doubtful that the general, in his condition, saw most of this busy traffic. But he was awakened by cavalryman Pleasonton in midafternoon to take a message from a worried Abraham Lincoln, and the response had Hooker's personal touch.

"We have news here that the enemy has reoccupied heights above Fredericksburg," the president wired. "Is that so?"

Hooker sat thinking in silence. Then he dictated an answer: "I am informed that it is so, but attach no importance to it." [37]

During the dialogue between Sedgwick and Hooker's command post, Butterfield had been carrying on the same kind of exchange with Gibbon in Fredericksburg. Gibbon already had moved one of his two brigades back across the river. Soon after Early retook the heights behind the town, Gibbon suggested that if Sedgwick had departed, maybe he should withdraw completely and take up his bridges. Butterfield told him, "Hold on to the last extremity, until further orders." But less than an hour later, he said perhaps Gibbon should take up his lower bridge and be ready to move the others. "Use your discretion," he added. Barely eight minutes after that, at 10:35 A.M., there was a sarcastic corrective from Hooker's headquarters: "The general says that Gibbon's command is to remain where it is. The bridges, of course, are to remain. It would seem from your dispatch that Gibbon and the enemy are retreating from each other." [38]

No time is noted on Butterfield's later message to Gibbon:

> Make your dispositions so that no confusion or panic ensues. ... You ought to be able to manage the position so as, if compelled to retire, to do so gracefully and sound. ... Short of the loss of every man of your command, do not permit the enemy to cross. In case you retire from the town, be vigilant. ... Keep an eye out for the pontoon train that was reported at Hamilton's Crossing. Much may depend on you, and I have no doubt you will prove yourself, as you have always heretofore, fully equal to the responsibility. [39]

With Gibbon's instructions fully garbled, Butterfield said he was leaving Falmouth to join Hooker. Just when he did so is unclear. So, to everyone involved, was the remarkable crisscross of messages that determined what Sedgwick would finally do.

Ten minutes before midnight, Sedgwick sent to Hooker:

> My army is hemmed in upon the slope, covered by the guns from the north side of Banks Ford. If I had only this army to care for, I would withdraw it tonight. Do your operations require that I should jeopard it by retaining it here? An immediate reply is indispensable, or I may feel obliged to withdraw. [40]

But just before or after getting that urgent appeal, Butterfield got Sedgwick's response to one of Hooker's earlier messages. In that one, Sedgwick said:

> I shall hold my position, as ordered, on south of Rappahannock.

Alarmed, at one o'clock Butterfield told Sedgwick:

> Dispatch this moment received. Withdraw. Cover the river, and prevent any force crossing. Acknowledge this.

At 2:00 A.M., Sedgwick got that order and replied:

> General Hooker's order received. Will withdraw my forces immediately.

But 20 minutes after that withdrawal order, Hooker had just read Sedgwick's previous promise to hold. He shot back:

> Yours received, saying you should hold position. Order to withdraw countermanded. Acknowledge both.

That dispatch took two hours to reach Sedgwick. At 3:20, he responded:

> Yours just received, countermanding order to withdraw. Almost my entire command has crossed over.

At 5:00, he followed up:

> The bridges at Banks Ford are swung and in process of being taken up. The troops are much exhausted. The dispatch countermanding my movement over the river was received after the troops had crossed.[41]

Thus, when Robert E. Lee awoke on Tuesday, May 5, to order the grim work of driving Sedgwick's corps across the Rappahannock, he found that "General Sedgwick had made good his escape and removed his bridges. Fredericksburg was also evacuated, and our rear no longer threatened. . . ."[42]

Lee's official report suggests neither great satisfaction that his rear was safe nor disappointment that Sedgwick had gotten away. Only later did he learn what else had been going on at Union headquarters while Sedgwick was being jerked around at the end of the telegraph line.

AT MIDNIGHT, Hooker called the six Union corps commanders above Chancellorsville to his headquarters tent for a council of war. Reynolds, Couch, Sickles, Meade, and Howard got there in time. Slocum did not arrive from his camp near the river until after the talking was over. Chief of Staff Butterfield and Engineer Warren were with the commanding general.

Hooker's opening statement left no doubt where the meeting was headed. His orders, he said, obliged him to cover Washington, and not to risk his army. Laying out the situation, he implied his lack of confidence in the troops along his line, noting their haphazard firing at imaginary Rebels during the day. "It was seen by the most casual observer that he had made up his mind to retreat," Couch wrote.

Hooker and Butterfield stepped out of the tent, leaving the corps commanders to consult among themselves. Warren remained. Meade was for fighting, partly because he did not think the army could get its guns across the river if it pulled out. Howard wanted to fight, too, saying the army was in this predicament because of his corps' bad conduct, "or words to that effect." He clearly wanted to remove the stain from his own and his troops' reputations. Couch felt as Meade did about fighting to save the guns, but not with Hooker in command: "I would favor an advance if I could designate the point of attack." Reynolds spoke from where he stretched resting on the ground. His corps had not been deeply involved, so he would not press his opinion, but he too wanted to advance. Sickles, saying he was not a professional military man, made the political case for withdrawing instead of risking worse defeat. Even he, still Hooker's favorite corps commander, seemed to resent that Hooker had laid the decision on his subordinate generals. Warren, hearing these suggestions of criticism against Hooker, walked out.

When Hooker returned, he said he was confident he could withdraw the army without loss of men or guns. To Couch, this meant that whatever happened, Hooker would be in charge. A vote was called for. The tally was three to two: Reynolds, Meade, and Howard for advancing against the Confederates, Couch and Sickles against. But to Hooker, the count was moot. He said he would take on himself the responsibility for pulling the army back across the river.

Couch stalked out of the tent. Reynolds, just behind him, asked, "What was the use of calling us together at this time of night when he intended to retreat anyhow?" [43]

Chapter Eighteen

LET US CROSS OVER THE RIVER

IN EARLY MAY, Fairfield plantation seemed truly named. Lilac and apple bloomed on the terraces stepping down from the main house toward Guiney Station. On the other side, locust and buttonwood framed the sky toward the fighting at Fredericksburg, 11 miles north. Until war came, Thomas Coleman Chandler and his family had lived at Fairfield as in a Stephen Foster ballad, while ninety slaves worked the 1,200 acres of surrounding farmland.

One morning in the fall of 1862, the Chandlers looked out to see their fields covered with wagon trains and thousands of soldiers. Stonewall Jackson's corps of the Army of Northern Virginia had moved in overnight and set up camp by the R.F.&P. railroad. Mrs. Chandler rushed out to invite the general to use one of her parlors as his headquarters. Jackson politely thanked her, saying he "never wished to fare better than his soldiers." He even declined to come in out of the cold to have his meals with the family. Mrs. Chandler, insisting she would not be "outgeneraled," repeatedly had her servants take food to his tent. Each time he sent it back, with thanks. Jackson's orderly, Jim Lewis, explained to the lady that "the general was mighty peculiar." On Thanksgiving, she sent turkey, ham, and all the trimmings, with instructions for Jackson to divide it among his troops if he would not eat it himself. Soon afterward he came to thank the Chandlers for their kindness, and rode away to the first battle of Fredericksburg.

Now, this first week in May, the family's old Virginia hospitality was stretched beyond capacity. Winding south from the battlefield, new thousands of soldiers had come, some limping afoot, some groaning in hardbottomed wagons, in all degrees of misery. Wounded Confederates were squeezed into the upstairs rooms of Fairfield house. The boggy lowlands were full of Union prisoners waiting for trains to take them to Richmond.

Rumors of raiding Yankee cavalry flashed up the telegraph line from the Confederate capital, and the mutter of faraway battle made them seem credible.

Late Monday afternoon, a courier came riding hard to the porch and told Mrs. Chandler and her daughter Lucy that Jackson had been wounded and was in an ambulance on the way to Fairfield. Mrs. Chandler mobilized her house servants, Mammy Phyllis and Aunt Judy, to prepare a front parlor in the brick main house as Jackson's sickroom. Just as they made up the bed, Jackson's chaplain, Tucker Lacy, arrived. When he heard noise from the wounded soldiers upstairs, he said Jackson would need absolute quiet. Surgeon McGuire came and was told some of those soldiers were feverish with erysipelas. Outside in the yard, there was a little frame house once used as an office, newly whitewashed inside, now unoccupied. Lacy decided it would be a safer place for Jackson. Mrs. Chandler and her servants hurried to set it up for him. A brief rain had spotted the windows; she built a fire in the grate to cut the chill.[1]

THE CONCUSSION of Sunday morning's battle around Chancellorsville had made the taut walls of the hospital tent near Wilderness Tavern vibrate like a gently struck drumhead. At about ten o'clock, the uncomplaining Jackson had asked Dr. McGuire to examine his right side. He believed that in his fall from the litter the night before, his side had struck a stone or a sapling stump. Now it was painful. McGuire found no broken skin or visible bruise, and Jackson's lungs seemed to function normally. The doctor applied some palliative treatment, assuming the hurt would soon go away.

When the noise of fighting rose louder, Jackson ordered all his aides except Lieutenant Smith back to the battlefield where they were needed. By evening the pain in his side had subsided, and he asked detailed questions about the fight, lighting up when told some officer or outfit had performed nobly. "Good, good," he said when he heard how his old brigade had charged. "The men of that brigade will some day be proud to say to their children, 'I was one of the Stonewall brigade.' "

That afternoon he balked at Lee's suggestion that he be carried away from danger and at the idea that McGuire might accompany him, which would take the surgeon away from the troops still fighting. But later, Lee heard from Stuart that Union wagon trains were moving beyond Chancellorsville. That could mean a new threat on the far left. It also could menace Jackson. This time Lee sent an order, not a suggestion, for Dr. McGuire to take

Jackson out of danger. When told that Lee had directed McGuire to go with him, Jackson relented. "General Lee has always been very kind to me," he said, "and I thank him."[2]

Jackson slept easily Sunday night. Next morning, Tucker Lacy aroused mapmaker Jed Hotchkiss to guide the two-horse ambulance that would take the general and Colonel Crutchfield, the wounded artillerist, to Guiney Station. A mattress was placed on the hard floor of the wagon to ease the journey. Hotchkiss rode ahead with a few engineers to clear the road of logs, boulders, and plodding wagons. He reversed the course of Jackson's flank march along Brock Road, then rode by Todd's Tavern and Spotsylvania Court House. The trip to Guiney was about 27 miles. Covered at a walk to keep from jouncing the ailing patient, it took close to 14 hours.

Occasionally teamsters with loaded wagons scorched Hotchkiss with language usually used on stubborn mules, refusing to move over until told who was following in the ambulance. Then they gave way and stood by the roadside with hats off, some weeping. The word raced ahead; along the way, men and women came out offering country delicacies and tearful prayers. Wounded troops trudging to the rear seemed cheerful until they heard who was passing.[3]

Jackson was in good spirits, talking about the battle. He had indeed intended to cut the Federals off from U.S. Ford, he said, and then Hooker would have had to attack him: "My men sometimes fail to drive the enemy from a position, but they always fail to drive us." He praised Robert Rodes, whose division had led the flank attack Saturday night, and hoped he would be promoted. He spoke highly of Col. Edward Willis of the 12th Georgia, in Rodes's assault line, and of E. F. Paxton and J. K. Boswell, both killed. In the rough wagon on the warm, damp day, Jackson was slightly nauseated. He suggested that McGuire spread a wet towel over his midsection, and that seemed to help.[4]

It was twilight, almost eight o'clock, when Hotchkiss led the way across the railroad track at Fairfield, past a paling fence to the little house in Chandler's yard. Thomas Chandler was there waiting. Soldiers lifted Jackson from the wagon. Chandler told the general he was glad to have him, but sorry to see him wounded. Jackson apologized for not shaking hands because one arm was gone and his other hand wounded.[5]

McGuire supervised as the soldiers carried Jackson's stretcher into a room to the right of the entry hall. They eased him onto a double rope-trellis bed with pine runners and headboard, and acorn posts at the corners. On the mantel over the low fire, a Gothic-arched Ingraham clock made in Bristol, Connecticut, ticked loudly, as if to hurry Stonewall on his way.

THE SUFFERING ARMIES resigned themselves to one last fight. The fighting already done had scattered vignettes of agony and tenderness over miles of battlefield. Almost all the disputed ground was now retaken by the Confederates, but surgeons of both armies worked or shunned work there, on troops Blue and Gray. Soldiers and chaplains looked after prisoners and corpses, often with greater attention to the dead.

After a clash, troops searched for fallen comrades, brought them in, laid them side by side. "We unbuckled their cartridge belts, took off their canteens and haversacks, then took from their pockets such articles as might be used or treasured as momentoes pocket knives bibles photographs letters from Mothers wives sisters sweethearts," recalled a soldier in the 10th Georgia. "We gave all these to a comrade who would send them to the loved ones at home, then taking a last look at our dead companions we wrapped their stark forms in blankets and hid them away beneath the bloodstained soil of Salem Heights, their linked souls unsevered by death, Comrades forever more."[6]

A Pennsylvania chaplain told of burying thirteen men in one place— eleven Federals and two Rebels. "There their bodies rest together in peace," he said. "Death has established a bond . . . at least between their bodies. Do their spirits still strive with each other? Do they go off quarreling into the unseen land? Union or Rebel, lay him down tenderly. Spread his bloody blanket lightly over him, it is all the shroud he has. Bring some small cedar twigs and lay on those dirty rags that are to be his last pillow." He told of offering a brief prayer while the workmen who dug the grave took off their hats but kept smoking, and then covered the bodies with two feet of clay.

But the gravediggers, after seeing so many, were not always so reverent toward the dead. That Monday, the chaplain had them dig a hole for five bodies to be laid side by side. One corpse was unusually tall, and did not fit, so the workmen were told to make the grave longer. One of them was "a Catholic Irishman," said the obviously Protestant minister. This man "swore he would not spend all day burying a d—d heretic, and at once raised an axe and struck one of the limbs a blow to cut them off, to shorten him." The chaplain, without thinking, "drew his fist and knocked the heathenish fellow in the head and sent him reeling into the hole he had just dug. All this was only a momentary interruption of the burial ceremony."[7]

To be cruel to the unfeeling dead seemed forgivable to some who had witnessed the well-meant cruelty inflicted on the wounded who were not yet dead. Civil War field surgeons knew nothing of sepsis and other fundamentals of modern medicine, and except for amputation, any active treatment by them was likely to make things worse instead of better. They used the same bloody swabs from patient to patient. Field hospitals swarmed with flies. In their clench-jawed fatigue, doctors routinely sawed off seriously wounded arms and legs with little thought of whether they might be saved. For body wounds, the most effective remedy was hope.

Federal surgeons left behind when the Confederates retook the Talley house, west of Chancellorsville, joined in trying to care for wounded of both armies scattered on the ground. "The operating tables were like butchers' blocks," said an Ohio captain. "The dying and dead lay among the living, and burial parties were very slow in removing the dead. Finally food gave out and many must have starved but for the supply of whiskey and condensed milk which had been sent for our relief by permission of General Lee, it being our only resource. . . ."[8]

Salem Church, so recently a fortress, became a hospital. Col. Robert McMillen of the 24th Georgia wrote that "The scenes of death and carnage witnessed here, no human tongue or pen can adequately describe"—but he tried: "After the house was filled, the spacious church yard was literally covered with wounded and dying. The sight inside the building, for horror, was perhaps never equalled within so limited a space. Every available foot of space was crowded with wounded and bleeding soldiers. The floor, the benches, even the chancel and pulpit, were all packed almost to suffocation with them. The amputated limbs were piled up in every corner almost as high as a man could reach; blood flowed in streams along the aisles and out at the doors; screams and groans were heard on all sides, while the surgeons, with their assistants, worked with knives, saws, sutures and bandages to relieve or save all they could from bleeding to death."[9]

Hard as it was on patients, the endless trauma became more than some of the surgeons could handle. To blur exhaustion and despair, they sought aid from their medicinal stores. The Pennsylvania chaplain saw only the weak side of such physicians. Some patients went untreated because surgeons behaved "in such a way as to deserve being booted out of the army," he wrote. "The chief part of the liquors provided by the Sanitary Commission for the sick and wounded is drunk by the surgeons, especially when a battle is at hand." There are exceptions, he granted, who labor day and night while other surgeons "are eating and drinking and sleeping, or *skedaddling.*"

Every standing building had become a hospital, every field a graveyard, yet to the troops it seemed the generals meant to make more wounded and dead.

JOHN SEDGWICK was lucky that from the blizzard of contradictory orders sent his way Monday night and Tuesday morning, he eventually chose to obey the ones that said withdraw. Unknown to him, even while Hooker was encouraging him to stay, promising to take the offensive in the morning, the Union commander was deciding to take the rest of the army back across the river.

All night Lee's guns pounded Sedgwick's crossing at Scott's Ford, and at dawn Confederate infantry found the pontoon bridges there cut loose at the near end, swung by the current against the far bank. "Behold, when morning came the buggers had left," said one of Gordon's Georgians. "Shortly after daylight we saw a white flag approaching and 72 of them bluebirds came in and gave themselves up and told us there was any quantity down in the woods near the river and we sent scouts out and soon had over 500 bagged. . . ." [10] At Fredericksburg, the 19th Massachusetts fought as rearguard for Gibbon before a detail chopped the shore lines of the bridge there and it drifted into the stream just ahead of pursuing Rebels.

Now both Federal forces were gone from Lee's rear, and he could turn back to Hooker. But he was aware that Sedgwick could try to cross again, if only to divert him. To prevent that, Lee assigned Early to re-occupy Fredericksburg and the heights with his division and Barksdale's brigade. After that he headed McLaws, then Anderson, back toward Chancellorsville.

Some of McLaws's division had been skirmishing till 4:00 A.M., combing the woods above the Sedgwick bridgehead, catching a few stragglers. In the morning the Confederates collected abandoned weapons and equipment from the rough country over which they had chased the Federals in the dark. They were bone-weary when word came about noon to march west. Despite this, it took them only two and a half hours to reassemble and reach the River Road–Mine Road area where Henry Heth's division had been watching the left of Hooker's line. Arriving with them, Lee sent Heth's relatively rested command to the other side of Chancellorsville. [11]

Anderson's division, strung out toward Early, was harder to round up when he got orders at 4:00 P.M. to head west. He set out, but at dark, most of his troops were still in column along the Turnpike, and he halted them after one of the most miserable marches of the campaign.

It was miserable because as they marched, the clouds burst. "I do not think that in all my life I ever saw a grander electrical display, heard more continuous or louder thunder, or was in a greater downpour of rain," one Georgian recalled. "The vivid lightning was blinding—not in quick brilliant flashes, but as if we were in a great sea of livid light, the deep continuous thunder shook the earth and the rain poured down in torrents."[12]

Driven by a northwest wind, it came down for hours. Along Hooker's lines, trenches filled with water and every low spot became a pond. Campfires were impossible. Canvas and oilcloth leaked, new streams gushed along the furrows where men had slept.

Dozens of wounded Federal prisoners around the cabin near Chancellorsville were unprotected by any cover, not even a blanket. As the storm mounted, they found out the cabin was in a slight hollow, which turned into a pool inches deep. Only the strongest of them could sit up out of it. Rice Bull of the 123rd New York was told that two of his disabled comrades drowned where water cascaded down on them from the cabin roof.[13]

Lee's troops, on the march and in their rifle pits, were no better off than the Yankees. His drive to get them in place to attack before nightfall subsided into the muck. To move them, to coordinate them in the dark in such a storm was hopeless. Attack would wait till morning.

But if nature denied Lee his chance to advance, it provided Hooker cover to retreat. Engineer Warren laid out a final, compact defensive semicircle from Scott's Dam on the Federal left to the mouth of Hunting Run on the right, to protect the bridges at U.S. Ford. Each corps would cut new roads through the woods to speed the move. Pleasonton's cavalry would cover the fords above and below. All guns except those rimming Warren's new inner line would get over before the fog lifted on Wednesday morning. Hooker let Butterfield break the news gently to Lincoln:

> General Hooker is not at this moment able, from pressing duties, to write of the condition of affairs. He deems it his duty that you should be fully and correctly advised. He has intrusted it to me. These are my words, not his.
>
> Of his plans you were fully aware. The cavalry, as yet learned, have

failed in executing their orders. . . . General Sedgwick failed in executing his orders, and crossed the river at Banks Ford last night; his losses not known.

The First, Third, Fifth, Eleventh, Twelfth and two divisions of Second Corps are now on south bank of Rappahannock, intrenched between Hunting Run and Scotts Dam. . . . Position is strong, but circumstances, which in time will be fully explained, make it expedient, in the general's judgment, that he should retire from this position to the north bank of the Rappahannock for his defensible position. Among these is danger to his communication by possibility of enemy crossing river on our right flank and imperiling this army, with present departure of two-years' and three-months' [nine-months'] troops constantly weakening him. The nature of the country in which we are prevents moving in such a way as to find or judge position or movements of enemy. He [Hooker] may cross tonight, but hopes to be attacked in this position.[14]

Lincoln did not get these tidings until Wednesday morning. They were still withheld from the public. The New York *Evening Post* asserted that "The whole country is in an agony of expectation to know the progress of the tremendous combat which is going on in Virginia," and suggested that news was held back to benefit stock speculators.[15]

THE RAIN FELL and the river rose. Union troops cut pine branches and laid them across the three pontoon bridges at U.S. Ford to soften the rumble of artillery crossing. The first stirring of activity on Tuesday had given some junior officers hope that at last Hooker was taking the offensive. "I was sanguine of success," wrote Maj. James Biddle, an aide to Meade. "I was completely mystified when I saw so many movements indicating a retreat. . . . I even then thought it was intended to send a portion of the army to Sedgwick." Biddle realized the truth in late afternoon when he went with Meade to headquarters and learned their corps had been assigned as rear guard for the withdrawal.[16]

At nightfall, soon after seven o'clock that stormy evening, the artillery started moving first, to clear the bridges for the following infantry. "It was darker than Erebus," Alpheus Williams said.[17]

James Coburn huddled against the rain with his friends in the 141st Pennsylvania, "but we consoled ourselves with the idea that it was as bad for the Rebs as for us—and with many a sympathizing thought for the poor suffering mangled bleeding wounded we tried to make ourselves as comfortable as possible. But as night closed in on us, how heartsick it made us to hear the order, 'Pack up everything quietly and be ready to move at a moment's notice.' It was the first intimation that we had but that all was going well on our right and left. We supposed that our men still held the heights of Fredericksburg—that although we were lying comparatively quiet our men were doing a big thing elsewhere. And then the thought, *must* we lose this battle? Have these brave comrades who have fought so bravely and died at their post died in vain?"[18]

In regiment after regiment, word came to pack up, fall in, move quietly. But before some of them started to march through the mud, orders rippled back to hold up. With all the supply trains and about half the artillery over the river, rising water was straining the three bridges. Guns and caissons were backed up more than a mile along the roads approaching the ford. Disaster loomed again. General Slocum sent his provost marshal, Capt. C. F. Morse, to the ford to see what was wrong. There, Marsena Patrick, provost marshal-general, said the order for retreat was suspended, and every command should return to its position on line. Morse ran his horse back to tell Slocum. Slocum wrote a message saying that unless the move was continued, the army would have to surrender within twenty-four hours. He dispatched it by an orderly, telling him to "kill his horse carrying it."[19]

With Hooker and Butterfield already across the river, the corps commanders were left without central direction. It was "Every corps for itself, no one to give orders," said Washington Roebling; Hooker was "probably asleep somewhere."[20] Meade, Couch, Sickles, and Reynolds conferred at Meade's headquarters. When Meade heard of the holdup and orders to refill the old line, his reaction was the opposite of Slocum's. "What an act of Providence!" he said. "Perhaps the salvation of the country will be brought about by this."[21] He sent Biddle to the ford to report on what was happening. Biddle found one bridge in operation, with artillery still moving. Unable to crowd his horse onto it, he walked across to discover Hooker in a house half a mile uphill, wrapped in a blanket on the floor. Butterfield, speaking for Hooker, said another bridge would be ready in ten minutes. By one account, the Rappahannock had risen six feet eight inches in two hours. The engineers were taking up one bridge to piece out the other two, making them long enough to span the high water.[22]

Biddle realized that the corps commanders were unaware of being leaderless. Returning, he woke up Meade, and Meade in turn sent word to Couch and Sickles that Hooker was across the river, out of touch. Couch, the senior corps commander, wrote that "I immediately rode over to Hooker's headquarters and found that I was in command of the army, if it had any commander." Meade dispatched Biddle to consult with Reynolds, who was asleep in his tent. Reynolds "advised a delegation being sent over the river to wake some one up to take command"—then more diplomatically said to tell Meade "he thought that if the army moved at once it could get over by daylight."[23]

But Couch, believing there was danger of losing the bridges, suspended the crossing, saying the army would stay and "fight it out." Then he turned in, but at 2:00 A.M. got a "sharp message" from Hooker—or Butterfield still speaking for Hooker—ordering the withdrawal to continue.[24]

Infantrymen who had been told to pack up, then stood in the rain for hours, then returned to their rifle pits, heard new orders in the blackness: "Fall in! Hurry up! Fall in!" Some had unwisely taken off their soaked shoes and were unable to pull them on fast enough. They set off half asleep and barefooted through the mud. Stragglers had coaxed bonfires alight at intervals along the roads. Reynolds's artillery chief, Charles Wainwright, stopped several times to warm himself on the way to the ford. Wherever he stopped, "All appeared to feel that our retreat was a disgrace, and . . . each conversation concluded the same: 'If Little Mac [McClellan] had been here we never should have gone off this way.' "[25]

At the bridges, Reynolds rode up to Meade and offered one last gesture: "General, I will remain with you and if there is any battle to be fought we will fight it together." But everything around them made clear the futility of his offer.

"Hurry and confusion all around was maddening as the blue masses sloshed through mud and water, hurrying to cross the river. Officers were more excited and fearful than the soldiers were." Bill Southerton of the 75th Ohio saw no need to hurry. "God Almighty! There were no Johnnies around. I took my time. Sloshing along, my boots coated with mud, breeches sodden, blouse dripping, pockets heavy with ammunition, soggy hardtack and raw pickled pork . . . I was in no mood to be yelled at. . . . The bridge was almost submerged by the torrent madly rushing like a mill race tumbling through a gorge." An officer yelled again, "Hurry up!" But the weary Ohioan thought the officers were not worried about the strong bridge cables—"they were afraid Lee would come up and complete his victory."[26]

By daybreak, thousands of Federal troops were jammed up at the bridgehead. A few random Rebel shells sprinkled the area, but caused no panic. Captain Morse thought "a very little extra strain" would have carried off the upstream bridge, sweeping away the lower one and cutting

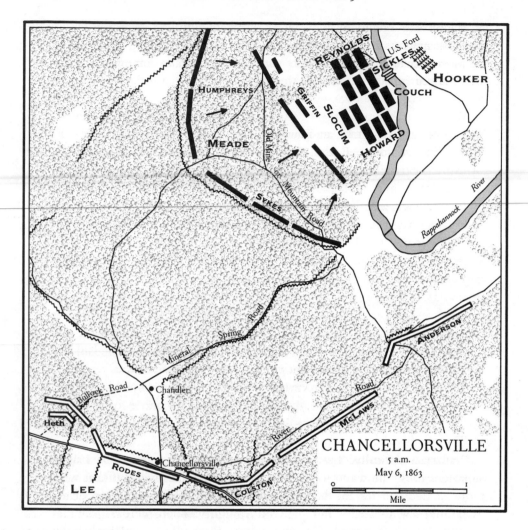

18. Admitting Defeat. *Hooker, effectively out of action, pulls his army back across the Rappahannock behind a shortened protective line manned by Meade's corps. Lee, surprised by this, does not have to make the final, inevitably costly assault he has intended.*

off the retreat. The hours from five to seven or eight that morning "were the most anxious I ever passed in my life," he wrote. Biddle said, "if we had been attacked the result might have been terrible, as there were 50,000 men massed in a hcap, waiting to cross."[27]

BENEATH A FLY-TENT at Fairview, Lee awoke Wednesday ready to throw five divisions—Rodes, Colston, Heth, McLaws, and Anderson—against the powerful Union line anchored at Chandler's. After sweeping the previous days' battlefield, his soaked and chilled soldiers had better rations for breakfast than usual, but little time to enjoy them. Skirmishers moved out toward where the Federal pickets had been the day before. Before battle lines were formed, Lee sat in his tent and wrote to Richmond:

> General Hooker did not recross the Rappahannock after his defeat on Sunday, but retreated to a strong position in front of the United States Ford, where he is now fortifying himself, with a view, I presume, of holding a position this side of the Rappahannock. I understand from prisoners that he is awaiting re-enforcements. . . . I had hoped that Longstreet would have been here before this time. . . . I hope every effort will be made to restore the railroads, else we will have to abandon this country.[28]

Uncharacteristically, Lee was paying attention to rumors of Union reinforcements, the way Hooker and his generals had worried that new divisions were joining the Southern command. He was admitting concern that Stoneman's cavalry had cut the rail line to Richmond. But his reaction, unlike Hooker's, was to keep attacking.

He checked the lineup of his troops: Heth on the left, a short way up the Bullock Road; Rodes along the Plank Road to Chancellorsville; Colston from there to half a mile up the River Road; McLaws along almost a mile of River Road, and Anderson from Mine Road right toward Hayden's house. The weight of the attack would be on the right, the shortest way to U.S. Ford.

Lee understood that this assault would be costly, but he showed no doubt that it would succeed. He was about to give the order when Dorsey Pender rode up, leaped off his horse, and announced that his skirmishers had moved ahead and found the Union trenches abandoned.

Hooker was gone.

Lee's anger at being surprised overrode any elation at the news. Pender's finding meant the battle was over. Instead of triumph, what Lee saw for the moment was complete victory slipping out of his grasp, and he was furious.

"Why, General Pender!" he said. "That's the way you young men always do. You allow those people to get away. I tell you what to do, but you don't do it! Go after them! Damage them all you can!"[29]

But it was too late.

Confederate skirmishers pushed on, harassed by Federal pickets, until they came within range of artillery drawn up beyond the Rappahannock. Meade's Fifth Corps manned the line around the bridgehead as masses of Union infantry retreated across the river. The last brigade to cross was James Barnes's, of Griffin's division. When some pickets of his 118th Pennsylvania climbed back into the rain-slippery works behind them, they were astounded to see campfires burning "and not a living soul around any of them to enjoy them." Suddenly, "It flashed on our minds that the army had retreated during the night and I tell you we felt very sad as we trudged through the mud," past stragglers and troops struggling to help wounded friends. Some pickets never did get the word, and were captured.[30]

When the last of Barnes's rear guard fell back down the slope and across the bridges, it was near 9:00 A.M. Engineers hurriedly cut the cables and let the pontoons drift to the Union shore. Barnes's men helped lift off and load the boats and planking, unhappy that "each plank weighed about half a ton, as half an inch of mud" coated it. Six to twelve mules strained to pull each wagon up the slope. Some of the wagons slipped and overturned with their teams into the deep gullies. To save time, they were left and the mules shot. Veteran troops who had seen comrades mutilated in battle complained at this—"Cruel! And this is war!"[31]

LINCOLN GOT Butterfield's telegram with the first ambiguous warning of retreat at 10:45 Wednesday morning, 23 hours 45 minutes after it was sent. By that time he knew Richmond papers were reporting that Lee had defeated Hooker, but also that Union cavalry was within five miles of the Confederate capital, destroying locomotives and bridges between there and the battlefront. In a 12:30 wire to Hooker, the president suggested that this news, together with the great rainstorm, "Puts a new face upon your case, but you must be the judge."[32]

Despite that vaguely hopeful dispatch, Lincoln admitted to Noah Brooks at the White House that in his own mind, he felt sure "Hooker has been licked." Still there was no certainty—until about three o'clock, when Lincoln got Butterfield's 1:00 P.M. message relaying this from Hooker: "The army has recrossed the river. . . . the bridges are up, and all are under orders to return to camp." [33]

"Had a thunderbolt fallen upon the President he could not have been more overwhelmed," wrote Brooks. "One newly risen from the dead could not have looked more ghostlike. [34]

"I shall never forget that picture of despair. He held a telegram in his hand, and as he closed the door and came toward us I mechanically noticed that his face, usually sallow, was ashen in hue. The paper on the wall behind him was of the tint known as 'French gray,' and even in that moment of sorrow and dread expectation I vaguely took in the thought that the complexion of the anguished President's visage was almost exactly like that of the wall."

Lincoln handed Brooks the telegram. As the correspondent read it, the president looked on with a "piteous" expression. "Never, as long as I knew him, did he seem to be so broken, so dispirited, and so ghostlike," wrote Brooks. "Clasping his hands behind his back, he walked up and down the room, saying:

"My God! My God! What will the country say? What will the country say!" [35]

Lincoln hurried out, leaving Brooks and the president's friend Dr. A. G. Henry together in the room. Empathizing with Lincoln, Henry wept. Brooks tried to console him. As they talked, out the window they saw General Halleck roll up in a carriage. Lincoln boarded it and the two drove away. Just after dark, Secretary of War Stanton advised Hooker:

> The President and the General-in-Chief left here this afternoon at
> 4 o'clock to see you. They are probably at Aquia by this time. [36]

In a gray rain, they boarded a special steamer at the Navy Yard. News of what had happened swept the capital. "The effect was indescribable," wrote Brooks. "The panic spread, and by night the town was well-nigh demented with excitement." Public places like Willard's Hotel "were in a state of siege." Rumors raced through the crowds: Hooker was arrested, Halleck was taking command, Stanton had resigned, Lee was approaching Washington, McClellan was coming to the rescue and so were a raft of other generals. McClellan boosters and Copperheads did not try to hide their satisfaction. [37]

· · ·

LEE'S GREATEST VICTORY had ended in anticlimax. If there had never
been a Seven Days, Second Manassas, Fredericksburg, Spotsylvania Court
House, or Cold Harbor, his performance at Chancellorsville would assure
his place in military history. The odds against him had been heavier than
they would be in any campaign until the last days before Appomattox. The
enemy's opening move onto the Confederate flank had been as menacing
as the Union presence on Richmond's doorstep the year before. The bold
resourcefulness that turned danger into triumph would be studied around
the world: among soldiers, the name "Chancellorsville" would evoke
tactical brilliance for decades to come.

But Lee dwelt on what might have been. He had prepared to end the
fight with a roar, with all-out assault on an entrenched, still numerically
superior Union army, and he was disappointed when Hooker got away.
If only Jackson had started his flank march earlier, he might have panicked
the Yankees back across the river Saturday afternoon. If Anderson had
linked up with Early to attack Sedgwick sooner on Monday, they might
have destroyed the Sixth Corps before dark. If the rainstorm had not come
on Tuesday, Lee might have pitched into Hooker's bridgehead before he
had time to slip away.

Battles always end with ifs. And if the rain had not come, if Hooker's
generals had been able to persuade him to stick and fight, if Lee had
attacked Hooker's concentrated position, the battle of Chancellorsville
might have ended with the Confederate army shattered and Lincoln
rejoicing. Lee won with daring, with skill—and with luck, which usually
blesses the bold.

As Hooker's army slogged back to its camps, Lee's dragged wearily
back downriver to its old defenses. It would be ready if Hooker, with his
superior numbers, his many still unbloodied regiments, should try again.
But all movement the rest of Wednesday, then Thursday, was away from
battle. For the commanders, creative thinking was reduced to paperwork.
Hooker, back at Falmouth, issued General Orders No. 49:

> The major-general commanding tenders to this army his congratu-
> lations on its achievements of the last seven days. If it has not
> accomplished all that was expected, the reasons are well known to the
> army. It is sufficient to say they were of a character not to be foreseen
> or prevented by human sagacity or resource.
> In withdrawing from the south bank of the Rappahannock before
> delivering a general battle to our adversaries, the army has given

renewed evidence of its confidence in itself and its fidelity to the principles it represents. In fighting at a disadvantage, we would have been recreant to our trust, to ourselves, our cause, and our country.

Profoundly loyal, and conscious of its strength, the Army of the Potomac will give or decline battle whenever its interest or its honor may demand. It will also be the guardian of its own history and its own fame.

By our celerity and secrecy of movement, our advance and passage of the rivers were undisputed, and on our withdrawal not a rebel ventured to follow.

The events of the last week may swell with pride the heart of every officer and soldier of this army. We have added new luster to its former renown. We have made long marches, crossed rivers, surprised the enemy in his intrenchments, and whenever we have fought have inflicted heavier blows than we have received.

We have taken from the enemy 5,000 prisoners; captured and brought off seven pieces of artillery, fifteen colors; placed *hors de combat* 18,000 of his chosen troops; destroyed his depots filled with vast amounts of stores; deranged his communications; captured prisoners within the fortifications of his capital, and filled his country with fear and consternation.

We have no other regret than that caused by the loss of our brave companions, and in this we are consoled by the conviction that they have fallen in the holiest cause ever submitted to the arbitrament of battle.[38]

It was a far cry from General Orders No. 47, issued six days earlier, in which Hooker declared that "our enemy must either ingloriously fly, or come out from behind his defenses and give us battle on our own ground, where certain destruction awaits him." The figures he gave for Confederate casualties were closer to his own losses. His report of destruction and consternation behind enemy lines was based on the long ride of his cavalry, which he himself insisted had failed in its mission. If the overall results were not up to expectations, as he said, "the reasons are well known to the army." But they were not necessarily the ones Hooker would propose.

Twenty-one divisions of Union infantry moved achingly into their huts, many of them "dejected, demoralized and disgusted," wrote John Smith of the 118th Pennsylvania. "They were satisfied in their minds that the army was not whipped in this case, but the army had been badly handled. Where 50,000 men should have been rushed into a fight the army only fought in detail, and I say it boldly and fearlessly that whiskey, and whiskey alone, was the cause of failure in this battle, as there is no doubt it was one of the best planned battles of the war so far. . . ."[39]

Lee, in his General Orders No. 59, issued Thursday, felt no need to make excuses:

> With heartfelt gratification the general commanding expresses to the army his sense of the heroic conduct displayed by officers and men during the arduous operations in which they have just been engaged. Under trying vicissitudes of heat and storm, you attacked the enemy, strongly intrenched in the depths of a tangled wilderness, and again on the hills of Fredericksburg, 15 miles distant, and, by the valor that has triumphed on so many fields, forced him once more to seek safety beyond the Rappahannock. While this glorious victory entitles you to the praise and gratitude of the nation, we are especially called upon to return our grateful thanks to the only Giver of victory for the signal deliverance He has wrought. It is, therefore, earnestly recommended that the troops unite on Sunday next in ascribing to the Lord of hosts the glory due unto His name.
>
> Let us not forget in our rejoicing the brave soldiers who have fallen in defense of their country; and, while we mourn their loss, let us resolve to emulate their noble example.
>
> The army and the country alike lament the absence for a time of one to whose bravery, energy and skill they are so much indebted for success.

With his order, Lee issued a letter from Jefferson Davis, "giving praise to God for the success with which He has crowned our arms" and thanking Lee and his troops for this addition to their "unprecedented series of great victories."[40]

WHEN THE REST of Lee's army moved back to and below Fredericksburg, he left two brigades around Chancellorsville to care for the wounded and clean up the field. Altogether his army brought in 19,500 small arms, tons of ammunition, uncounted coats, blankets, tents, packs, and rations—and almost 6,000 Union prisoners.[41]

In the hours and first days after battle, these Yankees found that the Rebels who had fought them so fiercely became friendly and considerate as captors. New Yorker Rice Bull recalled how they sat and talked, and "did not in the least object to our standing up for our side of the argument over the war." One of Ramseur's North Carolinians cut a laurel bush to make Bull a cane so he could limp off the field—and the prisoner still cherished that cane "as a memento of my Johnnie friend" fifty years later. But as time wore on, "there was no food, no nursing, and no medicine to dull the pain of those who were in torture."[42]

What the Confederate line troops could give was kindness; they could not give what they did not have. And the farther prisoners moved behind the lines, the less they felt of soldiers' camaraderie. Young Lt. Clay MacCauley of the 126th Pennsylvania marched with a column of captives back through Sporsylvania Court House toward Guiney Station. A pretty, furious woman rushed out of one house, shaking her little fists and shouting "Kill 'em all, colonel! Kill 'em all right here for me!" That night the swarm of prisoners slept on the muddy ground near Guiney.

When they awoke and saw wagons racing back and forth, they thought for a while that their side had won after all, and they might be recaptured. But that flurry of hope died quickly, and thoughts turned to food. Angrier and hungrier, the prisoners demanded it. Late in the day a wagon came, and their captors dumped a half barrel of salt beef and a barrel of flour on the ground. The prisoners tried to eat it, but had no fire and no kettle. The beef "took on an ironical red, white and blue tint," MacCauley wrote. The next day, four of the captives begged permission to go to a plantation house in search of food. At an outlying cabin they bought an old hen from a slave woman for five dollars. They did not reach the main house, because Stonewall Jackson was nearby.

JACKSON HOPED to rest a few days at Fairfield, then go to Richmond and home to Lexington to recover before returning to the army. But before he reached Guiney by ambulance wagon, Stoneman's marauding Union horsemen had cut both railroads from the Rappahannock to Richmond.

Lt. Col. Hasbrouck Davis, leading the 12th Illinois Cavalry, struck the R.F.&P. at Ashland. "Words cannot describe the astonishment of the inhabitants at our appearance," he reported. His force cut the telegraph to Richmond, disabled two engines, tore up rails, and started a huge bonfire. While the cavalrymen were at it, a train of seven cars rolled in unawares from Guiney. Aboard it were 250 sick and wounded Confederates, plus ranking officers. After questioning them, Davis let them go on parole. Riding east, Davis's troopers cut the Virginia Central line at Hanover Station, and claimed they burned 100-plus wagons and a thousand sacks of flour and corn. From there they turned south and bivouacked Sunday night seven miles out of Richmond. After that they were fought off by a trainload of Confederate infantry at Tunstall Station east of Richmond, and groped their way to Gloucester at the mouth of the York River.[43]

Col. Judson Kilpatrick with the 2nd New York Cavalry told an even more exciting tale, of breaking the R.F.&P. at Hungary Station at daylight Monday, then charging the outer defenses of Richmond itself. He reported driving a battery back within two miles of the city, capturing prisoners within the fortifications, burning a bridge, running a train of railroad cars into the Chickahominy River and destroying a ferry just ahead of pursuing cavalry. He reported that along the way he surprised another force of 300 Rebel cavalrymen, capturing 35, and burned 56 wagons and a storehouse of more than 60,000 barrels of grain. After this his troops ruined another wagon train and depot near Tappahannock, and beat a pursuing cavalry force back to the York River. Continuing down the York to Gloucester, after the battle he crossed the Rappahannock at Urbanna and returned up the Northern Neck to Falmouth. Thus Kilpatrick was able to say that he, like Jeb Stuart, had encircled an enemy army, though at a distance.[44]

After tearing up track and bridges northwest of Richmond, the rest of the Federal raiders roughly retraced the route they had taken on their way south, recrossing the Rapidan and the Rappahannock at fords well above the battlefield.

Stoneman's expedition had thrown lightly defended Richmond into a flutter. Convalescent soldiers were called out of the hospitals there, issued muskets and sent to the outskirts. Telegraph messages from Lee had to be routed via Lynchburg to Richmond. Citizens were armed, trees were cut to block roads—and then the raiders were gone.[45]

There had been scattered panic in the capital, but none where Hooker had hoped to create it: in the mind of Robert E. Lee. Knowing the railroad behind him was cut, Lee also knew he could do nothing about it, and focused on the main chance in front of him. Thus, strategically, Hooker's grand right hook turned out to be a psychological blow to civilians in Richmond, a temporary severance of Confederate communications and supplies, and little more.

THE RAIL LINE up to Guiney Station was briefly "a country full of wild rumors," sending teamsters, commissary soldiers, and transients scattering when they heard that Stoneman was heading north up the tracks. In the confusion, Union prisoners in the rain-soaked fields were loaded aboard trains, started south hoping for a decent meal, then brought back, turned into the fields, loaded again and so treated that they were glad at last to arrive at Richmond's infamous prisons.

The morning after Jackson came to Fairfield, another rumor of approaching Union cavalry swept through. Wagonmasters hitched up to flee the station, and Jed Hotchkiss came to tell the general goodbye. Jackson seemed cheerful, hopeful he would be back in uniform soon, and sent regards to Lee. Learning what caused all the bustle, he showed "the most perfect calmness," and confidence that if he were captured, God would see that the Federals treated him kindly.[46]

Jackson's brother-in-law, young Joe Morrison, was aboard the train that rolled into Ashland while Davis's Illinois cavalry was tearing up the tracks and depot. When the train was captured, Morrison went to get water from a nearby well, and was hidden by the woman of the house. While the Yankee raiders were listing their prisoners, he slipped away, and when they departed he made his way to Richmond to fetch his sister, Anna Jackson. Despite the panicky rumors still swirling, they set out for Guiney as soon as the rails were repaired, arriving before noon on Thursday.

In tender times away from camp and battle, Jackson liked to call his wife his "Sunshine." When she reached Fairfield, bringing the infant Julia, she tried to live up to that. But, for an hour, the doctors kept her from seeing him. He had asked for lemonade; somebody suggested that while she waited, she make it for him. His aide Smith took it in, and when Jackson tasted it he said quickly, "You didn't mix this; it's too sweet. Take it back." That was not like him. Nor, when Mrs. Jackson came in shortly afterward, was he like the man she had last seen only eight days before. His eyes were sunken, his face flushed with fever and scraped by the underbrush of the Wilderness. His voice was weak. When he saw her expression, he told her gently to cheer up—"Don't wear a long face; you know I love a bright face in a sickroom." And that was what she showed him when she was there. But beyond his room, she often wept.[47]

Dr. McGuire had thought Jackson was doing "remarkably well" on Wednesday. The stump of the left arm was healing. McGuire splinted the right hand, which was not painful. Jackson wanted to know how long he would be out of action. To Smith, he said that many might regard his wounds as a great misfortune, but "I regard them as one of the blessings of my life."

"All things work together for good to those who love God," Smith said.

"Yes, that's it, that's it," Jackson nodded.

Jim Lewis went back and forth to the Chandler house, bringing whatever food Jackson could digest, mainly milk. McGuire asked that Mrs. Chandler send ice milk made with a little vanilla. Jackson slipped in and out of sleep, eased by the doctor's opiates, asking how the battle was going, now and then talking unconsciously as if he were still there. Once he said distinctly, "Major Pendleton, send in and see if there is higher ground back of Chancellorsville!" [48]

Again, perfectly composed, he talked religion with Smith, of how prayer helped man in whatever he was doing. The Bible, he said, offered soldiers rules to cover every eventuality. He asked Smith, "Can you tell me where the Bible gives generals a model for their official reports of battles?" It might never occur to military men to look in the Scriptures for such models, he said, but they were there. "Look, for instance, at the narrative of Joshua's battle with the Amalekites; there you have one. It has clearness, brevity, fairness, modesty, and it traces the victory to its right source, the blessing of God." [49]

Wednesday night, an exhausted McGuire fell asleep on a couch in Jackson's room. About 1:00 A.M., Jackson felt nauseated again, and whispered for Lewis to bring a wet towel to place over his stomach. Lewis wanted to rouse the doctor, but Jackson would not let him be disturbed. At daylight, McGuire awoke and found the general in severe pain. Examining him, he found what he called pleuropneumonia of the right side. He sent for Dr. Samuel Morrison, the general's old friend, and Anna's relative.

Chaplain Lacy went to the heights behind Fredericksburg to find Dr. Morrison. While there, he reported to Lee on Jackson's condition.

"Give him my affectionate regards," said Lee, "and tell him to make haste and get well, and come back to me as soon as he can. He has lost his left arm, but I have lost my right. . . ." [50]

McGuire believed Jackson's painful side was from his fall from the litter the night he was wounded, rather than simple pneumonia. Dr. Morrison, who arrived about 5:00 P.M. Thursday to find Mrs. Jackson already there, apparently agreed. McGuire thought the ailment began too soon to have been brought on by the application of cold cloths. In his opinion, the fall deeply bruised the chest and caused internal bleeding.*

---

*McGuire's detailed records were lost in an ambulance when Jubal Early's troops were driven up the Shenandoah Valley by Union general Philip Sheridan in 1864. In 1975, Dr. Beverly C. Smith of New York examined the surviving descriptions of Jackson's condition and sent them to ten prominent surgeons for comment. Almost all believed Jackson had some condition below the diaphragm in addition to the pulmonary problem

Anna was given a room in the Fairfield mansion, but spent almost all her time with her husband. Jackson could see the anguish in her eyes. He told her quietly, "I know you would gladly give your life for me, but I am perfectly resigned. Do not be sad. I hope I may yet recover. Pray for me, but always remember in your prayers to use the petition, 'Thy will be done.' "

When Dr. Morrison walked in, the general was in pain and at times delirious. But he welcomed the newcomer, raising his right arm and saying to Anna, "There's an old familiar face." McGuire subjected him to cupping, raising a blister on his skin with the vacuum in a heated glass, and gave him mercury with antimony and opium. That evening, soothed by his wife and charmed by his baby daughter, Jackson felt better, and hope rose in those around him.

On Friday, the sharp pain in his side was gone, but breathing was hard and he felt deeply tired. One of the doctors who had come from Richmond to advise McGuire and Morrison said he thought cupping would help again, and Jackson agreed. Jackson told Dr. Morrison that he believed he would recover. "I believe God has yet a work for me to perform," he said. "I am not afraid to die. . . . I am resigned to abide [by] the will of my Heavenly Father."

He played with little Julia and petted her, calling her "my comforter." But he was weaker. For a few moments he raised his right arm above his head and silently prayed. Opening his eyes, he looked around and said, "I see from the number of physicians that you think my condition is dangerous, but I thank God, if it is His will, that I am ready to go."[52]

Dr. Morrison left for five hours to check on casualties in Early's division. When he returned late Friday afternoon Jackson was more often delirious, though he recognized all around him and understood what they said. When the doctor offered him medicine, Jackson said, "Do your duty, do your duty." Repeatedly, he wanted to know when he would be able to move to Richmond. He asked Dr. Morrison to advise Governor Letcher that he would not be there to accept his hospitality "for some days."[53]

Jackson grew weaker, and slept little on Friday night. Saturday morning, Anna read to him from the Book of Psalms. That afternoon, he called for Tucker Lacy to make sure the chaplain was keeping up observance of

---

diagnosed by McGuire. One theory was that a clot had moved from the amputation site to a lung. Others mentioned possible bladder, duodenal, pancreatic, or kidney injuries.[51]

the Sabbath in the corps. In the evening, he asked his wife to sing some hymns, and she did. At his request, she and her brother ended with "Shew Pity, Lord," which paraphrased the Fifty-first Psalm: "Shew pity, Lord; O Lord, forgive; Let a repenting rebel live. . . ."[54]

Though Jackson insisted he would be better in the morning, he was restless all night as his doctors and friends sat sponging his forehead. When he awoke Sunday, Anna told him he might not recover. He had said to her before that while he was willing to go whenever called, he would like to have some notice to prepare himself. She asked if he were ready "if He wills you to go today."

He thought a moment. "I prefer it," he said. "I prefer it. It will be infinite gain to be translated to Heaven." In late morning he slumped, and Anna knelt beside his bed, saying that before sundown he would "be with his Saviour." "Oh, no," he said calmly. "You are frightened, my child. Death is not so near. I may yet get well." Unable to hold back, Anna fell across the bed weeping, saying the doctors offered no hope.

He asked her to call McGuire. "Doctor," he said, "Anna informs me that you have told her that I am to die today. Is it so?" McGuire had to say yes. Jackson gazed at the ceiling, then told the doctor, "Very good, very good. It is all right."

When Sandie Pendleton came in about one o'clock, Jackson wanted to know who was preaching at corps headquarters that day. Tucker Lacy, Pendleton told him, adding that the whole army was praying for his recovery.

"Thank God," breathed Jackson. "They are very kind. It is the Lord's day; my wish is fulfilled. I have always desired to die on Sunday."

To Anna's questions, he said that if he died, she should go to live with her father in North Carolina. But he wanted to be buried in Lexington, in his beloved Valley of Virginia. She brought in the baby Julia, and for a moment his eyes lit up. He called her "little darling," and tried to embrace her with his shattered right hand.

Soon he seemed to fade. He muttered as his thoughts wandered to the battlefront, to the mess tent, to a council of war, to his family, to prayer. Then he focused on those beside him, and McGuire offered him brandy and water. No, said Jackson, it would only delay his departure, and he wanted his mind to be clear to the last. At 1:30, McGuire said he had about two hours left. "Very good," said Jackson. "It's all right."

Just after 3:00, his mind was back at Chancellorsville. He cried out, "Order A. P. Hill to prepare for action! Pass the infantry to the front. Tell Major Hawks . . ."

McGuire described the next moments:[55]

"Presently a smile of ineffable sweetness spread itself over his pale face, and he cried quietly and with an expression as of relief:

" 'Let us cross over the river and rest under the shade of the trees.'

"And then, without pain or the least struggle, his spirit passed from earth to the God who gave it."

Chapter Nineteen

Up Like a Rocket, Down Like a Stick

THE NIGHT AFTER Hooker's withdrawal across the Potomac, a shaken Lincoln landed at Aquia. There was none of the fanfare of his visit in early April. In the morning, a locomotive pulled his single car along the curving track to Falmouth Station. A lone cavalryman on each flank escorted his carriage from the station to Hooker's command post. With Halleck, Lincoln rode past riddled regiments, their officers puzzling over how to reorganize to make up for terrible losses—and other commands intact, puzzled over how they could have lost without ever fighting.

On both sides of the river, foot-slogging privates and sleepless generals, those who had sung "Joe Hooker is our leader" a week before and those who had tried to shirk the fight, all were thankful it was over. It had been the bloodiest battle of the war to date, worse than both battles of Bull Run combined, worse than Antietam or Fredericksburg, Fort Donelson or Shiloh. Hooker's army had lost more than 17,000 killed, wounded, and missing—5,000 more than at Antietam or in the December debacle at Fredericksburg. Lee's victorious divisions had lost nearly 13,000, almost as many as at Antietam, more than double the number at Fredericksburg. But as a fraction of strength, a measure of impact on battles ahead, Lee's losses were worse—22 percent against Hooker's 13 percent. The Union could make up those casualties much more easily than the Confederacy could find replacements in its dwindling pool of manpower.*[1]

Except for the empty bunks, the fresh graves, and full hospitals, the strategic situation was as it had been when the first dogwood blossomed in the valley of the Rappahannock. Lee and his army had won their most spectacular victory, their reputation had been assured for the ages. Yet tens

---

*See Appendix 2.

of thousands of Union soldiers refused to think they were beaten—their general, perhaps, but not his army.

At Army headquarters, Lincoln and Halleck talked with Hooker and his staff, and called the corps commanders together. Lincoln told them he feared that the effect of the defeat at home and abroad would be more serious than any other setback of the war. In Washington, Senator Charles Sumner had stomped into Secretary of the Navy Gideon Welles's office crying, "Lost, lost, all is lost!" In New York, Horace Greeley had moaned in the *Tribune* that the reputedly finest army on the planet had been defeated again by "an army of ragamuffins." But at Falmouth, Lincoln surprised the officers by not asking for their assessments of what had happened. There and then he blamed no one, and gave the generals no chance to unload their feelings about Hooker. He simply asked about the morale and condition of the army.[2]

Looking ahead, Hooker told Lincoln and Halleck that despite his battle losses and the discharge of many troops whose terms were expiring, he still would have about 100,000 under his command, all he could advantageously use. What Lincoln said when he and Hooker talked privately was not recorded. But that afternoon when the president headed to Washington, he left "Old Brains" Halleck behind, telling him to stay until he learned "everything."[3]

On the way back, the president composed a message for Hooker. This was a habit of his; after visiting the army, talking to generals or inspecting troops, he liked to have a little time to think to sum up his impressions. The campaign had ended "without effecting its object," he wrote, except perhaps for cutting Rebel communications. "What next?" asked the president. He would be glad of some early move to "help to supersede the bad moral effect" of the recent battles. But nothing should be done rashly, he cautioned. If Hooker had anything specific in mind, he should go ahead without interference from the White House. If not, Lincoln would like to know, "so that I, incompetent as I may be, can try and assist in the formation of some plan. . . ."[4]

Hooker answered promptly. He made the week-long clash of arms seem just a preliminary to further ventures. "A cause which could not be foreseen" had reduced prospects of success, he said, so he felt he should adopt another plan "which would be more certain in its results." Before deciding when to advance again, he wanted to "learn the feeling of the troops." The soldiers "should not be discouraged or depressed, for it is no fault of theirs (if I may except one corps) that our last efforts were not crowned with glorious victory." He had a plan, but would withhold details. "It has this to recommend it," Hooker concluded. "It will be one in which the operations of all the corps, unless it be a part of the cavalry, will be within my personal supervision."[5]

Perhaps subconsciously, Hooker in that sentence confirmed the least disputed, most charitable explanation of why his generalship failed at Chancellorsville. He was proven competent as commander of a division, whose movements he could direct first-hand, often out front on his white horse. But he could not direct seven corps, fighting on two or more fronts. It was too complicated. He could not fight a battle on a map.

Halleck put his sharp legal skills to work in questioning Hooker's subordinates and returned to Washington with more explanation than that. He, Secretary of War Stanton, and the president met at the War Department. Halleck reported that the halt at Chancellorsville and the final retreat both had been "inexcusable," and Hooker should not be allowed to lead the army into another campaign. Halleck also brought a message from Hooker that seemed to match the general's aim of keeping future operations within his personal grasp: Astonishingly, Hooker said he had never sought the army command, after all, and so he could if desired resign without embarrassment. He would be happy to stay on at the head of his old division.[6]

Congress and the cabinet split over whether Hooker should stay or go. On May 13, Lincoln advised Hooker that "I have some painful intimations that some of your corps and division commanders are not giving you their entire confidence." Several of the corps commanders had called on the president. Couch and Reynolds, at least, urged Hooker's removal. But Couch said he did not want the job. He recommended Meade instead. Reynolds said he would accept command only if he had total control of the army. Only Sickles, Pleasonton, and Butterfield sided with Hooker. Still, Lincoln decided to keep him, at least until the debate died down. Couch, furious, asked to be relieved.[7]

Neither cabinet investigators, congressional hearings, nor the perspective of time have changed the analyses of Hooker's performance that his corps commanders were able to offer one another and the president within hours of recrossing the Rappahannock. And as fast as Hooker's soldiers assured their families that they were still among the living, their letters spread scathing assessments of his generalship across the Union.

"Every tongue in the army seems today to be wagging its fastest," wrote Col. Charles Wainwright.[8] And one man's name was on every tongue.

At Pleasonton's headquarters across from Fredericksburg, twenty-three-year-old Capt. George Armstrong Custer wrote to the absent General McClellan, on whose staff he had served during the Peninsula campaign. "To say that everything is gloomy and discouraging does not express the state of affairs here," he wrote. "Hooker's career is well exemplified by that of a rocket, he went up like one and came down like a stick. It is reported that at two different times Hooker was *wounded* or injured by a shell and that this interfered with his success. . . . If anything except his lack of ability interfered or prevented him from succeeding, it was a wound he received from a projectile which requires a cork to be drawn before it is serviceable. . . .

"Even Hooker's best friends are clamoring for his removal, saying that they are disappointed in him. . . . You will not be surprised when I inform you that the universal cry is 'Give us McClellan.' . . . Jackson and A. P. Hill are as usual killed. I do not believe they will remain dead long." [9]

A month later, two years after graduating from West Point and thirteen years before dying at Little Bighorn, Custer became the youngest general in the Union army.

The upright John Gibbon was not so transparently ambitious. He told McClellan that Hooker, "so well known to possess personal bravery, seems to have yielded entirely to his nerves and to have shown a complete want of backbone at the wrong moment, to the surprise of every one. . . . The great trouble with us is that *principle* is wanting, and a certain set headed by such Maj. Gens. as Dan S. [Sickles] and Dan B. [Butterfield] is all powerful in its influence. God will not favor a cause where men without character and without principle are placed in the highest positions to the exclusion of high minded and honorable men." Good soldiers, he said, "cannot help making comparison between them and such men as Lee, Longstreet & Jackson." [10]

Up and down through the ranks, "Nearly all are very bitter on Hooker," wrote Charles Wainwright, "and many accuse him openly of being drunk." But Wainwright himself had seen no such signs. He focused on Hooker's congratulatory order, just issued: The general "goes on to boast of our achievements, captures and so on, while the balance is altogether on the other side, and the army more nearly disgraced than it has ever been before. Such braggadocio is worse than ridiculous." [11]

Whether he was drunk or sober, Hooker's bombast cost him after the battle. "The commander of our army gained his position by merely brag and blow, and when the time came to show himself, he was found without the qualities necessary for a general," wrote Captain Morse, Slocum's provost marshal. "I doubt if ever in the history of this war another chance will be given us to fight the enemy with such odds in our favor. . . ."[12]

The tart-tongued engineer Washington Roebling was glad "the astounding farce had come to an end. . . . If Hooker had gone bodily over to Lee he could not have helped him more than he did. . . . Hooker was simply a moral fraud. He had always posed. When it came to the supreme test, he failed utterly. He would have liked to hide in the bushes, but with thousands of eyes upon you the commander has not the privilege of the private. . . . When a general has done his very best and is defeated fairly and squarely, he is entitled to a nervous collapse. But when a man breaks down absolutely before the battle has even begun, he does not deserve the name of soldier."[13]

The bitterness many Union soldiers felt when they looked around at empty bunks came through when Edward H. C. Taylor of the 4th Michigan wrote to his sister in upstate New York: "What a pity that the bravery of such men should be thrown away—that so many lives be lost. . . . Is Hooker only 'getting his hand in'? And are men to be sacrificed for his practicing? Is he capable of the position? I can't answer the questions, but I know that fearful blunders were made and many lives thrown away—for what? . . .

"I can't trust Hooker. Most of the winter I have lived within ten rods of his quarters and know him to be a whiskey 'bloat'—one of the most profane men I ever knew and a terrible braggadocio. . . ." Later, Taylor added, "A victory is no victory at all unless you can show some great advantage to compensate for so many lives lost and so many wounds received. Otherwise the dead and the friends of the dead can judge the General whether he be guilty of murder or no."[14]

Not everyone who had survived the campaign condemned Hooker, but his defenders had to strain. Captain, later Colonel, Charles P. Mattocks of Sickles's corps reviewed the entire course of the battle, giving Hooker the benefit of the doubt at each turn. "That he was bitterly criticized may perhaps have resulted from one great defect in his own character, and that was his proneness to criticize others," Mattocks wrote after the war. "He may have stirred up enmities which brought to him their bitter fruit."[15]*

Immediately after Chancellorsville, Hooker had his opportunity to set

*In Hooker's retirement, when there was less doubt about his drinking habits, he talked publicly about his former colleagues the way he had always talked in private. In 1872, he read in the San Francisco *Chronicle* that Howard had accepted blame for the rout of his corps. Howard told a reporter that he had been newly appointed to command, and "felt a delicacy about interfering with the details of my subordinates . . . trusting entirely to them, until I should be better acquainted. It was a fearful mistake." Hooker leaped on the record favorably straight. Most expected him to do it in his official report of the campaign, and awaited that document with curiosity. Maj. Gen. Carl Schurz was one such. Schurz wrote in his own report that since so much blame had been heaped on the Eleventh Corps, every officer in it had a right to a fair investigation of his conduct. "I would therefore," he said, "most respectfully and most urgently ask permission to publish this report." Hooker did not respond. Schurz wrote to the War Department, asking that either his report be published or a court of inquiry be ordered to judge the performance of his division. Hooker said he could not approve publishing "an isolated report" until all were ready. Schurz persisted, meantime withdrawing an earlier request that his division be transferred away from Hooker's army. "I consider it a duty to myself and my men to stand right here until the mist that hangs over the events of the 2d of May is cleared up," he wrote. Still, General-in-Chief Halleck returned his request, saying, "Publication of partial reports not approved till the General commanding has time to make his report."[17]

But the general commanding never made his report. Neither that spring nor at any time in the future did Hooker try to rebut on paper all the things that others said about his performance in the most important week of his life. Beginning almost ten months after the battle, the Joint Committee on the Conduct of the War, dominated by anti-Lincoln radical Republicans, began hearings on the campaign. Those hearings went on for fourteen months, but only in the closing weeks did Hooker's demands bring him on as witness. His testimony covered sixty-seven pages.

---

this, and invited the *Chronicle* man to hear his version. "This statement [by Howard] appears to exonerate me from any reverse at Chancellorsville, not to say failure, as I had none," he asserted.

The reporter found Hooker in his room at San Francisco's Grand Hotel, looking his old self, though partially disabled by a stroke. The general maintained that "The only failure on my part was in not bringing General Howard to a strict account for his culpability. . . . He's a very bad man, but he's a pious character. O, I know him so well! He wrote to me in New York, offering me a professorship in his darkey college [the freedmen's school in Washington that later became Howard University]."

Howard, insisted Hooker, had never passed on his, Hooker's, Saturday morning warning to protect his flank. "He pocketed the telegram without reading it, said he was tired, and went to sleep. He seems to have been under the impression that Jackson was retreating." That, of course, was just what Hooker himself had assumed at the time.

From perfecting the record of the battle, Hooker slid into *ad hominem* remarks about Howard. When the reporter asked if Howard was a brave man, Hooker said, "Howard is a very *queer* man. . . . He was always a woman among troops. If he was not born in petticoats, he ought to have been, and ought to wear them. He was always taken up with Sunday Schools and the temperanth [*sic*] cause. Those things are all very good, you know, but have very little to do with commanding army corps. . . ."[16]

He explained how most everyone besides himself, especially John Sedg-wick, was responsible for what happened. If any blame was due Hooker, those listening had to deduce it on their own. "Our artillery had always been superior to that of the rebels," he testified, "as was also our infantry except in discipline, and that, for reasons not necessary to mention, never did equal Lee's army. With a rank and file mostly inferior to our own, *intellectually and physically,* that army has, by discipline alone, acquired a character for steadiness and efficiency unsurpassed, in my judgment, in ancient or modern times."

Discipline, of course, is the commander's responsibility.

Hooker contended—well after Sedgwick's death—that if Sedgwick had driven on to Chancellorsville, Lee would have been forced to retreat westward, which would have thrown the Confederates off the direct road to Richmond and the Union troops onto it. Hooker's sympathetic ques-tioners did not dwell on his mistakes; he and the committee left objective judgment for others, who still debate his conduct today.

HOOKER'S STRATEGIC plan to move onto Lee's flank was brilliant, and brilliantly executed. Its mistake, his first of the campaign, was sending almost all the Union cavalry far beyond the battlefield, out of touch with headquarters. Although Stoneman's raid caused excitement in Richmond, it had virtually no effect on the fight along the Rappahannock. Lee's cavalry numbered less than 40 percent of Hooker's, and that had to be split in order to harass Stoneman while screening and scouting for the main Rebel army. But close around the battlefield, each side had only four regiments of cavalry, and after the fight started, the Confederates under Stuart performed to near perfection.

After achieving his opening surprise, Hooker proceeded to make at least one major mistake a day. On April 30, when his troops reached Chancel-lorsville, he should have pushed on to Banks' Ford as planned, thus connecting the wings of his army by the shortest route. Instead he halted. Then, on May 1, confronted by Jackson's smaller but more aggressive force, he infuriated his own generals by ordering them to pull back on Chancellorsville.

Hooker cited the shattering of the Eleventh Corps by Jackson's flank attack on May 2 among key reasons for his defeat. That was merely the most embarrassing aspect of it. He should have seen to it that his right flank and rear were protected to prevent what happened. So should the corps commander, Howard, the division commander, Devens, and the brigade commander, von Gilsa. None did. Even if Hooker bore no blame for the rout of the Eleventh Corps, he could not credibly claim that that decided the battle, for he had more troops at hand and a stronger position in the days after the rout than before.

When the Confederate flank attack ground down in the moonlit tangles of the Wilderness, it fell short of Jackson's hopes. Jackson had been late starting that morning, consumed extra hours deploying his divisions through the Wilderness, and was unhappy when Rodes held up the attack because of darkness and confusion. Impatient to push on, he rode out beyond the lines.

His stunning but incomplete success that night left the Rebels themselves in a most dangerous situation; Hooker might have turned either way and overpowered the force confronting him. Although Jackson's attack shattered one corps and bloodied two others, its greatest impact was psychological, confirming Hooker's defensive mindset. Thus, the morning of May 3, Hooker surrendered a key element in his advantageous position when he ordered the abandonment of Hazel Grove. That move was never reasonably explained except for the vague purpose of consolidating his lines around Chancellorsville.

Hooker contended that his army did not have its supply trains on hand, and indeed some of his regiments ran out of ammunition in the fierce battle Sunday morning. That was largely because devastating Rebel artillery fire from Hazel Grove prevented resupply. But Hooker had a huge backup of material loaded and waiting just across the river.

He also maintained that the dense woods around Chancellorsville would have forced his advancing units into vulnerable columns along the narrow roads, so he did not attack east against Lee when the Confederate commander turned back toward Salem Church on May 3 and 4. The thickness of the forest discouraged Hooker's subordinates as well; at first they did not believe any troops could attack abreast through such a wilderness. But repeatedly, the Confederate infantry did. That may have been because Southern soldiers were more woods-wise, and unafraid of ripping their clothes and themselves crashing through the brush. Mostly it was because the Rebels were asked to do it, as Hooker's troops were not.

Thus Hooker did not continue his advance beyond Chancellorsville, and did not risk striking Lee while the Rebel commander was occupied with Sedgwick. He was satisfied to hold his shrinking bridgehead while urging Sedgwick to come to him. Yet even that passivity seemed to fit

Hooker's revised plan, of inviting Lee to fight him on his chosen ground—and Lee was about to oblige him when the Union general made his final mistake, withdrawing across the Rappahannock.

One of the reasons that Hooker cited was fear that the rising river, fed by the rainstorm of Tuesday, May 5, would cut him off from his supplies and communications. But he had announced the decision to recross in the meeting with his corps commanders in the early morning darkness, more than twelve hours before the storm. On May 6, if Hooker had still been in his formidable lines above Chancellorsville, Lee probably would have attacked them as fiercely as Stuart attacked on Sunday morning. Whoever ended holding the ground, the cost to the Confederacy would have been appalling, and might have shortened the war.

That attack could have become Lee's worst mistake. Because it never took place, his most serious errors of the campaign remain those made before the battle was joined. His first was allowing Longstreet to keep Pickett's and Hood's divisions south of Richmond until too late to join the fight. The mere threat that they might come, the rumor that they had come, influenced Hooker and Butterfield throughout the campaign. If that fear was intentionally fed by the Confederates, as repeated Yankee reports from captured Rebels suggest, it was one of the war's most important, little-recognized disinformation successes.

Second, by inadequately picketing the fords of the upper Rappahannock and Rapidan, Lee allowed Hooker to move a massive force onto his western flank. He hesitated—once, and only once—before deciding that that was Hooker's main advance. After that, he confounded Hooker by daring to divide his smaller army three times: in shifting to confront Hooker's enveloping force; in sending Jackson around the far flank; and in ordering McLaws and Anderson back to head off Sedgwick. Yet repeatedly, Lee brought more muskets to bear at the point of impact.

Lee was blessed by interior lines, so that—except for Jackson's flank march—his troops had shorter distances to cover than Hooker's did. He was more blessed by responsive lieutenants. His orders were concise, leaving detailed execution to men he trusted. Yet, unlike the voluminous, often contradictory messages that flowed from Hooker's headquarters, they were seldom misunderstood—the most memorable instance being the miscarried order for Early to withdraw from the Fredericksburg front on Saturday.

Some analysts have said that Lee's moves would have been disastrous instead of brilliant if he had been facing anyone but Hooker—that a strong

Union response to any one of them might have defeated him before he could complete the series. Lee understood that better than anyone studying his tactics in the leisure of later years. But in every battle from the Seven Days through Chancellorsville, he read his opponent perfectly. Perhaps he remembered Hooker from Mexico. Perhaps he found an inner weakness in Hooker's prewar dissolution. Perhaps he could see through the boasting of "Mr. F. J. Hooker," as he sometimes called Fighting Joe.

But the determining moment was when Hooker pulled back on Chancellorsville, forfeiting the advantage of his masterful flanking move. Starting then, Lee was master. Never again in American history has one general's ascendancy over another been so clear. Lee saw Hooker falter, and on that signal took chance after chance, each so promptly that it was done before Hooker's bemused brain and ponderous command machinery could counter it.

Yet Hooker's true failure did not lie in any one tactical error or combination of errors. He himself pinpointed the root cause in that rare admission of fallibility, when he said to Doubleday that he was not drunk, that "for once I lost confidence in Hooker, and that is all there is to it." But what caused him to lose his nerve, after winning his nickname with boldness on other fields, after inspiring his army with words like those he sent forth with Stoneman, about how "celerity, audacity and resolution are everything in war"?

He, at long last, was in command. He would be able to blame no one above him for whatever happened. He was in charge of an entire army, with too many corps commanders reporting directly to him. As he effectively admitted, he could not handle the complications, the concepts, of a battle fought beyond his personal vision. And all of these truths sank in on him when he realized that now he was man-to-man against Robert E. Lee. At the first sign that Lee was not going to cooperate by retreating according to Union plan, Hooker stopped thinking of winning the battle and switched his concern to not losing it. Hooker's moves were not all wrong, and Lee's were not all right. But Lee's were made with the quick authority of a general used to dominating the battlefield: he dominated Hooker with tactics, with brilliant subordinates, with determined soldiers, but mostly with moral force.[18]

The other Union generals who understood this also realized that the congressional hearings long after the battle were politically predetermined to clear Hooker. They bit their tongues rather than say officially what so many of them had said privately. Thus, when the Joint Committee on the

Conduct of the War finally issued its report the month after Appomattox, it fulfilled expectations. It praised Hooker. It blamed his defeat at Chancellorsville on the collapse of the Eleventh Corps, the cannonball that injured him, and the failure of Sedgwick and Stoneman to carry out orders.[19]

But long before then, Joe Hooker had left the Army of the Potomac.

Epilogue

THE LOST, LOST FIGHT

Whither depart the souls of the brave
that die in the battle,
Die in the lost, lost fight,
for the cause that perishes with them?

—ARTHUR HUGH CLOUGH, *Amours de Voyage*

AT FAIRFIELD, Stonewall Jackson's aides dressed his body in a dark civilian suit, then a blue military overcoat. For a shroud, Jefferson Davis sent from Richmond the first example of the newly approved Confederate national flag, white with the familiar red, white, and blue battle-flag design in the upper corner. The morning after Jackson died, the body in its coffin was taken to the parlor of the main house. As Mrs. Chandler stood looking down at her departing guest, Jim Lewis came in and gave her a lock of Jackson's hair that he had cut before the body was moved. The Chandlers' daughter, Lucy, brought a bunch of lilacs from the garden and placed them with the lilies of the valley already beside the body. In late afternoon, a special railroad car arrived bringing Governor Letcher and other dignitaries. The coffin was taken down the terrace, past the blossoming shrubs to the train. With Anna, Julia, Jim, the governor, the doctors, and aides, it left for Richmond.

When it was on its way, fifteen-year-old James Chandler and his sister went into the Jackson sickroom. The boy sat in the window, facing the railroad. Below him on the grass he saw a bloodstained military jacket. He went out and picked it up. Its left arm was cut away, and all its buttons were missing. Jim Lewis had brought it in the ambulance from Wilderness Tavern and, not knowing what else to do with it, had dropped it out the window the night Jackson arrived, and forgotten about it. The Chandler children kept it till their mother returned from Richmond. She realized it was a relic to be cherished, but when the wounded soldiers staying there heard about it, every man begged for a piece of it. She cut it into swatches for them, keeping only a small corner for herself. More than seventy years later, her daughter still had that fragment, subdividing it into strands for special admirers of Jackson.*[1]

Approaching Richmond, the train stopped for Mrs. Jackson to board a carriage with the governor's wife. Then the train rolled on, slowly. Business was halted, and the whole city surged around. As the coffin was carried into the governor's mansion, cannon boomed and a dirge drifted past Thomas Jefferson's Capitol building, down toward the James and the listening Union soldiers at Belle Isle and Libby prison.

That day, Lee issued General Orders No. 61:

> With deep grief, the commanding General announces to the army the death of Lieut. Gen. T.J. Jackson, who expired on the 10th inst., at 3.15 P.M. The daring, skill, and energy of this great and good soldier, by the decree of an all-wise Providence, are now lost to us. But while we mourn his death, we feel that his spirit still lives, and will inspire the whole army with his indomitable courage and un-shaken confidence in God as our hope and strength. Let his name be a watchword to his corps, who have followed him to victory on so many fields. Let his officers and soldiers emulate his invincible deter-mination to do everything in the defence of our beloved country.[3]

On Tuesday, to the strains of the "Dead March," two of Pickett's regiments marched with the hearse past the brick row houses of downtown Richmond. Troops of the Stonewall Brigade had wanted to come from the Rappahannock, but Lee, wary of another Union attack, regretfully told them they could not be spared. He himself would not leave the front long enough to say goodbye to Jackson's body at Guiney. Instead of the brigade, some of its wounded soldiers, recovering in Richmond, limped along with cavalry horses, Jackson's staff and fellow generals, and a company of civilian officials led by President Davis. They moved through

---

*Jackson's amputated arm was taken by Chaplain Lacy to be buried in the family cemetery at Ellwood, the farm of the preacher's brother, Maj. J. Horace Lacy, near Wilderness Tavern. The general's aide James Power Smith later placed a stone over it. In 1922, Brig. Gen. Smedley Butler of the U.S. Marines was there with troops staging a mock battle for President Warren G. Harding. Told about Jackson's arm, Butler said "Bosh!" and told a squad to dig there. When the surprised general saw the unearthed bones, he ordered them reburied and a bronze plaque made for the stone. The plaque later fell off.[2]

the silent streets, then back to the Capitol. Longstreet, Jackson's brother corps commander, headed the pallbearers. By nightfall some 20,000 people had filed through the House chamber to look into Jackson's face. As officials cleared the hall and started to close the coffin, a wounded veteran of Jackson's old division pushed forward. When he was held back, told he was too late, tears flooded down his bearded face. He raised the stump of his right arm. "By this arm, which I lost for my country, I demand the privilege of seeing my general once more," he cried. Governor Letcher interceded and waved him through to the coffin, banked with spring blossoms left by those come to mourn.

By Jackson's dying wish, his body was taken to Lexington. It went by train to Gordonsville, then Lynchburg, with Virginians strewing flowers along the way. At Lynchburg it was placed on a canalboat to follow the valley of the James through the Blue Ridge, to the Shenandoah Valley Jackson had made his own. VMI cadets carried the coffin to the classroom where, as an awkward major, he had taught war to boys now leading regiments and brigades. On Friday, a funeral was held at the Presbyterian church, to which he had committed himself so completely. All Lexington followed to the cemetery.[4]

ALL THE SOUTH wanted to be there, to see, to touch, to have some lock of his hair or thread of his uniform. The newspapers were full of the Confederacy's greatest victory, yet no one could bear to celebrate. Jackson, said one paper, was as valuable as a whole brigade, or a division. Another made him the equal of 50,000 fresh troops. After his wounding, the Richmond *Whig* had insisted that he could not die, because he had been put on earth for a purpose, and that purpose was not yet fulfilled.

More than 1,500 Confederates had been killed outright in the battle, and hundreds died afterward. Except in their own homes, their deaths were overshadowed by that of a martyr who had never been seen by most of his mourners. Like Lee, Jackson became an almost sacred figure to the South.

In the ranks of Lee's recuperating divisions, many soldiers were convinced by victory over the odds that they too had a special connection with heaven. Because Lee and Jackson were so publicly reverent and successfully aggressive, the army began to feel that its cause was blessed, and so its soldiers were unbeatable.

R. A. Pierson of Louisiana wrote, "With such soldiers and our present leaders our enemies can never accomplish the unwholy design which they have formed for our subjugation. If we are only true to our selves and God be for us, the time will surely soon come when we shall be redeemed from the miseries of this horrid war. . . ."[5]

Gradually, as the days lengthened, the armies along the Rappahannock relaxed. Sgt. L. Calhoun Cooper, a Georgian in the Troup Artillery, wrote that most of his comrades were spending their time fishing and sleeping. Yet "Everything around F. [Fredericksburg] seems desolate and forsaken. Even the birds are seldom heard with their cheerful voices. Insects of every description, except the most unwelcome, have gone to a better land. . . .

"The Confederacy ought to be grateful indeed to the armies of Virginia for its suffering and trials in the great [struggle]. Do you ever look back and think how many battles it has fought and against what good odds? Do you ever think and remember in all their fights they have ever been victorious? Certainly never was there such an Army in ancient or modern times. Had the Army in the west only done one tenth what our Army has done I believe Peace would have been dawning over our beloved country. If they will only hold Vicksburg all is well. If Gen. Lee's veteran Army was there all would be safe. With such defenses they would hold out against the world."

Cooper, who fought in McLaws's division and Longstreet's corps, was one of the few who committed to paper any resentment of Jackson-worship. "A great man has fallen," he conceded. But "It is wrong to make so much noise about one man, when thousands of privates have been killed unknown to glory. . . . It is disgusting and sickening to hear men say twas better to have lost 25,000 men than Jackson. This is all nonsense and toadyism."[6]

Despite competition and envy between outfits, Lee's troops in both corps were confident of their own superiority over the enemy. Yankees outnumbered Confederates three to one, wrote Frederick West, adjutant of the 51st Georgia, "but they were outrageously thrashed. This is the best army in the world I expect. We are all satisfied with Gen. Lee and he is always ready for a fight. He fights so fast when he gets the enemy where he wants them that they never recover from the first [blow]. . . ."[7]

The feeling was mutual. Lee, concerned over how to restaff his command structure before the next campaign, had no reservations about the troops in the ranks. "I agree with you," he wrote to division commander John B. Hood, "in believing that our army would be invincible if it could be properly organized and officered. There never were such men in an army before. They will go anywhere and do anything if properly led. But there is the difficulty—proper commanders—where can they be obtained? But they are improving—constantly improving. Rome was not built in a day, nor can we expect miracles in our favor."[8]

They were memorable words. It is essential that soldiers have confidence in their generals; is it possible for a general to be too confident of his soldiers?

WHILE THE CANALBOAT bearing Jackson's body was approaching the Valley, Lee was summoned to Richmond to talk of what came next. Confederate arms were victorious on the Rappahannock, but elsewhere the outlook was grim. Along the far Mississippi, U. S. Grant was slowly closing on Vicksburg. William Rosecrans was fencing with Confederate Braxton Bragg in eastern Tennessee. On the coast of Virginia and North Carolina, Federal troops threatened vital railroads, supplies, and perhaps the Southern capital itself.

Jefferson Davis, Mississippian, was concerned that Vicksburg would fall and Union control of the great river would cut the Confederacy in two. Joe Johnston had appealed for more troops there. Longstreet, who enjoyed his independence away from Lee, had stopped in Richmond and urged that he take two divisions west. In conferences with Davis, Secretary of War Seddon, and the cabinet, Lee acknowledged these far-flung threats but said the simple choice was between holding Mississippi and holding Virginia. The way to relieve pressure on Richmond was to take his underfed troops north again, into fat, unravaged Pennsylvania. That way he could threaten Washington and Baltimore, encourage foreign backing for the Confederacy, and fight the Union army in open country. Despite Davis's concerns for the West, the president and most of the cabinet endorsed Lee's idea. The only figure whose balkiness would matter was Longstreet, Lee's sole surviving corps commander.

Before doing battle again, Lee had to reorganize his army from corps level down. The Chancellorsville campaign had devastated his officer ranks; 12 brigade commanders were killed or wounded. But the first question was who would take Jackson's corps. "I know not how to replace him," Lee wrote. "God's will be done. I trust He will raise up someone in his place."[9]

Whether God spoke or not, Lee had to raise someone to corps command, and do it immediately. Some said Jackson had voiced a wish on his deathbed that his old lieutenant, Maj. Gen. Richard S. Ewell, would take his place. This was disputed by those who thought A. P. Hill deserved promotion on the basis of consistent and fiery performance. There is no record that Lee considered Jackson's alleged dying wish, but when he reviewed the generals available, Ewell and Hill, plus cavalryman Stuart, were the strongest contenders. Others might be as talented, but were not yet ready. Lee did not want to lose Stuart as his eyes and ears. In one of the most important decisions of his career, he chose Ewell, who had won his reputation in the Valley before losing his leg at Second Manassas. Then, before that news circulated in the army, Lee told Hill that he was creating a third corps, and Hill would be its commander.

By promoting Hill, Lee bypassed Lafayette McLaws, who was senior. By choosing Ewell, he brought back to active service a character who was the sentimental favorite of those who had fought under him. A West Pointer from Virginia, Dick Ewell, forty-six, had been spectacularly profane until he moderated his vocabulary under Jackson's influence. He also was spectacularly combative, and a near-match for Jackson in his personal peculiarities and diet. Yet he dared make light of Jackson's eccentricities, suggesting that his leader was insane when he heard that Jackson never used pepper because it made his left leg weak. It was Ewell who said, "I never saw one of Jackson's couriers approach without expecting an order to assault the North Pole!" [10] "Old Bald Head" Ewell was still on the rise when he lost his leg. He would never be quite the same. On getting Lee's order to take Jackson's corps, Ewell abandoned his bachelorhood and married his widowed cousin. With her, he reported on the Rappahannock May 20. Two weeks later, his aides lifted and strapped him into the saddle as Lee's army started for Pennsylvania. [11]

WHEN HOOKER realized that Lee was about to move, he asked Washington for reinforcements—though after Chancellorsville he had said he had as many troops as he could manage. Washington said no. When it became clear that Lee was heading north, Hooker wanted to attack the tail of the Confederate army. Lincoln told him to stay north of the Rappahannock: "I would not take any risk of being entangled up on the river like an ox jumped half over the fence and liable to be torn by dogs front and rear, without a fair chance to gore one way or kick the other." [12]

Hooker asked that all the Union troops who might figure in stopping Lee be put under one commander, not necessarily himself. Washington withheld an answer. When Lee approached the northern end of the Shenandoah Valley, Lincoln urged Hooker to go at him. "If the head of Lee's army is at Martinsburg and the tail of it is on the Plank Road between Fredericksburg and Chancellorsville, the animal must be very slim somewhere. Could you not break him?"[13]

Hooker shifted his headquarters north. But his every decision had to be checked with Washington, and repeatedly the answer was no. Eventually he wired Lincoln that as long as he failed to have Halleck's confidence, "we may look in vain for success."[14] Lincoln promptly ended the special arrangement by which Hooker had reported directly to him, ignoring Halleck. Henceforth, said the president, Hooker's relationship to Halleck would be strictly that of any army commander to the general-in-chief. Perhaps with that, Hooker finally realized that Lincoln and Halleck were trying to force him to resign, without the political fuss that would come with firing him outright.

The showdown came when Hooker decided to cross the Potomac to stay abreast of Lee. Under the circumstances, he saw no need to hold Harper's Ferry. Halleck disagreed. Defiantly, Hooker wrote an order to General French at Harper's Ferry, then waited with him for Halleck's reaction. It came quickly: "Pay no attention to General Hooker's orders."

As Hooker saddled up, an officer said action seemed sure. "Yes, but I shall not fight the battle," said Hooker. "Halleck's dispatch severs my connection with the Army of the Potomac."

At 1:00 P.M. on June 27, he asked to be relieved. Lincoln quickly complied, and ordered Maj. Gen. George G. Meade to command the Union army as it followed Lee north.*[15]

THUS, WHEN the Army of the Potomac and the Army of Northern Virginia groped into each other July 1 outside the farm town of Gettysburg, the Union force was under Meade, new as commanding general but familiar to the officers around him. One of the reorganized Confederate corps was led by Ewell, a man who had never worked directly with Lee. Yet when the first clash there took place, it seemed to some of them a continuation of the drama at Chancellorsville. After desperate fighting, the Confederates converged on Gettysburg, sweeping two Union corps out toward the hills south of town and taking almost 5,000 prisoners.

Lee, following his troops, had not wanted to risk a general engagement

---

*Hooker was ordered west, where he was cited for his action commanding one wing of Grant's army at Chattanooga in the autumn of 1863, and served with distinction through the siege of Atlanta. When Howard was named to command the Army of the Tennessee in July 1864, Hooker again asked to be relieved, and held fringe commands until retiring from the regular army after a slight stroke in 1868. He died in 1879.

until he could bring his army together. But when the opening clash broke
so dramatically in his favor, he looked beyond Gettysburg and saw Blue
infantry straggling onto a low ridge that dominated the imminent battlefield. He could not tell how well organized the Yankee troops were, but
figured that a prompt move might oust them before they recovered.

Dick Ewell could see this, too, from much closer. Yet, without instructions to move, he waited for orders. The officers around him, used to
Jackson's boldness, were amazed, then angered. John B. Gordon, whose
brigade had led Early's division in driving the Federals from the town,
wanted to go after Cemetery Hill, at the northern end of the long ridge.
Ewell would not consent. The two of them rode together into town. A
few Yankees were still there; musket balls whizzed past. Gordon heard one
strike home, and looked anxiously to Ewell, asking if he was hurt.

"No," said Old Bald Head. "But suppose that ball had struck you. We
would have the trouble of carrying you off the field, sir. . . . It don't hurt
a bit to be shot in a wooden leg."

The spirited Gordon may have hoped this nonchalance under fire meant
the old Ewell was back. Not so. Ewell kept waiting, to be told what
to do.

Maj. Gen. Isaac R. Trimble, just recovered from a severe wound and
without a command, was there as a volunteer aide. He asked if Ewell was
going to follow through his opening success. Ewell said he was waiting
for orders. Trimble, incredulous, rode away to look over the ground, then
hurried back. He was pointing now to Culp's Hill, at the same end of the
ridge, insisting that it commanded the field and should be taken immediately. Trimble is reported to have said, "Give me a brigade and I will
engage to take that hill."

·Ewell did not answer.

"Give me a good regiment and I will do it!" declared Trimble.

Ewell shook his head.

An aide reported Early's saying that the capture of the high ground was
imperative. Ewell sent for Early, who arrived to say so in person. Finally,
Ewell dispatched word to Lee that he would attack the hill if supported
from the west. Before he got an answer, Lee's adjutant general arrived to
say the commander could see the Federals falling back, that if they were
pressed, the heights could be taken. Ewell should do it if possible. Within
minutes, Ewell's own messenger returned from Lee with the same orders:
Ewell should take Cemetery Hill "if practicable."

Those two words loomed large as Ewell rode with Early to take a closer look. There were still sharpshooters in town; Union cannon were shuffling about; there were unconfirmed reports of Federals coming from the east. Ewell decided that taking the hill was not, for the moment, practicable. He would wait till Lee and reinforcements arrived.

When Lee came, he barely hid his dismay at Ewell's inaction. He was used to giving his generals discretion. Discretion, for Jackson, usually meant license to attack. But Ewell, as Jackson's lieutenant, was used to firm and specific instructions. Without them, for the moment his old fire seemed gone. He and Lee discussed possibilities, and agreed to shift Ewell's corps to the right and attack there in the morning. But later, Ewell got word that Culp's Hill was unoccupied. He rode to Lee to suggest taking it after all. Though the hour was past midnight, Lee, glad to hear any initiative from him, said go ahead. Ewell sent a newly arrived division toward Culp's, but scouts found the hill full of Federals. Not only that, but a captured message disclosed another enemy division coming up behind it.

July 2 dawned with the Union army in place along Cemetery Ridge from Culp's Hill toward two knobs at the south called Round Top and Little Round Top. There Lee would fight the rest of the battle of Gettysburg, and lose it, and after that it was downhill to Appomattox.

There were other reasons for how the battle ended. Jeb Stuart's absence, east of the field, deprived Lee of intelligence about the converging Federals. Ewell lagged again on the second day. Longstreet's balkiness delayed the Confederate attack then, and Pickett's climactic charge the next day. But the two most important factors at Gettysburg were the direct result of what happened along the Rappahannock in the first week of May.

One was Jackson's death, forcing the reorganization of Lee's army, putting Dick Ewell where Stonewall would have been. Jackson needed no more than a hint to do things others would not dare. Lee had said of him, "Such an executive officer the sun never shone on. I have but to show him my design, and I know that if it can be done it will be done. No need for me to send or watch him. Straight as the needle to the pole he advances to the execution of my purpose." [16] Lee's instructions to take the hill "if practicable" would have been a bugle call to Jackson, like the invitation to march across Hooker's front to assail the flank at Chancellorsville. Jackson was missed on every march, in every clash of arms, after he was cut down by those remorseful Tar Heels in the moonlit wilderness. Douglas Southall Freeman, Lee's biographer, says flatly that "the death of Jackson was the turning point in the history of the Army of Northern

Virginia." James Longstreet, both rival and colleague to Jackson, wrote that when Jackson fell, "The dark clouds of the future began to lower above the Confederates." [17]

The ordinary soldiers of Lee's army contributed the other clinching reason for the repulse at Gettysburg.

Two months before, they had collapsed Hooker's flank and hammered through his fiercely defended breastworks, driving away an army twice their size. They had convinced Lee that, as he said, "There never were such men in an army before"—and in that, he may have been right. He also said, "They will go anywhere and do anything if properly led"—and in that, the key words were "if properly led." Properly led on the decisive afternoon at Gettysburg, George Pickett's Virginians and Johnston Pettigrew's Carolinians would not have been sent across the killing fields from Seminary to Cemetery Ridge, against the massed Union army. But their bravery at Chancellorsville had persuaded their general that they were invincible, and so he sent them. And so Gettysburg was lost, and so the war.

Appendix 1

ORDER OF BATTLE

Army of the Potomac
Maj. Gen. Joseph Hooker

GENERAL HEADQUARTERS
Provost Marshal-General
Brig. Gen. Marsena R. Patrick

Patrick's Brigade
Col. William Rogers

Engineer Brigade
Brig. Gen. Henry W. Benham
(Brigade loss: k, 1; w, 6; m, 1 = 8)*

Signal Corps
Capt. Samuel T. Cushing

Artillery
Brig. Gen. Henry J. Hunt

Artillery Reserve
Capt. William M. Graham
Brig. Gen. Robert O. Tyler

---

*k, killed; w, wounded; m, missing; mw, mortally wounded; c, captured. Losses shown in the Order of Battle are incomplete, and do not add up to overall totals for either army. Sources: Order of Battle—*Official Records* 25, pt. 1, 156–70, 789–94; Brigade losses—*Battles & Leaders* 3, 233–38.

First Army Corps
Maj. Gen. John F. Reynolds

1ST DIVISION
Brig. Gen. James S. Wadsworth

1st Brigade
Col. Walter Phelps, Jr.
(w, 37)

3rd Brigade
Brig. Gen. Gabriel R. Paul
(k, 1; w, 15 = 16)

2nd Brigade
Brig. Gen. Lysander Cutler
(k, 3; w, 25; m, 5 = 33)

4th Brigade
Brig. Gen. Solomon Meredith
(k, 11; w, 46; m, 3 = 60)

Artillery
Capt. John A. Reynolds
(w, 9; m, 2 = 11)

2ND DIVISION
Brig. Gen. John C. Robinson

1st Brigade
Col. Adrian R. Root
(w, 5)

2nd Brigade
Brig. Gen. Henry Baxter
(k, 1; w, 16; m, 5 = 22)

3rd Brigade
Col. Samuel H. Leonard
(k, 2; w, 13; m, 1 = 16)

Artillery
Capt. Dunbar R. Ransom
(k, 7; w, 25 = 32)

3RD DIVISION
Maj. Gen. Abner Doubleday

1st Brigade
Brig. Gen. Thomas A. Rowley
(k, 1; w, 12; m, 36 = 49)

2nd Brigade
Col. Roy Stone
(w, 3)

Artillery
Maj. Ezra W. Matthews
(w, 9; m, 2 = 11)

SECOND ARMY CORPS
Maj. Gen. Darius N. Couch

1ST DIVISION
Maj. Gen. Winfield S. Hancock

1st Brigade
Brig. Gen. John C. Caldwell
(k, 36; w, 196; m, 46 = 278)

3rd Brigade
Col. Samuel K. Zook
(k, 13; w, 97; m, 78 = 188)

2nd Brigade
Brig. Gen. Thomas F. Meagher
(k, 8; w, 63; m, 31 = 102)

4th Brigade
Col. John R. Brooke
(k, 19; w, 64; m, 446 = 529)

Artillery
Capt. Rufus D. Pettit
(k, 2; w, 25 = 27)

2ND DIVISION
Brig. Gen. John Gibbon

1st Brigade
Brig. Gen. Alfred Sully
Col. Henry W. Hudson
Col. Byron Laflin
(w, 16; m, 4 = 20)

2nd Brigade
Brig. Gen. Joshua T. Owen

3rd Brigade
Col. Norman J. Hall
(k, 3; w, 56; m, 8 = 67)

3RD DIVISION
Maj. Gen. William H. French

1st Brigade
Col. Samuel S. Carroll
(k, 29; w, 182; m, 57 = 268)

2nd Brigade
Brig. Gen. William Hays (c)
Col. Charles J. Powers
(k, 26; w, 242; m, 61 = 329)

3rd Brigade
Col. John D. MacGregor
Col. Charles Albright
(k, 8; w, 80; m, 11 = 99)

THIRD ARMY CORPS
Maj. Gen. Daniel E. Sickles

1ST DIVISION
Brig. Gen. David B. Birney

1st Brigade	*2nd Brigade*
Brig. Gen. Charles K. Graham	Brig. Gen. J. H. Hobart Ward
Col. Thomas W. Egan	(k, 11; w, 124; m, 113 = 248)
(k, 72; w, 490; m, 194 = 756)	

3rd Brigade
Col. Samuel B. Hayman
(k, 30; w, 283; m, 253 = 566)

Artillery
Capt. A. Judson Clark
(k, 6; w, 26; m, 3 = 35)

2ND DIVISION

Maj. Gen. Hiram G. Berry (k)
Brig. Gen. Joseph B. Carr

1st Brigade	*2nd Brigade*
Brig. Gen. Joseph B. Carr	Brig. Gen. Joseph W. Revere
Col. William Blaisdell	Col. J. Egbert Farnum
(k, 52; w, 387; m, 65 = 504)	(k, 26; w, 160; m, 131 = 317)

3rd Brigade
Brig. Gen. Gershom Mott (w)
Col. William J. Sewell
(k, 57; w, 422; m, 48 = 527)

Artillery
Capt. Thomas W. Osborn
(k, 12; w, 68 = 80)

3RD DIVISION
Maj. Gen. Amiel W. Whipple (mw)
Brig. Gen. Charles K. Graham

1st Brigade	*2nd Brigade*
Col. Emlen Franklin	Col. Samuel M. Bowman
(k, 47; w, 304; m, 32 = 383)	(k, 51; w, 290; m, 236 = 577)

3rd Brigade
Col. Hiram Berdan
(k, 11; w, 61; m, 12 = 84)

Artillery
Capt. Albert A. von Puttkammer
Capt. James F. Huntington
(k, 2; w, 26; m, 9 = 37)

FIFTH ARMY CORPS
Maj. Gen. George G. Meade

1ST DIVISION
Brig. Gen. Charles Griffin

1st Brigade
Brig. Gen. James Barnes
(k, 4; w, 40; m, 4 = 48)

2nd Brigade
Col. James McQuade
Col. Jacob B. Sweitzer
(k, 9; w, 46; m, 7 = 62)

3rd Brigade
Col. Thomas B. W. Stockton
(k, 2; w, 18 = 20)

Artillery
Capt. Augustus P. Martin
(k, 2; w, 4; m, 2 = 8)

2ND DIVISION
Maj. Gen. George Sykes

1st Brigade
Brig. Gen. Romeyn B. Ayres
(k, 4; w, 17; m, 30 = 51)

2nd Brigade
Col. Sidney Burbank
(k, 17; w, 108; m, 22 = 147)

3rd Brigade
Col. Patrick H. O'Rorke
(k, 4; w, 29; m, 38 = 71)

Artillery
Capt. Stephen H. Weed
(k, 2; w, 13; m, 1 = 16)

3RD DIVISION
Brig. Gen. Andrew A. Humphreys

1ˢᵗ Brigade
Brig. Gen. Erastus B. Tyler
(k, 21; w, 166; m, 53 = 240)

2ⁿᵈ Brigade
Col. Peter H. Allabach
(k, 4; w, 31; m, 2 = 37)

Artillery
Capt. Alanson M. Randol

Sixth Army Corps
Maj. Gen. John Sedgwick

1ˢᵀ DIVISION
Brig. Gen. William T. H. Brooks

1ˢᵗ Brigade
Col. Henry W. Brown (w)
Col. William H. Penrose
Col. Samuel L. Buck (w)
(k, 66; w, 359; m, 86 = 511)

2ⁿᵈ Brigade
Brig. Gen. Joseph J. Bartlett
(k, 101; w, 368; m, 143 = 612)

3ʳᵈ Brigade
Brig. Gen. David A. Russell
(k, 35; w, 197; m, 136 = 368)

Artillery
Maj. John A. Tompkins
(k, 2; w, 5 = 7)

2ᴺᴰ DIVISION
Brig. Gen. Albion P. Howe

2ⁿᵈ Brigade (cq)
Col. Lewis A. Grant
(k, 39; w, 295; m, 97 = 431)

3ʳᵈ Brigade
Brig. Gen. Thomas H. Neill
(k, 52; w, 394; m, 404 = 850)

Artillery
Maj. J. Watts de Peyster
(w, 8; m, 1 = 9)

3ᴿᴰ DIVISION
Maj. Gen. John Newton

1ˢᵗ Brigade
Col. Alexander Shaler
(k, 7; w, 86; m, 67 = 160)

2ⁿᵈ Brigade
Col. William H. Browne (w)
Col. Henry L. Eustis
(k, 42; w, 278; m, 22 = 342)

3rd *Brigade*
Brig. Gen. Frank Wheaton
(k, 48; w, 237; m, 200 = 485)

Artillery
Capt. Jeremiah McCarthy
(k, 1; w, 4; m, 4 = 9)

LIGHT DIVISION
Col. Hiram Burnham
(k, 99; w, 99; m, 99; 99 99)

ELEVENTH ARMY CORPS
Maj. Gen. Oliver O. Howard

1ST DIVISION
Brig. Gen. Charles Devens, Jr. (w)
Brig. Gen. Nathaniel C. McLean

1st *Brigade*	2nd *Brigade*
Col. Leopold von Gilsa	Brig. Gen. Nathaniel C. McLean
(k, 16; w, 117; m, 131 = 264)	Col. John C. Lee
	(k, 45; w, 348; m, 299 = 692)

Artillery
Capt. Julius Dieckmann
(w, 11; m, 2 = 13)

2ND DIVISION
Brig. Gen. Adolph von Steinwehr

1st *Brigade*	2nd *Brigade*
Col. Adolphus Buschbeck	Brig. Gen. Francis C. Barlow
(k, 26; w, 229; m, 228 = 483)	(w, 9; m, 14 = 23)

Artillery
Capt. Michael Wiedrich
(k, 1; w, 10; m, 2 = 13)

3RD DIVISION
Maj. Gen. Carl Schurz

1st *Brigade*	2nd *Brigade*
Brig. Gen. Alex. von Schimmelfennig	Col. Wladimir Krzyzanowski
(k, 84; w, 215; m, 120 = 419)	(k, 36; w, 219; m, 153 = 408)

Unattached: 82nd Ohio
(k, 8; w, 48; m, 25 = 81)

Reserve Artillery
Lt. Col. Louis Schirmer
(w, 3)

TWELFTH ARMY CORPS
Maj. Gen. Henry W. Slocum

1ST DIVISION
Brig. Gen. Alpheus S. Williams

1st Brigade
Brig. Gen. Joseph F. Knipe
(k, 5; w, 53; m, 394 = 452)

2nd Brigade
Col. Samuel Ross
(k, 42; w, 253; m, 204 = 499)

3rd Brigade
Brig. Gen. Thomas H. Ruger
(k, 81; w, 465; m, 68 = 614)

Artillery
Capt. Robert H. Fitzhugh
(k, 7; w, 30; m, 9 = 46)

2ND DIVISION
Brig. Gen. John W. Geary

1st Brigade
Col. Charles Candy
(k, 58; w, 314; m, 151 = 523)

2nd Brigade
Brig. Gen. Thomas L. Kane
(k, 16; w, 90; m, 33 = 139)

3rd Brigade
Brig. Gen. George S. Greene
(k, 49; w, 219; m, 260 = 528)

Artillery
Capt. Joseph M. Knap
(k, 3; w, 15 = 18)

CAVALRY CORPS
Brig. Gen. George Stoneman

1ST DIVISION
Brig. Gen. Alfred Pleasonton

<table>
<tr><td>

1st Brigade
Col. Benjamin F. Davis
(k, 1; w, 8; m, 22 = 31)

</td><td>

2nd Brigade
Col. Thomas C. Devin
(k, 12; w, 54; m, 134 = 200)

</td></tr>
</table>

2ND DIVISION
Brig. Gen. William W. Averell

<table>
<tr><td>

1st Brigade
Col. Horace B. Sargent
(w, 6; m, 2 = 8)

</td><td>

2nd Brigade
Col. John B. McIntosh

</td></tr>
</table>

3RD DIVISION
Brig. Gen. David McM. Gregg

<table>
<tr><td>

1st Brigade
Col. Judson Kilpatrick
(k, 1; w, 1; m, 24 = 26)

</td><td>

2nd Brigade
Col. Percy Wyndham
(k, 2; w, 3; m, 40 = 45)

</td></tr>
</table>

Reserve Cavalry Brigade
Brig. Gen. John Buford
(k, 1; w, 3; m, 75 = 79)

Artillery
Capt. James M. Robertson

Army of Northern Virginia
Gen. Robert E. Lee

FIRST ARMY CORPS
Lt. Gen. James Longstreet
(Commanding divisions of George E. Pickett and John B. Hood,
detached to southeast Virginia)

MCLAWS'S DIVISION
Maj. Gen. Lafayette McLaws

<table>
<tr><td>

Wofford's Brigade
Brig. Gen. W. T. Wofford
(k, 74; w, 479; m, 9 = 562

</td><td>

Kershaw's Brigade
Brig. Gen. Joseph B. Kershaw
(k, 12; w, 90; m, 2 = 104)

</td></tr>
<tr><td>

Semmes's Brigade
Brig. Gen. Paul J. Semmes
(k, 85; w, 492; m, 26 = 603)

</td><td>

Barksdale's Brigade
Brig. Gen. William Barksdale
(k, 43; w, 208; m, 341 = 592)

</td></tr>
</table>

Artillery
Col. H. C. Cabell
(k, 5; w, 21; m, 2 = 28)

ANDERSON'S DIVISION

Maj. Gen. Richard H. Anderson

Wilcox's Brigade
Brig. Gen. Cadmus M. Wilcox
(k, 72; w, 372; m, 91 = 535)

Mahone's Brigade
Brig. Gen. William Mahone
(k, 24; w, 134; m, 97 = 255)

Wright's Brigade
Brig. Gen. A. R. Wright
(k, 25; w, 271 = 296)

Posey's Brigade
Brig. Gen. Carnot Posey
(k, 41; w, 184; m, 65 = 290)

Perry's Brigade
Brig. Gen. E. A. Perry
(k, 21; w, 88 = 109)

Artillery
Lt. Col. J. J. Garnett
(k, 1; w, 13 = 14)

Artillery Reserve

Alexander's Battalion
Col. E. P. Alexander
(k, 6; w, 35; m, 21 = 62)

Washington Artillery
Col. J. B. Walton
(k, 4; w, 8; m, 33 = 45)

SECOND ARMY CORPS

Lt. Gen. Thomas J. Jackson (mw)
Maj. Gen. A. P. Hill (w)
Brig. Gen. Robert E. Rodes
Maj. Gen. J. E. B. Stuart

HILL'S DIVISION

Maj. Gen. A. P. Hill
Brig. Gen. Henry Heth (w)
Brig. Gen. W. Dorsey Pender (w)
Brig. Gen. James J. Archer

Heth's Brigade
Brig. Gen. Henry Heth
Col. J. M. Brockenbrough
(k, 33; w, 270 = 303)

McGowan's Brigade
Brig. Gen. Samuel McGowan (w)
Col. O. E. Edwards (w)
Col. Abner Perrin
Col. D. H. Hamilton
(k, 46; w, 402; m, 7 = 455)

Thomas's Brigade
Brig. Gen. Edward L. Thomas
(k, 21; w, 156 = 177)

Archer's Brigade
Brig. Gen. James J. Archer
Col. B. D. Fry
(k, 44; w, 305; m, 16 = 365)

Lane's Brigade
Brig. Gen. James H. Lane
(k, 161; w, 626; m, 122 = 909)

Pender's Brigade
Brig. Gen. W. Dorsey Pender
(k, 116; w, 567; m, 68 = 751)

Artillery
Col. R. L. Walker
Maj. William J. Pegram
(k, 5; w, 20 = 25)

RODES'S DIVISION

Brig. Gen. Robert E. Rodes
Brig. Gen. S. D. Ramseur

O'Neal's Brigade
Col. Edward A. O'Neal (w)
Col. J. M. Hall
(k, 90; w, 538; m, 188 = 816)

Doles's Brigade
Brig. Gen. George Doles
(k, 66; w, 343; m, 28 = 437)

Colquitt's Brigade
Brig. Gen. Alfred H. Colquitt
(k, 9; w, 128; m, 312 = 449)

Iverson's Brigade
Brig. Gen. Alfred Iverson
(k, 67; w, 330; m, 73 = 470)

Ramseur's Brigade
Brig. Gen. S. D. Ramseur (w)
Col. F. M. Parker
(k, 151; w, 529; m, 108 = 788)

Artillery
Lt. Col. T. H. Carter
(k, 9; m, 37 = 46)

EARLY'S DIVISION

Maj. Gen. Jubal A. Early

Gordon's Brigade
Brig. Gen. John B. Gordon
(k, 16; w, 145 = 161)

Smith's Brigade
Brig. Gen. William Smith
(k, 11; w, 75 = 86)

Hoke's Brigade
Brig. Gen. Robert F. Hoke (w)
(k, 35; w, 195 = 230)

Hays's Brigade
Brig. Gen. Harry T. Hays
(k, 63; w, 306 = 369)

Artillery
Lt. Col. R. S. Andrews

COLSTON'S DIVISION
Brig. Gen. Raleigh E. Colston

Paxton's (Stonewall) Brigade
Brig. Gen. E. F. Paxton (k)
Col. J. H. S. Funk
(k, 54; w, 430; m, 9 = 493)

Warren's Brigade
Col. E. T. H. Warren (w)
Col. T. V. Williams (w)
Lt. Col. S. T. Walker
Lt. Col. S. D. Thruston (w)
Lt. Col. H. A. Brown
(k, 128; w, 594; m, 80 = 802)

Jones's Brigade
Brig. Gen. John R. Jones
Col. Thomas S. Garnett (k)
Col. A. S. Vandeventer
(k, 52; w, 420 = 472)

Nicholls's Brigade
Brig. Gen. Francis T. Nicholls (w)
Col. J. M. Williams
(k, 47; w, 266; m, 10 = 323)

Artillery
Lt. Col. H. P. Jones

Corps Artillery Reserve
Col. Stapleton Crutchfield

Brown's Battalion
Col. J. Thompson Brown

McIntosh's Battalion
Maj. David G. McIntosh

GENERAL ARTILLERY RESERVE
Brig. Gen. William N. Pendleton

Sumter (Ga.) Battalion
Lt. Col. A. S. Cutts

Nelson's Battalion
Lt. Col. William Nelson

CAVALRY
Maj. Gen. J. E. B. Stuart

1st Brigade
Brig. Gen. Wade Hampton
(detached)

3rd Brigade
Brig. Gen. W. H. F. Lee

2nd Brigade
Brig. Gen. Fitzhugh Lee
(k, 4; w, 7 = 11)

4th Brigade
Brig. Gen. William E. Jones
(detached)

Horse Artillery
Maj. R. F. Beckham
(k, 4; w, 6 = 10)

Appendix 2

CASUALTIES

THE CASUALTY FIGURES included in the Order of Battle (Appendix 1) demonstrate the problem of breaking down losses precisely for this or any other campaign of the Civil War. This is especially true in the Army of Northern Virginia, because most of its reports did not routinely include numbers captured and missing. The best efforts to sift and correlate such statistics for the war were made by William Fox in 1889 and Thomas Livermore in 1909. Both these studies were available for John Bigelow's analysis in 1910, and while his may be the most carefully considered calculations for higher command levels in the Chancellorsville campaign, he commits errors, too. He concedes, for example, that his day-by-day casualty figures "are in a measure conjectural"—and his own daily table mistakenly indicates that Early's division had zero losses on May 3, the day it fought the second battle of Fredericksburg.

In such a military situation, with deserters and malingerers aplenty, every effort to make casualty figures exact will be "in a measure conjectural." The tables on the following pages show where Bigelow comes out, down to the level of Federal corps and Confederate divisions.

Jackson's corps, biggest in either army, had the longest casualty list and the highest percentage of loss in the campaign. Sedgwick's Sixth Corps had the greatest loss on the Federal side, but Sickles's Third Corps suffered more by percentage. The way losses are spread throughout Lee's army shows how he brought all his outnumbered force into action, while the minimal losses in two of Hooker's corps prove that he did not follow Lincoln's instructions to "in your next fight, put in all of your men."

Birney's division of Sickles's corps took 1,605 casualties, more than any other Federal division. On the Confederate side, Hill's division suffered the most killed and wounded, while with missing included he and Rodes lost almost exactly the same number. But the percentage of loss in Colston's small division was highest.

Among Federal brigades, Neill's command of Howe's division lost 850 men, but that total included 404 missing, most of them captured in Sedgwick's hasty withdrawal to Scott's Ford Monday night. Burnham's brigade-sized "Light Division" lost 808, but 310 of those were missing. More were killed in Bartlett's brigade of Howe's division, heavily involved in Sedgwick's fight at Salem Church.

The two most battered Southern brigades were Lane's of Hill's division, in the thick of the Chancellorsville melee both Saturday night and Sunday morning, and Ramseur's of Rodes's division, which fought itself out in Sunday's assault. According to Fox's study, Ramseur lost 52.2 percent of his command.

The Federal regiment most severely hurt was the 12th New Hampshire of Bowman's brigade, Whipple's division. It lost 317 in the struggle around Chancellorsville. At Salem Church, the 121st New York of Bartlett's brigade lost 48 killed, 173 wounded, and 55 missing, a total of 276 men. At Marye's Heights, the 5th Wisconsin of Burnham's "Light Division" lost 193.

Confederate regiments did not offer figures for their missing. The 37th North Carolina of Lane's brigade lost 34 killed and 193 wounded, a total of 227, and the 2nd North Carolina of Ramseur's lost 47 killed and 167 wounded, totaling 214. All four of Ramseur's and four of Lane's five regiments lost more than 130 men each. According to Fox, the seven Southern regiments with highest losses were all from North Carolina. The Tar Heels, with 25 infantry regiments engaged, suffered more casualties than any other Southern state in the campaign (as they did in the entire war). Georgia, with 32 regiments in the campaign, came next, and Virginia, with 26 regiments, was third in losses.

Army of the Potomac

ORGANIZATION	AGGREGATE PRESENT FOR DUTY EQUIPPED	KILLED AND WOUNDED		KILLED, WOUNDED, AND MISSING	
		number	*percent*	*number*	*percent*
General headquarters, cavalry escort	60	0	0	0	0
I Corps	16,908	245	1	299	2
II Corps	16,893	1,193	7	1,925	11
III Corps	18,721	3,023	16	4,119	22
V Corps	15,824	541	3	700	4
VI Corps	23,667	3,145	13	4,610	19
XI Corps	12,977	1,618	12	2,412	19
XII Corps	13,450	1,703	13	2,824	21
General Artillery Reserve	1,610	0	0	0	0
Cavalry Corps { Active force	9,060	81	1	389	4
Cavalry Corps { Depot force	2,481	0	0	0	0
Provost Guard	2,217	0	0	0	0
ARMY OF THE POTOMAC	133,868	11,549	9	17,278[1]	13

Army of Northern Virginia

ORGANIZATION	AGGREGATE EFFECTIVE	KILLED AND WOUNDED		KILLED, WOUNDED, AND MISSING	
		number	*percent*	*number*	*percent*
1 Div., Anderson	8,370	1,189	14	1,445	17
2 Div., McLaws	8,665	1,395	16	1,775	20
Corps Artillery	720	52	7	106	15
I CORPS	17,755	2,636	14	3,326	19
1 Div., A. P. Hill	11,751	2,616	23	2,948	26
2 Div., Rodes	10,063	2,228	22	2,937	29
3 Div., Early	8,596	846	10	1,346	16
4 Div., Colston	6,989	1,870	27	2,078	30
Corps Artillery	800	69	9	80	10
II CORPS (Jackson)	38,199	7,629	18	9,381	25
General Artillery Reserve	480	3	1	3	1
Cavalry	2,500	25	1	111	4
ARMY OF NORTHERN VIRGINIA	60,892	10,293	17	12,821[2]	22

Source: Bigelow 473, 475.
[1] Plus 8 staff and engineers = 17,287.
[2] Plus 5 at HQ II Corps = 12,826.

Notes

1. WINTER ALONG THE RAPPAHANNOCK

1. Haydon, *Aeronautics in the Union and Confederate Armies*, 310–24; Hoehling, *Thaddeus Lowe*, 18–27.
2. Unknown 140th Pa.; *Berry Benson's Civil War*, 35.
3. Herbert, *Grandfather's Talks*, 154.
4. Todd, "Reminiscences," 78.
5. Brooks, *Mr. Lincoln's Washington*, 134.
6. DAB 2:309–; Boatner, *Civil War Dictionary*, 107.
7. Basler, *Works of Lincoln* 6:13.
8. Williams, *Lincoln and His Generals*, 200–204.
9. Ibid., 348; Botkin, *Treasury*, 233–34, from Rochester *Express*.
10. Moore, *Rebellion Record* 1863, 30.
11. Isaac Plumb, Jan. 1, 12, 1863.
12. David Beem to wife, Jan. 4, 1863.
13. William M. Dame to mother, Feb. 10, 1863.
14. Samuel Fisher to sister, Jan. 18, 1863.
15. C. R. Johnson, n.d.
16. Jacob Haas to brother, Jan. 3, 1863.
17. Tapert, *Brothers' War*, 127–8.
18. Unknown 140th Pa., Jan. 15, 1863.
19. Moore, *Rebellion Record* 1863, 396, from *N.Y. Times*.
20. Ibid.
21. Ibid., 398.
22. Stevens, *Three Years in the Sixth Corps*, 176.
23. Moore, *Rebellion Record* 1863, 399.
24. William A. Moore, 11.
25. James Coburn, diary, Jan. 21, 1863.
26. John L. Smith to mother, Jan. 25, 1863.
27. Raymond, "Journal," 703–6.
28. OR 21:998–99.
29. Sandburg, *Prairie Years and War Years*, 356; OR 25, pt. 2, 4.

2. MAN ON A WHITE HORSE

1. Hassler, *Commanders of the Army of the Potomac*, 126.
2. John B. Dunbar to Bigelow, Jan. 30, 1911.
3. Hebert, *Fighting Joe Hooker*, 18–19.
4. Ibid., 20–21; Bigelow, *The Campaign of Chancellorsville*, 5.
5. Hebert, 25.
6. Ibid., 34–35.
7. Hassler, *Commanders*, 130.
8. Hebert, 36–45.
9. Ibid., 47–49.
10. Ibid., 50–73.
11. Webb, *The Peninsula*, 71–76.
12. Bigelow, 6.
13. Hebert, 97–99.
14. Ibid., 114.
15. Pope, "The Second Battle of Bull Run," 465.
16. Hebert, 128.
17. Sears, *Landscape Turned Red*, 212, 223–24.
18. Hebert, 142–45.

19. William Farrar Smith, "Franklin's 'Left Grand Division,'" *B&L* 3:129.
20. Tucker, *Hancock the Superb*, 112–13.
21. Jt. Comm. Conduct of the War, *Report* (1865) 1:668.
22. Brooks, *Mr. Lincoln's Washington*, 42–43.
23. Hassler, *Commanders*, 132.
24. OR 25, pt. 2:15; Bigelow, 36.
25. Unknown 140th Pa., Jan. 25, 26, 1863.
26. Dunbar to Bigelow, Jan. 30, 1911.
27. G. F. Baer to J. H. Wilson, Mar. 26, 1911.
28. DAB 2:372.
29. Washington A. Roebling to Bigelow, Jan. 9, 1910.
30. San Francisco *Chronicle*, May 23, 1872.
31. OR 25, pt. 2:12–13.
32. Charles Littlefield to wife, Jan. 17, 1863.
33. Lord, *They Fought for the Union*, 11.
34. H. N. Hunt to wife and children, Apr. 17, 1863.
35. Tucker, 116.
36. Charles H. Veil, 36–37.
37. Jt. Comm., *Report*, 38th Cong., 2nd sess. 73–74.
38. Miller, *Spying for America*, 136.
39. Mattocks, "Major General Joseph Hooker," 215.
40. Huntington, "Battle of Chancellorsville," 151.

14. Ibid., 598.
15. "General Lee at the Battle of the Wilderness," from La Bree, *Confederate Soldier*, 304.
16. Wickwire, *Cornwallis*, 286.
17. Freeman, *R. E. Lee* 1:217.
18. Ibid., 294–98.
19. Ibid., 371–73.
20. Ibid., 420–22.
21. Ibid., 424–42.
22. Ibid., 442–76.
23. Alexander, 110–111.
24. Freeman, *R. E. Lee* 2:462.
25. Wills Lee, 7.
26. Freeman, *R. E. Lee* 2:484.
27. Ibid., 497–98.
28. Alexander, *Memoirs*, 318–19; Stuart, "Samuel Ruth," 35–.
29. Freeman, *R. E. Lee* 2:494–95.
30. Bigelow, *The Campaign of Chancellorsville*, 132–36.
31. Westwood Todd, 81–82.
32. McKay, *The National Tribune Scrap Book*, 124.

3. AUDACITY ABOVE ALL

1. W. B. Jennings, 42.
2. Henry C. Roney, 22.
3. J. Wilson to father, Apr. 21, 1863.
4. *Berry Benson's Civil War*, 36.
5. Jennings, 45.
6. Westwood Todd, 80–81.
7. Ibid., 82–83.
8. Douglas, *I Rode With Stonewall*, 208.
9. Robertson, *Stonewall Brigade*, 176.
10. Daly, *Portrait of a Man*, 91–93.
11. Alexander, *Military Memoirs*, 318.
12. Unknown 140th Pa., March 17, 1863.
13. Henderson, *Stonewall Jackson*, 608.

4. THE COUNTRY SAYS "MOVE"

1. Freeman, *Lee's Lieutenants* 2:397–409.
2. Bigelow, *The Campaign of Chancellorsville*, 73.
3. Ibid., 89–96.
4. Mercer, *The Gallant Pelham*, 91–92, quoting John Esten Cooke's *Surry of Eagle's Nest*.
5. Freeman, *Lee's Lieutenants*, 2:457–65.
6. OR 25, pt. 1:58.
7. Hess, "First Cavalry Battle at Kelly's Ford," 12.
8. Lonn, *Foreigners in the Union Army and Navy*, 117–25.
9. Galwey, *Valiant Hours*, 77–79.
10. Unknown, Will ———, 27th Conn., to Alzana, Mar. 18, 1863.
11. Hassler, *Commanders*, 134.
12. Small, *Road to Richmond*, 81.
13. Albinus Fell to Lydia, Apr. 5, 1863.
14. Unknown 140th Pa., Apr. 4, 1863.

15. John S. Robinson to Newton, Apr. 2, 1863.
16. Joe Critz to John, Apr. 2, 1863.
17. W. L. Masten to brother, Mar. 16, 1863.
18. OR 25, pt. 2:683.
19. Milo Grow to wife, Mar. 28, 1863.
20. OR 25, pt. 2:686–87.
21. Abernathy, "Our Mess."
22. OR 25, pt. 2:683–88.
23. Andrews, *The South Reports the Civil War*, 290–91.
24. Bigelow, 121.
25. Moore, *Rebellion Record 1863*, Documents 517–18.
26. William M. Dame to father, Mar. 28, 1863.

5. WHEN WE GET TO RICHMOND

1. Brooks, *Washington, D.C.*, 51–52.
2. Brooks, *Mr. Lincoln's Washington*, 153–54.
3. Ibid., 154–58.
4. Brooks, *Washington, D.C.*, 55–60.
5. Eisenschiml and Newman, *The American Iliad*, 381.
6. Brooks, *Washington, D.C.*, 54–55.
7. Eisenschiml and Newman, 382.
8. William Southerton, 2.
9. Brooks, *Washington, D.C.*, 56.
10. Darius M. Couch, "The Chancellorsville Campaign," *B&L* 3:155.
11. Brooks, *Washington, D.C.*, 56–58.
12. Bigelow, *The Campaign of Chancellorsville*, 139.
13. OR 25, pt. 2:199–200.
14. Ibid., pt. 1:1066–1067.
15. John Follmer, Apr. 13, 1863.
16. OR 25, pt. 2:214.
17. Weigley, *American Way of War*, 82–87.
18. Montross, *War Through the Ages*, 581–85.
19. OR 25, pt. 2:239–41, 289–90, 316.
20. Ibid., 855.
21. Unknown 140th Pa., Apr. 2, 1863.
22. Paullin, "Early Use of Balloons," 535–41.

6. THAT CRAZY OLD PRESBYTERIAN FOOL

1. Hotchkiss, *Make Me a Map of the Valley*, 126.
2. Sheeran, *Confederate Chaplain*, 39; Jones, *Louisiana Tigers*, 246.
3. Jones, *Christ in Camp*, 157–58.
4. J. G. Webb to mother, n.d.
5. Jones, *Christ in Camp*, 94.
6. Dabney, *Life and Campaigns of Jackson*, 649.
7. Jones, *Christ in Camp*, 89.
8. Vandiver, *Mighty Stonewall*, 55; Henderson, *Stonewall Jackson*, 126; DAB 5:558.
9. Freeman, *Lee's Lieutenants* 1:xlii.
10. Hotchkiss, *Make Me a Map*, 124.
11. Jones, *Christ in Camp*, 302–6.
12. Dabney, 658–59.
13. James Power Smith, "Stonewall Jackson and Chancellorsville," 359–60.
14. Abernathy, "Our Mess."
15. R. A. Pierson to father, Mar. 8, 1863; to sister Apr. 13, 1863.
16. Ibid., to sister, Apr. 5, 1863.
17. La Bree, *Confederate Soldier*, 88.
18. Dabney, 1–40.
19. Henderson, 35.
20. Dabney, 53–57.
21. Ibid., 82.
22. Vandiver, 125–26.
23. Ibid., 124–32.
24. J. J. White to May, June 30, 1861.
25. Vandiver, 152.
26. Boatner, *Civil War Dictionary*, 99.
27. Henderson, 106–13.
28. DAB 5:557.
29. Henderson, 405.
30. Douglas, *I Rode With Stonewall*, 147–58.
31. A. P. Hill to J. E. B. Stuart, Nov. 14, 1862.
32. Hotchkiss, 99.
33. Henderson, 588–89.
34. Douglas, 205.
35. Andrews, *The South Reports the Civil War*, 294–95.
36. Lonn, *Foreigners in the Confederacy*, 475.
37. OR 25, pt. 2:720, 725–26.

38. Ibid., 719.
39. Freeman, *Lee's Lieutenants* 2:519.
40. Ibid., 518–23.

7. INTO THE WILDERNESS

1. William Southerton, 5.
2. Bigelow, *The Campaign of Chancellors-ville*, 132–38. (Bigelow's overall figures are based on Federal returns of April 1863 and Confederate returns of March 1863.)
3. Southerton, 4.
4. Luther B. Mesnard, 25–26.
5. Silliman, *A New Canaan Private*, 25.
6. OR 25, pt. 2:263.
7. Ibid., pt. 1:796.
8. Ibid., pt. 2:273–74.
9. J. Ansel Booth to mother, May 9, 1863.
10. Bigelow, 187–88.
11. John Follmer, Apr. 30, 1863.
12. Von Borcke, *Memoirs of the Confederate War*, 205–6,
13. John Marshall to parents, May 14, 1863.
14. Bull, *Soldiering*, 40; Pittman, "Chancellorsville Campaign," 8; Meysenberg, "Reminiscences of Chancellorsville," 298.
15. J. W. McFarland to editor, May 9, 1863, in Bartlett, *Aunt and the Soldier Boys . . .*, 85.
16. James Houghton, 4.
17. Bacon, "A Michigan Surgeon," 317–18.
18. McFarland, May 9, 1863.
19. Booth, n.d.
20. Bigelow, 191.
21. Unknown 16th N.Y., 2–3.
22. Bigelow, 204–5; Jacob Haas, 27.
23. Wainwright, *A Diary of Battle*, 186.
24. Elon Brown, Apr. 29, 1863.
25. Ibid.
26. Rollin P. Converse to niece, May 13, 1863.
27. Wainwright, 186.
28. Brown, Apr. 29, 1863.
29. OR 25, 1:266–72; Bigelow, 206; Early, *War Memoirs*, 193.

8. HURRAH FOR OLD JOE!

1. Freeman, *Lee's Lieutenants* 2:523.
2. James Power Smith, "Stonewall Jackson's Last Battle," *B&L* 3:203.
3. E. P. Miller, Apr. 29, 1863.
4. Malone, *Whipt 'Em Everytime*, 76.
5. Dickert, *Kershaw's Brigade*, 208.
6. Henry C. Walker to John, May 9, 1863.
7. OR 25, pt. 2:757–58.
8. Freeman, *Lee's Lieutenants* 2:524–25.
9. Early, *War Memoirs*, 194–95.
10. Lafayette McLaws to wife, Apr. 29, 1863.
11. Sue Chancellor, "Recollections of Chancellorsville," 214.
12. Bigelow, *The Campaign of Chancellorsville*, 213; John F. Sale to aunt, May 10, 1863.
13. OR 25, pt. 1:862; Bigelow, 215.
14. Chancellor, 214.
15. Darwin D. Cody to father and mother, May 9, 1863.
16. OR 25, pt. 1:1046.
17. Ibid., pt. 2:305.
18. Alpheus Williams, *From the Cannon's Mouth*, 185.
19. OR 25, pt. 1:171.
20. Swinton, *Campaigns of the Army of the Potomac*, 275.
21. Bull, *Soldiering*, 43.
22. Couch, "Chancellorsville Campaign," *B&L* 3:157.
23. James P. Coburn to folks at home, May 1, 1863.
24. Charles Parker to Edgar, May 15, 1863.
25. Small, *Road to Richmond*, 101–2.
26. OR 25, pt. 2:312.
27. Ibid., 306–15.
28. Ibid., 759, 761.
29. Vandiver, *Mighty Stonewall*, 457.
30. Dabney, *Life and Campaigns of Jackson*, 660.
31. Freeman, *Lee's Lieutenants* 2:527.
32. OR 25, pt. 2:762.
33. Von Borcke, *Memoirs*, 202–3.
34. Bull, *Soldiering*, 41.
35. OR 25, pt. 1:1045–1047.
36. Von Borcke, 208–9.

37. T. T. Munford to J. W. Daniel, Mar. 22, 1907, Bigelow Papers, LC.
38. Bigelow, 226.
39. Von Borcke, 211.
40. Heermance, "Cavalry at Chancellorsville," 224.
41. Munford to Daniel, Mar. 22, 1907.
42. Coxe, "In the Battle of Chancellorsville," 138–41.

9. KEEP CLOSED ON CHANCELLORSVILLE

1. Thomas Herndon, 15.
2. Freeman, *Lee's Lieutenants* 2:528.
3. William K. Calder to mother, May 10, 1863.
4. Norman, *A Portion of My Life*, 169.
5. OR 25, pt. 2:322.
6. Ibid., 336–37.
7. Ibid., 302.
8. Gibbon, *Recollections of the Civil War*, 112–16.
9. OR 25, pt. 1:351–52.
10. Ibid., 198; Bigelow, *The Campaign of Chancellorsville*, 240.
11. OR 25, pt. 1:324.
12. Couch, "The Chancellorsville Campaign," *B&L* 3:159.
13. Freeman, *R. E. Lee* 2:514.
14. Bigelow, 242–45; Freeman, *Lee's Lieutenants* 2:530–33.
15. OR 25, pt. 1:862.
16. Ibid., 863.
17. Westwood Todd, "Reminiscences," 93–95.
18. OR 25, pt. 1:871.
19. Bigelow, 246.
20. Ibid., 250.
21. Couch, B&L 3:159; OR 25, pt. 1:198–99, 525–26.
22. J. Ansel Booth to mother, May 9, 1863.
23. OR 25, pt. 1:670.
24. Bigelow, 248.
25. Washington A. Roebling to Bigelow, Dec. 9, 1910.
26. OR 25, pt. 1:507.

27. Bigelow, 254.
28. Couch, B&L 3:170.
29. Bigelow, 477–478n.
30. OR 25, pt. 2:326.
31. Ibid., pt. 1:800.
32. Freeman, *R. E. Lee* 2:518.
33. Freeman, *Lee's Lieutenants* 2:533–34.
34. Ibid., 535; OR 25, pt. 1:866.
35. Freeman, *Lee's Lieutenants* 2:535–36; Bigelow, 252–53; Moorman, "Narrative of Events," 127; Micajah Martin to father, May 8, 1863.
36. Daly, *Portrait of a Man*, 99–101.
37. OR 25, pt. 2:328.
38. Ibid., 327.
39. Ibid., 329.
40. Ibid., 338.
41. Ibid., 329–39.
42. Bigelow, Map 15, 262.
43. Monat, "Three Years in the 29th Penna. Volunteers," May 1, 1863.
44. Eisenschiml and Newman, *The American Iliad*, 384–85.
45. Meysenberg, "Reminiscences," 299.
46. Weigley, *American Way of War*, 102.
47. Freeman, *R. E. Lee* 2:518–20.
48. Ibid., 516–24; Freeman, *Lee's Lieutenants* 2:538–48; Bigelow, 262–65; Vandiver, *Mighty Stonewall*, 463–68.

10. YOU CAN GO FORWARD, THEN

1. Carlton McCarthy, *Detailed Minutiae of Soldier Life*, 23; Confederate Ordnance Manual, 51.
2. Bigelow, *The Campaign of Chancellorsville*, Map 17, 280.
3. Henderson, *Stonewall Jackson*, 234.
4. Bigelow, 271.
5. Bigelow, Map 16, 274.
6. Oliver O. Howard, "The Eleventh Corps at Chancellorsville," *B&L* 3:195.
7. Bigelow, 276–77.
8. OR 25, pt. 2:360.
9. Ibid., pt. 1:362.
10. DAB 9:150; Hebert, *Fighting Joe Hooker*, 175.
11. OR 25, pt. 1:385–86.

12. Ibid., 408.
13. Lord, *They Fought for the Union*, 144, 160–65; Wiley, *They Who Fought Here*, 112.
14. Eisenschiml and Newman, *The American Iliad*, 392.
15. Jeter Talley, n.d.
16. Bigelow, 281; OR 25, pt. 1:387.
17. Ibid., 980, 934.
18. Ibid., 924.
19. Ibid., 980, 502.
20. Ibid., 387.
21. *Berry Benson's Civil War Book*, 37.
22. Robertson, *A. P. Hill*, 183; Alexander, *Military Memoirs*, 330.
23. William K. Calder to mother, May 10, 1863.
24. Freeman, *Lee's Lieutenants* 2:550.
25. James Power Smith, "Stonewall Jackson's Last Battle," *B&L* 3:206.
26. John L. Collins, "When Stonewall Jackson Turned Our Right," *B&L* 3:183.
27. OR 25, pt. 2:351–53.
28. Bigelow, 329.
29. Early, *War Memoirs*, 199–202.
30. OR 25, pt. 2:355.
31. Early, 202–4.
32. OR 25, pt. 1:645–46, 652–54; Bigelow, 288.
33. Osborn, "On the Right at Chancellorsville," 184–86.
34. OR 25, pt. 1:660–61.
35. Lonn, *Foreigners in the Union Army and Navy*, 180–81.
36. Lonn, 217–18; Rice, *Afield With the Eleventh Army Corps*, 29.
37. Rice, 23–24; Bigelow, 288.
38. Osborn, 186; Bigelow, 288.
39. Bigelow, 291.
40. OR 25, pt. 1:1080.
41. T. T. Munford to Bigelow, Jan. 5, 1909, Bigelow Papers, LC.
42. DAB 8:71–72.
43. Freeman, *Lee's Lieutenants* 2:551.
44. Vandiver, *Mighty Stonewall*, 470.
45. Freeman, *Lee's Lieutenants* 2:552–53; Munford to Bigelow, Jan. 15, 1909, Bigelow Papers, LC.
46. Smith, *B&L* 3:206.
47. Bigelow, 290–92.
48. OR 25, pt. 1:654.
49. A. B. Searles, *Boston Journal*, n.d.
50. OR 25, pt. 1:363.
51. OR 25, pt. 1:941–42.
52. Freeman, *Lee's Lieutenants* 2:558.
53. Smith, *B&L* 3:208.

11. Such a Stampede Never Was Seen

1. William Southerton, 11–13; Luther B. Mesnard, 28–29.
2. Osborn, "On the Right at Chancellorsville," 187; Rice, *Afield With the Eleventh Army Corps*, 2.
3. Lanier, *Tiger-Lilies*, quoted in Solomon, *The Faded Banners*, 53.
4. A. B. Searles, *Boston Journal*, n.d.
5. Rice, 24–25.
6. Silliman, "A New Canaan Private," 31.
7. OR 25, pt. 1:639.
8. Mesnard, 28.
9. Peabody, "Battle of Chancellorsville," 52–53.
10. OR 25, pt. 1:636.
11. Southerton, 13–15.
12. Moore, *Rebellion Record* 1862, 10; ibid., 1862–63, 31.
13. Darwin Cody, 2–3.
14. Freeman, *Lee's Lieutenants* 2:560–61; Vandiver, *Mighty Stonewall*, 476; J. P. Smith, "Stonewall Jackson and Chancellorsville," *B&L* 3:372.
15. W. B. Haygood (?) to Mrs. and Miss Jackson, May 18, 1863.
16. Curtis, "Chancellorsville," 303.
17. OR 25, pt. 1:641–42.
18. Mesnard, 28–29.
19. Ibid., 29–30.
20. Howard, "The Eleventh Corps at Chancellorsville," *B&L* 3:198.
21. San Francisco *Chronicle*, May 23, 1872.
22. OR 25, pt. 1:630; Meysenberg, "Reminiscences of Chancellorsville," 302.
23. Osborn, 188.
24. Peabody, 54.
25. Howard, *B&L* 3:198–99.
26. Cody, 2–3.

27. OR 25, pt. 1:655–56.
28. Ibid., 656.
29. Ibid., 647.
30. Cody, 2–3.
31. Bigelow, *The Campaign of Chancellors-ville*, 301.
32. Washington A. Roebling to Bigelow, Dec. 9, 1910.
33. San Francisco *Chronicle*, May 23, 1872.
34. Hebert, *Fighting Joe Hooker*, 207.
35. Bigelow, 302–3.
36. OR 25, pt. 1:657.
37. James D. Emmons to sister, May 12, 1863.
38. Bigelow, 303–4.
39. OR 25, pt. 1:679; Bigelow, 304–10.
40. Bigelow, 304–5.
41. Pennock Huey, "The Charge of the Eighth Pennsylvania Cavalry," *B&L* 3:186.
42. Bigelow, 317.
43. Andrew B. Wells, *B&L* 3:187–88.
44. John L. Collins, "When Stonewall Jackson Turned Our Right," *B&L* 3:183–84.
45. Wells, 188.
46. OR 25, pt. 1:773.
47. Ibid., 784–85.
48. Ibid., 941.
49. William K. Calder to mother, May 10, 1863.
50. OR 25, pt. 1:975.
51. Osborn, 189.
52. OR 25, pt. 1:984–85.
53. John C. Ussery to father, May 8, 1863.
54. OR 25, pt. 1:951.
55. Ibid., 960–61.
56. Bigelow, 309–10; Capt. James P. Huntington, "The Artillery at Hazel Grove," *B&L* 3:188.
57. Alfred Pleasonton, "The Successes and Failures of Chancellorsville," *B&L* 3:179–80.
58. Huntington, *B&L* 3:188.
59. OR 25, pt. 1:787.
60. Ibid., 249, 504.
61. Ibid., 970.
62. Haygood, May 18, 1863.

12. CHAOS IN THE MOONLIGHT

1. Freeman, *Lee's Lieutenants* 2:562.
2. Lucius B. Swift, "An Enlisted Man in the Chancellorsville Campaign."
3. Moorman, "Narrative of Events," in Webb, *Crucial Moments*, 128–129.
4. OR 25, pt. 1:919.
5. Ibid., 687; Bigelow, *The Campaign of Chancellorsville*, 316.
6. Moorman, 129–30.
7. Kyle, "Jackson's Guide When Shot," CV, May 1896, 308; Dabney, *Life and Campaigns*, 684.
8. Freeman, *Lee's Lieutenants* 2:564; Joseph G. Morrison to R. L. Dabney, Oct. 29, 1863.
9. Kyle, CV, Sept. 1896, 308.
10. Clark, *North Carolina Regiments* 2:100.
11. Freeman, *Lee's Lieutenants* 2:568; Dabney, 656.
12. Freeman, *Lee's Lieutenants* 2:568.
13. Robertson, *A. P. Hill*, 187; Murray Forbes Taylor to CV, n.d., 6.
14. Freeman, *Lee's Lieutenants* 2:569; Dabney, 687–88; Robertson, 188–89.
15. Dabney, 688; Robertson, 188–89.
16. Freeman, *Lee's Lieutenants* 2:572–73.
17. J. P. Smith, "Stonewall Jackson's Last Battle," *B&L* 3:212; Cooke, *Stonewall Jackson*, 425–26.
18. J. P. Smith, *B&L* 3:212.
19. Ibid., 212–13; Freeman, *Lee's Lieutenants* 2:575–76.
20. Robertson, *A. P. Hill*, 189.
21. Bigelow, 323,
22. OR 25, pt. 1:942–43.
23. Von Borcke, *Memoirs*, 228–30; John Follmer, 9; OR 25, pt. 1:1076; Freeman, *Lee's Lieutenants* 2:582.
24. OR 25, pt. 1:389.
25. Theodore Castor, 26.
26. Ibid., 26; Hamlin, *The Battle of Chancellorsville*, 119–22; OR 25, pt. 1:437.
27. Hamlin, 119–22; Williams, *From the Cannon's Mouth*, 194; Bigelow, 326–27; OR 25, pt. 1:418.
28. Hamlin, 120.
29. OR 25, pt. 1:390.
30. Ibid., 887.

31. Jones, *Lee's Tigers*, 146.
32. Dickert, *History of Kershaw's Brigade*, 214, quoting J. F. J. Caldwell, *History of a Brigade of South Carolinians* . . .
33. George W. Hall, diary.
34. Francis S. Johnson, Jr., to Emmie, May 5, 1863.
35. Lane, "How Stonewall Jackson Met His Death," SHSP 8:495.
36. Richard Reeves, memoir.
37. Clark, *N. C. Regiments* 2:100.
38. Joseph Saunders to Editor *Observer*, Jan. 30, 1880.
39. Moorman, "Wounding of Stonewall Jackson," 131; Freeman, *Lee's Lieutenants* 2:577.
40. Dr. Hunter McGuire, "Death of Stonewall Jackson," in *The Confederate Soldier in the Civil War*, 158.
41. Ibid., 158–59; Freeman, *Lee's Lieutenants* 2:581.
42. Freeman, *R. E. Lee* 2:534.
43. OR 25, pt. 2:769.
44. R. E. Wilbourn to Jubal Early, Feb. 12, 1873, in Early, *War Memoirs*, 213–17; Hotchkiss, *Make Me a Map*, 138.
45. Bigelow, 345.

13. So Perfect a Slaughter

1. OR 25, pt. 1:887.
2. Bigelow, *The Campaign of Chancellorsville*, 346; OR 25, pt. 1:925.
3. Alexander, *Military Memoirs*, 342.
4. Huntington, "The Battle of Chancellorsville," *B&L* 3:178.
5. OR 25, pt. 1:414, 924.
6. Alexander, 346; Bigelow, 347–48.
7. J. M. Hood, CV 13:1915.
8. Williams, *From the Cannon's Mouth*, 196–97.
9. OR 25, pt. 1:904, 907.
10. Lane, "How Stonewall Jackson Met His Death," SHSP, 1880, 8:495–96; Bigelow, 349; OR 25, pt. 1:791.
11. Bakeless, *Spies of the Confederacy*, 300.
12. Daniel D. Macomber to Eben, May 15, 1863.

13. Ridge ———, unknown member of Birney's HQ, to Uncle Bloom, May 9, 1863.
14. Bigelow, 350–51; Hassler, *Commanders*, 145–46.
15. OR 25, pt. 1:935.
16. Ibid., 363.
17. Ibid., 712.
18. C. F. Morse to Bigelow, Jan. 13, 1912, Bigelow Papers, LC.
19. OR 25, pt. 1:921.
20. Leroy Cox, 15.
21. OR 25, pt. 1:908.
22. Freeman, *Lee's Lieutenants* 2:592–93.
23. Ibid., 589.
24. OR 25, pt. 1:902–3.
25. Ibid., 1005–1006.
26. Douglas, *I Rode With Stonewall*, 217–18; OR 25, pt. 1:1013.
27. OR 25, pt. 1:1016–1018; Robertson, *Stonewall Brigade*, 186–87.
28. Morse to Bigelow, Jan. 13, 1912.
29. Nick Weekes to Capt. T. C. Witherspoon, Jan. 11, 1903, in Battle, "The 3d Alabama Regiment," 71–75.
30. James H. Lane to A. C. Hamlin, n.d., Lane Papers, Auburn University.
31. OR 25, pt. 1:996; Freeman, *Lee's Lieutenants* 2:596; William Calder to mother, May 10, 1863.
32. Norman, *A Portion of My Life*, 174.
33. OR 25, pt. 1:996, 1014; Freeman, *Lee's Lieutenants* 2:596–97.
34. Calder, May 10, 1863; OR 25, pt. 1:808; Norman, 174–75.
35. J. H. S. Funk to Stephen Dodson Ramseur, May 9, 1863; Ramseur to Funk, May 22, 1863, N.C. Archives, No. 138; OR 25, pt. 1:994–98.
36. George W. Beavers, 1–2.
37. OR 25, pt. 1:488, 993.
38. John C. Ussery to father, May 8, 1863.
39. Griffith, *Battle Tactics of the Civil War*, 85.
40. MacCauley, "From Chancellorsville to Libby Prison," 185–90.
41. Lucius B. Shattuck to mother, May 4, 1863; J. Ansel Booth to mother, May 9,

1863; William Peacock to Sarah, May 6, 1863.
42. OR 25, pt. 2:377.
43. Ibid., 377.

14. LEE'S SUPREME MOMENT

1. Sue Chancellor, "Recollections of Chancellorsville," 214; Darius Couch, "The Chancellorsville Campaign," *B&L* 3:167.
2. Bigelow, *The Campaign of Chancellorsville*, 362.
3. Samuel P. Bates, "Hooker's Comments on Chancellorsville" during an 1876 tour of the field, *B&L* 3:221.
4. Couch, B&L 3:167–68; OR 25, pt. 1:675.
5. OR 25, pt. 2:387–88.
6. Bigelow, 363–64.
7. Couch, *B&L* 3:169–70.
8. OR 25, pt. 1:875.
9. Unknown soldier of 16th Miss., 28–29.
10. W. B. Jennings, 49.
11. OR 25, pt. 1:872, 875, 862–64.
12. Bigelow, 365–66; Boatner, *Civil War Dictionary*, 550.
13. Freeman, *R. E. Lee* 2:538.
14. OR 25, pt. 1:925.
15. Freeman, *Lee's Lieutenants* 2:598.
16. James T. Miller to sister, May 10, 1863.
17. Samuel Lusk to father and mother, May 8, 1863.
18. OR 25, pt. 1:878, 999–1000; Alexander, *Military Memoirs*, 348.
19. Hays, *Under the Red Patch*, 185–86.
20. Chancellor, CV 29:214, 1922.
21. OR 25, pt. 1:490.
22. J. L. Smith to mother, May 5, 1863.
23. Tucker, *Hancock the Superb*, 121–23.
24. OR 25, pt. 1:314; Bigelow, 370; Unknown soldier of 140th Pa., May 3, 1863.
25. David R. E. Winn to wife, May 9, 1863.
26. Marshall, *An Aide-de-Camp of Lee*, 173.
27. Freeman, *R. E. Lee* 2:542.
28. Dabney, 695–96.
29. Dabney, 706–7.
30. Douglas, *I Rode With Stonewall*, 219–20. (Douglas says he himself had this conversation, lasting an hour; Dabney, 708–9,

says Douglas talked to Smith, who relayed it to Jackson.)
31. OR 25, pt. 2:769; Freeman, *R. E. Lee* 2:542–43.
32. OR 25, pt. 2:768.

15. WE'RE GOING TO CUT OUR WAY THROUGH

1. OR 25, pt. 2:365.
2. Ibid., 364–65.
3. OR 25, pt. 1:558.
4. Urbanus Dart to Horace, May 4, 1863.
5. OR 25, pt. 1:558; pt. 2:363.
6. OR 25, pt. 1:353; pt. 2:385; Gibbon, *Recollections of the Civil War*, 112–16; Bigelow, *The Campaign of Chancellorsville*, 383–84.
7. Bigelow, 382; OR 25, pt. 2:385.
8. Charles H. Brewster to Mary, May 10, 1863.
9. Ibid.
10. OR 25, pt. 1:617.
11. Bigelow, 385; Huntington W. Jackson, "Sedgwick at Fredericksburg and Salem Heights," *B&L* 3:227.
12. OR 25, pt. 1:358.
13. Ibid., 559.
14. Jacob Haas to brother, May 12, 1863.
15. Lewis Van Blarcom, reunion speech; OR 25, pt. 1:590.
16. Freeman, *Lee's Lieutenants* 2:613; Early, *War Memoirs*, 204–6.
17. OR 25, pt. 1:856.
18. Ibid., 559, 599)
19. Early, 206–7; Bigelow, 386–87.
20. Brewster, May 10, 1863.
21. Morton Hayward to sister, May 24, 1863.
22. Jackson, *B&L* 3:228–29; Bigelow, 389–91.
23. OR 25, pt. 1:599–600, 602–3, 609; Jones, *Lee's Tigers*, 152–53.
24. William F. Stowe to parents, May 15, 1863.
25. Thomas J. Lutman and Union soldier, May 2, 3, 1863.
26. Unknown soldier of 16th N.Y., n.d.
27. Jackson, *B&L* 3:230.
28. Stowe to parents, May 10, 1863.

29. Freeman, *Lee's Lieutenants* 2:617–18.
30. Ibid., 623–24.
31. OR 25, pt. 1:857.
32. Marius Oestreich, May 3, 1863.
33. Eisenschiml and Newman, *The American Iliad*, 405–6.
34. McGlashan, "Battle of Salem Church," 90–91.
35. R. E. Colston, "Lee's Knowledge of Hooker's Movements," *B&L* 3:233.
36. OR 25, pt. 1:1007.
37. OR 25, pt. 2:377.
38. Ibid., 379.
39. Ibid., 378.

16. FIRE IN THE PULPIT
1. OR 25, pt. 1:856–57.
2. Ibid., 826–27.
3. Unknown soldier of 16th N.Y., n.d.
4. OR 25, pt. 1:858.
5. Unknown soldier of 16th N.Y.
6. Mollie Orrock.
7. Jacob Haas to brother, May 12, 1863.
8. Unknown soldier of 10th Ga., 4–5.
9. McGlashan, "Battle of Salem Church," 92.
10. Unknown soldier of 16th N.Y.
11. OR 25, pt. 1:586, 618, 835, 858–59; Charles H. Brewster to Mary, May 10, 1863.
12. Unknown soldier of 10th Ga.
13. McGlashan, 92–93.
14. OR 25, pt. 2:381.
15. OR 25, pt. 1:1060.
16. E. W. Rowe to William McCauley, May 11, 1863.
17. Isaac Dunkelberger, memoir.
18. OR 25, pt. 1:1060–1061.
19. OR 25, pt. 2:769.
20. Ibid., 770.
21. Ibid., 770.
22. Von Borcke, *Memoirs* 2:244–46.
23. Bigelow, *The Campaign of Chancellorsville*, 403.
24. OR 25, pt. 1:203.
25. Bigelow, 403.
26. Couch, "The Chancellorsville Campaign," *B&L* 3:170.

27. Washington A. Roebling to Bigelow, Jan. 9, 1910.
28. Robert G. Carter, notes to Dodge's *Campaign of Chancellorsville*. Carter makes the same case almost as forcefully in his *Four Brothers in Blue*.
29. Hitchcock, *War from the Inside*, 228–29.
30. Wainwright, *A Diary of Battle*, 197.
31. OR 25, pt. 2:402–4.

17. EVERY HAT RAISED HIGH
1. DAB 4:424.
2. Stiles, *Four Years Under Marse Robert*, 212; Urbanus Dart to Horace, May 4, 1863.
3. Henry C. Walker to John, May 9, 1863.
4. Early, *War Memoirs*, 221–24.
5. William C. Mathews to father, May 8, 1863.
6. Early, 225.
7. DAB 9:361.
8. Early, 226.
9. Ibid., 226–27; OR 25, pt. 1:827.
10. OR 25, pt. 1:879–80, 852; Williams, *From the Cannon's Mouth*, 200.
11. OR 25, pt. 1:801–2.
12. Ibid., 802; Freeman, *R. E. Lee*, 552.
13. Bigelow, *The Campaign of Chancellorsville*, 416.
14. Wainwright, *A Diary of Battle*, 199.
15. Marcus L. Green, diary.
16. OR 25, pt. 2:414–15; William F. Stowe to parents, May 10, 1863.
17. W. B. Jennings, 51.
18. Early, 227–28; OR 25, pt. 1:802.
19. Jones, *Lee's Tigers*, 152–53; R. A. Pierson to father, May 8, 1863.
20. Jones, 155.
21. Dart, May 4, 1863.
22. Mathews, May 8, 1863.
23. George M. Bandy to William Strain and family, May 8, 1863.
24. Early, 229–30; OR 25, pt. 1:610; Dart, May 4, 1863.
25. Stowe to parents, May 10, 22, 1863.
26. Early, 229–30; Pierson to sister, May 9, 1863.

27. Micajah Martin to father, May 8, 1863; OR 25, pt. 1:869.
28. OR 25, pt. 1:872, 876.
29. Ibid., 828.
30. Freeman, *R. E. Lee,* 2:554–555.
31. Unknown soldier of 16th N.Y.
32. Luther C. Furst, diary.
33. OR 25, pt. 1:828, 802.
34. OR 25, pt. 2:407–8.
35. Ibid., 408.
36. Ibid., 409–10.
37. Ibid., 409; Bigelow, 411–15.
38. OR 25, pt. 2:412.
39. Ibid., 412–13.
40. Ibid., 412.
41. Ibid., 418–19.
42. OR 25, pt. 1:802.
43. Ibid., 802.
44. Couch, "The Chancellorsville Campaign," *B&L* 3:171; Bigelow, 419.

18. LET US CROSS OVER THE RIVER

1. Lucy Chandler Pendleton, Reminiscences to E. T. Stuart, May 30, 1930, 1; Freeman, *Lee's Lieutenants* 2:641.
2. Freeman, Lee's *Lieutenants* 2:635.
3. Hotchkiss, *Make Me a Map,* 140.
4. Dr. Hunter McGuire, "Death of Stonewall Jackson," *Confederate Soldier in the Civil War,* 159.
5. Pendleton, 2–3.
6. Unknown soldier of 10th Ga., 3–4.
7. J. W. McFarland to editor, May 9, 1863, in Bartlett, *Aunt and the Soldier Boys . . . ,* 85.
8. Osborn, "On the Right at Chancellorsville," 190–91.
9. Robert McMillen, memoir.
10. Urbanus Dart to Horace, May 7, 1863.
11. OR 25, pt. 1:829.
12. Unknown soldier of 10th Ga., memoir.
13. Bull, *Soldiering,* 75–76.
14. OR 25, pt. 2:421–22.
15. Bigelow, *The Campaign of Chancellorsville,* 423.

16. James C. Biddle, letter May 8, 1863, in A. S. Webb, "Meade at Chancellorsville," 234–35.
17. Williams, *From the Cannon's Mouth,* 201.
18. James P. Coburn to folks at home, May 8, 1863.
19. C. F. Morse to Bigelow, Jan. 13, 1912.
20. Washington A. Roebling to Bigelow, Jan. 9, 1910.
21. Wainwright, *A Diary of Battle,* 200.
22. Biddle, May 8, 1863, in A. S. Webb, 235; Bigelow, 427.
23. Biddle, May 8, 1863, in A. S. Webb, 235–36; Couch, "The Chancellorsville Campaign," *B&L* 3:171.
24. Couch, 171.
25. William Southerton, 17; Wainwright, 201.
26. Biddle, May 8, 1863, in A. S. Webb, 236; Southerton, 18.
27. Morse, Jan. 13, 1912; Biddle, May 9, 1863, in A. S. Webb, 236.
28. OR 25, pt. 2:779.
29. Freeman, *R. E. Lee,* 557.
30. J. L. Smith to mother, May 8, 1863.
31. Bigelow, 432; Smith, May 8, 1863.
32. OR 25, pt. 2:434.
33. Brooks, *Washington, D.C.,* 60; OR 25, pt. 2:434.
34. Brooks, *Mr. Lincoln's Washington,* 179.
35. Brooks, *Washington, D.C.,* 60–61.
36. OR 25, pt. 2:435.
37. Brooks, *Mr. Lincoln's Washington,* 180–81.
38. OR 25, pt. 1:171.
39. J. L. Smith, May 8, 1863.
40. OR 25, pt. 1:805.
41. Hotchkiss and Allan, *Chancellorsville,* 101.
42. Bull, *Soldiering,* 68, 73.
43. OR 25, pt. 2-1086–1087.
44. Ibid., 1083–1084.
45. OR 25, pt. 1:777–78.
46. Hotchkiss, *Make Me a Map,* 140; MacCauley, "From Chancellorsville to Libby Prison," 196–98; Dabney, *Life and Campaigns of Jackson,* 715.
47. Dabney, 716–17.

48. Lucy Chandler Pendleton to E. T. Stuart, May 30, 1930; Dabney, 715.
49. Dabney, 714–15.
50. Ibid., 716.
51. Beverly C. Smith to Col. Beverly M. Read, May 19, 1975.
52. McGuire, 159–60; Samuel B. Morrison to uncle, May 13, 1863.
53. Morrison, May 13, 1863.
54. Dabney, 721.
55. McGuire, 160.

15. George B. Walcott to uncle and aunt, May 13, 1863; Mattocks, "Major General Joseph Hooker," 219.
16. San Francisco *Chronicle,* May 23, 1872.
17. OR 25, pt. 1:658–60.
18. This section is based on Bigelow, *The Campaign of Chancellorsville,* 473–88; Freeman, *Lee's Lieutenants* 2:644–48; Freeman, *R. E. Lee* 2:584–89, and *R. E. Lee* 3:1–7; Henderson, *Stonewall Jackson,* 698–713; Stackpole, *Chancellorsville,* 359–72; and other studies.
19. Hebert, 223.

19. UP LIKE A ROCKET, DOWN LIKE A STICK

1. Bigelow, *The Campaign of Chancellorsville,* 505; OR 25, pt. 1:192, 809.
2. Welles, *Diary* 1:291–93; Sandburg, *Abraham Lincoln* 2:97.
3. Williams, *Lincoln and His Generals,* 243; Sandburg, 364; Charles F. Benjamin, "Hooker's Appointment and Removal," *B&L* 3:240–41.
4. OR 25, pt. 2:438.
5. Ibid., 438.
6. Benjamin, B&L 3:241; Hebert, *Fighting Joe Hooker,* 226.
7. Hebert, 227–29.
8. Wainwright, *A Diary of Battle,* 202.
9. George A. Custer to George B. McClellan, May 6, 1863.
10. John Gibbon to McClellan, May 18, 1863.
11. Wainwright, 202–3.
12. C. F. Morse to Bigelow, Jan. 13, 1912, quoting his letter of May 7, 1863.
13. Washington A. Roebling to Bigelow, Jan. 9, 1910.
14. Edward H. C. Taylor to sister Lottie, May 7, 12, 1863.

EPILOGUE. THE LOST, LOST FIGHT

1. Lucy Chandler Pendleton to E. T. Stuart, May 30, 1930.
2. Gordon W. Jones, "Ellwood," 20.
3. Dabney, *Life and Campaigns of Jackson,* 728–29; OR 25, pt. 2:793.
4. Ibid., 729–33; Freeman, *Lee's Lieutenants* 2:683–86.
5. R. A. Pierson to father, May 8, 1863.
6. L. Calhoun Cooper to mother, May 18, 1863.
7. Frederick H. West to sister Maggie, May 18, 1863.
8. Freeman, *Lee's Lieutenants* 3:16.
9. Freeman, *R. E. Lee* 2:690.
10. Henderson, *Stonewall Jackson,* 331–32.
11. Freeman, *Lee's Lieutenants* 2:695–96.
12. OR 27, 3:31.
13. Ibid., 1:39–40.
14. Ibid., 1:45.
15. Hebert, *Fighting Joe Hooker,* 239–45.
16. Henderson, 699.
17. Freeman, *R. E. Lee* 3:153; James Longstreet, "Lee's Invasion of Pennsylvania," *B&L* 3:245.

Sources

For their patient cooperation, I owe special thanks to the staff of the Fredericksburg and Spotsylvania National Military Park. I also am grateful for the promptness and professionalism of those at the U.S. Army Military History Institute at Carlisle Barracks, the Library of Congress, the National Archives, and the institutions below.

For soldiers whose letters, diaries, or personal reminiscences are quoted, I have tried to cite their units at Chancellorsville. For memoirists who later advanced in seniority, I have tried to note their ranks during this campaign. When the documents of a single soldier have been collected or edited by someone else, I have listed them by writer rather than editor. The following abbreviations are used for the collections and publications most frequently cited:

B&L *Battles and Leaders.*
CV *Confederate Veteran.*
CWRT Civil War Roundtable.
CWTI *Civil War Times Illustrated.*
DAB *Dictionary of American Biography.*
Duke William R. Perkins Library, Duke University.
FSNMP Fredericksburg and Spotsylvania National Military Park.
GDAH Georgia Department of Archives and History.
LC Manuscripts Division, Library of Congress.
MOLLUS Military Order of the Loyal Legion of the United States.
OR *War of the Rebellion,* Official Records.
SHC Southern Historical Collection, University of North Carolina.
Tulane Howard-Tilton Memorial Library, Tulane University.
USAMHI U.S. Army Military History Institute.

Alabama Department of Archives and History.
Emory University.
Georgia Room, University of Georgia.
Hill Memorial Library, Louisiana State University.
Indiana Historical Society.
Kennesaw Mountain National Military Park.
Bentley Historical Library, University of Michigan.

William L. Clements Library, University of Michigan.
Mississippi Historical Society.
University of Mississippi.
New Jersey Historical Society.
New-York Historical Society.
Northampton Historical Society.
Ohio Historical Society.
University of Rochester.
Alderman Library, University of Virginia.
Virginia Historical Society.
West Virginia and Regional History Collection, West Virginia University.

Manuscripts

Abernathy, W. M., Co. B, 17th Miss. "Our Mess: Southern Army Gallantry and Privations, 1861–1865." Mississippi Department of Archives and History.
Adams, C. E., Sgt., 2nd Va. Cavalry. Letter. Bigelow Papers, LC.
Baer, George F. Letter. Bigelow Papers, LC.
Barron, Alfred Benton, Co. K, 24th Ga. Letter. CW Miscellany, Personal Papers, GDAH.
Barton, Randolph. Letter. Bigelow Papers, LC.
Battle, Cullen Andrew, Col., 3rd Ala. "The 3d Alabama Regiment," written 1905. Papers of Rev. J. H. B. Hall. Alabama Department of Archives and History.
Beavers, Sgt. Geo. W., Co. D, 44th Ga. Memoir. GDAH.
Beem, Capt. David, 14th Ind. Letters. Beem Collection, Indiana Historical Society.
Bellows, Henry W., Chairman of Sanitary Commission. Letter. Bigelow Papers, LC.
Blackford, Eugene, Maj., 5th Ala. Letters. Confederate Mss., USAMHI.
Booth, J. Ansel, Co. D, 140th N.Y. Letters. Vol. 123, FSNMP.
Brett, Martin W., Co. F, 12th Ga. Memoir. Vol. 26, FSNMP.
Brewster, Charles H., adjutant 10th Mass. Letter. Northampton Historical Society, Northampton, Mass.
Brown, Elon F., 2nd Wis. Account of Chancellorsville written in hospital at Frederick, Md. CWTI Collection, USAMHI.
Calder, William K., 2nd N.C. Letters. Calder Papers, SHC.
Carter, Robert G., 22nd Mass. Annotations to C. A. Dodge's *Chancellorsville*. Vol. 32, FSNMP.
Castor, Theodore, Co. C, 3rd Mich. Memoir. Vol. 46, FSNMP.
Chandler, Silas, Woolfolk's Battery, Va. Artillery. Letter. Vol. 5, FSNMP.
Coburn, James P., 141st Pa. Letters and Diary. Coburn Family Papers, USAMHI.
Cody, Darwin Dianthus, 1st Ohio Light Battery. Letter. Vol. 37, FSNMP.
Converse, Rollin P., Capt., 6th Wis. Letter. Chicago Historical Society.
Cooper, L. Calhoun, Sgt., Troup Artillery. Letters. No. Ga.-15, Kennesaw Mountain NMP.
Cox, Leroy W., 46th Va. "Memoirs of Leroy Wesley Cox, Experiences of a Young Soldier of the Confederacy," as related to Ruth Ritchie. Virginia Historical Society.
Critz, Joe, N.Y. Letter. Vol. 46, FSNMP.
Crocker, John S., Col., 93rd N.Y. Letters. Brockett Collection, Dept. of Manuscripts and University Archives, Cornell University.
Cross, Fred Wilder. "Historic People and Places in the Chancellorsville, Wilderness and Spotsylvania Court House Region." FSNMP.

Custer, George Armstrong, Capt. Letter. McClellan Papers, Reel 35, LC.

Dame, William Meade, Pvt., 1st Co., Richmond Howitzers. Letters. Virginia Historical Society.

Dart, Urbanus, Jr., Pvt., 26th Ga. Letter. Dart Family Papers, Letters of Horace Dart, GDAH.

Dunbar, John B. Letter. Bigelow Papers, LC.

Dunkelburger, Isaac R., 1st U.S. Cavalry. Memoir. Michael Winey Collection, USAMHI.

Emmons, James D., 154th N.Y. Letter. Michael Winey Collection, USAMHI.

Evans, William J., Capt., 7th N.J. Letters. Evans Papers, Ms. Group 1149, New Jersey Historical Society.

Fell, Albinus R., 6th Ohio Cavalry. Letters. CW Miscellaneous Collection, USAMHI.

Firebaugh, Samuel Angus, Co. H, 10th Va. Diary. SHC.

Fisher, Samuel, 4th N.J. Letter. Lewis Leigh Collection, Book 24, USAMHI.

Follmer, John, 16th Pa. Cavalry. Diary. Bentley Historical Library, University of Michigan.

Funk, J. H. S., Col., 5th Va. Letter. Ramseur Papers, N.C. Archives.

Furst, Luther C., 39th Pa. Diary. Harrisburg CWRT Collection, USAMHI.

Gibbon, John. Letter. Reel 35, McClellan Papers, LC.

Giles, J. E., Letter. Nov 21, 1908. Bigelow Papers, LC.

Gillespie, Jasper A., Co. B, 45th Ga. Letter. GDAH.

Gilpin, E. N. Letter. Bigelow Papers, LC.

Gouldsberry, Thomas, Co. H, 84th Pa. Letter. Vol. 37, FSNMP.

Green, Marcus L., Pvt., Phillips Legion. Diary. Kennesaw Mountain NMP.

Haas, Jacob W., Capt., Co. G, 96th Pa. Diary and Letters. Harrisburg CWRT Collection, USAMHI.

Hadaway, W. K., Co. K, 24th Ga. Letter. GDAH.

Hall, George W., Co. G, 14th Ga. Diary. Hargrett Rare Book and Manuscript Library, University of Georgia.

Hall, Woodbury, Lt., 3rd Me. Letter. Leigh Collection, USAMHI.

Haskell, Alexander Cheves, Capt., McGowan's adjutant. Letters. Haskell Papers, SHC.

Haygood, W. B., Capt., Co. C, 44th Ga. Unsigned letter believed by him. Edward Harden Papers, Duke.

Hayward, Morton, 7th Mass. Letters. Lewis Leigh Collection, Book 24, USAMHI.

Herndon, Thomas, Capt., Co. L, 14 Tenn. Diary including will. Vol. 130, FSNMP.

Higley, Albert E., 22nd N.Y. Letters. Vol. 47, FSNMP.

Hill, Ambrose Powell. Letter. Stuart Papers, Virginia Historical Society.

Hillyer, Francis Lorraine, 3rd Ga. Letter. Vol. 26, FSNMP.

Hillyer, Isaac, 28th N.J. Letter. Vol. 33, FSNMP.

Houghton, James, 4th Mich. Journal. Bentley Historical Library, University of Michigan.

Huidekoper, Frederic L. Letter. Bigelow Papers, LC.

Hunt, H. N., 64th N.Y. Letter. Vol. 17, FSNMP.

Hunt, Isaac P., Capt., 161st N.Y. Diary. CW Miscellaneous Collection, USAMHI.

Jennings, W. B., Co. G, 22nd Ga. Memoir. Presented to United Daughters of the Confederacy, Georgia. Vol. 127, FSNMP.

Johnson, Charles R., 16th Mass. Letter. Harrisburg CWRT and William Prince Collections, USAMHI.

Johnson, Francis Solomon, Jr., Co. F, 45th Ga. Letters. Special Collections, Hargrett Rare Book and Manuscript Library, University of Georgia.

Kelly, Reuben, 12th U.S. Infantry. Letters. Vol. 123, FSNMP.

Kirkpatrick, James J., 1st Sgt., Co. C, 16th Miss. Diary. Vol. 125, FSNMP.

Laird, James, 24th Mich. Letters. Vol. 33, FSNMP.

Lee, Wills, 2nd Co., Richmond Howitzers. Memoir. Vol. 138, FSNMP.

Lemont, Frank Lindley, Capt., 5th Me. Letters. Vol. 33, FSNMP.

Lewis, John, 17th Conn. Letter. Leigh Collection, USAMHI.

Littlefield, Charles H., 21st Conn. Letters. CW Miscellaneous Collection, USAMHI.

Lusk, Samuel R., Sgt., 137th N.Y. Letter. Vol. 117, FSNMP.

Lutman, Thos. J., Cpl., 1st Co., Washington Artillery. Diary with Federal soldier's entry after Lutman's death. Civil War Library and Museum, Philadelphia.

McArthur, Charles W., Maj., 61st Ga. Letters. Kennesaw Mountain NMP.

McCarthy, Dennis J., 104th N.Y. Letters. McCarthy Papers, Folder 1863, USAMHI.

McIntosh, David G., Maj., CSA. Letter. Bigelow Papers, LC.

McLaws, Lafayette, Maj. Gen., CSA. Letter. McLaws Papers, No. 472, SHC.

McMillen, Robert, Col., 24th Ga. Memoir. CW Miscellany, Personal Papers, GDAH.

Macomber, Daniel D., 1st Mass. Letter. Lewis Leigh Collection, Book 6, USAMHI.

Marshall, John, 123rd N.Y. Letter. New-York Historical Society.

Marshborne, Samuel W., Capt., Co. C, 53rd Ga. Letter. Vol. 113, FSNMP.

Masten, W. L., Lt., Co. D, 21st N.C. Letter. FSNMP.

Mathews, William C., Co. G, 38th Ga. Letter. *The Central Georgian*, June 3, 1863. Vol. 128, FSNMP.

Mesnard, Luther B., Co. D, 55th Ohio. Memoir. CW Miscellaneous Collection, USAMHI.

Miller, E. P., Lt., Co. K, 17th Miss. "Life in the Camp and on the Field." Diary. Vol. 63, FSNMP.

Miller, James T., 111th Pa. Letters. Schoff Civil War Collection, Soldiers' Letters Series, Clements Library, University of Michigan.

Mitchell, John R., 140th Pa. Diary. Mitchell Collection, USAMHI.

Monat, David, 29th Pa. "Three Years in the 29th Pennsylvania Volunteers." Journal. Vol. 43, FSNMP.

Moore, Joseph Addison, Capt., Co. B, 147th Pa. Memoir. CW Miscellaneous Collection, USAMHI.

Moore, William A., 82nd N.Y. and 3rd N.Y. Artillery. Memoir. CW Miscellaneous Collection, USAMHI.

Morrison, Joseph Graham, Capt., 57th N.C. Jackson's aide and brother-in-law. Letter. Charles William Dabney Papers, SHC.

Morrison, Samuel Brown. Letter. Special Collections, Florida Atlantic University.

Morse, C. F., Capt., Twelfth Corps. Letter. Bigelow Papers, LC.

Munford, Thomas T., Col., 2nd Va. Cavalry. Letters. Bigelow Papers, LC.

————. Letters. John W. Daniel Papers, Duke.

Oestreich, Marius, 96th Pa. Diary. Harrisburg CWRT Collection, USAMHI.

Orrock, Mollie. Salem Church historical materials in possession of Miss Mollie Orrock, June 1977. Vol. 4, FSNMP.

Paige, Charles C., Co. I, 11th N.H. Diary. Wendell W. Long Collection, USAMHI.

Parker, Charles, HQ Root's Brigade, First Corps. Letter. Schoff Civil War Collection, Letters and Documents Series, Clements Library, University of Michigan.

Peacock, William H., Sgt., 5th Mass. Battery. Letters. Vols. 34, 108, FSNMP.

Pendleton, Lucy Chandler. Reminiscences to Edward T. Stuart at Jackson Shrine, Guiney Station, May 30, 1930. Vol. 51, FSNMP.

Pennington, George W., 141st Pa. Letters. Vol. 121, FSNMP.

Pierson, R. A., 9th La. Letters. Rosamonde E. and Emile Kuntz Collection, Manuscripts Section, Howard-Tilton Memorial Library, Tulane University.

Plumb, Isaac, Capt., Co. C, 61st N.Y. Diary. CW Miscellaneous Collection, USAMHI.

Powers, Kenneth H., 67th N.Y. Vol. 45, FSNMP.

Price, R. Channing, Maj., Stuart's adjutant. Letter. Price Papers, SHC.

Pryor, Shepard Green, 12th Ga. Letters. Pryor Papers, University of Georgia.

Ramseur, Stephen Dodson, Brig. Gen., CSA. Letters. Ramseur Papers, N.C. Archives.

Reeves, Richard Martin Van Buren, Co. E, 18th N.C. "Our Confederate Veterans." Memoir. Cape Fear Chapter, United Daughters of the Confederacy. Confederate Veteran Papers, Duke.

Robinson, John S., 27th Conn. Letter. Vol. 117, FSNMP.

Rodenbaugh, Theophilus F., Capt., 2nd U.S. Cavalry. Letter. Bigelow Papers, LC.

Roebling, Washington Augustus. Letter. Bigelow Papers, LC.

Rowe, E. W. Letter. SHC.

Sale, John F., Co. H, 12th Va. Letter. Vol. 3, FSNMP.

Saunders, Joseph H., Col., 33rd N.C. Letter. Saunders Papers, SHC.

Shattuck, Lucius B., 24th Mich. Letter. Michigan Historical Collection, Bentley Library, University of Michigan.

Sickles, Daniel E., Maj. Gen. Letter. Bigelow Papers, LC.

Smith, John L., 118th Pa. Letters. Vol. 44, FSNMP.

Southerton, William B., 75th Ohio. Reminiscences. Ohio Historical Society.

Stanley, Thomas W., 5th N.J. Letter. Vol. 32, FSNMP.

Steffan, Edward W., Sgt., 121st Pa. Letters. Vol. 115, FSNMP.

Stephenson, Luther, 32nd Mass. Letter. Bigelow Papers, LC.

Stilwell, W. R., 53rd Ga. Letters. WPA Project 5993, Letters from Confederate Soldiers, Vol. 11, GDAH.

Stowe, William F., 2nd Vt. Letters. Vol. 47, FSNMP.

Strouse, Ellis C., Co. K, 57th Pa. Letter. *CWTI* Collection, USAMHI.

Swift, Lucius B., Sgt., 28th N.Y. "An Enlisted Man in the Chancellorsville Campaign." Bigelow Papers, LC.

Tallman, William H., 66th Ohio. Memoir. Charles Rhodes Collection, USAMHI.

Taylor, Edward H. C., 4th Mich. Letters. Taylor Papers, Michigan Historical Collection, Bentley Library, University of Michigan.

Taylor, Murray Forbes. Letters. Bigelow Papers, LC.

Tiffany, John, Lt., Co. D, 27th Va. Letter. Vol. 139, FSNMP.

Tilton, William, Col., 22nd Mass. Account of Chancellorsville. Joshua Chamberlain Papers, LC.

Tinsley, Davis, Lt., Co. H, 4th Ga. Letter. United Daughters of the Confederacy. Vol. 10, GDAH.

Todd, Joseph, Battery F, Pa. Light Artillery. Diary. CW Miscellaneous Collection, USAMHI.

Todd, Westwood A., Co. E, 12th Va. "Reminiscences of the War Between the States 1861–1865," SHC.

Toffey, John James, Co. C, 21st N.J. Letters. Vol. 68, FSNMP.

Treichler, James M., Sgt. Maj., Co. H, 96th Pa. Memoir. Vol. 41, FSNMP.

Tyler, Cyril H., 7th Mich. Letter. Tyler Papers, Duke.

Unknown: Ridge ———, officer in HQ Birney's Division. Letter. Archives & Manuscripts Section, West Virginia Collection, West Virginia University Library.

Unknown: Will ———, 27th Conn. Letter. Vol. 119, FSNMP.

Unknown: Soldier of 10th Ga. Memoir of Salem Church. CW Unit File, 10th Ga., GDAH.

Unknown: Soldier of 16th Miss. Memoir. Louisiana Historical Association Collection, Tulane.

Unknown: Soldier of 16th N.Y. Memoir, "Fredericksburg During the Civil War." Schoff Collection, Bentley Library, University of Michigan.

Unknown: Laird ———, 4th Ohio. Letter. Geo. S. Lester Papers, Dept. of Archives and Manuscripts, Louisiana State University.

Unknown: Soldier of 140th Pa. Letters. Timothy Brookes Collection, USAMHI.

Ussery, John C., 23rd N.C. Letter. Vol. 130, FSNMP.

Veil, Charles Henry, Co. G, 38th Pa. Memoir, "An Old Boy's Personal Reminiscences of the Civil War." CW Miscellaneous Collection, USAMHI.

Wade, Edward H., 14th Conn. Letters. Schoff Civil War Collection, Soldiers' Letters Series, Clements Library, University of Michigan.

Walcott, George B., Co. E, 44th N.Y. Letter. Vol. 110, FSNMP.

Walker, Henry C., Co. K, 13th Ga. Letter. CW Miscellany, Personal Papers, GDAH.

Wallace, John G., Capt., Co. C, 61st Va. Diary. Vol. 3, FSNMP.

Webb, John G., Co. D, 9th Ga. Letter. Lewis Leigh Collection, Book 32, USAMHI.

West, Frederick H., Adjutant, 51st Ga. Letter. Vol. 4, FSNMP.

White, James Jones, 4th Va. Letter. White Papers, SHC.

Wilbur, Joshua G., Surgeon, 18th Mass. Letters. Vol. 70, FSNMP.

Williams, Albert B., 122nd N.Y. Letter. Williams Papers, University of Rochester.

Wills, Henry H., Bedford Artillery. Letters. Vol. 65, FSNMP.

Wilson, J., 16th Miss. Letters. University of Mississippi microfilm.

Winn, David R. E., Lt. Col., 4th Ga. Letter. Emory University.

Printed Letters and Memoirs

Abernathy, W. M., 17th Miss. "Our Mess: Southern Army Gallantry and Privations, 1861–1865." Mississippi Dept. of Archives and History.

Alexander, Edward Porter, Col., CSA. *Military Memoirs of a Confederate.* New York: Scribner's, 1907.

Armstrong, Thomas A., Co. I, 139th Pa. Dispatch to Pittsburgh *Chronicle* in "The Road to Cold Harbor." *The History of Pennsylvania Volunteers 1861–65,* by Samuel P. Bates. Vol. 116, FSNMP.

Bacon, Cyrus, Surgeon, 14th Mich. "A Michigan Surgeon at Chancellorsville One Hundred Years Ago." *University of Michigan Medical Bulletin* 29, 1963.

Bandy, George M., Co. D, 60th Ga. Letter, May 15. *The Strain Family.* Toccoa, Ga.: Commercial Printing Company, 1985.

Bartlett, William H., Col., USA Ret. Ed., *Aunt and the Soldier Boys from Cross Creek Village, Pa. 1856–1866.* Santa Cruz, Calif.: Moore's Graphic Arts, n.d.

Benson, Berry, 1st S.C. *Berry Benson's Civil War Book: Memoirs of a Confederate Scout and Sharpshooter.* Athens: University of Georgia, 1966.

Bull, Rice C., 123rd N.Y. *Soldiering in the Civil War: The Diary of Rice C. Bull, 123rd N.Y. Volunteer Infantry.* San Francisco: Presidio, 1977.

Chancellor, Sue. "Recollections of Chancellorsville." CV 29, 1921.

Coxe, John, Co. B, 2nd S.C. "In the Battle of Chancellorsville." CV 30, 1922.

Curtis, Finley Paul, Jr. "Chancellorsville." CV 25, 1917.

Cushing, Wainwright, Lt. "The Charge of the Light Division at Marye's Heights." *War Papers.* Vol. 3. Portland: MOLLUS Maine, 1908.

Dame, William Meade, 1st Richmond Howitzers. *From the Rapidan to Richmond.* Baltimore: Green Lucas Company, 1920.

De Trobriand, Regis, Col., 38th N.Y. *Four Years With the Army of the Potomac.* Boston: Ticknor & Co., 1889.

Dickert, D. Augustus. *History of Kershaw's Brigade.* Reprint. Dayton: Morningside, 1976.

Early, Jubal Anderson, Maj. Gen., CSA. *War Memoirs: Autobiographical Sketch and Narrative of the War Between the States.* Bloomington: Indiana University, 1960.

Farley, Porter, Capt., 140th N.Y. "Reminiscences of the 140th Regiment New York Volunteer Infantry." *Rochester in the Civil War.* Rochester: Rochester Historical Society, 1944.

Fitzpatrick, Marion Hill, Sgt. Maj., 45th Ga. *Letters to Amanda.* Culloden, Ga.: Mansell Hammock, Inc., 1976.

Galwey, Thomas Francis, Lt., 8th Ohio. *The Valiant Hours: Narrative of 'Captain Brevet,' an Irish-American in The Army of the Potomac.* Harrisburg: Stackpole, 1961.

Gibbon, John, Maj. Gen., USA. *Recollections of the Civil War.* New York: Putnam, 1928.

Giles, J. E., Capt., 8th Pa. Cavalry. "The Famous Charge of the 8th Pennsylvania Cavalry at Chancellorsville." *Grand Army Scout and Soldiers' Mail,* March 10 and April 14, 1883.

Gordon, John B., Brig. Gen., CSA. *Reminiscences of the Civil War.* New York: Scribner's, 1903.

Grow, Milo, Co. D, 51st Ga. Letters. Published for Grow family reunion at Lake Seminole, Ga., 1986. Vol. 128, FSNMP.

Hamlin, Augustus C., Eleventh Corps. *The Battle of Chancellorsville.* Bangor: Privately printed, 1896.

Heermance, W.L., Capt., 6th N.Y. Cavalry. "The Cavalry at Chancellorsville," in *Personal Recollections of the War of the Rebellion,* 2nd series, MOLLUS, New York: 1897.

Herbert, Hilary A., Lt. Col., 8th Ala. "Grandfather's Talks About His Life Under Two Flags." Privately printed, 1903. SHC.

Hess, Frank W., Maj., 3rd Pa. Cavalry. "The First Cavalry Battle at Kelly's Ford, Va." *First Maine Bugle.* Rockland: First Maine Cavalry Association, 1893.

Hitchcock, Frederick L., Maj., 132nd Pa. *War from the Inside.* Philadelphia: Lippincott, 1904.

Hood, J. M., Sgt., 1st S.C. "The Battle of Chancellorsville." CV 23, 1915.

Hooker, Joseph. Maj. Gen. " 'Fighting Joe' Hooker: He Fights the Battle of Chancellorsville Over Again." San Francisco *Chronicle,* May 23, 1872.

Hotchkiss, Jedediah, Jackson's topographical engineer. *Make Me a Map of the Valley.* Dallas: Southern Methodist University, 1973.

Huntington, James F., Capt., 1st Ohio Light Artillery. "The Battle of Chancellorsville." *Papers of Military History Society of Massachusetts* 3. Boston: The Society, 1903.

Jones, Gordon W. "Ellwood: The Years of the Willis-Jones Dynasty." Vol. 60, FSNMP.

Kelley, George E., Co. B, 14th Ga. Letter to Macon *Telegraph,* May 16, 1863. Vol. 127, FSNMP.

Key, John C., Maj., 44th Ga. "Reminiscences of the Civil War." *Jasper County News,* Nov. 24–Dec. 15, 1898. Vol. 126, FSNMP.

Kitchen, J. C., Lt., Co. B, 132nd Pa. "Burnside's Mud March." Unidentified newspaper in James A. Stahl Papers, Harrisburg CWRT Collection, USAMHI.

Kyle, David. "Jackson's Guide When Shot." *CV* 9, 1896.

Lane, James H., Brig. Gen. CSA. "How Stonewall Jackson Met His Death." *Southern Historical Society Papers* 8, 1880.

McAllister, Robert, Col., 11th N.J. *The Civil War Letters of Gen. Robert McAllister.* New Brunswick: Rutgers University, 1965.

MacCauley, Clay, Lt., 126th Pa.. "From Chancellorsville to Libby Prison." *Glimpses of the National Struggle.* St. Paul: MOLLUS Minnesota, 1887.

McGlashan, Peter, Capt., later Col., 50th Ga. "Battle of Salem Church." Address to Confederate Veterans of Savannah, Ga. Savannah: Breid & Hutton, 1893.

McKay, Charles W., Co. C, 154th N.Y. Memoir. *The National Tribune Scrap Book: Stories of the Camp, March, Battle, Hospital and Prison Told by Comrades.* Washington: National Tribune, 1909.

Malone, Bartlett Y., Co. H, 6th N.C. *Whipt 'Em Everytime: The Diary of Bartlett Jancey Malone.* Jackson, Tenn.: McCowat-Mercer, 1960.

Martin, Micajah D., Sgt., Co. D, 2nd Ga. Battalion. "Chancellorsville: A Soldier's Letter." *Virginia Magazine of History and Biography* 37, 1929.

Mattocks, Charles P., Capt., 17th Me. "Major General Joseph Hooker." *War Papers.* Vol. 3. Portland: MOLLUS Maine, 1908.

Mead, Christopher C., Co. H, 12th N.J. Letter. *Manuscripts* magazine 35, no. 1, winter 1983.

Meysenberg, T. A., Maj., U.S. Volunteers. "Reminiscences of Chancellorsville." *War Papers and Personal Reminiscences.* Vol. 1. St. Louis: MOLLUS Missouri, 1892.

Moorman, Marcellus N., Capt., Stuart's Horse Artillery. "Narrative of Events and Observations connected with the Wounding of General T. J. (Stonewall) Jackson." Richmond: Southern Historical Society Papers 30, 1902.

Morrison, Robert Hall, II. Memoir of Joseph Graham Morrison, 1955. N.C. Collection, University of North Carolina.

Norman, Wm. M., Lt., Co. A, 2nd N.C. *A Portion of My Life.* Written while prisoner at Johnson's Island, 1864. Winston-Salem: John F. Blair, 1959.

Oden, John P., Capt., 10th Ala. *The End of Oden's War: A Confederate Captain's Diary.* *Alabama Historical Quarterly* 43, Summer 1981.

Osborn, Hartwell, Capt., 55th Ohio. "On the Right at Chancellorsville." *Military Essays and Recollections.* Vol. 4. Chicago: MOLLUS Illinois, 1907.

Patterson, Josiah B., Lt., Co. E, 14th Ga. Letters. "The Road to Spotsylvania." *Atlanta Weekly,* Oct. 16, 1983.

Peabody, J. H., 1st Sgt., Co. B, 61st Ohio. "Battle of Chancellorsville." *G.A.R. War Papers.* Cincinnati: Fred C. Jones Post No. 401, Department of Ohio, Grand Army of the Republic, 1901.

Pittman, Samuel E., Capt., U.S. Volunteers. "Chancellorsville Campaign: Operations of Gen. Alpheus S. Williams." *War Papers.* Vol. 1. Detroit: MOLLUS Michigan, 1893.

Raymond, Henry J. "Journal." *Scribner's Monthly* 19, 1880.

Rice, Owen. Capt., Co. A, 153rd Pa. *Afield With the Eleventh Army Corps at Chancellorsville.* Cincinnati: H. C. Sherick, 1885.

Rogers, Horatio, Col., 2nd R.I. *Personal Experiences of the Chancellorsville Campaign.* Providence: N. B. Williams, 1881.

Roney, Henry Clay, 22nd Georgia. "Reminiscences . . ." *Richmond County* (Ga.) *History* 2, no. 1 (Winter) 1979.

Searles, A. B., Capt., 45th N.Y. "On Picket at Chancellorsville." *Boston Journal* 49, n.d. FSNMP.

Silliman, Justus M., 17th Conn. *A New Canaan Private in the Civil War.* New Canaan: New Canaan Historical Society, 1984.

Small, Abner R. *The Road to Richmond: The Civil War Memoirs of Major Abner R. Small of the Sixteenth Maine Volunteers.* Berkeley: University of California, 1939.

Smith, Beverly C., M.D. Letter about diagnoses of precise cause of Jackson's death. *VMI Alumni Review,* Summer 1975.

Smith, James Power, Capt., CSA. "Stonewall Jackson and Chancellorsville." *Papers of the Military History Society of Massachusetts* 5. Boston: The Society, 1906.

Snead, Claiborne, 3rd Ga. *History of the 3rd Georgia*. Augusta: Chronicle & Sentinel, 1874.

Stephens, Thomas W., Sgt., Co. K, 20th Ind. *The Civil War Diary of Thomas White Stephens*. Lawrence, Kans.: University of Kansas, 1985.

Stevens, George T., Surgeon, 77th N.Y. *Three Years in the Sixth Corps*. Albany: S. R. Gray, 1866.

Talley, Jeter. Reminiscence of Catharine Furnace. *Infantry Journal*, n.d., quoted in unidentified newspaper account. Vol. 135, FSNMP.

Taylor, Murray Forbes. Letter in *CV* 12, Oct. 1904.

Thayer, George A., Capt., 2nd Mass. "History of the Second Massachusetts Regiment of Infantry—Chancellorsville." Paper read at officers' reunion, Boston, May 11, 1880.

Thompson, Alfred, Sgt., 49th Pa. Letter. Luvaas Collection, USAMHI.

Thompson, William McKenzie, Co. G, 15th N.J. Letter to Hunterdon *Republican*. CW Miscellaneous Collection, USAMHI.

Unknown: Henry ———, Co. B, 11th N.J. Letters. "Federal Soldier Writes of Battle of Chancellorsville." Fredericksburg *Free Lance-Star*, May 1, 1935. Vol. 17, FSNMP.

Van Blarcom, Lewis, Capt., 15th N.J. Reunion Speech, 15th Regiment New Jersey Volunteers. Unidentified newspaper, Vol. 109, FSNMP.

Voorhees, Lucian A., Co. A, 15th N.J. Letters to Hunterdon *Republican*. CW Miscellaneous Collection, USAMHI.

Wainwright, Charles S., Col., 1st N.Y. Artillery. *A Diary of Battle: The Personal Journals of Col. Charles S. Wainwright 1861–1865*. New York: Harcourt Brace & World, 1962.

Webb, Alexander S., Lt. Col., Fifth Corps. "Meade at Chancellorsville." Boston: Massachusetts Historical Society, 1903.

Wickersham, Charles I., 8th Pa. Cavalry. "Personal Recollections of the Cavalry at Chancellorsville." *War Papers*. Vol. 3. Milwaukee: MOLLUS Wisconsin, 1903.

Wilbourn, R. E., Capt., CSA. "Campaigns in Virginia, Maryland and Pennsylvania, 1862–1863." Boston: Massachusetts Historical Society, 1903.

Williams, Alpheus S., Maj. Gen., USA. *From the Cannon's Mouth: The Civil War Letters of General Alpheus S. Williams*. Detroit: Wayne State University, 1959.

Books and Articles

Anderson, Nancy Scott, and Dwight Anderson. *The Generals: Ulysses S. Grant and Robert E. Lee*. New York: Knopf, 1987.

Andrews, J. Cutler. *The South Reports the Civil War*. Princeton: Princeton University, 1970.

Bakeless, John. *Spies of the Confederacy*. New York: Lippincott, 1970.

Basler, Roy P. *The Collected Works of Abraham Lincoln*. Vol. 6. New Brunswick, N.J.: Rutgers University, 1953.

Bates, Samuel P. *The Battle of Chancellorsville*. Meadville, Pa.: T. E. Bates, 1882.

Battles and Leaders of the Civil War: 4 vols. Robert U. Johnson and Clarence C. Buel, eds. New York: Century, 1887–1888.

Beale, James B. *Chancellorsville*. Philadelphia: J. Beale, 1892.

Bigelow, John, Jr. *The Campaign of Chancellorsville*. New Haven: Yale University, 1910.

Boatner, Mark Mayo. *The Civil War Dictionary*. New York: McKay, 1959.

Botkin, B. A. *A Civil War Treasury of Tales, Legends and Folklore*. Reprint. New York: Promontory Press, 1981.

Brooks, Noah. *Mr. Lincoln's Washington*. New York: Thomas Yoseloff, 1967.

————. *Washington, D.C., in Lincoln's Time*. Chicago: Quadrangle, 1971.

Caldwell, J. F. J. *The History of a Brigade of South Carolinians Known as "Gregg's" and Subsequently as "McGowan's Brigade."* Philadelphia: King and Baird, 1886.

Canby, Courtlandt, ed. *Lincoln and the Civil War*. New York: Braziller, 1960.

Carter, Robert G. *Four Brothers in Blue: A True Story of the Great Civil War from Bull Run to Appomattox*. Washington: Gibson Press, 1913.

Catton, Bruce. *The Army of the Potomac: Glory Road*. Garden City: Doubleday, 1952.

Chambers, Lenoir. *Stonewall Jackson*. 2 vols. New York: Morrow, 1959.

Clark, Walter, ed. *Histories of the Several Regiments and Battalions from North Carolina, in the Great War 1861–'65*. 5 vols. Raleigh: E. M. Uzzell, 1901.

Cooke, John Esten. *Stonewall Jackson: A Military Biography*. New York: G. W. Dillingham, 1866.

Crane, Stephen. *The Red Badge of Courage*. Reprint. New York: Knopf, 1952.

Cunningham, H. H. *Doctors in Gray: The Confederate Medical Service*. Baton Rouge: Louisiana State University, 1958.

Dabney, R. L. *Life and Campaigns of Lieut.-Gen. Thomas J. Jackson*. Reprint. Harrisonburg, Va.: Sprinkle, 1983.

Daly, Louise Haskell. *Alexander Cheves Haskell: The Portrait of a Man*. Norwood, Mass.: Plimpton Press, 1934.

Davis, Burke. *Jeb Stuart: The Last Cavalier*. New York: Rinehart, 1957.

De Peyster, John Watts. *Chancellorsville and Its Results*. New York: L. W. Payne, n.d.

Dickert, D. Augustus. *History of Kershaw's Brigade*. Newberry, S.C.: E. H. Aull, 1899.

Dodge, T. A. *The Campaign of Chancellorsville*. Boston: J. R. Osgood, 1881.

Dooley, Louise K. "A War-horse for Stonewall." *Army* magazine, April 1975.

Doubleday, Abner. *Chancellorsville and Gettysburg*. New York: Scribner's, 1882.

Douglas, Henry Kyd. *I Rode With Stonewall*. Chapel Hill: University of North Carolina, 1940.

Eisenschiml, Otto. *The Hidden Face of the Civil War*. Indianapolis: Bobbs-Merrill, 1961.

————, and Ralph Newman. *The American Iliad: The Epic Story of the Civil War as Narrated by Eyewitnesses and Contemporaries*. Indianapolis: Bobbs-Merrill, 1947.

Fox, William Freeman. *Regimental Losses in the American Civil War*. Albany: Albany Publishing Co., 1889.

Franklin, John Hope. *The Emancipation Proclamation*. Garden City: Doubleday, 1963.

Freeman, Douglas Southall. *R. E. Lee: A Biography*. 4 vols. New York: Scribner's, 1935.

————. *Lee's Lieutenants: A Study in Command*. 3 vols. New York: Scribner's, 1942–1944.

Gough, John E. *Fredericksburg and Chancellorsville: A Study of the Federal Operations*. London: H. Rees, 1913.

Gould, Edward K. *Major General Hiram K. Berry*. Rockland, Me.: Courier Gazette, 1899.

Griffith, Paddy. *Battle Tactics of the Civil War*. New Haven: Yale University, 1989.

Hamlin, Augustus C. *The Battle of Chancellorsville, Jackson's Flank Attack*. Bangor, Me.: Privately printed, 1896.

Happel, Ralph. "The Chancellors of Chancellorsville." *Virginia Magazine of History and Biography* 72, no. 1, Jan. 1963.

Harrison, Noel G. *Gazetteer of Historic Sites Related to the Fredericksburg and Spotsylvania National Military Park*. Vol. 1. Fredericksburg: FSNMP, 1986.

Hassler, Warren W., Jr. *Commanders of the Army of the Potomac*. Baton Rouge: Louisiana State University, 1962.

Haydon, F. Stansbury. *Aeronautics in the Union and Confederate Armies*. Vol. 1. Baltimore: Johns Hopkins University, 1941.

Hays, Gilbert Adams. *Under the Red Patch: The Story of the 63rd Regiment Pennsylvania Volunteers*. Pittsburgh: 63rd Pa. Volunteers Regimental Association, 1908.

Hebert, Walter H. *Fighting Joe Hooker*. Indianapolis: Bobbs-Merrill, 1944.

Henderson, G. F. R. *Stonewall Jackson and the American Civil War*. New York: Longmans, Green, 1936.

Hoehling, Mary. *Thaddeus Lowe: America's One-Man Air Corps*. Chicago: Kingston House, 1958.

Hotchkiss, Jed, and William Allan. *The Battle-fields of Virginia: Chancellorsville*. New York: Van Nostrand, 1867.

Howard, Oliver Otis. *Autobiography of Oliver Otis Howard*. New York: Baker & Taylor, 1908.

Johnson, Allen, and Dumas Malone, eds. *Dictionary of American Biography*. New York: Scribner's, 1928–1936.

Jones, Gordon W. "The Years of the Willis-Jones 'Dynasty.' " Vol. 60, FSNMP.

Jones, J. William. *Christ in the Camp, or Religion in the Confederate Army*. Reprint. Harrisonburg, Va.: Sprinkle, 1986.

Jones, Terry L. *Lee's Tigers: The Louisiana Infantry in the Army of Northern Virginia*. Baton Rouge: Louisiana State University, 1987.

La Bree, Ben, ed. *The Confederate Soldier in the Civil War*. Louisville: Courier-Journal, 1895.

Lanier, Sidney. *Tiger-Lilies*. New York: Hurd & Houghton, 1867.

Lee, Fitzhugh. *General Lee*. Reprint. Greenwich, Conn.: Fawcett, 1961.

Leech, Margaret. *Reveille in Washington 1860–1865*. New York: Harper & Brothers, 1941.

Linderman, Gerald F. *Embattled Courage: The Experience of Combat in the American Civil War*. New York: Free Press, 1987.

Livermore, Thomas Leonard. *Numbers and Losses in the Civil War in America, 1861–1865*. Boston: Houghton Mifflin, 1909.

Long, E. B. *The Civil War Day by Day: An Almanac*. Garden City: Doubleday, 1971.

Lonn, Ella. *Foreigners in the Confederacy*. Gloucester, Mass.: Peter Smith, 1965.

———. *Foreigners in the Union Army and Navy*. Baton Rouge: Louisiana State University, 1951.

Lord, Francis A. *They Fought for the Union*. New York: Bonanza, 1960.

Luvaas, Jay, and Harold W. Nelson, eds. *The U.S. Army War College Guide to the Battles of Chancellorsville & Fredericksburg*. Carlisle, Pa.: South Mountain Press, 1988.

McCarthy, Carlton. *Detailed Minutiae of Soldier Life in the Army of Northern Virginia 1861–1865*. Richmond: Privately printed, 1882.

McDaid, William Kelsey. *"Four Years of Arduous Service: The History of the Branch-Lane Brigade in the Civil War."* Ph.D. diss., Michigan State University, 1987.

McIntosh, David Gregg. *The Campaign of Chancellorsville*. Richmond: W. E. Jones' Sons, 1915.

McPherson, James M. *Battle Cry of Freedom: The Civil War Era*. New York: Oxford University, 1988.

McWhiney, Grady, and Perry D. Jamieson. *Attack and Die: Civil War Tactics and the Southern Heritage*. University, Ala.: University of Alabama Press, 1982.

Marshall, Charles. *An Aide-de-Camp of Lee*. Boston: Little, Brown, 1927.

Mercer, Philip. *The Gallant Pelham*. Macon, Ga.: The J. W. Burke Company, 1929.

Miller, Francis Trevelyan, ed. *The Photographic History of the Civil War 9, Poetry and Eloquence from the Blue and Gray*. New York: Review of Reviews, 1911.

Miller, Nathan. *Spying for America*. New York: Paragon House, 1989.

Mitchell, Reid. *Civil War Soldiers*. New York: Viking, 1988.

Montross, Lynn. *War Through the Ages.* New York: Harper & Row, 1960.

Moore, Frank, ed. *The Rebellion Record, A Diary of American Events.* Vol. 3. New York: G. P. Putnam, 1863.

———. *The Civil War in Song and Story.* New York: Collier, 1865.

Nelson, H. A. *The Battles of Chancellorsville and Gettysburg.* Minneapolis: 1909.

Ordnance Bureau, Richmond. *The Field Manual for the Use of the Officer on Ordnance Duty.* Richmond: Ritchie & Dunnavant, 1862.

Paullin, Charles Oscar. "Early Use of Balloons in War—Thaddeus S. C. Lowe." *United Service Magazine,* Aug. 1909 (London).

Richardson, Charles. *The Chancellorsville Campaign.* New York: Neale, 1907.

Robertson, James I., Jr. *General A. P. Hill: The Story of a Confederate Warrior.* New York: Random House, 1987.

———. *Soldiers Blue and Gray.* Columbia: University of South Carolina, 1988.

———. *The Stonewall Brigade.* Baton Rouge: Louisiana State University, 1963.

Sandburg, Carl. *Abraham Lincoln: The War Years.* New York: Harcourt, Brace, 1939.

Sears, Stephen. *Landscape Turned Red: The Battle of Antietam.* New Haven: Ticknor & Fields, 1983.

Sheeran, James B. *Confederate Chaplain: A War Journal.* Milwaukee: Bruce Publishing Company, 1960.

Solomon, Eric, ed. *The Faded Banners.* New York: Sagamore Press, 1960.

Stackpole, Edward J. *Chancellorsville: Lee's Greatest Battle.* Harrisburg: Stackpole, 1958.

Stern, Philip Van Doren, ed. *Soldier Life in the Union and Confederate Armies.* Greenwich, Conn.: Fawcett, 1961.

Stiles, Robert. *Four Years Under Marse Robert.* New York: Neale, 1903.

Stuart, Meriwether. "Samuel Ruth and Robert E. Lee: Disloyalty and the Line of Supply to Fredericksburg 1862–1863." *Virginia Magazine of History and Biography* 72, no. 3, Jan. 1963.

Swinton, William. *Campaigns of the Army of the Potomac.* New York: Scribner's, 1882.

Symonds, Craig L. *A Battlefield Atlas of the Civil War.* Annapolis: Nautical and Aviation Publishing Company, 1983.

Tapert, Annette. *The Brothers' War.* New York: Times Books, 1988.

Taylor, Walter H. *General Lee: His Campaigns in Virginia 1861–1865.* Reprint. Dayton, Ohio: Morningside, 1975.

Thomas, Emory M. *The Confederate Nation 1861–1865.* New York: Harper & Row, 1979.

Townsend, Geo. Alfred. *Campaigns of a Non-Combatant.* New York: Blelock, 1866.

Truby, J. David. "War in the Clouds: Balloons in the Civil War." *The Civil War.* Los Angeles: Mankind Publishing Co., n.d.

Tucker, Glenn. *Hancock the Superb.* Indianapolis: Bobbs-Merrill, 1960.

———. *High Tide at Gettysburg.* Indianapolis: Bobbs-Merrill, 1958.

———. *Lee and Longstreet at Gettysburg.* Indianapolis: Bobbs-Merrill, 1968.

U.S. War Department. *The War of the Rebellion: A Compilation of the Official Records of the Union and Confederate Armies.* Washington: Government Printing Office, 1889.

Vandiver, Frank. *Mighty Stonewall.* New York: McGraw-Hill, 1957.

Von Borcke, Heros. *Memoirs of the Confederate War of Independence.* Reprint. Dayton, Ohio: Morningside, 1985.

War Department, Richmond. *Regulations for the Army of the Confederate States, 1863.* Richmond: J. W. Randolph, 1863.

Webb, Alexander S. *The Peninsula: McClellan's Campaign of 1862.* New York: Scribner's, 1881.

Webb, Willard, ed. *Crucial Moments of the Civil War.* New York: Bonanza, 1961.

Weigley, Russell F. *The American Way of War*. New York: Macmillan, 1973.

Weisberger, Bernard A. *Reporters for the Union*. Boston: Little, Brown, 1953.

Welles, Gideon. *Diary of Gideon Welles*. 3 vols. New York: Norton, 1960.

Whitman, Walt. *Specimen Days in America*. London: Oxford University Press, 1931.

Wickwire, Franklin, and Mary Wickwire. *Cornwallis: The American Adventure*. Boston: Houghton Mifflin, 1970.

Wiley, Bell Irwin. *The Life of Billy Yank, The Common Soldier of the Union*. Garden City: Doubleday, 1971.

————. *The Life of Johnny Reb*. Indianapolis: Bobbs-Merrill, 1943.

Williams, T. Harry. *Lincoln and His Generals*. New York: Knopf, 1952.

Williamson, James J. *Mosby's Rangers*. New York: Kenyon, 1896.

Index

abolitionists, 13, 42

Adams, Charles Francis, 32

Adams, R. H. T., 207, 208

Alabama infantry, 167, 232, 235, 245, 267, 275; *3rd,* 230; *5th,* 5, 163, 166, 171, 238; *6th,* 238; *8th,* 10, 274, 277; *9th,* 273, 277; *10th,* 261, 266, 274, 277; *11th,* 274; *12th,* 191; *14th,* 274

Albright, Charles, 287

Aldie (cavalry clash at), 51

Alexander, E. Porter, 45, 124, 139, 155, 211, 218, 221, 222, 299, 300

Alexander, Peter, 84

Alexandria *Gazette,* 43

Allen, Thomas S., 264, 265

Alrich farm, 127, 129

Alsop's farm, 116, 117, 118

amputation, 250–1, 310, 342 *n.*

Anderson, Richard H., 25, 74, 104–8, 114–16, 123, 124, 142, 153, 185, 216, 243–7, 252, 269, 291–9, 311, 312, 317

Antietam (Sharpsburg), battle of, 8, 11, 26, 27, 45, 47, 53, 89, 92, 128, 150, 163, 236, 330

Appomattox, 273, 340, 349

Aquia, 7, 330

Archer, James J., 154, 169, 211, 218, 221–3, 245

Arlington (estate), 41, 42, 44

Army of Northern Virginia, 35, 37, 38, 39, 44, 134; *see also* Confederate Army

Army of Tennessee, 85

Army of the Ohio, 69

Army of the Potomac, 11, 18, 19, 25, 29–35, 61, 64, 69, 87–90, 321; *see also* Union Army

Arrowsmith, Charles, 188

artillery, 48–9, 88, 227, 262

Ashby, Turner, 162

Asmussen, Charles, 181

Atlanta, siege of, 347 *n.*

Averell, William W., 52–4, 56, 162, 208

Avery, Isaac E., 298

Bacon, Cyrus, 96

Baker, Edward D., 24

balloons (Union intelligence), 6–8, 25, 34, 69, 70, 86, 87, 113, 121, 155–7, 223, 296

Ball's Bluff, battle of, 159

Bandy, George, 298

Banks, Nathaniel P., 80

Banks, Robert, 126

Banks' Ford, 16, 67, 108, 122, 123, 130, 131, 274, 285, 300, 301, 302, 313

Barksdale, William, 74, 101, 102, 115, 157, 158, 261, 266–8, 284, 289, 290, 311

Barlow, Francis C., 154, 158, 159, 187

Barnes, James, 318

Barr, Richard R., 204

Barry, John D., 202, 212

Bartlett, Joseph J., 258, 276, 363–4

Bates, Edward, 60

Beauregard, Pierre G. T., 23, 80

Beavers, George W., 235

Beckham, R. F., 134, 175

Bee, Barnard E., 80

A Note About the Author

A descendant of Confederate soldiers, Ernest B. "Pat" Furgurson served as a U.S. Marine officer before embarking on a long career as a foreign correspondent and Washington columnist for the Baltimore *Sun*. A native of Danville, Virginia, he graduated from Columbia College (1952) and the Columbia School of Journalism (1953) and is the author of biographies of General William C. Westmoreland and Senator Jesse Helms. He is the father of two children, and lives with his wife in Washington, D.C.

A Note on the Type

The text of this book was set in a digitized version of Fournier, a typeface originated by Pierre Simon Fournier *fils* (1712–1768). Coming from a family of typefounders, Fournier was an extraordinarily prolific designer both of typefaces and of typographic ornaments. He was also the author of the celebrated *Manuel typographique* (1764–1766). In addition, he was the first to attempt to work out the point system standardizing type measurement that is still in use internationally.

The cut of the typeface named for this remarkable man captures many of the aspects of his personality and period. Though it is elegant, it is also very legible.

Composed by ComCom, a division of
The Haddon Craftsmen, Inc., Allentown, Pennsylvania.
Printed and bound by Fairfield Graphics,
Fairfield, Pennsylvania.
Designed by Anthea Lingeman